Selected Sermons of Norman Nagel

Selected Sermons of Norman Nagel

FROM VALPARAISO TO ST. LOUIS

CONCORDIA PUBLISHING HOUSE • SAINT LOUIS

Copyright © 2004 Concordia Publishing House
3558 S. Jefferson Avenue
St. Louis, MO 63118-3968

All rights reserved. No part of this publication may be reproduced, stored in a retrieval system, or transmitted, in any form or by any means, electronic, mechanical, photocopying, recording, or otherwise, without the prior written permission of Concordia Publishing House.

Edited by Frederick W. Baue

Unless otherwise noted, Scripture quotations are taken from the King James or Authorized Version of the Bible.

Scripture quotations marked RSV are taken from the Revised Standard Version of the Bible, copyright 1952 [2nd edition, 1971] by the Division of Christian Education of the National Council of the Churches of Christ in the United States of America. Used by permission. All rights reserved.

Quotations from Luther's Small Catechism are from *Luther's Small Catechism with Explanation* (St. Louis: Concordia, 1986, 1991).

The sermon on p. 45 is amended from Gail McGrew Eifrig and Frederick Niedner, eds., *Our Hope for Years to Come: The Valparaiso University Prayer Book* (Valparaiso Ind.: Valparaiso University, 2001). Used with permission.

Manufactured in the United States of America

Library of Congress Cataloging-in-Publication Data
Nagel, Norman Edgar.
 [Sermons. Selections]
 Selected sermons of Norman Nagel : the Valpariso years, 1968-1983.
   p. cm.
 Includes bibliographical references and index.
 ISBN 0-7586-0123-9
 1. Lutheran Church—Sermons. 2. Church year sermons. 3. Occasional sermons. 4. Sermons, English—20th century. I. Title.
BX8066.N23S452 2004
252'.041—dc22   2004003456

---

3 4 5 6 7 8 9 10 11 12   27 26 25 24 23 22 21 20 19 18

Contents

Publisher's Preface   11

Sundays of the Church Year

First Sunday in Advent (Luke 19:28–38)
Luther-Tyndale Memorial Church, London, 1954   13

Second Sunday in Advent (Matthew 3:1–12)
Valparaiso University, 1977   18

Third Sunday in Advent (Matthew 11:2–14)
Concordia Seminary, 1998   21

Fourth Sunday in Advent (Philippians 4:5)
London, 1954   23

Christmas Day (Luke 2:1–20)
Valparaiso University, 1975   28

First Sunday after Christmas (Luke 2:33–35)
Valparaiso University, 1968   32

Second Sunday after Christmas (1 Samuel 2:1–10)
Valparaiso University, 1973   35

The Epiphany of Our Lord (Matthew 8:5)
Valparaiso University, 1971   41

The Baptism of Our Lord (Mark 1:9–11)
Concordia Seminary, 1990   43

Second Sunday after the Epiphany (John 1:43–51)
Valparaiso University, 1979   45

Third Sunday after the Epiphany (Romans 12:20–21)
London, 1949   48

Fourth Sunday after the Epiphany (John 6:51–59)
Concordia Seminary, 1986   55

Fifth Sunday after the Epiphany (Mark 1:29–31)
Concordia Seminary, 1988   56

Sixth Sunday after the Epiphany (Mark 1:40–45)
Valparaiso University, 1979   58

Seventh Sunday after the Epiphany (Matthew 19–20)
Valparaiso University, 1971   62

The Transfiguration of Our Lord (Luke 9:28–36) Valparaiso University, 1977	66
Ash Wednesday Valparaiso University, 1969	71
Lenten Midweek 1 Valparaiso University, 1969	74
Lenten Midweek 2 Valparaiso University, 1969	77
Lenten Midweek 3 Valparaiso University, 1969	80
Lenten Midweek 4 Valparaiso University, 1969	83
First Sunday in Lent (Matthew 4:1–11) Concordia Seminary, 1995	86
Second Sunday in Lent (Mark 12:1–12) Concordia Seminary, 1996	89
Third Sunday in Lent (Luke 11:20) London, 1954	92
Fourth Sunday in Lent (Matthew 26:51–54) London, 1957	97
Fifth Sunday in Lent (Mark 10:32–45) Concordia Seminary, 1990	101
Palm Sunday (John 12:20–26) London, 1951	104
Maundy Thursday (Mark 14:12–25) Valparaiso University, 1974	109
Good Friday (Mark 15:33–47) London, 1957	113
The Resurrection of Our Lord (Matthew 28:1–10) Valparaiso University, 1981	118
Second Sunday of Easter (John 20:26–31) Luther-Tyndale Memorial Church, London, 1964	121
Third Sunday of Easter (1 John 3:20) Concordia Seminary, 1993	125
Fourth Sunday of Easter (John 16:16–23) Valparaiso University, 1971	128

Fifth Sunday of Easter (James 1:13–18)
Cambridge, 1967 … 132

Sixth Sunday of Easter (John 16:23)
London, 1957 … 137

The Ascension of Our Lord (Luke 24:50–53)
Cambridge, 1965 … 143

Seventh Sunday of Easter (Luke 24:44–49)
Valparaiso University, 1970 … 146

The Day of Pentecost (Matthew 10:16–23)
Concordia Seminary, 1986 … 150

The Holy Trinity (Romans 11:33–36)
London, 1955 … 152

Second Sunday after Pentecost (Galatians 1:1–10)
Concordia Seminary, 1998 … 158

Third Sunday after Pentecost (Luke 14:15–24)
Zion Academy, 1996 … 161

Fourth Sunday after Pentecost (Luke 15:1–7)
London, 1954 … 166

Fifth Sunday after Pentecost (Luke 6:41–42)
Holden Village, 1971 … 169

Sixth Sunday after Pentecost (Luke 21:25–38)
Concordia Seminary, 1984 … 172

Seventh Sunday after Pentecost (Matthew 11:25–30)
Holden Village, 1978 … 175

Eighth Sunday after Pentecost (1 Corinthians 10:13b)
London, 1955 … 177

Ninth Sunday after Pentecost (Matthew 7:16b–18)
London, 1954 … 182

Tenth Sunday after Pentecost (Ephesians 4:1–16)
Concordia Seminary, 1997 … 188

Eleventh Sunday after Pentecost (Matthew 14:13–21)
Valparaiso University, 1981 … 190

Twelfth Sunday after Pentecost (Luke 18:9–14)
London, 1954 … 194

Thirteenth Sunday after Pentecost (Luke 12:49–53)
Valparaiso University, 1980 … 200

Fourteenth Sunday after Pentecost (Galatians 3:15–22)
London, 1955   203

Fifteenth Sunday after Pentecost (Luke 14:1, 7–14)
Valparaiso University, 1977   208

Sixteenth Sunday after Pentecost (Matthew 6:28)
London, 1954   212

Seventeenth Sunday after Pentecost (James 2:1–5, 8–10, 14–18)
Concordia Seminary, 1991   217

Eighteenth Sunday after Pentecost (Genesis 8:18–22)
Valparaiso University, 1971   219

Nineteenth Sunday after Pentecost (Ephesians 5:19)
London, 1955   223

Twentieth Sunday after Pentecost (Matthew 21:33–45)
Valparaiso University, 1975   228

Twenty-first Sunday after Pentecost (Ephesians 5:15, 17)
London, 1956   233

Twenty-second Sunday after Pentecost (Luke 18:1–8)
Valparaiso University, 1980   238

Twenty-third Sunday after Pentecost (Colossians 1:9–10)
London, 1955   241

Twenty-fourth Sunday after Pentecost (Matthew 25:1–13)
Valparaiso University   246

Twenty-fifth Sunday after Pentecost (Matthew 25:14–30)
Valparaiso University, 1978   251

Twenty-sixth Sunday after Pentecost (Exodus 32:1–20)
Concordia Seminary, 1990   255

Minor Festivals

The Circumcision of Our Lord (Numbers 6:22–27)
Valparaiso University, January 1, 1978   257

The Confession of St. Peter (Matthew 16:13–23)
Concordia Seminary, January 18, 1999   261

St. Timothy, Pastor and Confessor (John 21:15–17)
Concordia Seminary, January 24, 1992   263

Polycarp, Bishop and Martyr (Revelation 2:8–11)
Council of Presidents, February 23, 1978   266

St. Matthias, Apostle (Acts 1:15–26)
Concordia Seminary, February 24, 1995   268

The Nativity of St. John the Baptist (Luke 1:57–80)
Holden Village, June 24, 1971   270

St. Peter and St. Paul, Apostles (Matthew 16:13–20)
Holden Village, June 29, 1971   273

The Visitation (Luke 1:39–56)
Holden Village, May 31, 1971   277

St. Mary Magdalene (Luke 22:14–23)
Concordia Seminary, July 22, 1987   280

Formula of Concord (1 Timothy 6)
Central Lutheran, Minneapolis, July 24, 1977   283

St. James the Elder, Apostle (Acts 11:27–12:3)
Concordia Seminary, July 25, 1996   288

Holy Cross Day (John 12:20–33)
Concordia Seminary, September 14, 1992   290

St. Michael and All Angels (Psalm 103:19–22)
London, September 29, 1957   293

St. Luke, Evangelist (Luke 1:1–4; 24:44–53)
Concordia Seminary, October 18, 1983   298

St. Simon and St. Jude, Apostles (John 14:21–27)
Concordia Seminary, October 28, 1997   300

Reformation Day (Matthew 18:20)
Westfield House, October 31, 1963   302

Reformation Day
Valparaiso University, October 31, 1967   307

All Saints' Day (Matthew 5:1–12)
Valparaiso University, November 1, 1981   314

Harvest Festival (Deuteronomy 16:13–15)
London, 1954   318

The Holy Innocents, Martyrs (Matthew 2:16–18)
London, December 28, 1956   324

Occasional Sermons

Memorial Service (1 Corinthians 15:56)
Valparaiso University, 1980   329

Funeral Sermon (John 6:68)
Valparaiso University   331

Wedding Sermon (Philippians 4:4–6)
Cambridge, December 11, 1966   332

Wedding Sermon (Matthew 19:3)
Valparaiso University   337

Church Anniversary (Exodus 20:3)
Good Shepherd, Coventry, 1966   339

Pledge Sunday (Genesis 28:10–22)
London, 1957   344

Mission Festival (Isaiah 35)
St. Paul's, Borehamwood, 1963   349

Synod (Hebrews 11:31; James 2:25–26)
1967   354

Confessional Address (John 20:11a, 14–17a)
London, 1955   357

Confirmation (Revelation 3:11)
London, 1951   359

Dedication of Westfield House (Luke 8:4–15)
Cambridge, February 25, 1962   364

Publisher's Preface

This collection contains selected sermons of Rev. Norman Nagel from 1949 to 1999, a fifty-year period. The earliest sermon dates from his vicarage in London. Upon graduation from Concordia Seminary, St. Louis, in 1953, Rev. Nagel returned to London, where he served Luther-Tyndale congregation in all aspects of pastoral ministry. This book contains many sermons from those years. In 1957 Rev. Nagel went up to Cambridge to pursue doctoral studies, receiving his doctoral degree in 1962. He was appointed the first preceptor of Westfield House in 1962 and continued in that position until 1967. Because he was not preaching every Sunday, this book contains fewer sermons from this period.

In 1967 Valparaiso University extended the call as Dean of the Chapel of the Resurrection to Rev. Nagel. As American society in general and The Lutheran Church—Missouri Synod in particular faced turbulent times, Rev. Nagel returned to regular preaching.

In the 1970s, Rev. Nagel became an occasional guest lecturer and preacher at Holden Village, a Lutheran retreat center on Lake Chelan in Washington. This collection includes a few sermons from those years.

Returning to his alma mater, Concordia Seminary, in 1983, Rev. Nagel taught systematic theology and was also a preacher in the newly constructed Chapel of St. Timothy and St. Titus. Several sermons from these years appear in this volume.

Rev. Nagel would like to thank Debbie Roediger at Concordia Seminary for all the work she did on the sermons, as well as Lorraine Thune at Valparaiso University. Concordia Publishing House wishes to thank Rev. Naomichi Masaki and Rev. Al Collver for collecting many of Rev. Nagel's seminary chapel sermons, as well as Nancy Prigge, Brandy Overton, Susan Turner, Carolyn Guelbert, and Lou Ann Oberto who accurately keyed in the many sermons from the pre-computer years.

The sermons in this volume have been edited with a light hand, for the most part only changing British spellings, such as *colour*, to conform to standard American style.

The Editor

First Sunday in Advent

LUKE 19:28–38

LUTHER-TYNDALE MEMORIAL CHURCH, LONDON (1954)

"And when He was come into Jerusalem, all the city was moved, saying, 'Who is this?' " (Matthew 21:10). When Jesus rides past the crowd, they must either grasp a palm branch or, with frowning, hate-filled eyes, turn their backs. Many people say that they couldn't care less about Christ, yet they use His name to curse. They don't curse by Zeus or Thor or Brahma but by Christ. Thereby they witness to Christ's inescapable power, though in our age, which is so empty of faith, a genuine curse is becoming rather difficult. Only a believer can be guilty of a 100 percent curse.

A cool, dispassionate denial of Christ is virtually impossible. Regardless of whether we believe in Him, we are moved by Christ. He is either welcomed with joy or crucified with a hate that blurs and fuddles the coldest atheist. If it were announced that Jesus was arriving on the 11:05 at Waterloo, would there be a Londoner who wouldn't hear of it or be excited about it? All the people in the crowds that would run out to see and cheer certainly wouldn't be Christians, but the whole city would be moved—not as it would by a French president or Alexander the Great but by some mysterious power that excites and grips and cannot be accepted or denied without passion. The Christian shouts glad, selfless, childlike hosannas. The person who scowls and curses is like a moth fascinated by a light, round which it performs the gyrations of blasphemy to death. We may well ask, "Who is this?"

The Propers for today present a contrasting, paradoxical answer. The Epistle tells of Him who, being God, became man and, as a servant, was obedient unto death, even the death of the cross. In the Collect we prayed that following the example of such humility we might, with such patience, be made partakers of the resurrection of the Son of God who died on the cross. The Gospel tells of a King who rides into the capital on another man's donkey. He weeps over the city that received Him with royal and divine honor. "All the city was moved, saying, Who is this? And the multitude said, This is Jesus the prophet of Nazareth of Galilee" (Matthew 21:10–11).

Many in this multitude were from Galilee. Jesus was their hometown man, and it was good to see Him going over big in proud Jerusalem—probably a similar emotion to that which colonials feel when one of their own achieves spectacular success in London. Jesus was one of them and had done them great good, but when challenged by a frowning Pharisee, the multitude called Him no more than a prophet. When Jesus grew bigger and His claims of loyalty total, then they changed their tune. Prophet Jesus certainly was—but if only that, then He was a most rash and foolish one who was committing suicide by entering Jerusalem. He was either a sorry sort of prophet or something infinitely more than a prophet.

Jesus is a king—a king who has complete possession and rule over all things. Did Lazarus walk that day from Bethany in the company of the disciples? Did the new and wondering eyes of Bartimaeus behold the fair city of Zion for the first time as he joined the multitude who began to "rejoice and praise God with a loud voice for all the mighty works that they had seen" (Luke 20:37)? This Lord of life and death sends two of His disciples to fetch a colt and its mother, for the colt had never been ridden. The disciples are just to go up and take the animals. This would be daylight robbery for anybody but God, who owns all things. God can't steal; that can only be done by humans who have rather foolish notions about possessing things. Humans talk about this or that being "mine" without realizing that it is a foolish way of talking about something they have use of for a bit. If anybody challenged the disciples while they were making off with the donkey, they were simply to say, "The Lord hath need of him" (Luke 19:34). That is that. You can't argue with the Lord when He claims the donkey that He Himself made. And the owner of the donkey nobly comes through the test of his faith, though he probably had to walk or work harder in consequence.

Here is Jesus, a sovereign king who owns all things, and all knowledge is also His possession. He told the disciples just where they would find the ass and colt, and there they were. This seemingly trivial manifestation of divine omniscience was, of course, not without its purpose. In the next few days each disciple would be sorely tempted to think of Jesus only as a prophet who failed, so Jesus gives this extra prop to their faith. He did the same thing when He gave miraculous directions for the Passover arrangements, identifying the man carrying the water jug on his head as the means to acquire a room. Jesus was a king almighty, all-knowing, whose rule and possession embrace all things.

But look. Now Jesus enters His city on another man's donkey, not on a magnificent prancing horse with the flashing splendor of the spears and swords of a great army. His path is strewn with the palms of peace. He rides the animal of peace with the black cross on its back, for here rides the Prince of Peace who is hailed by the glad voices of children. Jesus' throne is not His by shedding the blood of others but by shedding His own blood. Clearly His kingdom is not of this world. Jesus does not destroy but weeps over the city that will crucify Him. He goes into that city, for now is its great day of grace. Now it may behold its Messiah king clearly set forth. He comes unto His own Jerusalem, the sacred city so abundantly blessed, the glory of Israel to which He had so often mercifully stretched out His hands. Jesus comes into Israel, the chosen of God, with whom God had made His covenant, to whom God had given the Law, the true ways of worship, and God's own promises. Now as her crowning privilege, Israel received the Messiah king. This was her greatest and also her last chance. These were the days of decision. It was rare in His life that Jesus did something as a demonstration, but He rode triumphantly into Jerusalem. If that city would receive Him, she would find her peace in Him. God wanted to gather her under His wings as a hen gathers her chicks. But Jerusalem would not. He came unto His own and His own received Him not. The wings of God were spurned, and after a little while came the talons of the Roman eagle.

But did not Jerusalem gladly receive Jesus? Ah, yes, she did, but it was the welcome of a crowd. The song of welcome to the entering pilgrims had been swelled to greater acclamation for Jesus. It was a grand day. The sun shone and Jerusalem lay in all her ancient splendor. The host of Galilean pilgrims cheered their Galilean prophet. They didn't look at the mean and humble donkey that bore the black cross on its back. They saw Jesus of Nazareth, the miracle worker. He had done great things for them, and He was from Galilee. We do not presume to judge the sincerity of their praise, but we know that the disciples themselves had no clear notion of what it was all about and the purest praise was perfected out of the mouths of babes and sucklings. The crowd was only a fickle mob. On Sunday they cry, "Hosanna"; on Friday they cry, "Crucify Him." Such is not the kingdom of God.

The kingdom of God is not of this world. It is not bound by lines on a map or built with a sword. Christ's kingdom is Christ's people, but not people in a crowd. The kingdom of Christ is within you, each one of you. Christ never deals with us by the dozen or by the thousand. That is left to the Christless who make of others a commodity or a tool of comfort. Christ deals with individuals, and it is only in the dealing of Christ that we have value. Otherwise we are merely rather sad and pointless creatures. Today Christ is hailed as a king by a crowd, but the excitement and the shouting are not near the heart of His kingdom. As a king who would rule in our hearts, we see Christ in His dealings with the owner of the donkeys and the two disciples who went on such an extraordinary mission. The kingship of Christ was not in Galilean shouts for the hometown man who had become a public figure. It was in our Lord's eyes when He turned to Peter. It was in our Lord's voice when He said "Mary" to the weeping Magdalene. It was in our Lord's thrice-repeated question, "Simon, son of Jonas, lovest thou me?" (John 21:17).

Jesus doesn't enter a city as a king. He enters into your hearts, one at a time. He knows all your background, all your twists and problems. He even knows how many hairs grow on your head. It is into your heart that Jesus would ride. You can close the gate of your heart against Him, and He will not force an entry. He will weep over the city of your heart. How often He would gather you close to Himself, even as a hen gathers her chick, but you would not have it. You were too busy with the house, the business, the radio, or the motor car—too tired to be bothered. When He would speak with you, you shut His mouth. You let dust gather on your shiny new Bible. You said worship together with God's family was too much effort. Or you looked for the wrong things in Jesus. Like Jerusalem's crowd, you thought that He was a king, someone with whom it is worthwhile to be associated. If you expect Jesus to be this sort of bread king, then you will certainly be let down. His kingdom is not of this world.

If Jesus comes into your heart, He comes "meek, and sitting upon an ass" (Matthew 21:5). He is a king that would set up the rule of His love and humility in your heart. That means the rejection of the pride and glory of all the kingdoms of this world. Jesus won't turn stones to bread for you. And if He rules, He rules alone. His rule rises above every earthly claim, even that of a father, mother, brother, sister, or spouse. You are in His kingdom because of an oath of allegiance that binds even if He commands you to do something unusual. You bear the badge of His subjects and that badge is a cross. "If any man will come after Me, let him deny himself, and take up his cross daily, and follow Me. . . . whosoever will lose his life for My sake, that same shall save it" (Luke 9:23–24).

There are no reservations in loyalty to Jesus. He wants His love to rule in every house and shop, in every alley and gutter in the city of your heart. To each one of you the Advent king says: "Come unto Me, all ye that labour and are heavy laden, and I will give you rest. Take My yoke upon you, and learn of Me; for I am meek and lowly in heart: and ye shall find rest unto your souls. For My yoke is easy and My burden is light" (Matthew 11:28–30). We were constructed to fit under that yoke. Without it we are like a car without a battery. We can't get started. Under that yoke, in Christ's kingdom, we first become ourselves. Then, for the first time, we become a real individual, for Christ has dealt with us personally, in and for ourselves. It was for you, just you (not for a thousand million people), that Christ died. That is the sweet, personal, life-giving message of the cross. As one redeemed by Christ, you belong to Him, to His kingdom. You have a place, value, and meaning, and unto your soul is given rest and peace.

Now no one can say, "Who am I? What do I matter, a trifling nobody among millions?" So great was the love of God for you, just you, that the Son of God went the way of sorrows to the cross that you might be His, be in His kingdom, and that He might be the king of your heart. Once He is the king of our hearts, we can't ever say in frustration or despair, "What do I matter?" So also when the rule of His love has taken over from the usurping, false, and evil self, we may never say, "What can I do?"

What this world despises, Jesus takes and uses to accomplish His great purposes of love. Out of the mouths of babes and sucklings He perfects praise. He had need of a donkey; so also He has need for me and you.

AMEN.

Second Sunday in Advent

Matthew 3:1–12

Valparaiso University (1977)

We need a whole lot more help to be cheerful than to be miserable. The latter comes sort of naturally. The things we have to be worried about usually make a longer list than the things that make us deep down happy. We are somehow afraid of being happy for fear of being cheated. From our past come the cautionary voices that prompt us to protect ourselves against expecting too much. Better settle for some manageable-size happiness that can be protected. Don't look for more.

In the wilderness, John cries "Repent!" upon all such protections (Matthew 3:2). Come free of them. Start again from zero. The waters of Baptism drown the old and give birth to the new. John's baptism is toward the new, toward what is coming, toward who is coming: the Lord, whose way is to be prepared by casting aside all that stands in His way so nothing blocks Him. Try to protect yourself against Jesus as against an enemy and you will then have Him as an enemy. Meet Him with demands of what you deserve and that is what you will get, and no escape. Some will receive of Jesus' might and His justice, others of His gentleness and life-engendering care, as was spoken by the prophet Isaiah: "Behold, the Lord God will come with strong hand, and His arm shall rule for Him: behold, His reward is with Him, and His work before Him. He shall feed His flock like a shepherd: He shall gather the lambs with His arm, and carry them in His bosom, and shall gently lead those that are young" (40:10–11). Jesus leads. He goes on ahead, leading to the more He always has in store for us. He was a whole lot more than John imagined or was ready to accept.

When Jesus comes, whose coming John proclaimed, He brings always more than we can imagine. Getting ready for what is coming is one way of describing your days at university. Yet there are those for whom the opposite is the case with regard to our coming Lord. University days bring alternatives, challenges, doubts, and denials regarding the Lord Jesus as we have come to know Him so far. The temptation is to cling tightly to this Jesus and protect Him against contact with what questions and threatens Him. We may put protections around Him to keep Him safe in some sort of compartment so we can visit Him from time to time. We feel secure with this Jesus we desperately want to keep because we see around us what can happen to people when they throw Him over. How else can we hold ourselves together without Jesus? This is the counsel of fear, for we are cowering back within the area of our own competence and control and its security.

Or, even worse, we reach back for our childhood Jesus and think of Him as more than where we are with Jesus now. This is particularly a temptation when Christmas comes. In the happy memories of childhood Christmases, ah, there was Jesus for us in a way that we long for again. At Christmas we may pretend it is so again. But pretending will not hold; it will leave a hole that pride will all too easily slip in to fill, smiling at our simple childish notions of Jesus and the world He came to save. But now we are older. We have lost our childish innocence and have become wise in the ways of a world in which Jesus has little place. At university we have come to know so many things that simply make that childhood Jesus impossible.

The Jesus whom Advent proclaims is the Jesus who is coming. Him you do not meet by looking backward or by smothering and embracing the Jesus you are trying to protect so you can somehow keep Him going. Him you meet ahead of where you are now. Repentance is the stripping away of everything that closes Jesus in, of everything that is unwilling to risk His being more for you. Instead, you are open, receiving of Him who is always on ahead, more.

Wednesday's *Monitor* had a picture of a bunch of German students. Please close your eyes and look at it with me. A couple of them are standing, more are sitting, and most are what you couldn't really call standing or sitting—just sort of drooping. All are wearing the jeans required by social/peer/herd pressure. One of them is rather languidly holding up a placard with his equivalent of "We are children of Abraham and have never been in bondage to anyone." Quite clearly they are not in bondage to their parents. If you go into their parents' homes, the monstrous rubber plant and plush oriental carpet shout at you, "We are rich, we are! We have made it!" The parents' homes are no longer home for these children. They are on the street, children of the wilderness.

Wilderness strips you down to the basics. Jeans go better in the wilderness than double-knits, velvet, or silk. They dress basic, these children of the wilderness—no frills. They reject the riches and attendant values of their parents. They make like they are poor, dressed like tramps in the wilderness. Their parents' rubber plants and oriental carpets have their correspondence, as Aristotle might observe, in the students' ostentatiously raggedy jeans, which are carefully bleached to different shades of fadedness and have patches in the oddest places where trousers just don't wear out. The patches are recognizably phony by where they are put and boast of poverty. Yet there is one more patch we can spot in the picture. It is pert and posteriorly placed and, quite frankly, chuckles with its bright red flowers. Love that patch. It is like the "nevertheless" in what the Large Catechism says of Baptism. Because these are German students, we may recall something that Goethe said, though they have pretty plainly rejected him too. Goethe said there is nothing on the outside that is not an expression of what is on the inside, and nothing on the inside that is not expressed in what is on the outside.

What are we to make of these students' ragged jeans? Honesty, and on to things more basic than their parents think important—"the whole middle-class trip," as we might say transatlantically. There are things they can count on one another for, things that matter more than rubber plants and oriental carpets. Some true things certainly. Then there is the phoniness too. The poor of the world, they are not. They have what they choose. Food is no real worry, and there is money if they want it from home. Yet there is a poverty that lots of money can make you feel more keenly. They are children of the wilderness in their grasp for what is basic. But they do not let the wilderness be all the way for them. That is too frightening to face.

John was a child of the wilderness; his garment of camel's hair was his jeans. "Behold, they that wear soft clothing are in kings' houses" (Matthew 11:8). His wilderness cry is to strip away all the frills, all the phoniness. Repent. What is for real? There is one who is coming. Jesus is for real. The only piece of clothing He ever had that came from Marshall Field's they cast dice for while He hung naked on the cross. That cross is for real. There is nothing in all the world more real than that cross. Out from the cross there is nothing that you need to hide from or try to cover up.

We are so used to jeans that they don't quite say for us what they do on the Continent, particularly behind the Iron Curtain. There are different shades of wilderness. There is a wilderness experienced in a regimented society; the wilderness experienced in a competitive, affluent society; and the wilderness you may know on a university campus or in your own heart.

This Advent spend some time in the wilderness, stripped of all frills and phoniness, stripped down to what is basic, naked—naked toward Him who comes. His Baptism gives who He is and what is His to do. Jesus has His time in the wilderness. His heart goes out to those in the wilderness with Him. He feeds them with His words of life and truth. When a boy gives up his lunch, He feeds them with those loaves and fish. With bread and wine He bodies and bloods us with Himself. As it goes with Jesus, so it goes with us—as real as death, as real as life, His and ours, together.

AMEN.

Third Sunday in Advent

MATTHEW 11:2–14

CONCORDIA SEMINARY (1998)

Pretty clearly the Sadducees and the Pharisees are not the ones to follow. They may be characterized by their opposite, those who confess their sins in Baptism. Those who do not confess their sins get a devastating blast of the Law; those who refuse to repent end up in unquenchable fire. Those who repent, confess their sins, and are baptized are gathered into the granary. The Lord is into bread, *lechem*.

This is not the first or the last call to repentance. The garments of camel's hair and the leather belt tell us that. King Ahaziah had an accident, a bad fall, and he figured the Lord should help him get over it. So he called up the man of God. And the man of God said, "No go" (or words to that effect). "What manner of man was he . . . ?" asked Ahaziah. "And they answered him, 'He was a hairy man, and girt with a girdle of leather about his loins.' And he said, 'It is Elijah the Tishbite' " (2 Kings 1:7–8).

Again and again there is an "Elijah job" to be done. We are already in the third week of Advent. The Lord has more than one Elijah. So He promises with the last words we read in the Old Testament: "Behold, I will send you Elijah the prophet before the coming of the great and dreadful day of the LORD: And He shall turn"—that is "repent"—"the heart of the fathers to the children, and the heart of the children to their fathers, lest I come and smite the land with a curse" (Malachi 4:5–6). The Lord is into families. Alternative to being in His family is the searing, individual loneliness of hell. For those who turn themselves away from God, there is nothing left to hold them together. They sink in pieces, dead, but for the echoing, fiery recriminations of those who insisted that they belong to themselves.

There is something honest about a straightforward unbeliever in contrast with those who confess the Name but abuse it in their attempts to bend it to their plans and purposes. Ahaziah, Pharisees, and Sadducees—that is, laity and clergy—you, me. The Advent message of John the Baptist faces us up to that question. Of him Jesus says, "This is Elijah, which was for to come. He that hath ears to hear, let him hear" (Matthew 11:14–15). "For the kingdom of heaven is at hand. For this is he who was spoken of by the prophet Isaiah, saying, The voice of one crying in the wilderness, prepare ye the way of the Lord, Make His paths straight" (Matthew 3:2–3). We have heard the voice of Elijah the Tishbite, the man of God, that is, the man called to speak the Lord's words. We have heard the voice of Malachi, prophesying another Elijah; the voice of Isaiah, prophesying the mission and message he is sent on; and the voice of Jesus. He is Elijah who is to come—the voice of one crying in the wasteland.

The mouth of the Lord has spoken it. How many mouths does the Lord put to His use? How many Elijahs? How many Sundays in Advent? How many calls to repent, to turn? As many as our sins that need repentance. The Lord is slow to give up on you. He calls you to repent again and again. But if you insist on holding on to your sins—perhaps just your favorite one or two—and try to run with both Him and your sins, He will finally put an end to that game. He tells you so. He issues a warning call to repent, to turn. Your sins are either with Jesus or with you. It is only the sins you hold and keep away from Him that can damn you. Jesus has already answered for your sins. You have to take them back from Him to be damned by them.

"Behold, the Lamb of God who takes away the sins of the world." The Agnus Dei invites us to Jesus' altar to eat His body and drink His blood, which are given into death for the forgiveness of your sins. Body and blood He has because He was born of Mary. This body and blood was given and shed as the Lamb of God. Jesus has borne all our sins. He gives His body and blood for you to eat and to drink for the forgiveness of all your sins. "This is My body which is given for you. .

. . This is My blood . . . shed for you" (Luke 22:19–20). Jesus says this to you—He who is king, He who is the Lamb, He who brings heaven in His kingly presence: "Repent ye: for the kingdom of heaven is at hand" (Matthew 3:2).

Amen.

Fourth Sunday in Advent

Philippians 4:5

London (1954)

People who have grown up with lots of money and feel assured of having all the money they may want use their money in a different sort of way than those who have just recently come into a pile. The latter want to convince themselves and others that they now have money. Hence we see the strident and proverbial demonstration of wealth of the newly rich. It is their attempt to certify and establish themselves as wealthy. The excess of demonstration is born of an uneasiness that they may not be equally accepted by those who have always had lots of money. Those who have always had lots of money tend to regard these ostentations of the newly rich as rather bad taste, for if people really felt assured of their wealth, they wouldn't feel any necessity of making a parade of it to convince themselves and others that it is really so.

Similarly, there is an ease and carefree attitude in the speech of those whose good grammar and vocabulary are inbred. They don't give great thought to each sentence and pronunciation; it comes naturally. They have the confidence of possession, whereas those who are uneasy about their language betray their uncertainty in excessive exactitudes and condemning criticism of other people's speech. Some foreigners achieve a good English that is correct according to the rules but never has the ease and confidence of those born English. The ease and confidence spring from the certainty of possession.

The proverbial modesty and politeness of the English gentleman is said, by some, to be based on the confident assumption of his own superiority. The superiority of being British is so beyond question that there is no need to assert it. It is taken for granted. Men of lesser countries may have to make loud noise about their significance, for they are uncertain about their prominence and power. But Britons have no such misgivings, therefore, the gentlemanly deference.

The point of all this is that when people are confident of possessing something, they have no need to convince themselves and others with a lot of obnoxious assertion. Rather, it is those who are uncertain about their possession who so painfully work to establish assurance and recognition. The previous examples are a curious mixture of good and bad, yet they do, in a way, illustrate this point, which is also the point of our text. Moderation, as used in Philippians 4:5, means the quiet confidence of being God's child who possesses God's riches and truth and lives in this confidence, awaiting the promised fulfillment.

In His First Advent, Christ achieved for us the possessions that are ours in Him. Chief among these possessions is that we have a Savior who came down and was born a man. Christ lived the life in our place that God expects each of us to live. As our replacement, Christ died the death for our sins. In Him we have forgiveness of sins. In Him we have the righteousness in which we are clothed as we stand before God. In Christ we have God as our gracious Father. He also gives us the Holy Spirit through whom we have the inspired Scriptures that speak the life-giving Gospel into our hearts. We have the Spirit as our Guide and Comforter. He empowers the Word of truth in us so it transforms us and our lives. We know ourselves to be God's people and that our lives have their achievement and meaning in being lived toward the fulfillment of Christ's Second Advent.

These are great possessions, indeed, but are we sure that we have them? If we look to ourselves, we may well have doubts, but our certainty is in Christ and in Him alone. In Christ we have unshakable confidence of possessing the treasures of the sons of God. Our text calls us to live the confidence of possessing the riches of the sons of God, and it calls such living "moderation."

Those who are sure of their possessions need no excess of demonstration to convince others of their riches. Likewise, the Christian confidence needs no proud vauntings. It has an inner composure and certainty. Christians do not need the recognition of others, for the basis is in Christ. If God calls me His child for Jesus' sake and in Jesus guarantees that I possess the riches of the sons of God, then my certainty is unshakable and quite free of the opinions of others. Nor do I have any need of the props that the ungodly use to give themselves some significance. God's people do not have that uneasiness that breeds self-assertion and quarrels. What is there to quarrel about? Christians do not have to show other people that they are wrong to bolster themselves and what they know to be true. What they know to be true is the truth that is Christ—and that truth needs no argument.

Yet this unquarrelsomeness and certainty of being right in Christ is the very thing that infuriates the ungodly. That anybody can be so sure of being right really irritates the ungodly, who know no such certainty and seek to do away with their uncertainty by pathetic demonstrations of mind or might or money. The ungodly seek rest for their souls, but they seek where rest cannot be found. Thus they go from one excess to another. Christians understand this. They know the ungodly to be those from whom they have been rescued, so Christians have ready sympathy for those still floundering. Christians do not scorn the excessive demands of the ungodly, for they know the uneasy hearts from which they come. Christians are patient and helpful, for they would bring healing to those unsteady hearts now striking out in all manner of excess. As Jesus said: If a man demands you walk a mile with him, go with him for two miles. If he asks you for your shirt, give him your coat too. Christ's people do not object: "But I am not your servant" or "This is my shirt." Christ's people have no doubt about who they are and what is theirs, but it is these poor people who don't know who they are or what is theirs in Christ.

The certainty of our riches in Christ enables us to be generous in the service of others. We don't have to strive for the recognition of our rank or place. All that is secure in Christ and beyond question. Therefore, we are free to act as servants. Only a completely free person can be a true servant. I once went to a party where there were some social climbers who wanted to establish their position. They insisted on being waited on while the lady with the title (who was the genuine article) was having a rollicking good time, making more sandwiches in the kitchen. She had no uneasiness about her rank. She took it for granted and felt free to lend a hand as a servant. The people who insisted on being served she may have thought rather sad, but she served them cheerfully nonetheless. In doing so, she showed them some of the quality of a true lady. If even in the social arena of the world we see such things, how much more ought not the royal sons of the heavenly King show forth the bearing, the moderation, of those who know that in Christ they have all things?

We must not take part in two treacheries that deny that we are the royal children of God. The first treachery is that we should not allow people to feel sorry for us because we are Christians. This is a particular temptation for those active in the work of the church. We work hard and grow weary for the church, then somebody says to us, "My, how you do the work of the church. You poor thing. You must be quite worn out." And we sigh, accepting their pity, because we are pleased with the recognition of what we have done. This is a fearful denial of our position as God's child, for whatever we do for Christ, it is our royal privilege to do. If anybody is to be pitied, it is those who do not have the privilege and joy of spending their energies for Christ. Whenever we show reluctance to play the part of a child of God, whenever we let others pity us for our actions as Christians as if we are the losers, we deny that we are children of the King. We admit that what the ungodly world values is more precious to us than the riches of the heavenly King.

This brings us to the other treachery, which is the acceptance of the standards of the ungodly world. We neglect the riches that God gives in Christ and bend our lives toward the acquisition of those things that the ungodly esteem and use to prop up their lives. We seek recognition, social rank, superior authority, power, or wealth, and in asserting our possession of these as giving significance to our lives, we betray our discontent with being merely the children of God. "Merely the sons of God"—that is what we are often afraid of. "Lest having Christ we have naught else beside." We are scared that we may lose out on some earthly thing. We mistrust God and fear that He may deprive us of the things we really want apart from Him. This is behind our lack of eagerness for His Second Advent. We may be the losers. We don't quite trust God.

Such distrust is treason. It slanders God and denies our royal position. Besides, the King won't put up with it. You can't have one foot in the kingdom of Christ and one foot in the kingdom of this world. Christ calls us out of the kingdom of this world into His kingdom. Therein He grants us not only citizenship but also sonship. We are made the sons of God. As God's children He has us continue on for a while in this world. But we are *in* the world, not *of* the world, for He would have us show forth His kingship. We are children of the King. As His children, we are to practice the way He once went through this world. One day we shall come into the kingdom, but now we are young and immature. God knows we need a lot of training in being His kind of princes and princesses.

Occasionally we hear about the owner of a big business who puts his son to work in his own factory. There the son has to work with the rest of the employees. His back aches and his hands blister, but his father knows he will be a better man for the firm if he has been through all this before he inherits the business. Similarly, God puts us through some hard training here. At times our hearts ache and our hands blister, but God knows we will be better for His kingdom.

That is one side of it; the other is the attitude of the son while he is working in the factory. He doesn't see his work as so much pointless drudgery only for the sake of the pay on Friday. He sees his work in relation to his father and his future. He knows he is coming into the business, and therefore there is no need for him to make a big noise among the employees to assert his position and rank. He is confident of that and gets on with the work. In the same way, if we are the children of the King, we have no need to make a lot of self-asserting noise to establish our position. What and who we are is settled by our relationship to the King: We are His children and heirs.

In quietness and confidence is our strength, for our strength and confidence are in Christ. Hence there is no excess of ostentation nor strutting in the pricey possessions of this world to cover the uncertainty of a soul adrift. Nor is there the excess of misery in looking for pity from ourselves and others, but we have moderation toward everyone, the moderation of those who are confident in being God's people for Christ's sake. The patience and generosity of those who live from God's resources. The cheerful acceptance of what Christ puts us to now because we know its meaning and purpose. The calm bearing of pain that knows nothing of the tearful, sentimental, beaten-dog attitude toward heaven as a coward's escape, but the courage, the composure, the balance, and the certainty of those who in Christ have all things.

In Christ we have the sonship and the victory. Christ's resurrection guarantees the victory of His brothers and sisters. Christ's second coming brings final fulfillment. And Christ, our Lord, is at hand.

AMEN.

Christmas Day

LUKE 2:1–20

VALPARAISO UNIVERSITY (1975)

"It happened." That is how the Christmas Gospel begins. "It happened." "It came to pass" has rather an aura around it. "It happened" is such a matter-of-fact and ordinary way of reporting an occurrence that most modern translations leave it out, regarding it as redundant. If you report what took place, you don't also have to say that it happened. True, but when the event has suffered such a lack of focus that it has been turned into a pretty myth to make shallow pretenses of a piece with reindeer in the sky and "all I want for Christmas is my two front teeth," then it is not redundant to hear the evangelist report matter-of-factly, "It happened."

What happened is told with bold simplicity and with no religification, but it is told really quite unprepossessingly. The government wanted more taxes. So what is new? That sounds familiar. This is the world in which we live—"as sure as death and taxes." In a census, people and property had to be listed, then on this basis the amount of tax was assessed. This listing is what is spoken of in our text. The latter part wasn't completed until A.D. 6, according to Josephus. In Gaul there was such opposition that the whole process took 40 years. Just think if they had to do it in Scotland! In Palestine there was opposition, especially in Galilee, the hotbed of the Zealots. But Joseph just sets out, traveling through a country raided by the Zealots, who would make short shrift of such collaborators with the hated Romans.

Caesar has nothing to fear from Joseph and Mary, a woman in the third trimester of her pregnancy. Or so it would appear. What difference could this couple make to mighty Caesar Augustus, ruler of the world? He was concerned about Herod the Great. Caesar had punished Herod for not toeing the line and had deprived him of his title "friend of Caesar." But a carpenter, a woman, and a fetus—even if he had known of them, what would Caesar care? His job was statistics and taxes, law and order. At all of these he was very good. But today we remember Caesar Augustus for something he neither knew about nor intended. He was instrumental in bringing Mary and Joseph and the unborn child to Bethlehem. The most powerful man in the world and an insignificant carpenter, without their choice, bring it about that Jesus' birth is in Bethlehem. (They do not really bring it about; they are instrumental, but that fact is made explicit only in the second part of today's Gospel.)

Bethlehem was hometown for "the house and lineage of David," technical terms with taxable significance. A decree of Caesar Augustus was executed by Quirinius so an unheard of man by the name of Joseph and the woman he was to marry, and she already in late pregnancy, would travel to Bethlehem. While they were there, Mary "brought forth her firstborn son, and wrapped Him in swaddling clothes, and laid Him in a manger; because there was no room for them in the inn" (Luke 2:7). They must have been poor, and she must have had an anxious time of it. Is there anything more to say? All over the world poor women are having anxious times every day. So a baby was born. It was a boy. Poor little guy in a manger. Who cares? His mother and Joseph. Nobody else. That is all there was to see.

But that is not all that happened. What happened you could not know by looking. You could only know if you were told, and you could only be told by someone who had seen it happen. The people asleep in Bethlehem did not know of this birth. But near Bethlehem there were some who were told, and they were told by those who knew, those who bring messages from God. He is moving things to the fulfillment of His promise.

Now if God has a message, it is only natural to expect that it would be given to those who understand that sort of thing: the theologians or the priests who have charge of His affairs. No, the message is given to shepherds. Nothing very likely about them, a rough lot, and notorious for their bad church attendance. They were scared stiff. Who wouldn't be? The pure brilliance of light signaled the presence of God: "The glory of the Lord shone round about them" (Luke 2:9). They couldn't run away, and they couldn't stand it. How could they protect themselves from God? What could they expect from Him? They could not imagine that He had come to give out prizes to reward what splendid chaps they were. They knew what sort of men they were, and they knew that from God they would have to take whatever He gave out. Everything depended on Him, and they were defenseless. They feared God above all else. All else could not hinder Him. They were exposed to God. Whatever came from Him, that is how it would be for them.

From God then comes His word through His messenger: "Fear not." Good news. "For unto you is born this day in the city of David a Savior, which is Christ the Lord" (Luke 2:10–11). So that is it. That is why Caesar Augustus and Quirinius and Joseph were where they were and did what they did: So these shepherds, as the first to be told, would know what had happened. The Good News is what happened. The angel does not discuss the attributes of God, the changes of His mercy outweighing His justice, that His justice is not all that hard and will bend in their favor if they make a sincere effort, that they are basically decent people who just haven't got it all together yet, or that all the things they have been yearning for are now on their way. No, the angel's message is simply what happened—a birth—and the identification of the one born—"a Savior which is Christ the Lord." Impossible? No, it has happened. God does not have to wait for clearance from us whether it is possible or not. It happened. A Savior born, Christ the Lord.

That is what the angel said in the unmistakable and fearful glory. Could it be so? The shepherds find it so when they follow the message of the angel. They go to Bethlehem and find the message to be true. With the message, they are given a sign. They might have stumbled on some other baby born in Bethlehem that night. They would not know by looking at the baby; all babies look pretty much alike, and Mary's Son was a baby like all the others. The one of whom the angels spoke was "wrapped in swaddling clothes, lying in a manger" (Luke 2:12). Only one baby like that could be found in Bethlehem, only by that sign could the shepherds know which one. They found that one. That is all we are told. That is what matters, and the shepherds carried that message. They did not have much to say about what they had seen of the baby. What can you say about a baby? Not much. A baby is a baby. What they told others was what had been "told them concerning this child" (Luke 2:17). The shepherds were next in proclaiming what had happened. The birth was the birth of the Savior who is Christ the Lord.

Impossible? No, with God nothing is impossible. But it is not with the possibility that anything is proven for our salvation. Almighty God can do what He likes. But can He love us so much—can holy God love us so much—as to put Himself into our messed-up lot, into what happens to us for our sake, to be our Savior? The heart of unbelief is to refuse to be loved so much. God can love others perhaps, but not me. Or we may think we deserve God's love, which is also refusal of His love. We would have God deal with us another way, not with undeserved love but in a way in which we would have ourselves to thank, at least for some of it.

Not so the shepherds. They feared God above all and from Him came the Good News, His Good News. The shepherds followed and found and carried on the telling of the message they had received. They took it from God. What He said had happened, and they believed, most incredible of all, that this birth was for them, the birth of a Savior who is Christ the Lord. For them and for you, yes, for you. That is how much God loves you. It happened, and you have been told.

The shepherds went proclaiming, but they also went back to their sheep—same old sheep but no longer the same old shepherds. While minding their sheep, they heard God's word, and now they went on minding their sheep, believing God's word that told them what was for them from God: "a Savior who is Christ the Lord." Joseph went back to his carpentry and Mary to caring for her child and her home. We are told she pondered these things in her heart. God knows her heart. We know she pondered the birth, the child, and the words that had been spoken of Him. The word *pondering* means "putting together." She pondered how this baby of hers could be the one of whom such things were spoken.

The words concerning Mary's baby are spoken to you also. To *you* is born a Savior who is Christ the Lord. That is who is for you from God. Such is God for you. Fear Him above all else and from Him hear the message. Nothing comes ahead of that; nothing is surer than that. Everything else comes after that, fits in with that, is illumined by that fact. You have it on the highest authority that Christ has been born. It is an authority not of power but of love. God is pleased with us; He loves us. If we fully believed that, then surely our hearts would burst, says Martin Luther. "Born in us today." Yes, Lord, I believe. Help my unbelief. Help me out of refusing to be loved so much. Let Your body and blood have their way with me so I know how incredibly You join me and love me to death and by Your death win forgiveness for me, who is accepted, embraced, joined with You.

Then we go back to what it is that we have in the way of sheep to tend, carpentry to do, child and home to care for. The same tasks, but different. That is where we carry and heed the message, and in living out our calling, God will do things through us that are beyond our knowing and planning, as He did through the shepherds, Mary and Joseph, and even Caesar Augustus and Quirinius. We are there for God as He may be pleased to use us. We are the "handmaid of the Lord"; therefore, no heroicising of yourself. That is only an impediment to our Lord. "I will do a Quirinius" or "I will do a Mary." No, God wants to do with you a Jim and a Susan. We let Him be the Lord. Would we wish to change Him or submit Him to doing things according to our prescriptions? Mary had to learn later that God had His own way of doing what was His to do—a cross and a sword through her heart. But she held to the words, good words, words of the Savior who is Christ the Lord in the stable and on the cross.

You came to hear the good words again, bringing along the parts of you that still say no, the parts from a world of death and taxes and all the things that threaten to wear away your life or trivialize it. The good words help us through to the rock bottom of what happened, and on that we can build, fitting in with that all the pieces and layers of our lives, the hard things and certainly the happy things too. We can let them be the happy things they are—family, home, friends together, gifts, food, drink, and all the fun and kindliness of Christmas—for they are liberated from having to cover a wretchedness or emptiness of heart. For our heart is now fixed where true joy is found, and that is more than anything that offers it a contradiction. "A Savior, which is Christ the Lord." It happened, and the words have carried it to you, and the bread and wine. Then return, proclaiming it, back to your sheep. While tending them, our Lord will have things to do with you that you have not planned.

AMEN.

First Sunday after Christmas

LUKE 2:33–35

VALPARAISO UNIVERSITY (1968)

According to Luke, Christmas concludes in the temple—the institutional church I suppose we could call it. The baby Jesus was brought there for the Service of Presentation forty days after His birth (so we celebrate the event on February 2). On the Sunday after Christmas, we ponder the prophetic words of Simeon that point forward to what lies ahead for this child's career: "Behold, this child is set for the fall and rising again of many in Israel; and for a sign which shall be spoken against . . . that thoughts of many hearts may be revealed" (Luke 2:34–35). This may not sound very Christmasy, yet since Christmas Day we have observed St. Stephen's Day, St. John's Day, and the Feast of the Holy Innocents, all of whom were martyrs. How shocked we are by these words of Simeon depends on what we traditionally have thought of Christmas.

Jesus, Simeon says, is one in response to whom people show if they have received or rejected God. Once again this Christmas, Luke has extolled Mary's baby as the Son of God. Gabriel told Mary she would have a son and Elizabeth greeted Mary as the mother of her Lord. Zechariah blessed God for the fulfillment of His promises and for John who would "go before the face of the Lord to prepare His ways" (Luke 1:76). The angels proclaimed the birth of "a Savior which is Christ the Lord" (Luke 2:11).

The shepherds went with haste and, shockingly, found a baby in a manger. Yet their hearts were glad, for they received what had been told them. They knew what was hidden there in the baby in the manger. For this child is a sign, as Simeon says. In the Bible a sign often means something that contains and conveys what God is doing and giving. At the same time a sign hides under what appears to be its opposite. The disclosure of a sign is by a word of God, which requires hearing and receiving, faith. God's dealing with us in this way reduces us to the point at which we are nothing but receivers. The shepherds received the words of the angel and embraced the baby in the manger as the Savior who is Christ the Lord.

Simeon received a word from God too. He would not die until he saw the Messiah. Each day Simeon grew older and older, yet he clung to God's word. When the sign of Mary's baby came to the temple, Simeon rejoiced. The messages contained in that sign were "now you will die" and "this is the Savior." A baby of the poor is the sign of Simeon's death and salvation. Simeon looked at his life and his death through this sign and departed in peace. For Simeon, this child was set for his falling and rising.

It was to Mary that Simeon's prophecy was spoken. Her child was also a sign of her falling and rising. Mary had to learn that she had a son, yet she did not have Him—He really had her. Sometimes, when Mary made the ordinary claims of a mother or misunderstood, she was pushed back by her son. To receive the sign of her son meant that Mary suffered loss. Simeon told her of a sword that would pierce her, and our hearts turn to the mother fallen at the foot of the cross of her son. Remember, a sign appears as the opposite of what it contains and conveys. The sign hidden under its opposite on the arms of the cross and in the arms of Simeon was God's salvation. God's way of giving this sign can only be received in the same lowly way. In that lowliness there is great mercy. We are not required to pull ourselves up to a level at which we become worthy of being dealt with by God. There is no point below this lowliness where we can fall beneath His reach. People are lost by refusing this lowliness, thinking it is an insult to their pride and insisting on ways of being dealt with that do them honor. These people want a god who will serve their purposes and meet their specifications.

Mary cried for her son in the stable. She cried for Him at Calvary with tears that washed away any demand and insistence of hers. When all of Mary was crumpled, when a sword went through her soul, she was raised up. For Mary and Simeon, Jesus was a sign for falling *and* rising. For many in Israel, He was a sign only for falling. In their response to Jesus, the Jews showed what they were. The thoughts of their hearts were revealed. He did not meet their self-honoring specifications. They had no use for such a lowly, weak, and beggarly Messiah. They wanted someone useful for their social, political, and religious purposes, and for these one needs power.

Mary's baby had power enough, but the power was hidden beneath its opposite. Jesus wins victories not by the exercise of power but by the exercise of redeeming love. His greatest victory was hidden under its opposite. The King on a donkey had His throne on a cross. Many in Israel spoke against that sign, stumbled, and fell. Simeon used words from Isaiah's prophecy to tell of the sign (Isaiah 8:9–15). Immanuel: When God is with us, when God deals with us, it is judgment and salvation, falling and rising, or it is falling only, judgment only.

When God deals with us, we are shown for what we are. When God deals with us, the thoughts of our hearts are revealed. If we cling to our thoughts, to our insistences about God and what He must produce for us, we are undone and remain under judgment. If we are shown what we are and come clean in repentance, we receive the gifts of salvation that raise us up. These gifts come in the unlikely sign of the puling infant on Simeon's arms, the sign of the man dying on the cross, the sign of the bread and wine. We fall in repentance; we are raised by forgiveness and quickened. We receive the body and blood of Christ hidden in the lowly sign of bread and wine. (*Sign* here has little to do with Huldrych Zwingli's *signify* or making pictures or pointers out of the Sacrament. The sign contains and conveys the body and blood of Christ as His words disclose, whether you believe it or not, whether you fall and rise or only fall.) God's messengers disclosed what was hidden in Mary's baby. Christ's own words disclose what is hidden in the bread and wine.

Simeon embraced the Savior in the sign of the baby that brought him his death and his salvation. You embrace the Savior in the sign of this Sacrament where the thoughts of your heart come clear. This sign means death to you in your self-affirmation and specifying of God. It means your rising, for you are joined more closely with Christ and share His life, which no sword through your soul nor anything can destroy. All this we rejoice in as we join in the Song of Simeon after the Sacrament, rejoicing in the Savior in whom we have our falling and rising, our departure and our salvation.

AMEN.

Second Sunday after Christmas

1 SAMUEL 2:1–10

VALPARAISO UNIVERSITY (1973)

We cannot imagine a year without Christmas. But who would miss a Second Sunday after Christmas? Well, here we have one. What are we to do with this out-of-the-ordinary Sunday? The Old Testament lesson leads us back through Christmas to a mother who had a baby. What is so remarkable about that? Women have babies every day. Each of us bears witness to that fact. In childhood, nothing is more ordinary than mother. She is always there. Yet being a mother is no ordinary thing for a woman. Each bearing of a child and rearing of a child is quite particular. This time is unique, this child is unique (especially the first time). Even the second and third child do not just bring more of the same events over again.

The repeated, the ordinary, the particular, the unique. How are these interrelated in our lives? Such interrelation is vital for healthy living. Those whose lives are ordinary and routine go under in boredom. Those who live only for each particular event move erratically from this to that without sustaining continuity. They don't feel like they are part of something larger.

For Hannah, motherhood was not ordinary because she was barren and it seemed she would never give all that she could as a mother. Hannah did not think of herself as an individual. She was a wife for her husband and would be a mother for their children. She did not think of herself as someone tossed into the world who landed where she was by happenstance or capricious fate. Hannah was a member of God's people to whom the promises were given of what the Lord would bring to fulfillment from and for His people. He was God who had committed Himself to them: "And [I] will be your God, and ye shall be My people" (Leviticus 26:12).

Hannah's particular family at Ramah was part of the larger tribe of Ephraim, which was part of the larger family of the people of Israel. The relationship with members of her immediate family and with those in the larger local family, within the people of Israel, was part of her everyday life. Hannah's identity—who she was, what she was part of—was in the everyday things of her home. Her identity was drawn and held together in the life of prayer and devotion. The people of Israel were nourished in the local congregation with corporate worship and prayer, the acknowledgment of the Lord who held them together as His. This feeling of belonging to the people who acknowledged the Lord who had covenanted with them "I will be your God and you shall be My people" came to comprehensive expression when the Israelites went up to Shiloh at the time of one of the three great festivals that drew together the year's rhythm of work and harvest with God the giver and God of the covenant and promise. In the carrying through of His purposes and promises, the Israelites knew themselves to be a part of God's people. Their lives were from God's hands, held together and sustained by Him—the lives of the people, of the tribe, of the family, of the person.

The gift and flow of those lives were celebrated in the great festivals at Shiloh and through the local congregation, in the family, and in private, personal prayer. Such a healthy flow of vigorous, lively belonging is expressed in the great word *peace*. Blockages of that flow inhibit that healthy functioning of things and of people working together in peace. The enemies of peace threaten and disrupt that flow of life for God's people, the tribe, the family, the person. Hannah's personal sorrow was that there was no flow of life from her barren womb. Her sorrow was made more bitter by the hostile comments of Elkanah's other wife, Peninah, who had children. Elkanah showed he felt sorrow, too, by the portion he gave Hannah in the celebration and fellowship meal at Shiloh. Then the priest insulted her because he took her for a babbling woman who had drunk too much wine at the festival meal.

The things that were blocking the flow of Hannah's life and peace did not cut her off into bitter isolation, for she poured everything out before the Lord in her prayer. She did not crawl under or dig in behind the barriers that blocked the flow of her life, for Hannah knew her life flowed from the Lord. Her prayer pleaded that her life might flow freely from the Lord, beginning from Him who could give the flow of life from her womb, and the life that might come she would give back to Him, her gift of flowing life. "Go in peace," said the priest, meaning that things would work together for healthy flow of life, "and the God of Israel grant thee thy petition that thou hast asked of Him" (1 Samuel 1:17).

> And they rose up in the morning early, and worshiped before the LORD, and returned, and came to their house in Ramah: And Elkanah knew Hannah his wife; and the LORD remembered her. Wherefore it came to pass, when the time was come about after Hannah had conceived, that she bare a son, and called his name Samuel, saying, Because I have asked him of the LORD. (1 Samuel 1:19–20)

Next time they were going to Shiloh, Hannah said she had to stay home for her child's sake. Elkanah was wise enough not to know better than the new mother about the care of her child. Hannah was doubtless feeling the weight of her vow to give her child into the Lord's service at Shiloh. She would keep Samuel with her as long as she could, though she knew he was hers yet not hers. Samuel was also Elkanah's, and he had made Hannah's vow his own. She had promised to give their child to the Lord. When she finally took him to Shiloh, Hannah said she was lending Samuel to the Lord—not hers yet still hers. Elkanah did the occasion proud with a special sacrifice of a three-year-old bull, an ephah of flour, and a skin of wine. Hannah spoke to the priest who had insulted her and told him how God had heard her prayer.

Then it all comes flowing out to the Lord in Hannah's prayer of thanksgiving, a psalm she may have learned from the liturgy or at Sunday school. Her prayer expresses that it is all to God, for Hannah knows that it is from Him that she has been given to. Her life flows freely to God as she has received from Him her flow of life that enlarges in her family, in her congregation, in her relationships, and among her people. It is God at the center, holding it all together and from whom the flow of life comes that lifts Hannah up in exultant thanksgiving. The gift of a son had overflowed her life with happiness and filled her emptiness. Hannah overflowed with all the good things of motherhood, and the waves of happiness washed through her family, the congregation, her little world at Ramah, and now at the center of the life of the people, at the tabernacle with the ark of the covenant at Shiloh, the pledge of the Lord's presence and promises for His people. Here Hannah empties herself again. She gives her happiest gift in her life back to the Lord, and from Shiloh she would leave empty.

The psalm with which Hannah says her prayers to the Lord recognizes that the Lord is her Lord not only through her happy days but also through all her days. In her bitter days she did not turn her back on the Lord and desert Him by saying that He does not care or He is no God. Hannah had cried to Him in her need and her unhappiness. The Lord gave her a child, and she overflowed with glad thanksgiving. But she did not say, "This proves that the Lord is for real." Had Hannah said that, when she lost her son, she would have disintegrated and said to the Lord, "No more of You." When people say they have lost their faith because of some great loss or pain, they are showing that they did not have much or any faith to lose. Those people do not believe God, His name, His Word, or His promises. First for them comes what they want, and God is their servant to see that they get and keep what they want. "You are my servant to see that I get or keep what I want" is the opposite of "You are the Lord."

Hannah kept her faith through the days of her emptiness, through the days of overflowing happiness, and through the days ahead when her child was with her no more. Her whole life, and all that was Hannah, her heart, were "in the Lord." The Lord was the rock foundation on which all her days and all the pieces of her life were integrated. "In the Lord" she knew that her life was where no enemies could invade and destroy her. They would have to destroy the Lord first before they could do her harm. "My heart rejoiceth in the LORD, mine horn is exalted in the LORD: my mouth is enlarged over mine enemies; because I rejoice in Thy salvation" (1 Samuel 2:1).

He is the only Lord. There is no other Lord, none greater than He. He is above all. We cannot call Him in question because whatever He does is right. "There is none holy as the LORD: for there is none beside Thee: neither is there any rock like our God" (1 Samuel 2:2). Those who proudly put their confidence in themselves and their strength, the Lord sees the folly they are. What anybody amounts to is by the Lord's assessment. "Talk no more so exceeding proudly; let no arrogancy come out of your mouth: for the LORD is a God of knowledge, and by Him actions are weighed" (1 Samuel 2:3). What is mighty and proud in its own strength the Lord turns upside down. The Lord shows the folly of our pride, of trusting in ourselves. "The bows of the mighty men are broken, and they that stumbled are girded with strength" (1 Samuel 2:4).

Then come the words in the psalm that fit Hannah most closely: "The barren hath born seven; and she that hath many children is waxed feeble" (1 Samuel 2:5). The details do not precisely fit Hannah's life, but they indicate her feelings at what was happening in her life. A hospitalized man who had come close to dying and was in great pain told his pastor, "I have known the psalms all my life; now I have learned to pray them as never before." The psalms indicated what was going on in this man's life. For Hannah the psalm speaks of her barrenness, of her happiness in giving birth to a child, and of her forlornness when her child was no longer with her. All her life was "in the Lord."

There is nothing that lies beyond the Lord. There is nothing outside of His reach. Even death does not lie outside His lordship but serves His purposes. "The LORD killeth, and maketh alive: He bringeth down to the grave, and bringeth up" (1 Samuel 2:6). There is special mention of the hungry, the poor, and the needy, for they express the emptiness that can be filled by the Lord. The Lord delights to fill emptiness with good things. Those who are full with their own proud strength are not givable to.

The Lord does not love you less if you are rich. He wants you to give thanks for your riches and use them as His. The Lord lends them to you, and you give them back to Him as Hannah did with her greatest riches, her child, in a continuity of living "in the Lord." Hannah was kept from boasting of her deprivation and loss, of how she suffered for what she gave to the Lord, because the Lord gave her three more sons and two daughters. "The LORD maketh poor, and maketh rich: He bringeth low, and lifteth up" (1 Samuel 2:7).

There is much more in the psalm Hannah prayed. Some of the words held her life in them; some of the words spoke of things that were not part of her life. The Lord did not give her to "sit with princes," but she prays this psalm for all its rejoicing of a life, the whole of it, lived "in the Lord." Hannah's life was in her prayer, in this psalm of the liturgy, and in her worship of the Lord at the tabernacle at Shiloh. From that center her life was "in the Lord" also in Ramah, in the congregation, and in her own home and family—all of one piece, a continuity of life, not of this and that or bits and pieces, but all fitting together, an organic vital wholeness "in the Lord."

Today we have the Word of God read and preached into our lives, and our lives fit closely into some of the words and not so closely into others. With prayers and hymns we acknowledge our lives to be "in the Lord." We use the name of God at the beginning of our service, and in the creed we confess that "You are the Lord." We hold nothing outside God's lordship, from Him our lives flow in their poverty and their riches, in our being brought low and in our being raised up. He is the Lord. "There is none holy as the LORD: for there is none beside Thee: neither is there any rock like our God" (1 Samuel 2:2). That rock certainly integrates our whole lives, holds them together, and keeps them flowing toward the Lord in worship. Our lives flow from Him and all He gives into our congregation, homes, families, and communities.

The year that lies ahead will have the oft repeated and the ordinary, as well as the new and the unique. We shall live it all "in the Lord"—the days we find ourselves overflowing with good things, we live them all "in the Lord." There is no other Lord. He has become one of us by way of little Mary, who sings much of the same psalm in her song of thanksgiving for the son that was born of her and who was pointed to at the end of Hannah's song—the Anointed One, the Messiah, the Christ. The love that brought Him to the manger and the cross is the love in which our lives are held and lived "in the Lord."

AMEN.

The Epiphany of Our Lord

MATTHEW 8:5

VALPARAISO UNIVERSITY (1971)

Epiphany arrived with a small point of light, a star, that led those strange characters called the Magi to Jesus. Where did they come from? Where did they return to? Nobody knows. These Gentiles, foreigners, outsiders were asking where is He who is born King of the Jews. Scriptures said the Messiah would be born in Bethlehem. What the Magi found there was a strange sort of Messiah, a quite ludicrous king. They fell down and worshiped Him, gave their best. The Magi were His men, then they were shepherded away. They had their little moment on stage, then they were heard of no more. Are they lost? No, they were the first of many people who would come from the East and sit at the table with Abraham, Isaac, and Jacob.

Sunday's Gospel includes two more outsiders, the leper and the centurion (Matthew 5–7). Jesus' sermon on the mountain teaches the way of life in the new Israel, just as old Israel had received its Law through Moses on the mountain. Old Israel, new Israel—more of the same Israel? No, for we have already heard of the Magi, and now we hear of two more who don't count in Israel. Jesus is there for the outsider too. With a movement to gasp at, Jesus reached out and touched the putrid leper, a thing forbidden in Israel. Healed, the leper is led back into the community of Israel. He is to go see the priest and offer what Moses commanded. It is the same Israel.

When Jesus came to Capernaum, a centurion stopped Him and blurted out his need for Jesus to heal his servant. Right away Jesus said, "I will come and heal him" (Matthew 8:7). This was too much for the centurion, a Roman and a heathen, whose home the Jews were taught never to enter. So in his rough soldier's way he tells Jesus, "This is too much. Orders are orders. Just say the word."

Then it is Jesus' turn to marvel at the centurion, and He puts it in terms of Israel. Sons of the kingdom will be cast out into the outer darkness, and many will come from the east and the west and sit at table with Abraham, Isaac, and Jacob in the kingdom of heaven—God's kingdom, His people, His Israel, Jesus' Israel—for Jesus is the Christ.

He fulfills God's plan, what God has in mind for people, the gathering of His Israel, those who call Him Lord.

In Matthew the first people to call Jesus "Lord" are the leper and the centurion. "Lord" is the name of the God of Abraham, Isaac, and Jacob. One Lord, one Israel. It is the same old Israel into which many come from the east and the west. Many who are members of Israel according to the flesh drop out, for they do not receive the Christ, they do not believe. Those who believe, those who receive Him, are Israel, the people of Abraham, who is the father of the faithful. Faith is first spoken of in Matthew's Gospel with this Gentile centurion's words. Faith is where Jesus is Lord. There is Israel, there is church, the congregation of believers gathered together by the Lord, the God of Abraham, Isaac, and Jacob; the God of the Magi, leper, and centurion; the God of you and me and that leper with whom you don't want to have any contact.

The Book of Matthew was written for people who were not at all sure that Gentiles belonged in Israel. Those people didn't have a doubt that they belonged, hence the blast against the sons of the kingdom. Sometimes that is where we fit into our text. We are in God's kingdom, naturally. But be warned, sons of the kingdom can be cast out, those who do not receive the Christ, those for whom He is not Lord, those who have another Christ, another Messiah of their own liking and construction. There is one Lord, one Christ, one Israel, one church, and one plan of God for our rescue and completion. They are gathered from the east and west to sit at the table with Abraham, Isaac, and Jacob.

Into this one purpose and company and kingdom of God we have been gathered so we are not torn apart by the discontinuities that would reduce us to pieces. We are not human fragments thrown in the air and blown about by blind and cruel chance. Our leprosy and looming death are touched and overcome by this man from Nazareth whom we believe, receive, call Lord, and who incorporates us into His Israel that He leads through history and brings to the consummation. Our worship this morning is not an isolated piece of time. It expresses the whole of who we are and what we are for together. You cannot be Israel by yourself or "just me and my friends." Israel is Christ's people, not sundered or destroyed by generation gaps or future shock. Ponder those glorious genealogies with their funny names and doubtful characters. They proclaim the continuity of God's Israel and show how the unlikeliest people are included.

Transfiguration Sunday is that burst of light with Moses, Elijah, Peter, James, and John. The light is transmitted for us through words and water, wine and bread, and we gather and move on together to the Lord's Table at which we are as one with angels, archangels, and all the company of heaven, Abraham, Isaac, and Jacob, and so on and on and on through today and tomorrow, on to the consummation.
AMEN.

The Baptism of Our Lord

MARK 1:9–11

CONCORDIA SEMINARY (1990)

Jesus came from Galilee to the Jordan to be baptized by John. That just didn't seem right to John when he had been blasting away at sinners and proclaiming fearful judgment on them. Then Jesus came along and acted as if He were a sinner, just like the rest of us. What John had been proclaiming concerning God's judgments didn't seem to fit with Jesus coming to a sinner's baptism. In fact, John should go to Him for baptism. Jesus must stay separate, and we must move to Him. He should not come and be a sinner with us.

Yet Jesus does become one of us. He takes on all that has gone wrong with us—all our sins. Jesus is most sinner, most Savior. With that sin, He belongs with us. There is no distance or separation between us and Christ. That is how God has decided His judgment and His righteousness is to go. Jesus answered, "Suffer it to be so now: for thus it becometh us to fulfill all righteousness" (Matthew 3:15). What John had seen as a necessary separation—"No sinner's baptism for you!"—Jesus gently pushes past and tells John, "We are in this together, this fulfilling of all righteousness." This is God showing how He is toward us, how His judgment falls, how His righteousness is fulfilled.

For the fulfilling of all righteousness, the Righteous One, one of the Messiah's names, had been promised. Another name of His in today's Gospel is Servant. Both names are in the promise in Isaiah: "Shall My righteous servant justify many; for He shall bear their iniquities" (53:11). That this is the Righteous One, who bears our iniquities, is shown when Jesus is baptized with sinner's baptism. There is a word of God put on the event so we may know and receive everything that is in this man for us.

The star led the Wise Men to Jerusalem in search of the one born to be King of the Jews. It was the wrong place, the wrong sort of king. To the star were added God's words of promise. Star and words of God led on to Bethlehem and to such a king as never was before or since. We only know for sure what is happening if there is a word of God put on it. "This is My beloved Son, in whom I am well pleased" (Matthew 17:6). These are God's own words of promise, declared fulfilled in Jesus. "Behold My Servant, whom I uphold; Mine elect, in whom My soul delighteth; I have put My Spirit upon Him: He shall bring forth judgment to the Gentiles" (Isaiah 42:1). Here justice is how God says things are, His righteousness. And the one baptized is the fulfiller of it so righteousness may be ours too. Where our sins are is where He is. Where His righteousness is, is where we are. His righteousness is as surely ours as our sins are surely His. Christ joins us in our sin, bears it, and fulfills all righteousness to make righteousness ours. We are righteous with His righteousness, and in that God has His delight.

The delight and pleasure of God are in His beloved Son, and that is where we are too. What is ours is His; what is His is ours. So God delights in us too. If our hearts would take this in, Martin Luther said, they would burst for joy into a hundred thousand pieces. In a world that is given over to sin, death, and the devil, there is one point where the delight of God dwells. "This is My beloved Son with whom I am well pleased." That is where we are in solidarity with Jesus. With Jesus there is God's delight. God, Christ, you—all together like one thing.

Do you live where Christ is, where God has His delight? Yes, for God has put His words on you too. With the water His name was put on you at your Baptism. You are not just a doubtful, ambiguous, meaningless, hopeless bunch of atoms bouncing around. You have the word of God put on you. At your Baptism, surely, and at Jesus' baptism too. For there Jesus is in solidarity with us and we with Him. Because He is the beloved Son, we with Him are beloved sons and daughters, delighted in and beloved of God. So you can't just drag along dreary, fearful, guilt-ridden, nobody-loves-me, me-against-the-rest, me-against-the-system, me-separate, all alone. When John saw Jesus separate, Jesus said, "No. Us." When Jesus says "us," He takes on what we are and gives us what He has. The Righteous One fulfills all righteousness, and you are in on that, where God says you are at—in His delight, with Jesus. As if that weren't enough, Christ now gives to you His body and His blood, together-ed with Him. "Us"-ed. It goes with you as it goes with Him.

AMEN.

Second Sunday after the Epiphany

JOHN 1:43–51

VALPARAISO UNIVERSITY (1979)

Who of us faced with the simple question "What would be a good place to have a Lutheran university?" would answer, "Nazareth"? This city was not exactly a crossroad of history or civilization. Besides, there wasn't the city of Fort Wayne nearby with a bunch of keen Lutheran laymen thinking it might be a good idea to have a Lutheran university. Nazareth was just Nazareth. Could anything good come out of Nazareth? Nothing much ever had before. There were no famous bank robbers or murderers to boast of, let alone a naval victory or heroic quantities of snow. No one from Nazareth had ever made it into the Top Ten list. Nazareth had not even made it into the Old Testament or the Apocrypha or Josephus or the Talmud. Nazareth was a one-donkey nothing of a town.

"Now Philip was of Bethsaida" (John 1:44), and he has something to tell his friend Nathanael. We know from the highest possible authority that Nathanael was a good man, and we also have supporting circumstantial evidence. Under a fig tree was a favorite spot for reading the Bible. Yet it is possible to read the Bible twice a day under a dozen fig trees and still miss the whole message. Indeed, you can read the Bible in such a way as to prevent yourself from getting the message. You can read it as a manual on how to be a good person because it contains lots of rules and models to follow. You can read the Bible as a manual on how to be a good god. The problem with Nathanael wasn't that he was a bad person, it was his theology, how he thought God was supposed to be a good God. *Nazareth* on Nathanael's lips means, "That is no way for God to be doing anything." There are ways that are fitting for God to do things, and doing them from Nazareth, out of that nothing of a town not even mentioned in the Old Testament, cannot possibly be one of them.

The Wise Men went to the capital to see the King. If a king is born, a palace is where it ought to happen and be known about. But the star led them to a stable. The Magi's problem, too, was in their theology. Their old gods had to die for God to be born for them in a stable, and that meant their dying, too, and their being born again. In the "Journey of the Magi," T. S. Eliot wrote of birth and death and the life-altering meeting of the Magi and the King. Upon their return to their earthly kingdoms, these Magi were confronted by the idolatry of their fellow citizens and wished to be reunited with their King, even if it meant death.

Death and birth were also necessary for Nathanael. The God who couldn't do anything for Nazareth had to die, and the God who could do everything for Nazareth had to be born for him, and that birth was birth again for Nathanael. New God, new Nathanael, Jesus of Nazareth, Nathanael His disciple. Jesus comes the stable way, the womb way, the Nazareth way.

What about the Valpo way? We, a university crowd, are more Wise Men than shepherds. We are expected to know the answers. We have a little planetarium and we study what makes the world go, how things work, and how to succeed. We need power and money, say the realists; we need love say, the romantics. With the biggest college chapel in the world and fig trees of our required theology, we think we have a pretty fair handle on God. There are standards that He has to meet, otherwise we'll flunk Him out. There are ways that are fitting for God to behave and ways that are not. When we lay it down for Him, it is ridiculous to suppose that we are then dealing with the living God.

Jesus knew how ridiculous it was to deal with God this way, so He gave Nathanael a poke about his fig tree. With a grin? Now a grin is not something God is supposed to do, neither is He supposed to come from Nazareth nor be born in a stable nor flee as a refugee nor make tables for the bumpkins of Nazareth the way they want their tables made.

What is God supposed to be like? Philip does not have an argument with Nathanael, though they could have had a real good theological one. But Philip was already a Jesus man. He knew there could be nothing persuasive of Jesus better than Jesus Himself. "Philip saith unto him, 'Come and see.' Jesus saw Nathanael coming to Him . . . Before that Philip called thee, when thou wast under the fig tree, I saw thee" (John 1:46–48). Nathanael wasn't seeing, but he was seen by Jesus of Nazareth, yes, Nazareth. The first question is not whether you believe in God but whether He believes in you. Jesus accepted Nathanael. Jesus saw Nathanael and had His man Philip say to him, "Come and see." Nathanael was seen. He came and he saw Jesus of Nazareth.

In the Gospel of John, seeing is not just rods and cones work. Nathanael's eyes saw the man from Nazareth, and that man came across to Nathanael, welcoming him. Then Nathanael saw Him personally and exclaimed, "Rabbi, Thou art the Son of God; Thou art the King of Israel" (John 1:49). This wasn't a cautious or guarded way of talking, but the best that could come from Nathanael when Jesus made him His man. Then perhaps there was a grin. Come on, you say big words, but you haven't seen anything yet! You will see the gate of heaven, the one who knows the way, the one who is the way, the one to be lifted up. That is certainly no way for a Son of God and the King of Israel to go.

Nathanael had called Jesus "Rabbi," "Son of God," and "King of Israel." Jesus picks up none of these titles but speaks of the Son of Man, the name that makes Him interchangeable with everyone and anyone. It is the title that Jesus uses when He speaks of His glory, the glory of the Son of Man. During Holy Week, Jesus said, "The hour has come that the Son of Man should be glorified," (John 12:23), then He spoke of His death, of His being lifted up from the earth. "The people answered Him, 'We have heard out of the law that the Christ abideth forever: and how sayest Thou, The Son of Man must be lifted up? Who is this Son of Man?' " (John 12:34). He is Jesus of Nazareth, the King of the Jews, INRI, the King of Israel who has a cross for His throne.

Jesus kept His promise to Nathanael: "Thou shalt see greater things than these" (John 1:50). Greater things than Nathanael could ever have imagined or wanted. He wanted no Christ that would come from Nazareth, let alone one that dies on a cross and has, as His throne, a cross by which He draws all to Himself. There Christ does for us what was ours for our sin, our sin of trying to make Him into another kind of God. He is the Calvary kind, the Nazareth kind. If Christ can have His way the Nazareth way, the Calvary way, then perhaps by way of Valpo too.

We lay aside our pride and guile, our trust in ourselves as altogether fitting channels for God's working, when we pray that this may be a university "under the cross." That is a Nazareth prayer from Nazareth hearts. These hearts are astonished that our Lord should see us under our fig trees and should care about us. Can anything good come out of Valpo, out of you, out of me? Our measuring of ourselves may not be at all encouraging. Do we judge the way the world judges? Do we judge the way natural religion judges? Do we judge with our own judgment? Do we judge with the judgment of Jesus of Nazareth? Who says yes to us? Our yes of pride and guile rings hollow, yet our "No, we really aren't worth much" comes into contradiction with Jesus' yes. The "Yes, you; I saw you" is spoken by the man from Nazareth.

> If they might guess his Bethlehem of birth . . .
> A Nazareth none after may despise!
> And there he dwells . . .
> In lanes or chambers is his gospel shown . . .
> The land's salvation hidden in the Name
> Which for his pilgrimage in time now hath
> Our bodies' hallowed region for his path,
> We his Capernaum, his Bethany,—
> But ah! We too his Mount, his Calvary!

His Nazareth, His Dau, His Scheele, His Brandt, His Neils, His Valparaiso.

AMEN.

Third Sunday after the Epiphany

ROMANS 12:20–21

LONDON (1949)

Our text presents a battle, a struggle against an enemy. Last Sunday's Epistle showed how Christ shines forth in our relationships within the family of God. Today's Epistle shows how Christ shines forth in our relationship with our enemy. Therefore, let us consider how our enemy got to be that way, how our enemy may win the victory, how we may win the victory, and, finally, how the battle goes.

Our Lord tells us that if we live as His disciples, we will be hated for no other reason than that we are His disciples. The Christian life is a constant reproach to those whose lives are empty of God and full of self. Christ's life was of such a quality that people saw their own lives as ugly and distorted compared to Him. They hated Him with a hatred that killed Him in their hearts and on the cross. Insofar as we are like Christ, others will hate us for the same reason. Jesus said, "Ye shall be hated of all men for My name's sake" (Matthew 10:22) and "If they have persecuted Me, they will also persecute you" (John 15:20). If we have not felt this persecution, doubt is not cast on the word of our Lord but on how much of our lives are lived as disciples of Christ. Persecution does not necessarily mean sword and cross and lions, though in our day there is no lack of that sort either. Just a few hours flight from here, thousands are suffering for Jesus' sake. To think only of the Lutherans who have been starved, shot, tortured, and enslaved in the last few years is to see the truth of our Lord's words with shuddering clearness, and then to wonder how we shall stand when our turn comes.

But our turn is now. As God's people we are engaged in battle all our lives, and this battle is more difficult because it is so unspectacular. Great Christians have said that it is easier to face the firing squad for Jesus' sake than to turn the other cheek. In the days ahead our Father may allow us the tests of bloody persecution, starvation, and torture, but our job now is to fight our present battle and train to grow strong so we may face any emergency without fear. We have not known prison and death for Christ, but we have experienced the freezing supercilious pity of those superior and enlightened moderns who hold in contempt what we as Christians hold most dear. It has hurt us keenly to be regarded as rather stupid, old-fashioned, simpleminded folk sadly behind the times in this enlightened twentieth century. It is not easy to be mocked as an enemy of fun and pleasure, to refrain from cursing when scorned as a holy Joe, or called a fine Christian with a love that ridicules you.

We live in a society in which, among polite Englishmen, religion is respected. But you must not allow your religion to interfere too much with business (close an eye, give a wink). It is not even a good topic to talk about too much. So the dynamite of our Lord's Gospel is diluted to become a part of our respectability. We think it is carrying things a bit too far to pick up drunks or beggars and help them—that is what we have police and ambulances for. The women of Leicester Square call forth self-righteousness or a sordid jest, and the children of the slums prompt only blame on their parents or the government. For us to take hold and tackle these problems personally, as Christ would do, would be to subject ourselves to the persecution of patronizing pity, a thousand petty obstructions, and thinly veiled contempt. If you walk and work with Christ, you will run into a lot of snags and scorn.

However, it would not be honest to assume that all the obstructions and enmity we meet are caused by the fact that we are Christians. From us, too, there goes out malice, ill will, selfishness, a love that is limited, and a sympathy that is narrow. These call forth a response of the same kind, and we cannot then say that we are suffering for Christ. As Scripture says, it is no credit to us if we suffer malice that is roused by our own lovelessness (1 Peter 3:17). We get our enemies because we are Christ's and because of our stumbling into lovelessness, ill will, and selfishness.

The victory our enemy seeks is to make us the same as himself. The reproach of a Christian life is unbearable, for it points toward a recognition of sin and the confession of worthlessness before God. These are they whom Jesus speaks of when He says, "And this is the condemnation, that light is come into the world, and men loved darkness rather than light, because their deeds were evil. For every one that doeth evil hateth the light, neither cometh to the light, lest his deeds should be reproved" (John 3:19). Light would destroy the darkness.

The highest human folly is to shrink from that cleansing light. Fearfully many love darkness, cherish their disease, and hate God, who alone can heal. In their darkness there is no contentment. They cannot be at peace with themselves because they are not at peace with God. They seek consolation in trying to discredit and destroy the children of light. Their highest pleasure is to see a righteous person fall. They may forget for a moment what is unclean in themselves by besmirching someone else.

Such a strategy of attack is seldom consciously known to the godless you meet or those with whom you work. They are only privates in the army of evil and scarcely aware of that. Their commander at hellish headquarters does his best to keep them befuddled. The godless must not see things too clearly because that is what the opposition wants. The devil knows that his most effective soldiers are the ones who think they are fighting on the other side—witness the Inquisition and the words of Jesus to His disciple, "The time cometh, that whosoever killeth you will think that he doeth God service" (John 16:2). Whether the devil's private realizes it or not, his great pleasure is to work the overthrow of a child of God. The methods of attack are multitude, frontal and invidious, brazen and subtle, but the victory aimed at is the same—to make evil like himself.

Our Lord charges us to be sober and watchful against every attack. The stand we take may be poisoned by our doing the right thing for the wrong reason. A frontal attack of anger or spite may trip us into the same. If somebody is angry with us and we lose our temper, the enemy has won the victory. We are conquered because we have sunk to anger, and his evil anger has confused and conquered us. If somebody makes a selfish demand on us and we make a selfish reply to defend our rights and interests, we have been beaten and captured by selfishness. The enemy has demonstrated that our thinking and actions are just as selfish as his own, so he congratulates himself on his victory by boasting that we are no better than he is. You may recall such defeats you have experienced like this.

How are we to defend ourselves or win the victory? Our text gives the answer: We are to defend ourselves with "coals of fire" (Romans 13:20). At first glimpse this looks like an efficient way of dispatching our enemy. It is efficient, but in a deeper, more powerful way. When anger stirs a responding anger, anger wins the victory and enmity is strengthened. If you reply to your enemy's selfishness with your own selfishness, you have been beaten and have made him more than ever your enemy. Our Lord gives us instructions concerning how to meet such attacks. At first, Matthew 5:38 looks like unconditional surrender to the enemy, and, in a way, it is. It is certainly not our common sense. By nature we think an eye for an eye and a tooth for a tooth. If people are kind to us, we will be kind to them. If we are kind to others, we expect them to be kind in return. If we are kind to someone and he or she isn't sufficiently thankful, we say we will remember that and not let ourselves be so foolish next time. We love and esteem those most who love and esteem us most. That is the way of human love, and at its center is self. Our Lord rejects this: "But I say unto you, That ye resist not evil" (Matthew 5:39). If someone strikes us and we don't strike back, we are called cowards, but our Lord calls us brave and heroic, for by so doing we do not surrender to malice but have won the victory as God's people, for our God is love. But the victory of love is even more complete. Not only do we hold out and not surrender but we can also win our enemy over to our side—the side of God's family. This is accomplished with "coals of fire."

As long as the godless receive anger for anger and self-assertion for self-assertion, they are within the narrow realm that they understand. But when anger is met with kindness and self-assertion is met with a selfless love, they are stumped. That is new, outside their realm of thought and action, and they are shaken by it. The godless will probably try to conceal their defeat behind a callous and mocking bravado. They will try and explain away that kindly love in terms of the selfish reasons that only they understand, but the shaft of your love may have pierced their selfish hearts. In the words of our text, you have heaped coals of fire on their head.

The coals of fire are the burning pangs of shame that smolder in their selfish hearts as the godless try to forget your discomforting, kindly love. Your love has shown them how ugly their own narrow self-seeking life is. You have lodged a coal in them that burns and cleanses. Often the godless will laugh at you for your kindness and call you a fool. That is the severest test for you: to believe that you are not a fool, or to confess, with glad peace in your heart, that you are Christ's fool. With undiminished concern for your enemies, you will sigh that their hour is not yet, and you will pray that it may be soon and you may help to bring it closer, cracking the selfish heart with the heat of your coals. As our text suggests, it is usually when our enemies are in great need that the coals of love burn hottest on their head. While they are getting along well enough, they may call you a fool. The coals may be covered over by the thoughtless bustle and preoccupation of what some call life—filling stomach, catching buses, turning handles, reading newspapers. But the fire in these coals is indestructible. God in His mercy may blow on it with a wind of grief or suffering. Then our enemies will see the size of their own strength and worth and we, despite the insults and ingratitude, continue to care for them with tender kindness. At this point, the coals of love will flame to brightest victory. People's minds may withstand our argument. People's hearts may rebel against our threats, but there is no defense against love.

In heaping on these coals of fire, we must beware of three things, lest we stain our love with sin. The first is that in heaping coals we dare not set ourselves up as judges, never be self-righteously shocked, never make our enemies feel that we are lowering ourselves to help them in a magnificent effort of charity. Who are we to judge creatures created for God's love and as unworthy of that love as we are? Our position is not to condemn. The Epistle says judgment is God's business. If the coals of our love are sufficiently hot, our enemies will be brought to condemn themselves, and we will have won over the enemy as David conquered Saul in the cave of Engedi and as our Lord did with the woman taken in adultery.

Second, we dare not enjoy our enemies' shame when we do them a kindness. We do not show them what foul wretches they really are and what shining lights of love we are. We do not return kindness for injury, thinking now they will have to feel ashamed of themselves. This is all hypocritical self-righteousness. The coals of fire must be poured from a heart that is aflame with sincere concern for the welfare of the enemy. Coals of healing shame come only from a heart of love.

The third danger is that we heap the coals of fire for our own benefit because it pays. Any businessperson will tell you that friendliness pays dividends and that, blow for blow, cutthroat competition is only wise when you are much bigger than the other people and they can't hurt you. A dog will lick the fingers that scratch it under the chin and bite the hand that holds a stick. The heathen philosopher tells us that kindness conquers malice, and we all admit that a friend is more than an enemy. It is a part of worldly wisdom to keep on the right side of people. It pays to be nice because we think, "I might need his help some day when I am in need." This niceness is an abomination to our God because at its center is self, a self that treats people as things to be used for personal benefit. It is only when we regard each person as one whose nature God's Son took to Himself and for whom He died, only when we thus see Christ in others, that we love with a love that helps and shames and heals and pleases our Father. Jesus said that in loving others we are loving Him. In our love for Him, there is no place for self-righteousness and self-assertion.

Finally, how goes the battle? This kind of sermon about turning the other cheek and heaping coals of fire on our enemies is fine and lovely in the pulpit and on paper, but in real life it is quite impossible to follow. Business is business. If this statement means anything, it is that we want Christ to stay in His place and leave the largest part of our lives to ourselves to be lived according to a different set of rules than His way and with a purpose that is the opposite of and a denial of His purpose in us. Christ's love that conquered sin, death, and the devil neither cares to be checked by our petty selfishness nor to be imprisoned in a narrow corner of our hearts. God wants the whole of us. He wants us to be afire with His love so we have abundant coals of love that help and shame, heal and win.

The battle is far from easy. It takes its toll on us. Love is like a poultice. As mother said, the hotter the better, even to the point of pain, because it draws out the bad and stirs the healing flow of blood. When you take a poultice off a boil or festered sore, you see that it has become dirty and soiled, but it has drawn out the bad and cleansed the wound so the sore is healing. So love draws out the bad; suffers anger, ill will, insult; and stirs the healthy flow of love. The coals of love burn, but the hotter the better. When we have taken people's anger and abuse with love, we have drawn out the bad in them, and their burning pain of shame is the first stage toward healing.

Another reason that makes it difficult for love to hope all things and to endure all things is that we don't see the immediate result. We get discouraged because of mockery and ingratitude. Yet every time we meet people, we make them something different because of their contact with us. We become a part of everybody that we meet. We are lodged in their memory and have influenced them. If we meet self-assertion with self-assertion, we push people farther from Christ. If in selfless love we turn the other cheek to their malice, they may see Christ through us, condemn their petty ill will, and come to know the love of Christ for them within the family of God.

Our greatest chance for effective coal heaping is in our need and want because there is less room then for silly pride and obstruction to the burning and healing power of love. The word translated as "feeding" in our text means to feed with your own hand as one does a child or invalid, that is, with personal concern and care of the person that is your enemy, the person who hates and abuses you. Notice also that the text says a heap of coals. We can't expect to win the victory by dropping one coal now and then. A spectacular gesture for Jesus is much easier than the sustained persistent heaping of loving coals despite ridicule and ingratitude.

That is the way the Lord said we could win the victory. It is the only way to really conquer the enemy, for love wins them over and makes the enemies our friends, our brothers and sisters in Christ. When discouraged, think of how Christ loved you, not because of anything lovable in you. Your sin made you God's enemy, hateful to God. Yet God gave proof of His love by sending Christ to die for us sinners. Through Christ we have been brought within the love of God. As God's children,

God is at work in us and through us, and God is love. Under the banner of the cross, we shall not fail. Jesus said, "Be of good cheer; I have overcome the world" (John 17:33). The hands of Christ sustain us, for in those hands is the print of the nails. O God, give us in Christ the strength and readiness of selfless love that we may not run short of coals.
AMEN.

Fourth Sunday after the Epiphany

JOHN 6:51–59

CONCORDIA SEMINARY (1986)

Today's message is a matter of life and death. The Gospel reading for today has the word *life* in it eight times, and each time it becomes richer and deeper with meaning. With each deepening of life, there is a corresponding deepening of death. Only from Jesus are we given the full reach of these meanings from the cross, where He gives His flesh for the life of the world. Chapter 6 culminates with a forward reference to Calvary by mention of Jesus' betrayal, and this comes as grounding, test, and content of Peter's confession: "Lord, to whom shall we go? Thou hast the words of eternal life" (John 6:68). Without Calvary, Peter's confession would be devil's talk, yet Judas is identified with the devil. There is the final culmination of death, which is hell.

In contrast with this view of life is the shallow view of death and along with it the shallow view of life. This shallow life is kept from shallow death by the bread that Jesus gave them to eat at the beginning of the chapter. The one who could keep them from such a death they wanted to make their king, a king who could sustain them in such a life, not to have to worry anymore where their next meal was coming from. The people wanted picnics every day in the green pasture beside the lake in Galilee. Now there is a king! We hear echoes of this in the rhetoric of politicians and advertisements—the felicity of the ultimate hamburger, the happiness that comes with drinking the best wine and squirting or rubbing on the right stuff here and there. Jesus withdrew from all that. He would draw them deeper—deeper life and so also deeper death.

The generation that was delivered out of Egypt all died in the wilderness, though the Lord gave them bread from heaven. Repeatedly in John, Jesus fulfills and bursts what is told us in the Old Testament. Jesus is bread from heaven of which a man may eat and not die. Here death is ultimate death and its counterpart is ultimate life. Jesus said, "I am the living Bread" (John 6:51). What could be a more "I am" statement of life? But there is more. There is life through and beyond the furthest reach of death. Death can reach no further than Calvary. That there was death in Calvary is shown by the fact that flesh and blood are spoken of separately. But they are Jesus' flesh and blood, so there is life with them beyond the furthest reach of death—life indestructible, life forever.

Statistically, John 6 begins with five thousand people and ends with only twelve. And one of them is the devil's man who will betray Jesus. They all deserted Him, and Peter denied Him three times. When everything is at stake, there is only Jesus. Everything hangs on Him—ultimate death. Then through and beyond its furthest reach—ultimate life. And that life Jesus gives to those who eat His flesh and drink His blood. "He that eateth My flesh, and drinketh My blood, dwelleth in Me, and I in him. As the living Father hath sent Me, and I live by the Father: so he that eateth Me, even he shall live by Me" (John 6:56–58). "Whoso eateth My flesh, and drinketh My blood, hath eternal life; and I will raise him up at the last day" (John 6:54).

Amen.

Fifth Sunday after the Epiphany

Mark 1:29–31

Concordia Seminary (1988)

Epiphany will soon end with a big, bright bang of glory. For this week we read about Peter's mother-in-law's flu. She had been coughing a lot and running a temperature, so she needed to stay in bed. That is the spot we are at in Epiphany this year, before the Transfiguration. Mark never leaves us standing around gawking. He uses the word *immediately* forty-five times. We are into the next event before we have finished the last one. Everything leads on to Calvary, the cross that was laid on Jesus at His baptism with the name Son/Servant.

If we only read Mark, everything in Jesus life would all happen in a year. We are only into the first chapter and Jesus has begun His ministry, His preaching, called for disciples, preached in the synagogue at Capernaum, and cast out an unclean spirit. The unclean spirit cries out, "I know Thee who Thou art, the Holy One of God" (Mark 1:24). Jesus did this on the Sabbath. "Who is this?" the people wonder. The answer to this question is next in our text.

"And forthwith, when they were come out of the synagogue, they entered into the house of Simon and Andrew, with James and John" (Mark 1:29). Into this lowly, little world of Peter's house comes the one who proclaims His coming as the coming of the kingdom of God, the one who calls men from their work to be His for His work. Here is one mightier than the unclean spirits who, in His presence, fear destruction. Jesus drives out the unclean spirit so He is all the big fuss. What is going on? From that blaze of flame, He stoops down into the dim and lowly house of Peter and Andrew accompanied by James and John. One can imagine Peter's family members: "If there are not enough chairs, we can sit on the floor. If we had known you were coming! And everything is such a mess! It has been enough taking care of mother-in-law, you know the bother she can be, and these fellows have been no help at all, off listening to some preacher chap. That is *you*."

Jesus goes to Peter's mother-in-law to check on her. They clear the way to the bed where the woman lies sick, not really the place for a man to be and certainly not something with which the Messiah should be bothered. But here is the Holy One of God, whose coming is the coming of the kingdom of God. Jesus simply assumes the freedom of the house. Nothing gives Him pause. To the bed and the feverish, flustered woman He comes.

There is nothing more important in all the world than for Jesus to be there for the sick woman. With all on Himself, He is there just for her. He took her by the hand and lifted her up, and the fever left her. The woman doesn't have an ecstasy or let fly with a sound or something we might expect. She simply puts the kettle on. Big deal. Yes, big deal. From that day she was never the same. She knew to whom she was precious. She, the supernumerary old mother-in-law, with all her crackling aches and pains, was precious. The kingdom of God had come to her with this man whom the boys had brought home with them and their other friends.

Peter's mother-in-law does the next thing for her to do, what is right there for her to do. She serves them. That is what the epiphany does with her and with Jesus. "Even as the Son of Man came not to be ministered unto, but to minister, and to give His life a ransom for many" (Matthew 20:28). "For many" and "ransom" are also referred to in Isaiah 53. The Holy One of God who was there as a servant for Peter's mother-in-law is among us also this morning as the servant at His Table, serving His body and blood that is given for you to eat and to drink.

Jesus went through the streets of Capernaum, to that house, and was at that happy table there. "If only I had known you were coming"—it would surely have been the best Peter's mother-in-law could provide, her most favorite recipe. Jesus knows of our coming to His Table this morning. And He serves His best. By God's grace you, too, are precious, worth the giving of His body and His blood. Jesus died for you "and for many."

AMEN.

Sixth Sunday after the Epiphany

MARK 1:40–45

VALPARAISO UNIVERSITY (1979)

Today's Gospel is about Jesus. Of course, every Gospel gives us something more of Jesus, but what is given to us of Him in today's Gospel is strange indeed. Jesus said, "See thou say nothing to any man" (Mark 1:44). Aren't we supposed to tell the whole world about Him? He said, "Go ye therefore, and teach all nations, baptizing them in the name of the Father, and of the Son, and of the Holy Ghost: Teaching them to observe all things whatsoever I have commanded you" (Matthew 28:19–20). But we read today: "See that you say nothing to any man."

Perhaps Jesus is using some clever psychology. The surest way to have something spread is to tell someone that it is a secret and not to tell anyone. That may be shrewd worldly wisdom, but we don't need

Jesus to teach us that or how to manipulate one another. The skill to use and manipulate others for our purposes we develop as infants. If screaming doesn't work for us, we soon develop subtler ways of manipulation to get food and attention. In Jesus we don't find anything of this—though He probably screamed His head off, too, when it was getting close to feeding time. When He says, "See that you say nothing to anyone," what He means is "See that you say nothing to anyone."

Jesus' meaning is clearly shown by the fact that the healed leper's blabbermouthing the miracle hinders Jesus. "Jesus could no more openly enter into the city, but was without in desert places" (Mark 1:45). The healed leper shouldn't have done it, but what does that mean for us? Is this a word of Jesus that is not for us? Is it a word that is spoken only to the healed leper? It is certainly spoken to him, and we must begin with Jesus saying it to the leper.

First, today's Gospel is about Jesus, not the leper or leprosy. There don't seem to be any lepers here this morning, and even if there were, we don't have a word of the Lord to us to miraculously heal them. At most, we have Jesus as an example (*imitatio Christi*). Jesus healed lepers. You must be like Jesus. Go and heal some lepers. That is not the message, so we go back to Jesus.

Jesus is a man to whom a leper comes, before whom a leper kneels and pleads, "If Thou wilt, Thou canst make me clean" (Mark 1:40). From the grammar, it is quite clear that the leper has no doubt that Jesus can accomplish this task. A bit before, Mark has told us:

> And at even, when the sun did set, they brought unto Him all that were diseased, and them that were possessed with devils. And all the city was gathered together at the door. And He healed many that were sick of divers diseases, and cast out many devils; and suffered not the devils to speak, because they knew Him. (Mark 1:32–34)

It all happens so easily, so casually, without any fuss. The healing flows from Jesus as if He can't help doing it. He gives no dramatic show or spectacular performance. These people need Him, need healing, and the healing Jesus does is as natural for Him as breathing. But "He suffered not the devils to speak, because they knew Him." These are strange words and a strange Jesus. Doesn't He want everyone to know He is the Savior of us all? What kind of a Savior?

Mark does not give us a list of those who were healed—four strep throats, two monos, one gout, and six influenzas. What a clinic Jesus could have set up, exceeding even our own university clinic, though He wouldn't have the use of the wonder drugs, antibiotics, and Librium. There were lots of people who would have loved it if Jesus had set up a clinic. Think of the medical fees they would save.

Jesus did not get much sleep that night. "And in the morning, rising up a great while before day, He went out, and departed into a solitary place, and there prayed" (Mark 1:35). We know something of how Jesus prayed: "Father, Abba, not My will but Thine be done." Jesus drew back from there. "And when they had found Him, they said unto Him, 'All men seek for thee.' And He said unto them, 'Let us go into the next towns, that I may preach there also: for therefore came I forth'" (Mark 1:37–38). "Came forth" is a strange way of talking.

Then comes today's Gospel. Jesus is a man to whom a leper comes with complete confidence that Jesus can heal him. But does Jesus want to heal him? He may care about others, but does Jesus care about me? There is nobody less worth caring about than a leper. The Law of Moses forbade anyone to have anything to do with a leper. A hard law, a socially beneficial law, and a law with divine sanction. The Law put a leper outside. He was excluded from the community of God's people. Jesus joins the leper and reaches out to take hold of that rotting man. He becomes unclean with the uncleanness of the leper. Jesus joins the leper in his uncleanness and shares it with him.

Does Jesus care about that man? Jesus cares like nobody else. Jesus is there for that man in his leprosy. This is the miracle. Jesus sets aside the Law that can identify the disease but cannot heal it. Only He who gives the Law may set it aside. That is who it is who takes hold of the leper cast out by the Law. "If You will," says the leper. "And Jesus, moved with compassion, put forth His hand, and touched him, and saith unto him, I will; be thou clean" (Mark 1:41). That is a miracle, too, a happy one, but a smaller one. That the Lord of all the world, and of the Law, should bother about someone so utterly worthless as a leper, cast out by the Law, is what is really incredible.

When you face the living God, the only question is whether He bothers about you. It is all up to Him, and in Jesus the answer is yes. I will; be clean. "Hey Jesus. You are something else. Let's You and me go off and start a commune. You and me for sure and perhaps a couple other ex-lepers. With You around, we shan't have any worries at all, and we can thumb our noses at the rest of the world grubbing its way along, but not us. Not You and me." Now that is not in the text. What is in the text is Jesus. He sends the healed man back into the community. If anyone tries to stop him, he had best have his piece of paper signed by the priest as testimony of being a leper no more.

However, it is now a whole lot of things that the healed man isn't anymore, far beyond what any priest of the Law can testify to, let alone effect. The healed man goes back into the community and has to find a place to live, food to eat, and clothes to wear. Will anyone advance him a month's rent? He has to find a job. Someday, perhaps, he will have a wife, a home, and a family. Death, taxes, and all that sweat will be his. Jesus sends him to do it. But the one whom Jesus sends is the one who has been at the Jesus point, where everything was up to Jesus: "If You will." And Jesus, the one who runs the whole show, says, "I will; be clean." Nothing can be bigger or more sure than that. That is fact number one, and all that Jesus sends to the healed man is lived out from that fact. He is a free son of the kingdom where Jesus is Lord, as Jesus showed Peter in the matter of the taxes they both had to pay— no, not had to pay but did pay. But what does the healed leper do? He goes blabbing all over the place just as Jesus told him not to do.

The first lesson we learn from today's Gospel is puzzling and hard to practice: When do we hinder Jesus by telling about Him? The healed leper was wrong. When in doubt, I suppose, it is better to tell than not to tell. We do have Jesus' words bidding us to tell of Him. But if you notice yourself getting carried away by bragging what a hot-shot Christian you are and what an "in" you have with Jesus, the questions to ask yourself are: Is this just to make me feel good? Is this a way of getting attention drawn to me, not to Jesus? Is this a promotion of my jack-in-the-box Jesus? Am I making such a splendid showing as a Christian that those listening might wonder whether my shiny Jesus could bother about little ol' them, who don't have much of anything to point to, before turning away because Jesus couldn't possibly be bothering about them? Remember, there is an easy, almost casual, no-big-fuss way Jesus did His miracles that evening. Then He could be using you for one of His big miracles. For Jesus to be using us, we shouldn't be getting in His way, hindering or misrepresenting Him.

The second lesson we learn from today's Gospel is Gospel Jesus. Is this Superman Jesus, Clinic Jesus, Jesus with all the clobber you had best get in on? No. Is this Friend of Lepers Jesus, Friend of Sinners

Jesus? Yes. At His baptism, Jesus was sinner with us, taking our sin on Himself, for it was a baptism for sinners. In today's Gospel, Jesus takes the leper's uncleanness on Himself and under the Law is unclean with him. The Law excludes and condemns. Jesus takes hold of the man outside. He goes under and beyond the Law. It is His. Jesus joins the man in his uncleanness and rejection. The leper cannot doubt that Jesus is for him.

You have sin. You have uncleanness. But Jesus joins you there. He bears the lot for you, even to Calvary. He is the Jesus to whom you, too, can pray, "If Thou wilt, Thou canst make me clean" (Mark 1:40). He was for the leper; Jesus is for you too.

Amen.

Seventh Sunday after the Epiphany

Matthew 19–20

Valparaiso University (1971)

The flights of angels at the end of *Hamlet* is said to ruin the tragedy. The less-Christian Goethe has a divine intervention at the end for Faust's felicity that doesn't seem to fit. Gustavus Adolphus died just in time to be a hero. Martin Luther King Jr. marches on more powerfully for having been shot. Hitler had dreams of dying Wagnerianly that didn't quite come off. With *Jesus Christ Superstar* we do see a grandiose death. Martin Luther did not quite have a dramatic death. In his last days he was writing to his dear Katie about the delicious trout the Counts of Mansfield were giving him to eat. (They were the brothers and princes whom he was helping to forgive each other). And he also wrote how much he missed her incomparable beer. We like Luther better as the heroic man at Worms; it would have been better still if he would have been burnt at the stake.

The disciples thought of themselves as making the big scene. They emphasized to Jesus their heroic self-sacrifice after the rich young ruler who had wanted to become Jesus' disciple had reservations and had failed. The rich young ruler thought he qualified because he had kept the commandments. Jesus said, "If thou wilt be perfect, go and sell all that thou hast and give to the poor" (Matthew 19:21). By the qualification route, there is always more to be done. You can never arrive at the point of "now I have done it all; now I qualify." Discipleship to Jesus does not exist with reservations: "If I can hang on to this, then I will be your disciple." For a disciple, everything is in Jesus' hands and from His hands. All gifts are from His hands.

In Matthew 19 we read first about Jesus' feelings concerning the magnitude of marriage. The disciples thought this sounded impossible. Jesus taught that marriage can only be received as a gift. After marriage come the children. They are blessed and to such is given the kingdom of heaven. After this is the story of the young man held captive by his possessions. He would like to be Jesus' disciple, but there are some things he wants to hang on to that he must give up if he is to be Jesus' disciple. "Impossible," say the disciples again. "Yes," says Jesus again, "only God can give it." To be a gift, something must be refusable. In Luke we are shown the pain in Jesus' eyes as He watched this young man go away from Him.

It is at this point that Peter speaks for the disciples and boasts, "We have left everything and followed You." The disciples have done what this young man refused to do, and they want to know what they qualify for. Jesus said that those who followed Him "shall sit upon twelve thrones, judging the twelve tribes of Israel. And every one that hath forsaken houses, or brethren, or sisters, or father, or mother, or wife, or children, or lands, for My name's sake, shall receive a hundredfold, and shall inherit everlasting life" (Matthew 19:29). Imagine the immense satisfaction on the faces of the disciples once they heard this. Jesus was talking their *quid pro quo* language. The more you give up, the more you will get.

Then Jesus speaks the demolition: "Many that are first shall be last; and the last shall be first" (Matthew 19:30). God operates backward of the way we calculate. The way He runs the show is like the householder, the owner of the estate, who has work for men to do in his vineyard. The owner hires laborers for a day's work and a day's pay. But there is more to do than those who work a day for a day's pay can complete. It is not possible for them to say they have done all that there is to do. There is more work, so others are needed. At nine o'clock and at noon, at three o'clock and again at five, when only one hour for work remains, the lord of the vineyard calls others to do his work. They follow his call, and they work.

So far everything has gone normally, except, perhaps, that the owner does seem extraordinarily keen to get the work done and to get every possible man doing it. Calculation of profit margin does not seem to limit the wage allocation. Now at the end of the day, things really start going backward. Those paid first are those who have done only an hour's work. They are given a full day's pay. That shoots any kind of cost accounting—can't run a business that way. "Impossible," we hear the disciples say again under their breath. "The more you sacrifice and do, the more you get" is what they had understood Jesus to say.

When the disciples first signed on, they thought they would receive more. For their day's work they received a day's pay. No injustice is done to them. They cannot claim breach of contract. It riles them to be made equal with other people. It is not the Lord's injustice but His generosity that infuriates them, for it destroys their whole case for themselves on the basis of their work and deserving. They deserve and can demand, which is the opposite of being given to. The way of the kingdom of heaven is not to demand things from God. Everything is in the hands of the Lord and from the hands of the Lord. Here are no reservations, qualifications, or demands but discipleship, faith, being given happy, generous gifts beyond calculation.

Just as the Sermon on the Mount is no resource for political science, so this parable is no resource for how to run a business. The parable speaks of a vineyard. A vineyard is for wine that makes glad the heart of man, as the psalmist says. A vineyard has been the picture of Israel, God's people, since Psalm 80 and Isaiah 5. "For the vineyard of the Lord of hosts is the house of Israel" (Isaiah 5:7). The parable tells of God's way with His people, His Israel, His church. From this we may learn discipleship—everything in His hands and from His hands with incalculable generosity for gladness of heart.

Yet have we heard all that the parable is saying? We know that we may not load every detail with meaning. The main point rings clear, yet we may not overlook the work and wages. There is no negative hint about them at all. How do the work and wages fit with the giving and receiving, grace and faith, that are the way of the kingdom? There can be no doubt that discipleship means work, labor, and sweat, the work that the Lord sets you to. Those who are found not working in the parable are called idle, which is the word James used to describe faith that is inactive and dead. At the end of the day there is reward. It is this fact that utterly demolishes the heroic posture of the disciples that is expressed by Peter. To his boast, "Look at all we have given up," we are apt to reply, "Yes, but look at all you get. It really pays off."

The disciples, however, are not as conditioned by Kant, by considerations of purity and virtue of motive, as we are. Do we do what we should for no other reason than that we should? When we serve God for His own sake and not for what we get out of Him, such a view can establish a basis for boasting, for displaying a pure and shining virtue. Consider the virtue displayed by protestation of what it rejects and repudiates. Such virtue can be so pure that it scorns God and any approval or reward from Him. That would only muddy the purity of motivation. Opposition and loss may be counted as evidence of the purity of virtue as can scorn for rewards, except perhaps the reward of satisfaction in itself. You may sometimes find such virtue in people who boast that they are motivated by nothing but love. But do not look too closely or you may find their love selective, or doing ugly damage to the person they say they love, or even excluding whole categories of people from their vaunted love. Love does not boast of itself; it is occupied with whom and what it loves. "Good works do not have a name," said Martin Luther. The moment we honor good works with a name, they are no longer good works, that is, they are no longer done in faith. They are no longer within and from the giving hands of the Lord. They are slipping toward becoming a basis for boasting and making demands.

When mother says, "Sally, will you polish the silver, please? Jim, nip over to Miller's and get some of that tutti frutti that we all like so much. Billy, do put away your toys; it's only an hour before they will be here for the party," do we stop to examine the purity of motives and the quality of virtue in each child? If we do, we may lose a glimpse of how things go in the kingdom of heaven.

There is another glimpse one step back in our context when Jesus tells of marriage among those that are His disciples. Husband and wife are there for each other without reservation, love's full sharing, with much work and happy rewards. The moment one spouse points to what has been given up for the other, what is put up with from the other, and demands some consideration, things are going wrong. Things are not going the kingdom of heaven way, the loving, giving, sharing, there-for-the-other way.

If you or I had directed Job, we probably would have ended this account with a climax of heroic death after the line "Though He slay me, yet will I trust in Him" (13:15). We are embarrassed by the fact that Job ends up better off than he started. Do not be embarrassed by God's generosity. Do not be displeased with Him that He does not sufficiently attend to the purity of your motives and virtue. That is the sort of God He is—the giver God, everything in and from His hands, which means freedom from piecemeal living and the constricting calculation of our worth. "Happy are those who know that they are poor; the kingdom of heaven is theirs."

God calls us to work, to spend our lives in discipleship. We work because He has called us. Some work through heavy burden and heat of day. Some seem to have it easier than we do, yet we are glad for them because we know each one of us is a worker in the vineyard. God has His own way with each one of us. He is the Lord; we are given to by Him who is bountiful beyond deserving or calculation.

After the parable, Jesus "was going up to Jerusalem," and He tells His disciples of His crucifixion and His resurrection. We are only seventy days from Easter. That is what we are heading toward with Him.

AMEN.

The Transfiguration of Our Lord

LUKE 9:28–36

VALPARAISO UNIVERSITY (1977)

An old Sunday school hymn I used to sing spoke of a "happy land" where Jesus would reign. This happy land may be just super for the angels and archangels and so on, but it is not where you and I go on. We go on here at a particular place and at a particular point in time. Fortunately that is where today's Gospel also goes on.

Our reading begins with the time location "about eight days after these sayings" (Luke 9:28). "These sayings" refers to the question from Jesus, "Who do you say that I am?" Peter, always ready with his mouth, says, "The Christ of God." Luke is gentle and doesn't tell how Peter really didn't understand this question. He also doesn't relate Jesus' devastating rebuke, but he does tell us Jesus' words: "The Son of Man must suffer many things, and be rejected of the elders and chief priests and scribes, and be slain, and be raised on the third day" (Luke 9:22).

Then comes today's Gospel story, placed a week later and up on the mountain. A further answer to the question "Who is this Jesus?" happened while Jesus was praying. The bright dazzling light that appeared signaled the glory that declared the presence of God, in Jesus, on the mountain. Further signaling the presence of God was the appearance of Moses and Elijah. The arrangements for their being present we can only leave to the one who is running the event. What they gave as an answer to the question "Who is Jesus?" is that He is what the Law and the Prophets are all leading toward. What they proclaimed brings us to this Jesus and who He is. Jesus is revealed most fully by what He does, and that is what they spoke about—the death that He would fulfill in Jerusalem.

To fulfill a death is something extraordinary. But that a death should be at the center of the glory that is Jesus, that is extraordinary beyond everything. Now it doesn't say "death" in the text. "Departure" is there as a translation of the Greek word *exodos*, a euphemism for death. The Latin equivalent would be *exit*. Refined gentleman that Luke is, as witness to his solicitude for Peter and for the ladies, he uses a polite euphemism. While Mark can be rude and crude, Luke is polished and polite. So Luke uses a euphemism that means plump and plain death.

The Living Bible uses the word death, which is not a translation, but then *The Living Bible* doesn't claim to be a translation. It is a paraphrase, as *Phillips* is a paraphrase, only more so. *The New English Bible*, which claims to be a translation, does a bit of paraphrasing itself. They "spoke of His departure, the destiny He was to fulfill in Jerusalem." *Destiny* is a heathen word, at home in Athens rather than in Jerusalem, and what Jesus, Moses, and Elijah speak of happens in Jerusalem. The Authorized Version uses the word *decease*, which captures the euphemism better than the Revised Standard Version's use of *departure*, but *decease* is now a bit old-fashioned. *The Jerusalem Bible* gets the euphemism best with "they were speaking of His passing." That is the current, contemporary, *Christian Science Monitor* euphemism for death.

However, we may be a bit uneasy about euphemisms for death in our day when there is so much cosmetic cover-up and pretense to avoid confronting death honestly. Noel Coward has one of his characters in *This Happy Breed* express this revulsion at refusing to face the fact of death. The man's son has been killed, and his friends give him sugary pious talk about his son's passing on. The grieving father can't stand it and cries out, "He didn't pass on, pass out, or pass over. He just bloody well died."

Jesus just bloody well died. Although such a way of putting it might offend the stylistic and refined sensibilities of Luke, his exodus euphemism refers to Jesus' death in Jerusalem. The word *exodos*, besides being a euphemism for death, also happens to be the title of the second book of the Greek Old Testament, the Septuagint. Perhaps Luke intended some echoes of this. We cannot be absolutely sure. What we can be sure of is that death that is fulfilled in Jerusalem. No doubt about that. It is there nine verses before and eleven verses later.

Luke is the only one who writes what was spoken about during the transfiguration, hence all this particular attention to it. Besides, with something so remarkable as the transfiguration, you have to stick close to the text for fear of going wrong. The easiest way to go wrong is the two-worlds way of Greek thinking: heavenly world and earthly world. The transfiguration is then a bursting in of the heavenly world, where God really goes on. We are kept from this way of thinking by sticking close to the text and to the evangelist's purpose for telling us something about Jesus. What we have picked up so far is: (1) Where Jesus is, there is the presence of God; (2) What God was doing in the Old Testament brings us to Jesus; and (3) What Jesus is for, what He is to do, is the death that He is to fulfill in Jerusalem. Death and Jerusalem are no heavenly world things. They are very down to earth, where we are, and where the saving action for us takes place.

On the ground where we are is also where our fellows, Peter, John, and James, are "heavy with sleep." The next time that happens is in Gethsemane, and there is an angel to strengthen Jesus toward His death. There Peter gets it all wrong, imagining that he can help Jesus with a sword. Gentle Luke doesn't mention that the swordsman was Peter. Today at the transfiguration Peter gets it all wrong again. He wants to make three booths, tents, tabernacles for the glory to dwell in as long ago in Israel. He blurts this out as Moses and Elijah were parting from Jesus. Peter wants to hang on to them, but they go. Jesus goes on beyond where Moses and Elijah bring things to. No tents for Moses and Elijah, and none for Jesus either. Jesus is the tent where the glory dwells, hidden and revealed.

The bright cloud signals the presence of God. The disciples find themselves within that cloud and are scared to death, which is how it is with sinful people in the presence of God. Then a voice speaks out of the cloud, "This is My beloved Son: hear Him" (Luke 9:35). We have heard that before at Jesus' baptism. The Son is proclaimed by the Father with a word that requires a double translation: Son and Servant. Consider Isaiah 53:11: "By His knowledge shall My righteous servant justify many; for He shall bear their iniquities." In solidarity with sinners Jesus is baptized, and the death for sin, His bearing our iniquities, is laid on Him at His baptism. The same word is spoken on Jesus at His transfiguration.

That is the Jesus who is there with the disciples when the bright glory has gone. But the glory has not really gone, for where Jesus is, there is that glory, whether hidden or shining forth. How do we know this? By heeding what the Father says. He says who Jesus is, and He bids us listen to Him. God has spoken; the men are silent. That is how it should be. When God speaks, you shut up. You receive what He says. From God to you in silent receiving is believing. God speaks Jesus to you. "This is My Son, My chosen; listen to Him!"

"And they kept it close and told no man in those days any of those things which they had seen" (Luke 9:36). If the disciples had maintained their silence, we would never know about Jesus. Their silence was only for those days, and when those days were accomplished, Jesus said to them:

> "These are My words which I spoke to you, while I was still with you, that everything written about Me in the Law of Moses and the prophets and the psalms must be fulfilled." Then He opened their minds to understand the Scriptures, and said to them, "Thus it is written, that the Christ should suffer and on the third day rise from the dead, and that repentance and forgiveness of sins should be preached in His name to all nations, beginning from Jerusalem. You are witnesses of these things." (Luke 24:44–48 RSV)

We have their witness, and through this we do the listening to Jesus that we are bidden to do today. "This is My Son, My chosen; listen to Him!"

Peter, who was always getting it wrong, did get it right in the end. Through his apostolic words also we do our Jesus listening. So listen to what comes to us from Peter when he was facing his death that Jesus had spoken about to him.

> Since I know that the putting off of my body will be soon, as our Lord Jesus Christ showed me. And I will see to it that after my departure [*exodos*] you may be able at any time to recall these things. For we did not follow cleverly devised myths when we made known to you the power and coming of our Lord Jesus Christ, but we were eyewitnesses of His majesty. For when He received honor and glory from God the Father and the voice was borne to Him by the Majestic Glory, "This is My beloved Son, with whom I am well pleased," we heard this voice borne from heaven, for we were with Him on the holy mountain. And we have the prophetic word made more sure. You will do well to pay attention to this as to a lamp shining in a dark place, until the day dawns and the morning star rises in your hearts. (2 Peter 1:14–19 RSV)

Now listen to today's Epistle: "The light of the glorious gospel of Christ, who is the image of God . . . the light of the knowledge of the glory of God in the face of Jesus Christ" (2 Corinthians 4:4–6). That face that was shown on the mountain and that was spat on in Jerusalem.

We are not bidden to the mountain nor to shattering experiences of the presence of God nor to attempts to booth Him with any construction of ours. We live where we are located. We live where death goes on, where Jesus is. We live where Christ is spat on. How many times a day do you hear His holy name tossed around as if it was worth nothing, meant nothing—as if Christ is worth nothing, means nothing? He suffers all our sins. He suffers for all our sins in the death He fulfills in Jerusalem. The one who does that for you is the one to whom you are bidden to listen. That listening is in receiving silence before the words of God, here together and when you read the Scriptures. God speaking to you is located for you there and happens at the particular times of your devotions.

Where are we? The Last Sunday after the Epiphany, the Transfiguration of Our Lord. If dated and located, then we do not float timelessly in some heavenly world to which we escape in spurious religiosity, nor are we plagued with anxiety about the things that may not be there tomorrow or a year from now. The continuities you can count on are of Jesus. We are here together, today, listening to Him, this first day of another week at Valpo. And in this particular week comes Ash Wednesday.

The dating and movement of our days is by Jesus. His sun and moon together give us the Passover date, the exodus date, and forty days before that is Ash Wednesday. All the world, every place in it that we may be, and all our days are different and have their character, their progression, their meaning, their glory from Jesus. They are ordained for listening to Him. Where His words are, where His name is, there He is. There is the glory—sometimes hidden (sometimes deathly hidden) and sometimes bursting through, but there, for He is there, as surely as it is to Him that you are listening. Have a glorious Lent!

AMEN.

Ash Wednesday

VALPARAISO UNIVERSITY (1969)

The trouble with considering deadly sins as separate pieces is that we may become so preoccupied with our sins that we get no further than the resolve that we really must try to do better. Those who think of Christianity as nothing more than a moral renovation program tend to think of sins as individual items that you can keep on a checklist and add up the score each day. But sins are not individual items as if at 11:15 this morning I did a sin. It was a corker, but I have not done that sin since.

Particular sins are symptoms of a disease. We sin because we are sinners; we are not sinners because we sin. A corrupt tree brings forth corrupt fruit. Its fault lies not in its being a tree but in its being corrupt. What is wrong with us is not that we are human but that we are gone wrong, we are sinners. We might get some notion of this from looking at ourselves and much more likely from looking at others, but even that is not compelling. You got your bag; I got mine. You do your thing; let me do mine. Nobody judge nobody for there isn't anything to go by. That is how it is when there are no standards, no oughts, or no more than socially relative oughts. Some things are socially obnoxious, but as long as I am not being a nuisance to anybody, I can do as I please. When I itch, I scratch myself, and that is nobody else's business but mine. Here we are still dealing with various items of behavior.

Such people God would shatter with His Law. Take a look at commandments four through eight. Have you kept all these? Look at commandments nine and ten, then the first three. Face up to the holy God, the generous Creator God whose wrath is on all ungodliness. Sin is ungodliness. Sin says no to God. Sin makes us think we are in charge. God doesn't matter, we do. *Puff.* He doesn't exist.

When we throw ourselves against God, it is not God that falls to pieces. "In pieces" rightly describes our society and the people in it. Instead of wholeness, we have pieces, and particular pieces are picked up and treated as if they were wholes. Christ came to put the pieces together. They can't stick together until they have been washed. Forgiveness washes clean and puts together, just as sin divides, separates, and shatters. Separation number one is from God, separation number two is from others, and separation number three is the going to pieces of a person. We see these examples in the Old Testament: (1) Adam separates from God. (2) Cain kills Abel. (3) Cain is torn with guilt and fear. (4) God spares Cain.

Where separation begins, there it must first be healed. But that is just what we are unwilling to face, that is what we are headed away from. We make up all sorts of notions to rationalize our direction away. In place of the living God we put ideas and project our thinking. If others treated us the same way we treat God, we would have nothing more to do with them; and we are not about to go crawling back. We have our pride.

Yet God, the real one, the living God, loved us so much that He sent His Son, born of a woman, made under the Law, to redeem those that are under the Law that we might be adopted as His sons and daughters. This is our redemption. God bought us back not with gold or silver, but with the holy, precious blood of Jesus Christ and with His innocent suffering and death that we may be His children. Christ's death on Calvary is the cost.

That is the way God did it. It is irreverent to inquire whether our redemption might not have been done another way or even to propose a more fitting and appropriate way. Some have suggested Satan as the recipient of the ransom; others dislike the evident injustice of the innocent one suffering for the guilty. The alternative is the guilty suffering for the guilty, and God did not choose that way. You can have that way if you insist.

Sin breaks with God; sin brings death, real death, separation-from-God death. That is our lot. There is no hope in us. Another takes that death of ours on Himself and is forsaken of God. He takes our hell. When we stand at the cross, as it goes with Christ so it goes with us. If He breaks, if He goes under, so do we. He is there for us. Out of the dread darkness Jesus cries with a loud voice, triumphantly, "It is finished." He has done it. He is through. Then He goes on to make the way for us also through the little death of the grave.

My sin is answered for. It can no longer claim, condemn, or enslave me. Sin's dominion is overthrown. I am forgiven. Full atonement has been made; full and free forgiveness is ours, a sheer gift. What put us wrong with God, what separated us, is gone. Separation number one is overcome. God forgives and sees us in Christ, righteous, justified. Separations two and three are in the process of being overcome. The pieces here are to be put together again but now out from point number one, the same gift and forgiving way.

Here we run into trouble. Individual pieces resist being put together. They assert themselves and draw back from forgiveness, from Christ. We have our pride. Anything held back from Christ, from forgiveness, makes its claims and can enslave, warp, and disintegrate us.

This takes us back to where we started with sins being regarded as individual items or pieces—as if Christ did not answer and die for the whole of you but only for six of your seven deadly sins. Tragically, one often meets those who hug one sin as an individual item—isolated. They can tell you the time and the place it happened. This sin is outside forgiveness, too big, too dark to be forgiven. Great stretches of a life can then be overshadowed, warped, twisted, enslaved by that sin. Some sink even lower, attempting to pretend that the particular sin was not sin. As long as we are dealing in pieces, we are exposed to this sort of damnation. Perversity and pride can lead us to insist on our suffering for selected sins. This one, my special sin, I am going to make atonement for. This is a denial of Christ and Calvary. There is nothing of you that He left out of His atonement for you, left out of His forgiveness. Christ died for you, the whole person, for He would make you whole. There is fact here and there is process. You are forgiven; you are righteous with Christ's bestowed righteousness. He counts for you; you are justified. Now you are to become what you are.

The primary and ultimate fact about you is established by Christ and Calvary. You are forgiven, made God's holy child for Christ's sake. That fact is as solid as Christ and Calvary. But it is not an "abracadabra" formula. The drunkard that has rotted his liver is not, upon repentance, supplied with a new liver. Virginity surrendered to fornication cannot be restored. The damage done by a tyrant of a father or a trollop of a mother does not instantly disappear. The words that crush someone's chance for happiness cannot be unsaid.

Sin carries its damage along with it. We may not see the healing of the damage, but the sin can be forgiven, its dominion broken. Sin can no longer destroy us; it can no more destroy us than it can destroy Christ. He has answered for it all. You are free. When you go to Calvary, do not hide in your hip pocket or handbag some special sin that you think you can deal with yourself. Your sin is not this or that item. Your sin is you in alienation from God. The man on the cross at the center of it all is there for you—all of you.

AMEN.

Lenten I

MIDWEEK SERMON

VALPARAISO UNIVERSITY (1969)

There is nothing quite so shriveling as fear. The pervasiveness of fear is shown by its projection into the gods that humans make. Gods made in the image of us are focuses of fear. Thunder means a god is growling. Quick! Do or offer something to quiet his wrath. Religion is used as a device for averting or at least minimizing the threat of gods. The Greeks sophisticated their gods out of history into the realm of ideas, thus they entered the realm of human projection. When talking about the gods, you are really talking about humanity. Theology is anthropology, as the cognoscenti put it nowadays, repeating Feuerbach of a hundred years ago. However, this does not liberate us from fear, only traces fear to its source.

One popular theory about fear is that the source of our fear is the unknown. When we understand where thunder comes from, we are no longer afraid of it. Ignorant imagination supposes that unexplored planets are populated with ogres. When we have sent somebody to see what is really on the planet, that fear will die. At the same time, of course, we are stockpiling technology against the fear of somebody else getting more technology and being the first to set up a space station from which this ludicrously small planet might be dominated.

Knowledge does not always cast out fear. The monkeys who stole Jove's thunder would not be content with a frightening demonstration. They annihilated a city and were so satisfied with the result that they did it again. We put our trust in a balance of fears with, it is hoped, a margin in our favor. Socially the haves seek to exercise a larger fear than that of the have-nots. On campus, there is the fear of a crippling grade and the fear of ruinous revolt. We are not so much the victims of fear as its producers.

We may regard ourselves as sophisticated beyond the level of how the first chapters of the Bible put things, but it is difficult to imagine a more telling and penetrating statement of the basic facts. Adam and Eve are true to us, and the serpent, too, we know well enough, though he talks such a plausible line that we are in danger of not recognizing him as other than ourselves. The real shocker to us is God. He just loves people and is happiest giving them all sorts of good things and piling them up that they may have His kind of giving happiness. God, man, woman, children, people—more and more. "I am here for you. I am here for you." The embrace of love and its happy flow back and forth and to and fro, round about and back again. The dance of love. The dance of life.

The dance stops when we say, "No, I am for me," plant ourselves in the center, and arrange and manipulate things to our own advantage and service, for this is our idea of being a god. He won't be for anybody else, and this results in cutting off the flow of life from Giver God and its onward flow to others. Life is cut off; therefore, death comes in the profoundest and most ruinous sense.

When we take the center and death position, we have fear. Then everyone is a threat to us and our ability to sustain the center spot for ourselves. Even God becomes a threat and an enemy to be defended against, for we then project our fear onto Him also. The serpent suggests that God thinks only of Himself, occupying the number one spot and being big by keeping you down. God forbids you some good to keep you inferior and deprived while pretending to be your friend. You want the fruit? Take it. Adam and Eve took it and disobeyed God. They treated Him as an enemy.

God recognized the facts produced by their action but refused the role of enemy. He gave Adam and Eve a promise of liberation. When the promise is fulfilled, it is put to the test. The man from Nazareth has been called the Son of God at His baptism. The tempter has lost none of his subtlety. First, the tempter gives a suggestion of doubt regarding God's words. "If You be the Son of God" is followed by the suggestion of deprivation. God can't really want You to go hungry? Why be denied bread? You have power; use it for Your own benefit. Jesus is tempted to qualify as Son of God according to Satan's notion of God.

Jesus holds Himself to being man for us. He uses no other resources than those given to us. The words of God are all He uses, and with their strength, Jesus holds to His purpose. He refuses to play Satan's kind of God. Jesus holds to being man for us, so He holds to being true Son of God, one with the Father, God for us, Emmanuel, God our servant. Jesus is not raising Himself up by putting us down; instead, He lowers Himself to raise us up. Such is the will of God that Jesus obeys.

Jesus is not deflected at His temptation. When subsequently tempted to put on a show of power that would reveal a God who would fit our notions, Jesus resolutely refuses. He never uses His power for Himself. Jesus is the man for others. As such He has no basis for fear, for fear is self-regarding. Jesus came to do the Father's will that was "for us and for our salvation." It was the weight of what that involved, not fear, that brought Jesus low in Gethsemane. Yet He held to the Father's will and went on to Calvary. There Jesus did what only He could do. He did it for us, for if we had to bear our sin's burden that would be the end of us.

As we follow Christ and His way, obedient to the Father through Lent, He is not just a moral example for us: "Be brave, be fearless like Jesus." That would only make more clear how abysmally we fail to do the will of God. Because we quite obviously fail to be like Jesus, then we can only fear the consequences of our failure. In following Jesus we learn from Him, we see in Him what God is really like, for us. The fears we project onto God have no place in Him. They fall to the ground at Calvary. Here is no God that is God by subjugation and deprivation, but God that is God by giving Himself for us. We have no need to defend ourselves against such a God. We can laugh at all the dodges and subterfuges that humans raise against an enemy god. God is for us, and we are for Him. "For Me is what you do for your neighbor," He says. So our neighbor now is no longer a threat but is how we serve the man of Calvary in whom God is most God for us.

Our society, our whole economic system, our civilization, our way of life is shaped by fear. If we should ever grow brave and fearless in the will of God, what on earth would become of us?

AMEN.

Lenten II

"LOVE VS. LUST"

VALPARAISO UNIVERSITY (1969)

Jesus is uninterchangeable. This fact is borne in upon us ever more profoundly in our Lenten discipleship. All through the Gospels we know that Jesus is moving toward Calvary. John proclaimed Him the Lamb of God who takes away the sin of the world. Jesus identifies with sinners and is baptized. He is proclaimed Son of God and is tested by the devil's temptations. Jesus holds to being man for us and rejects any use of His power for proving He is God. The shadow of the cross is there all the time. The Gospels do not allow the cross to be thought of as a thing of chance. Jesus moves steadily toward it. The Gospels have been called accounts of Jesus' passion with a preface. He is what He is only as the crucified. There is only one Calvary in all the world, only one Christ crucified.

This does not fit our categories, whether we call them historical, scientific, or rational. Categories depend on like instances. When Jesus is put into some category, He differs from other instances in that category only by degrees. What if we put Him into a category such as "Great Men" or "Great Teachers"? When subordinated to our categories, Jesus becomes a teacher or illustration of some human truth or ideal. In Jesus we see how a good man is treated in the world. Or He is a paradigm, a noble martyr, or a stirring example. Could we put Socrates in the same category? The course of a great teacher's life or death makes no essential difference to his teaching. Socrates' death was noble indeed, but even if we did not know of it, his teaching would remain the same.

However, if we did not know of Jesus' death, we would not know Jesus. Any account of Jesus that does not collapse with the removal of the passion is not an account of Jesus. When Paul Tillich was asked if his teaching would collapse without Jesus, he answered no. A dispensable Jesus who merely serves to illustrate some idea or principle is an interchangeable Jesus, and that is not the Jesus of the Gospels, the Jesus who moves steadily to the cross. His uninterchangeability there is beyond the imagination and beyond the capacity of our understanding. When the limitations of these are exercised, the result is an interchangeable Jesus. The Jesus of the Gospels has then been "de-Jesused" by us.

We saw last week, in Jesus' holding to be man for us, that He was one with God as God is for us. He was not a Son of God according to our criteria or Satan's criteria. The meaning and size of God for us, the fact that God loves us, grows and grows as we follow Jesus to Calvary. That overwhelms us. There is no greater love than that. Jesus is identified with that love at His baptism: "This is My beloved Son." That is the love within which lies uninterchangeability, the love within which lies personhood, or the love that creates persons.

What about us? How pathetically interchangeable we have become—statistics for a sociologist. A factory injects units of labor, a nation needs a calculated quantity of cannon fodder, without a certain percentage of unemployed the economy gets out of kilter. But this week, we are concentrating on sex, prompted by, of all things, Reminiscere's Epistle, and interchangeability is the hallmark of lust. In German there is a saying: "In the dark all cats are gray."

We use a most unfortunate idiom when we say that a lustful man "wants a woman." Strictly speaking, a woman is just what he does not want. A woman happens to be the necessary piece of apparatus for the pleasure he wants. How much he cares about the woman is subsequently quite clear. Cambridge undergraduates seldom marry those whom they call their "mattresses." A common attitude is revealed by a conversation overheard on a Friday: "Had any sex this week, John?" "No, can't say that I have. I think I had perhaps better plan to relieve myself this evening."

All those thoughts we, of course, despise. Lust has to be rather more refined to get at us, or perhaps not so much refined as disguised as its opposite—Satan as an angel of light, love as a law unto itself. Anything goes in the name of love. We may betray a trust, betray a friend, risk damaging people if we do it in the name of love. Love may ride roughshod over truth and honor when two people willingly give themselves to each other, regardless of any other considerations. There is a splendor here as of a fallen angel. Angelic, indeed, yet fallen if deceiving, and deceiving if interchangeable. Love vows uninterchangeability, and that is marriage-size love. Anything less between a man and a woman is not yet full-grown or it is counterfeit. Even before love has grown uninterchangeable, there is a wonder and a mystery, a loss of self-regard, a caring for another. This is coupled with fluctuation and painful uncertainty, blissful and agonizing palpitation, an awareness of delights and dangers. It is felt in nerve and body chemistry. And discipline takes over that love may grow full-size. As love grows, the gambler's fear that would take its winnings and ruin the game declines. We play until we can pay in full. Then the game starts for real. Mrs. Franzmann said that after she was married she felt that all the years before she had been only half alive. But not everybody has a husband like hers. However, that is a silly thing to say. One man's meat is another man's poison. Some men seem remarkably happy with the most unlikely wives. Silly again, for only they are in their own uninterchangeability, and they have accepted each other and fitted together despite his snoring and her unspeakable hats. Within love's confident uninterchangeability, things find their place. Thus conjugation also has its easy, ardent, playful, happy home, liberated from the desperate clutching at personal realization and transcendent consummation.

That seems to have gone rather out of fashion of late, at least in lots of movies and books. In the bad old days, copulation was usually the climactic consummation after "God Save the Queen." Nowadays it is old stuff by the time the movie starts, or it is gotten out of the way early on so people can get down to the serious business of really getting to know each other. There has been a fearful devaluation of sex. Christians have the big and delightful job of restoring to sex its splendor. In a world in which man is generally thought of as an animal, his sexuality gives intimations and promptings that contradict this animality. We can witness the pallid casualness of the barnyard, the gray copulation for which the lights must be turned out and for which a necessary preliminary is the desensitizing and dehumanizing use of alcohol.

The interchangeable works of darkness we turn our backs on. We save ourselves for that glad casting off of our fig leaves with that person with whom in the bright light of day before God and others we vow uninterchangeability. This is the size of love and sexuality to which Christians are called and for which they are enabled by the uninterchangeable Jesus. He is not interchangeable with a self-validating idol of so-called love. He has shown us the size and nature of love by His unique interchange with us at Calvary, which makes Jesus utterly uninterchangeable for us, and it is His gift and bidding for a man and a woman that they live that uninterchangeability as husband and wife, as between Him and His bride for whom He died and with whom He banquets.

AMEN.

Lenten III

"LAYING ASIDE GREED"

VALPARAISO UNIVERSITY (1969)

India is brought near by lust for gain, said Herodotus (fifth century before Christ). Today he might observe that the moon is brought near by lust for power. A similar shift is observable in the understanding of Judas. The affluent are apt to think that it could not have been only 30 pieces of silver that prompted his betrayal of Jesus; Judas must somehow have been playing the power game. That is probably more our kind of Judas.

D. L. Sayers has persuasively given Judas such a characterization in her drama "The Man Born to Be King." Now there is something deceptive and penetrating here. Judas projects his ideals onto Jesus—noble, national, religious ideals. Judas had given up security, property, and money to follow Jesus. We cannot hold a candle to Judas on that score. But Jesus did not fulfill Judas's ideals. When ideals flounder, you need something to hang on to that is solid. As his hopes collapsed, Judas clutched at the pathetic 30 pieces of silver, a mere $20 to $30. The amount is derisory, but it is solid cash. In grasping that money, Judas gets his hands on a reality. Jesus ended in disillusionment for Judas, but this was money in his hand, hard currency. This you can calculate and rely on.

The higher a man's thinking rides in the air, the cruder the things he clutches at when he crashes. Our thinking rises above preoccupation with money. We have always had enough to get by, and some of us have demonstrated its worthlessness by profligate wasting of it. A university education will put you well above the bread line. One can indulge in contempt for money on a full stomach.

We have exalted ideals, and we may project them onto Jesus. But when the crunch comes and ideals crumble or are met with bitter frustration, when our Jesus doesn't pull off our ideals, what will we then use to try to steady ourselves? What will be the solid thing we grasp? What will we be willing to betray and sell to get our hands on something solid? At the moment we are not apt to think that it will be money, and there is much worldly wisdom supporting us as it shows the vanity of riches. We instinctively admire the ascetic and enjoy a righteous glow as we speak scornfully of money. This is good natural religion, but Jesus did not propound such otherworldly nonsense. He did not hold much property to be sure, but it was sensible to have something in the kitty to pay for supper, and, with a wry chuckle, He paid His taxes. He did not refuse an invitation to dinner just because it came from the arrogant rich. Jesus just will not fit into our ideals.

It has been claimed that Jesus stands for communism and its bastard brother socialism, by which the Swedes and English show how decadent they are. He is also claimed by the capitalists, free enterprise, and nowadays we hear sometimes that Jesus stood for revolution. Does this mean that Jesus is politically and socially useless? Yes and no. Dorothy Sayers supplies Judas with the best of motives and ideals. He was simply trying to force Jesus' hand, set Him up to turn on His power to accomplish the right things. The right things vary with the things we want to have Jesus do for us. At a lower level, we select a phrase from Jesus here and there to embellish or illustrate our point of view or to support our argument or program. We want to use Him as an ally when the only alternatives are "my Lord" or "my Judge." Jesus turned His back on every attempt to enlist Him into some party or program. He turned His face to go up to Jerusalem that all things might be accomplished that were spoken of by the prophets.

The greedy in search of power, position, and money recognized in Jesus a threat and disposed of Him. Power, position, and money provided objective justification for what men did to Jesus. They were the final recourse behind the high-flying talk. When pushed hard, people grasp for something solid, and the high talk disperses in the air from which it was generated.

Jesus had His job, and with steady and unhurried step, He went to it. Greed offered Him the world—a Christian society—but He was set to achieve a more profound and more thoroughgoing human revolution. He did not waft off with airy words, then thud down. He was integrated, a whole man. When all hell and sin bore down on Jesus, there was no emptiness in Him into which the waters of greed could flood and make Him clutch at something to save Himself from drowning. In His dereliction, He cried to God. Here was the man, full man, but He was not there for Himself, He was there for us. For us He died and rose again. Here (as we saw last week) is Jesus the utterly uninterchangeable, my Savior and my Lord. Now He gives us of His fullness that we may be full and whole, no longer empty and in peril of any buffet that may make a crack to let in the drowning waters of greed and make us desperately clutch at some spar to save us.

As Jesus' people, we deal with money, power, and position as things outside ourselves. There is no emptiness in us that they need supply. We are not dependent on them for who and what we are. That is fully from Christ. So we are no longer slaves to greed but lords. Power, money, and position are instruments and tools for living out our calling as Christ's people. We have no need to play the fool with them or be fooled by them. They are neither more nor less than what they are. We neither inflate them as idols on which our lives depend nor do we talk high-sounding nonsense in contempt of them. Money is an efficient instrument. We work hard for it, for as much as our training and equipment can honestly earn. The apostle exhorted those who were going otherworldly (1 Thessalonians 4:9–12; Ephesians 4:28; Acts 20:35). We work to give to those in need, which is a most Christlike thing. We do not need money to fill or prop us up, but there is so much good that money can be useful in achieving.

Similarly we seek power and position, for these, too, are useful tools for the work that Christ's compassion would have us do. Because they are not our idols, we do not have to talk hypocritical nonsense to keep up a pretense of their holiness. Nor do we have to sustain our holiness by the hypocrisy of refusing to do business in the dirty dog-eat-dog world of politics and social reform. Our holiness has its source in the Rock of Calvary. Therefore, in the kingdom of the left hand, where the choice is never for an absolute good but always which is the lesser of two evils, we sin bravely, for here we have no revelation, no divine specific directives, but we are Christ's free people, freed from filling ourselves and serving our own advantage, free to serve others.

This week our awareness of needs is being stretched. As Christ's people we cannot pass by on the other side. As Christ's people we are equipped to recognize hypocrisy and idolatry. Yet seeing things for the size that they are is not enough, awareness is not enough, and talking is not enough. We can be so busy talking and planning the remaking of society so there will be no more poor that we forget the poor of today, the specific persons within the unique grasp of poverty. A fellow student of yours took over the medical debts of a widowed mother. I only got to hear of this indirectly because the burden got so heavy. He is not much of a talker. This does not mean that we should not thunder against a system in which the kind of medical care you get depends on where you live and how much money you have. But talk is not enough. Social and political action are called for as well as present giving for the present needy. Give till it hurts, they say, or better yet, give until it feels good.

Here, too, unhypocritical honesty is called for. There is also a hypocritical Pharisaic honesty. The price of the pair of shoes you are wearing could save the life of a Biafran child, yet you cannot do without shoes. There may be other things that you could do without. A lot of money goes into your attendance at Valparaiso University. There are other universities at which you could learn calculus more cheaply, be honest and true to yourself, and cultivate your precious little me. You can answer for your being here as training, as enlarging your appropriation of God's bounty of skill and beauty, as learning to live as Christians in community, as equipping yourself to serve others and build Christ's kingdom with compassion and competence—saturated with the Gospel that liberates you from having to justify yourself, liberates you from motivations of fear and guilt and greed, and that through your life and witness may liberate some others for whom Christ also went through Calvary.

AMEN.

Lenten IV

"PRIDE"

VALPARAISO UNIVERSITY (1969)

One can't help but love Peter. You get it straight from Peter because he blurts things out. Christ loved him and gave it to him straight—right down the line, or better, right up the line. Jesus did not share the notion that straight talk meant only denunciation. When we begin a conversation with "I am going to be honest with you," it usually introduces something unpleasant. The buddiest words we have from Jesus were to Peter when He arranged (with a chuckle) for them to pay their taxes together. There was a bond between these two men that gave them honesty. True honesty, like true humility, is unself-regarding. The moment one points to honesty in oneself, you know it is not there.

Both honesty and humility seem to be in Peter when he recoils from having his feet washed by Jesus. But Jesus does not allow things to be as Peter reads them. To Peter it was utterly backward and upside-down that Jesus, his Lord and Master, should wash his feet. Peter wants to have things right side up. He can make sense out of Jesus as a Lord and Master, and Jesus ought to behave that way and not ridiculously get down on the floor to wash dirty feet. There was something similar in Peter's collapse after the staggering catch of fish. Peter said, "Depart from me; for I am a sinful man, O Lord" (Luke 5:8). In his mind, there was no reason, no deserving, of such abundance. Then Jesus asked three times, "Peter, do you love Me?" And the man who had denied Jesus three times was called to spend his love in the service of Christ's flock. There was no reason, no deserving, but only the love of Jesus.

For Peter, to let Jesus wash his feet was to be washed of his Lord-and-Master thinking. If Jesus, who qualified for Peter as Lord and Master, was one who washed feet as a lowly servant, there wasn't much alternative for Peter. To let his feet be washed was to be drawn into Jesus' servanthood. "If I wash thee not, thou hast no part with Me" (John 13:8). The magnificent thing in this is that Peter was past the point of wanting to hold some part of himself back, some part where he could still play the Lord-and-Master game. Have the lot then! There is total surrender here, but perhaps with something of a *harrumph*, as when Thomas said in response to Jesus' mad announcement that He was going to Jerusalem, "We may as well go along and get ourselves killed too." This is the point at which some get stuck, sighing with resignation, suffering for the Lord.

Stoic and humanist can get you as far as this. It is the furthest point to which Goethe could bring Faust. It is a joyless thing, for it is the ultimate refinement of pride: when a person can let things go and enjoy a complacent self-satisfaction. Greed and fear and lust are left behind in the proud mastery of resignation. If there was any of this in Peter, Jesus pulled him past it. Jesus will not leave Peter to think about his total surrender. Quantitative and self-regarding thinking Jesus pushes aside. "He that is washed needeth not save to wash his feet, but is clean every whit: and ye are clean, but not all" (John 13:10). The word *washed* rings with echoes of Baptism. What is written here is not just to tell us a story about Peter. It shows the way of Jesus with a man whom He loved, but He shows us that we also may be such a one who clings to Lord-and-Master thinking, one who denies Jesus, yet one who also may be restored, forgiven, and washed clean by Jesus, one who claims and lives out the life given in our Baptism.

A notable psychiatrist justified his exorbitant fees as therapeutically essential. When people have to pay a lot for something, they feel it has to do them good. They would not value the treatment if they received it free. While we applaud and are grateful for the achievements of this week for a better university, we must yet spot the resignation that sighs, "It could have been worse," and ask rather hopefully how it could have been better. There may be something there that calls for repentance. We may ask the foot-washing question. How much of it was there, or how much was it to insure that my feet get washed?

We cannot wash another's feet until we have let Jesus wash our own. Oh, we may do some foot washing with *harrumphs* and sighing resignation, but the heathen can do that also. Only when we have let Jesus be our servant and are drawn into servanthood with Him, only as we are cleansed of our Lord-and-Master thinking, only as He has washed us clean can we be freed from pride's last stand of resignation. In the Upper Room and at Calvary there is no reason for, no deserving of, such a love that makes a mockery of our pride. It is all gift. Baptism, as is so clear when an infant is baptized, is utterly a gift. Jesus' doing, His bestowal, His making us His own, His taking us into His servanthood is a gift. There is a death and a rising to life here. From the death of his denials, Jesus raised up Simon Peter with a look that pierced him through yet reached out to him. He asked, "Peter, do you love Me?" Then Peter understood what Jesus had done when He washed his feet and gladly went to the servant's task Jesus gave him and to the death with which he would glorify Christ.

This sermon was supposed to have been about pride. Hopefully pride got lost somewhere along the way. Perhaps that miracle of grace for some of you got you past the joyless pride of resignation into the glorious liberty of God's children who have nothing to prove but only a life given as a sheer gift, a life to be given away because of Jesus, to whom with the Father and the Holy Spirit be all praise, thanks, and glory, now and forever.

AMEN.

First Sunday in Lent

MATTHEW 4:1–11

CONCORDIA SEMINARY (1995)

The names put on Jesus at His baptism were Son of God and Suffering Servant. With those names came what was His to do. The voice from heaven spoke words from Psalm 2 and Isaiah 42. "Son of God" was used to describe the people of Israel; the people of Israel are gathered up in their king. The Davidic title, Son of God, is put on Jesus at His baptism, which is His anointing to kingship. "This is My beloved Son, in whom I am well pleased" (Matthew 3:17). "Beloved" and "with whom I am well pleased" were said in Isaiah of that Son of God, that Servant of God. We will hear the names "Son" and "Servant" again at Jesus' transfiguration as He stands with Moses and Elijah, speaking of the death that He would accomplish.

Then we are told Christ would make Himself a sacrifice for sin. He will make many to be accounted righteous, for He will bear their iniquities. Such is the Son, Servant of God, the King who stands for His people, the Christ, the Lamb of God who takes away the sin of the world. "This is My beloved Son, in whom I am well pleased." The next thing that Matthew tells us is that

> Jesus was led up by the Spirit into the wilderness to be tempted by the devil. And He fasted forty days and forty nights, and afterward He was hungry. And the tempter came and said to Him, "If you are the Son of God, command these stones to become loaves of bread." But He answered, "It is written: Man shall not live by bread alone but by every word that proceeds from the mouth of God." (Matthew 4:1–4 RSV)

The last words from the mouth of God to Jesus were "This is My beloved Son, in whom I am well pleased" (Matthew 3:17). The tempter casts doubt on these words: "If You are the Son of God." This is similar to the first temptation that involved us all: "Hath God said, 'Ye shall not eat of every tree of the garden?'" (Genesis 3:1). The devil is saying, "Doesn't God want you to have food? Doesn't He want you to have what is good for you? Doesn't God love you? So take the fruit." Eve did take the fruit. And with her sin, her taking, her unbelief, she brought all her children into bondage, one from which, try as they may, they can never get free. All their efforts bring them deeper into slavery, no matter how many styles of fig leaves they try.

In Jesus' temptation, when everything that is wrong with us hangs on Jesus, He did not sin. The words of God come first and are sure: "It is written: Man shall not live by bread alone, but by every word that proceedeth out of the mouth of God" (Matthew 4:4). Jesus' victory is not with some magical blast but in the strength of the words of the Lord. The same words have been given to you too. Jesus was tempted to slip away from the words of God, away from the cross, into the bondage and slaveries of power. For Him to grasp power as the way of being a Servant/Son/King would make bad news out of the Good News. It would mean that is indeed the way everything goes. Everybody wants power, even God. Those who look for a big power god get that kind of god. The ways of power are coercion and necessity. God does not want to deal with us with coercion. That is not His saving way with us in Jesus. Jesus came to set us free—no whip, no rope, no slaves.

In *The Brothers Karamazov*, Dostoyevsky has the Grand Inquisitor say to Jesus, "Thou didst not know that when man rejects miracles, he rejects God, too." There are many people we know who reject miracles, and in rejecting miracles, they reject God. We fall into the same bondage if the first thing we do is try to prove some miracles, as if then we would have proven God. The only God of whom we might find proof would be a god who does miracles. There are loads and loads of gods like that around. There is only one of the Calvary kind. The Grand Inquisitor continues by stating that man needs miracles so badly that he will "create new miracles of his own for himself." That is temptation, but Jesus turned away from miracles. When He healed in response to pleaded need, He often told people not to tell anyone about it. Those who come to Jesus because of miracles should stay at home with the gods they already have, gods who are kept as gods as long as they produce the desired miracles. If you go to church and the god who is being promoted there is the miracle-worker one, what hope is there for you?

At Calvary, Satan says the same thing, as also earlier through Peter, "If Thou be the Son of God, come down from the cross" (Matthew 27:40). At the consummation of His saving work for us and at its beginning, Jesus does not come down from the cross, for He is the Son/Servant of God. At His baptism He is already put to that task. At His temptation He holds Himself toward the cross. Can anyone be as free as that? Jesus is. And in Him is the Father's pleasure.

Religion comes in the next temptation. And what could be more religious than the temple and its pinnacle? The devil knows how to behave himself in church. A telling word of Scripture would be just the thing that is called for. He has one, but one fixed to fit his purpose. No captive is more delicious to the devil's taste than one he captures by using the words and the name of God. Verbal inspiration is not his primary problem. The devil can cite Scripture for his purpose, says Shakespeare. And every heretic can too, says Tertullian. So Satan tempts: "If You are the Son of God, throw Yourself down, for it is written, 'He will give His angels charge of you, and on their hands they will bear you up, lest you strike your foot against a stone'" (Matthew 4:6 RSV). You can trust God's promises, can't you? Satan certainly sometimes sounds like a reasonably good Lutheran, doesn't he?

Jesus sees it straight because He says God's words straight. There won't be any tempting of God, calling Him up for a miracle, or all those more subtle ways in which we try to get in on God's power and use it to our purpose—even good purposes, perhaps. But with us, getting control of God, binding Him, is the native meaning of the word *religion*. That can be a dirty word.

Jesus, who refused to do a spectacular miracle in the temple, could not be taken captive there. A few years ago it was quite the thing to say, "You won't find Jesus here in church. He is out there in the world doing what people need to have done for them there. That is the real Jesus." Satan seems to follow something of the same line of thought. The devil took Jesus to a high mountain, showed Him all the kingdoms of the world and their glory, and said to Him, "All these I will give You if You will fall down and worship Me. You can be king of the lot, Jesus. All the power that is mine I will put at Your disposal. The two of us together can hardly fail, if You will only do things a bit more my way."

Some years ago a sociologist said to The Lutheran Church—Missouri Synod: "You have all that good Bible stuff, but if you will just make a few adjustments, not really big ones . . . Don't let the Lord's Supper get in the way of speedily growing the church with selected people. Just a few adjustments, then you, too, can strike it big." The time when the church exercised great power in the world some called the Age of Faith. Try that out on the Jesus of the third temptation, the Jesus who moves steadily to Calvary.

Satan's sort of king is not the one who hangs on the cross, the one who resists temptation on His way to the cross. Along that way we follow again with Jesus this Lent, deeply rejoicing in what He does for us, in what is only His to do, in what He does that counts for us, in what He does on the cross by which we come to be forgiven and righteous. "By one man's obedience . . . shall many be made righteous" (Romans 5:19). Only God (who doesn't have to prove He is God) does it. So hidden, so human, so weak, so hungry, so declining to make it big in the church or in the world. Here is the way of the cross. That is the way Jesus does it.

One expectation of the Messiah would be that He would be invulnerable. Nothing could hurt Him, not even a fall from the pinnacle of the temple. Now there is a sensible sort of Christ. And Satan rides along on our natural way of projecting God and getting maximum mileage with our "religion." No wonder they had no use for a man who got Himself crucified! There was never such a way of being a king before, of being God's Son, the Suffering Servant, of being Christ, of being Savior, of being Jesus for you, even to His body broken and His blood shed—for you.

AMEN.

Second Sunday in Lent

MARK 12:1–12

CONCORDIA SEMINARY (1996)

Just give up, we would say to the master of the vineyard. Anybody else would after all that trouble. But the master does not give up. One failure after another does not deter him. He keeps on sending servants. Again, he sent another servant, and the tenants wounded him in the head and treated him shamefully. The master sent another to the vineyard, and the tenants killed him too. Thus it went with many others. Some servants were beaten; some were killed.

The Old Testament, whose history this parable recaps, can be depressing reading. There isn't much to show for an annual review. God's people spent forty years wandering in the wilderness. Nothing that the Lord did seemed to do much good, but He kept on trying. His people kept telling God how He should do His business—at least back in Egypt they knew what they could count on. They imagined that God was there to supply what they wanted and claimed they deserved.

But the Lord would not be such a God for them. That would be the end of Him and the end of His people. He did not bring them out of the house of slavery so He could be a slaveowner and have them as His slaves. God would have them as His people, His holy people, a priestly kingdom, free, rejoicing in the confidence of His covenant and His Torah, not having any other confidence that will not hold.

> A wandering Aramean was my father; and he went down into Egypt and sojourned there, few in number; and there he became a nation, great, mighty, and populous. And the Egyptians treated us harshly, and afflicted us, and laid upon us hard bondage. Then we cried to the LORD the God of our fathers, and the LORD heard our voice, and saw our affliction, our toil, and our oppression; and the LORD brought us out of Egypt with a mighty hand and an outstretched arm, with great terror, with signs and wonders; and He brought us into this place and gave us this land, a land flowing with milk and honey. And behold, now I bring the first of the fruit of the ground, which Thou, O LORD, hast given me. And you shall set it down before the LORD, your God, and worship before the LORD your God; and you shall rejoice in all the good which the LORD your God has given to you and to your house, you and the Levite, and the sojourner who is among you. (Deuteronomy 26:5–11 RSV)

There is delight in all the gifts received from God, who loves nothing as much as giving out His gifts. When His gifts are received as gifts, and recognized as coming from Him, He draws us into His gift-giving delight. Such is the rejoicing of the people who bring the firstfruit of the ground that God Himself gave them.

What Jesus is speaking about in this parable is the refusal of God's gifts, taking them over as if they were ours by right or by our measures and not as gifts. The Lord is speaking to those people who refuse God's gifts to bring them to repentance. He failed, but they got the message. They decided they would have no such God. The way they had God figured out was threatened by the God Jesus represented. To protect their God, Jesus would have to be gotten rid of. They left Him and went away. To fulfill the rest of the parable, God sent another servant to receive some of the fruit of the vineyard.

Gifts cease to be gifts when we think in terms of "the inheritance will then be ours." Those gifts are what we have gotten hold of, stacked up in our storehouses, and counted up. Doesn't that impress you? "All the kingdoms of this world and the glory of them"—can't we have that and Jesus too? Oh, come, let us fix our eyes on Jesus.

In Lent we follow Jesus. That is what God is like. Lent is not used up with trifling pieties. It is a facing up to God, the Jesus who does it His way. Jesus holds to God's way that was given to Him at His baptism, the way of the Suffering Servant, our sin-bearer, the way to Calvary. He holds to this even when tempted to do it some other way. Jesus declined to be taken over by Satan's "pure success" theology. Who could have any use for such a Jesus? Most of His own people rejected Jesus. By their definition of God, He was obviously a failure. In Matthew we read of a crescendo of rejection. In Mark nobody understands until Jesus hangs dead on the cross. Nevertheless, Jesus keeps on going to Calvary.

Those who had commandeered the Lord to their success-by-power program were not going to let Him get in the way of what they wanted. What they had taken over, they were going to hang on to. " 'This is the heir; come, let us kill him, let us seize on his inheritance.' And they caught him, and cast him out of the vineyard, and slew him" (Matthew 21:38-39). What does the owner of the vineyard do? He will not give up his vineyard. Those who would turn it into a place of bondage and turn him into the sanctioning reference of their enslaving takeover he shoves aside. Jesus also does not give up. He suffers Himself to be rejected and keeps on His way, the Calvary way. That is the sort of God that He is. That is the sort of vineyard Jesus doesn't give up on.

Jesus does fail to deliver on what we lay down for Him. By our prescriptions, He is a great failure. But not by His promises. Jesus' vineyard promise will be kept in His way of keeping it. "Remember, O Lord." The Old Testament lesson's love song tells of God laying waste to the vineyard. The Gospel tells of Jesus destroying those who took it over and of giving His vineyard to others. Who is that? If they reject God's gifts and insist on His being a god who meets their projections, He will be that, unrejectably. God's almighty power and His wrath are irresistible.

We are saved from the wrath of God by Jesus, who takes it in our place: "When we were enemies, we were reconciled to God by the death of His Son" (Romans 5:10). We rejoice in God through our Lord Jesus Christ. Isaiah rings in: "In that day sing ye unto her, A vineyard of red wine. I the LORD do keep it; I will water it every moment: lest any hurt it, I will keep it night and day. Fury is not in Me" (27:3–4). "Now will I sing to my well-beloved a song of my beloved touching his vineyard. My well-beloved hath a vineyard into a very fruitful hill" (5:1).

Could it ever be that Jesus would be such a God for you? A "love song" God? I am yours, and you are Mine. His vineyard, and more than vineyard, more than a love song for the vineyard, more than one flesh in husband and wife, deeper than child in the womb, deeper than into death for a friend, deeper than bread and wine. It is His body and His blood that He gives into you. Come to the feast. Hasten to the nuptial hall and celebrate the *Abendmahl*.

AMEN.

Third Sunday in Lent

LUKE 11:20

LONDON (1954)

This business about devils is certainly difficult. We Christians are reluctant to talk about the subject too much for fear of being laughed at. When devils do get mentioned, we tend to slide over the matter as if it doesn't mean anything to us or it embarrasses us. After all, who still believes in devils in this enlightened age? How many intelligent and educated people take the devil seriously? We assume it is just a lot of old-fashioned superstition. Modern people have outgrown such silly notions as the devil. When we can travel faster than sound and plan a trip to the moon, there really isn't any place for devils. No, the devil is now much discredited and something of a joke. Just think of the picture of the devil in black, with red tights, trident, pointy tail, and horns. He is a comic, laughable nonsense, and the word *devil* has gone all the way from dread to endearment, as when a fond father says of his son, "Isn't he a little devil?" A devil? No, there just isn't such a thing.

From this view of devils, we see one of Satan's most tremendous and strategic victories. Having gotten himself disbelieved in, he can go about his business, and people don't even suspect he exists, let alone is working on them. Rather shrewd, when you come to think of it! At the beginning of the century, when most people were captivated by the evolutionary theory, it was thought that we were well on the upward path of progress. From primeval slime we had attained to such a position of mastery over nature that it was only a matter of time before we would be amid prosperity and peace. Sin and Satan could be dispensed with. We would establish the kingdom of heaven on earth with roofs, shirts, and fair wages for all. Since then we have had two wars whose horrors and bestiality have shaken the world and have shaken also some of the smug complacency of the humanist worshipers. Because of this, there is now (in many people) a growing awareness of the devil and his achievements.

During our time, some 10 to 14 million Poles have been exterminated and only God knows how many Jews. Thousands of children were thrown into railway trucks and transported to hellish slavery, never to be heard of again. Fine respectable citizens became beasts who delighted to torture and to kill, and now the proudest national achievement is making bigger and better bombs. Confronted with such monstrous evil, our thinking, which goes by fashions, has come to suspect evil as a force in itself, powerful and demonic.

Yet these experiential things are seldom able to convince the doubters, especially people who fervently refuse to admit the possibility of devils. Such closed minds will never be convinced, and proofs of observation or history are not what really convince us either. As Christians, we look to the Bible for reliable information. We have found it reliable wherever it becomes a part of our lives. What is more, it has God's guarantee.

Now, when you look at the Bible, you find that there is surprisingly little about devils, especially when you compare the Bible with the other literatures among which it was written. But what there is in the Bible about devils is of extreme significance. The fall of man was decisive for us all, and in that the rebellious devil won the first of his many victories. We were made captive by the fateful triad—Satan, sin, death. In the First Adam's enslavement, the curse of evil came on all his children. The rescue of us from evil is the point that follows.

In the heart of every person is a throne. We were designed as dependent creatures, as the subjects of another. God intended to occupy that throne and by His rule give us the happiness, beauty, freedom, and strength that He wants us to have. But we dethroned God; we sinned. We thought we could climb onto the throne ourselves. This was the devil's lie: "Ye shall be as gods" (Genesis 3:5). We cannot mount that throne. It is as impossible as if a horse would try to mount the saddle on its own back. If God does not occupy the throne in our hearts, it is occupied by another, by the enemy of God, the devil.

This truth—that unless God is enthroned in your heart, the devil sits and rules there—is the hardest truth for us to swallow, yet it is only with this truth that our ways and the world's ways are in any way intelligible. What is more, that is the way Scripture says it is. When Jesus called Paul to be His apostle, He told Paul that his work was to open men's eyes, to turn them from darkness to light and from the power of Satan to God. Here you see the division: two parties, either of darkness or of light, either of Satan or of God. This "either/or" runs throughout Scripture. There is no third possibility, no middle ground, no neutral. It is unrelenting war, Satan against God, and the battleground is the human heart—your heart and mine.

The enemy is of an order of being we cannot understand. What is a fallen angel? What is Satan? We know so little about who he is, but we know a good deal more about what he does. Satan and his crew, thrown out of heaven, set themselves to overthrow the works of God. When God made people, whose hearts were to be ruled by His love, Satan sought God's dethronement and deceived us into thinking we could ascend the throne and be our own lord and master. Thus deceived, we came into the dominion of Satan. Satan became what Scripture calls "the god of this world" (2 Corinthians 4:4). And there, for all that we can do, we would remain forever lost, separated from God, and so dead.

But God in mercy looked on our plight and had pity. He promised one who would overthrow the dominion of Satan. He promised one who would restore the rule of God's love in the hearts of people, that is, establish the kingdom of God. Our text proclaims the fulfillment of that promise. Jesus of Nazareth has cast out the devil and restored the rule, the kingdom of God, in our hearts. "But if I cast out devils by the Spirit of God, then the kingdom of God is come unto you" (Matthew 12:28).

Christ came to dethrone the usurper. The first vital battle we considered a fortnight ago—the forty days conflict and the three crucial attacks. The decisive battle of the war comes in another three weeks—on the Friday we, for that reason, call good. The final action may come any minute. But a war consists not only of major offensives but also day-by-day fighting, loosing a little ground, gaining a little ground. Throughout His life, Christ was having skirmishes with the devil, one of which is reported in today's Gospel.

The Jews recognized that the things Jesus did could be done only by God or the devil. They were nearer the truth in this than those who deny all "this stuff of the devil," as they call it, and make Jesus into a sweet and lovely man who gave us rules of life that will make us sweet and lovely too. No, here was either the finger of God or the finger of Satan. The Jews refused to recognize God in this Nazarene; therefore, the only other possibility was that He was or had a devil.

The Jews referred Jesus' work to a specific devil called Beelzebub. In popular belief, there were stacks of devils, the product of wild speculation and morbid obsession. Jesus sets aside this whole world of thinking in which Beelzebub was produced and uses that name only in quotation. Jesus drives the matter home to the center and speaks of Satan as the enemy. The demons or devils are but his army. The New Testament teaches us that devils are personal beings with activity and purpose. They sometimes cause sickness, though not by any means every sickness. Jesus rebukes the disciples for thinking that a man's congenital blindness was caused by his or his parents' own special sin. The demons also have supernatural knowledge of Christ and His mission. Above all, they distort and destroy the functioning of a person as planned by the Creator. A devil can get such control of someone that when that individual speaks, it is said that the devil speaks. The purpose of all of this is to make wreckage of a creature designed by God for high happiness and achievement.

This operation of the devil on someone can happen to the best of us. Into the heart of one of the Twelve Satan entered and got control. Of Judas it is recorded, "Satan entered into him" (John 13:27). Jesus said, "Have not I chosen you twelve, and one of you is a devil?" (John

6:70). When Peter told Jesus that He should not go up to Jerusalem to suffer, Christ called him Satan. We are repeatedly told of Satan's untiring attacks on the church. And we are warned to beware of him. "Be sober, be vigilant; because your adversary the devil, as a roaring lion, walketh about, seeking whom he may devour" (1 Peter 5:8). If we mean to be of Christ, we, too, will certainly be subject to attack.

At the time of Christ and the founding of the church, the devil, seeing his dominion in peril by Christ, lashed out with particular violence. Such direct and frontal attacks we may not see nowadays, but that certainly does not mean that Satan has given up the struggle. It seems the devil has changed his strategy and is now more dangerous because of the current subtlety and unsuspected manner of his approach. But if we are alert, we shall not fail to discern his insidious efforts. Just try giving up some particular bad habit or try being kind to somebody you particularly dislike. You will see then the devilish difficulty and strange abundance of reasons that flood your mind to convince you not to bother with such a difficult and tiresome endeavor. Or think, for example, of the simple proposal of not going to church. How many reasons are immediately suggested in favor of staying away? Or in your prayers, how extraordinarily difficult is it for you to concentrate and keep your whole mind directed to your Lord? In reading the newspaper you encounter no difficulties in concentration. So in some of the simplest endeavors of the Christian life there is evidence of an extraordinary power hindering you. This power of evil is even more evident in our uglier sins. Think of the times when you quite completely lost your temper. You said and did things that you don't like to think yourself capable of doing or saying. You were given special aid by the devil.

At every turn we may see the efforts of Satan to dethrone Christ from our hearts. The more earnestly we mean to have the rule of Christ's love in our lives, the more we shall feel of the devil's efforts. For his purpose is to destroy the purposes of God and bring to wreckage God's sons and daughters. Hence it is that the greatest saints have known more of the devil than the most godless. The devil doesn't much bother with the godless for the time being. They are safe in his bag, so he bends his special attacks on the children of God. The more we strive for Christ, the more we shall suffer attack from Satan. The better we do, the harder it will get. But our gracious God will not let us stop growing. He wants us to be like Christ; therefore, we have to walk the same way of temptation.

This is our confidence: that Christ has walked this same way before us. He has made the path and shown the victory. If we stick close to Christ, we shall have the victory also; in Him we are secure. The decisive victory has already been won by Christ on Calvary. There the devil spent his utmost strength and was vanquished. That victory is for us also, but our Father suffers us to be tempted still so we may be tested and strengthened and cling ever closer to Christ.

Clinging to Christ and His victory, we can beat back the attacks of the devil. When he tries to claim us as his own and make us despair because of our much sinning, then we can boldly call the devil the liar that he is. "No, Satan, I am not yours. Christ has died for me and I am forgiven. He has conquered you, and so shall I." So when faith is strong, we can laugh in the face of the devil with blithe boldness. He cannot bear such scorn. The devil must then depart from us, for our Lord Jesus sits on the throne in our hearts. Then is the kingdom of God come upon us.

AMEN.

Fourth Sunday in Lent

MATTHEW 26:51–54

LONDON (1957)

Peter was first introduced to Jesus by his brother Andrew. A little later, while they were working at their fishing nets, Jesus called them to be His disciples, to leave everything, and walk His way with Him. He told them of that way and of His kingdom, but they understood it in their own way. Jesus gave Peter his name, not as a description of what he was but of what the love of Jesus would make him: first, the human love of a friend, then God's that suffers and dies.

What friends Jesus and Peter were we see in the comradely way in which they dealt with paying their taxes. Jesus said that as God's free men they were no man's slave but would gladly do their bit in paying their taxes. He told Peter where to find the money that would be enough for them both.

Most memorable of Peter's friendship was his confession at Caesarea Philippi: "Thou art that Christ, the Son of the living God" (John 6:69). He spoke with all the burning ardor of his loyalty to his friend Jesus. But when Jesus pointed toward His suffering, Peter protested, and Jesus vehemently rebuked him. Peter was thinking in the way of the world, not in the way of God. We saw the same passionate loyalty on the way to the garden. Although everybody else might desert Jesus, Peter would never fail Him. Peter would even die for Him. Now in our text the same ardent, misguided love seeks to protect Jesus from His passion, and again Peter is rebuked. He did not yet understand the love of God. Peter loved Jesus and didn't want Him to suffer. Jesus loved Peter and knew that He had to suffer, for only thus would He fulfill His saving work for Peter and for us all.

At Caesarea Philippi, Peter put his entreaty between Jesus and His passion and now in Gethsemane he interposes his sword to protect Jesus. But in doing that, Peter was standing in the way of Jesus accomplishing His mission. Like the other disciples, Peter had not understood the kingdom of God. He thought of it as an earthly kingdom, so he spoke and acted as if it were merely an earthly kingdom.

Peter's sword in the garden is the most blatant statement of his earthly thinking. When the men of earthly power came against Jesus, Peter bravely stood against them, but his weapon was an earthly one. His stand was no stronger than his weapon, and the victory he could achieve with it only a sword's victory.

Jesus had a far different and higher battle and victory before Him, and in the battle and victory He had no need of a sword, and to use a sword would have betrayed Him from His mission into something of which there is enough in the world already. The man who takes the sword steps into the realm of the sword, and in that realm things are settled by the sword, but this is not the settlement for which Jesus came.

Jesus does not reject the sword as such, but He rejects Peter's use of it in Gethsemane for the kingdom of Christ, for the sword is useless to the kingdom of Christ. There is another kingdom in which the sword belongs, and the use of it there Jesus confirms. No one may take the sword, snatch it into one's own hands, and use it. The person who does that justly comes under the sword of those to whom the sword has been entrusted.

All power belongs to God and derives from Him, but He ordains deputies and entrusts a use of power to them. We see this in the Fourth Commandment in which God delegates a use of power and authority to parents. Similarly, a use of power is entrusted to those who rule. Scripture is quite explicit about this: "For there is no power but of God: the powers that be are ordained of God. Whosoever therefore resisteth the power, resisteth the ordinance of God: and they that resist shall receive to themselves damnation. . . . he beareth not the sword in vain: for he is the minister of God" (Romans 13:1–4).

Peter was resisting the power. The sword was not entrusted to Peter but to the rulers. They had a right to use it—not Peter. How they used it was something they had to answer to God for. Peter's business was to be subject to the higher powers. One may not "take" the sword. It is not our job here to investigate the complex problems of obedience to our government. Nor is Peter's taking the sword merely an offence against the government; the worst of Peter's offence was that he thought he could serve the kingdom of Christ with a sword. What makes Peter's sin so horrible is that he acted against the kingdom of Christ.

God's victories are victories of love. God uses force only where love fails. If Jesus had approved Peter's sword or summoned the twelve legions of angels to get Him out of the predicament, it would have meant the failure of God's love that brought Him to put us right again. Jesus came to suffer and die for our sins, to drink the cup of God's wrath on sin for us. When we saw Jesus wrestling to hold Himself to the will of God, it was love that held Him to it. Loving God and loving us, Jesus triumphantly concluded, "Not as I will, but as Thou wilt" (Matthew 26:39). Jesus was there for God, He was there for us, and the victory of answering for our sins according to the plan of God was the victory of God, who was prepared to suffer our hell for us.

For such a victory a sword was worse than useless, not only Peter's little sword but also the twelve legions of angels. By mentioning these Jesus showed Peter how feeble his pitiful little sword was and how wrong he was in thinking of using force for the kingdom of Christ. If God wants to use force, He has plenty of it. But God does not want to be a tyrant; He would rather be our Father. God could blast all His enemies out of existence, but who then would be left? Because we have sinned, we have set ourselves against God. If He gave us force and justice, that would be the end of us. But God did not want that despite our rebellion. He wanted to rescue us from our sinful ruin.

You can't change a sinner by force, not even God. Suppose God rounded us all up with a whip or a sword—all He would have would be a rebellious herd of cattle or slaves. God wants a family. Free sons and daughters dwelling with Him in love. Force is quite hopeless for achieving that. Force cannot change people, make them better, make them free, make them love. Force can line people up and impose an external conformity, but force cannot get at someone's heart and change it.

Last week we saw Christ reaching into men's hearts with His words to Judas and His look to Peter. He could have taken them both captive by force. He then would have had two prisoners. Jesus wants no prisoners in His kingdom. There are no bars or chains there. You can run away anytime you like, for only those in His kingdom are there because they freely love Him. So both for the bringing in of the kingdom by the suffering of Christ and the building of the kingdom, a sword is worse than useless.

This has important implications for our lives and our serving the kingdom. Whenever we do anything merely because we have to, by compulsion, we are not acting as free sons and daughters of the kingdom. If we pay our taxes because we will go to jail if we don't, we act as slaves and not as God's free children, not as Peter and Jesus did when they paid their taxes together. The motive of Christian action is not force but love. We live from the Gospel, not from the Law.

Christ never gets behind His friends with a sword or a whip. He gets inside them with His love, a love that makes us free to want and achieve what God wants and plans. Therefore, Jesus goes to Gethsemane and moves toward the cross, not at the point of a sword but moved by love of God and love of us. "Willingly all this I suffer."

Love alone wins any worthwhile victory, and to do this it must be willing to forego force and to suffer. When a man strikes you with his fist or with his tongue and you strike back, you have been defeated by him. His enmity has won the engagement, and enmity is double. If he strikes and you do not retaliate, then enmity remains single and a little discomforted. By refusing to be made into his enemy, you have taken the first step toward love's victory of cleansing his heart of malice and making him your friend. Thus sin that sets us against each other is overcome. Only love can overcome sin, though it often means suffering long. The overcoming of the sin that divided us from God cost Calvary. Because it was love's victory, it achieved the true victory, not merely one of external appearances, which is the best force can do.

At times there is nothing left to us but the use of force. But when we use force, it is an acknowledgment of the failure of love. Only when love has exhausted its possibilities do we reluctantly resort to force. To protect against things getting worse, it can be a necessary but negative achievement. Positive good is the work of love. All our good hangs on Jesus going on to Calvary. Does no sword spell defeat? Through Lent we follow along with Jesus, His way, to be our Savior. But are we following ever closer or slipping from His way to something more reliable?

AMEN.

Fifth Sunday in Lent

MARK 10:32–45

CONCORDIA SEMINARY (1990)

In our reading we have the third and last prediction of the passion, the fifth Sunday in Lent, *Judica*, which comes from the Introit, "Judge me, O God." Who dares to pray such a prayer? Jesus does. Through Lent we have been following Jesus toward Calvary. Our *Judica* Gospel tells of the last stretch of that journey. "They were on the road going up to Jerusalem." Who dares that journey? Jesus does.

The disciples hung back in foreboding and fear. They were amazed and afraid. Twelve disciples, twelve tribes of Israel. He who leads the disciples is the Lord of Israel, just as the statement of His presence, the bright cloud, led Israel on her journey to the Promised Land, which was entered by way of Jericho. That is where Bartimaeus is given his sight. He sees as the Twelve had failed to see.

Jesus told the Twelve, "Behold, we go up to Jerusalem; and the Son of Man shall be delivered unto the chief priests, and unto the scribes; and they shall condemn Him to death, and shall deliver Him to the Gentiles" (Mark 10:33). The Twelve did not get it. They did not see. What blinded them was their lust for power and the fear that they might lose out or lose their lives. First James and John, then the others, were indignant that they might only get third or fourth place or even—perish the thought—the twelfth place, the bottom spot. They were looking to get the top spots. "One on Thy right hand, and the other on Thy left hand, in Thy glory" (Mark 10:37). The two brothers just wanted to keep it in the family. The fight about who gets the right-hand spot can wait until later, so long as it is one of them. When we see that sort of thing going on today—nepotism, influence-peddling, heads rolling, you scratch my back and I'll scratch yours, jostling for the power spots, simony, and its reverse, the top, that is, executive pastors, to the highest bidder, with that size of debt we simply can't take that man on this call—when we see that sort of thing going on, it makes us want to puke in disgust.

Jesus does not puke. He continues on His way to Jerusalem. And He draws us along with Him, which means leaving all that putrid and enslaving stuff behind. How gently Jesus draws the disciples on. "You do not know what you are asking," He tells the brothers. The place is at His right hand and at His left. We know who gets those places when Jesus is crowned, proclaimed king, and enthroned, as John says. Those at His right hand and at His left are those who are crucified with Him. All three of them are numbered among the transgressors.

One of the criminals who hung next to Jesus on the cross mocked Him, "If Thou be Christ, save Thyself and us" (Luke 23:39). The other rebuked the thief, saying, "And we indeed justly; for we receive the due reward of our deeds: but this man hath done nothing amiss" (Luke 23:41). The just for the unjust. Jesus is judged as the one who bears the iniquity of us all. He drinks the cup of God's wrath on sin, before which He shuddered at Gethsemane, "Abba, Father, all things are possible unto Thee; take away this cup from Me: nevertheless not what I will, but what Thou wilt" (Mark 14:36). Yet it was the will of the Lord to bruise Him. He put Him to grief when He made Himself an offering for sin.

"For Christ also hath once suffered for sins, the just for the unjust, that He might bring us to God" (1 Peter 3:18). That is Peter, preaching in his first Epistle. In Gethsemane Peter also slept, "for their eyes were heavy" (Mark 14:40). Then he thought power, swinging a sword, would help Jesus. At Caesarea Philippi, Peter spoke for Satan. Peter wanted no crucified Christ. In today's Gospel he is indignant with James and John for trying to get in first for the top spots. Jesus has a long way to pull them when He, walking ahead, goes up to Jerusalem. There is death for them in that Lenten journey.

Jesus speaks of the cup that is His to drink at His baptism, His death that is His to do. Are you able? We are able. "Yes," says Jesus, "they will be yours, and that will put an end to your worrying about who sits at the right hand and who at the left. When yours are the cup and the Baptism, you will no longer carry on as those who are not Mine. Those who are not Mine think themselves great by how many people they can push around, get on top of, κατακυριεύουσιν, lording it over them, laying it on them from above, great by how many you can make serve you." That is not where Jesus does His thing. Jesus is at the bottom of the pile. The whole weight of it comes down on Him. He is one lump with all sinners. All sins' enslavement He is slave to—judged, damned.

Jesus spoke of it as giving His life as a ransom for many. Ransomer is Redeemer, *go'el*, and the price is His life. For many, as in Isaiah 53, Jesus speaks His disciples into that many, as He does also when He gives His body to eat and His blood to drink into our mouths this morning. His blood is shed for many for the forgiveness of sins.

Our liturgy follows Luke at this point and says, "For you." The phrase "for you" evokes faith. Yes, for me too. Amen, we say, as Jesus gives into us His body and His blood. Those to whom our Lord gives His body and blood can pray, "Judge me, O God." If He tosses you out, He is tossing out the body and blood of His Son—and He cannot do that.

God did the judgment on you when He did the judgment for your sins on Jesus. That death for your sin was given you. It is yours at your Baptism. His cup, His Baptism—yours. There was a putting of you to death in your Baptism by words and water and a new "you" was born, a you no longer enslaved to sin. "I am crucified with Christ: nevertheless I live; yet not I, but Christ liveth in me: and the life which I now live in the flesh I live by the faith of the Son of God, who loved me, and gave Himself for me" (Galatians 2:20). It is no dead, inert stuff that the Lord gives into your mouth this morning. As He forgives and enlivens you with His body and His blood, His body and blood are alive in you in the same way when He spoke of them as the ransom for many, for you, not to be served but to serve.

AMEN.

Palm Sunday

John 12:20–26

London (1951)

On this day of hosannas and palms strewn in homage of Jesus, we join to acclaim the Son of David as our king. He is most surely king, yet a strange, unworldly king. All He has to ride on is a donkey. There is no splendid chariot, no swords flashing, no pomp and circumstance of state, but an ordinary man on a donkey, most acclaimed by children. A strange king, indeed, whom this world is at a loss to explain. Yet there was high excitement in Jerusalem that first Palm Sunday and not a little wonder. Would Jesus rally the people to throw off the Roman yoke? What was He planning? Curious questionings filled many a heart. Some Greeks were there who had been led by the star of God's promises in the Old Testament Scriptures. They came to Jerusalem to celebrate the Passover and heard talk of a Messiah, whom God had promised would deliver His people. They came to Philip and Andrew who brought them to see Jesus. In their hearts was the longing that their hope would be fulfilled and they would find the Messiah, their king.

Jesus' reception of them was royal in its warm kindness of welcome. Royal also were the words He spoke. Jesus called Himself the Son of Man, a name of the Messiah. Had their hope been fulfilled? These Greeks were men who had been drawn closer to God through the Old Testament, which they had come to know through Jewish friends and synagogues. The hope of Israel, the hope of a deliverer, a Savior, they had come to make their own hope, for it was the only hope. The religions of the world into which they had been born gave no food for the hunger of their souls, for like all heathen religions, they had man at their center—man who must save himself, must make himself worthy so he might avoid the anger of the gods. But when we try to save ourselves, we can never arrive at certainty. No matter how frantically we may try, how can we know when we have done enough? It is impossible to find salvation in ourselves in the very place where it is lacking. All man-centered religions end in despair, indifference, or shallow pride.

Let's look at the heathen. There are those who have given up, who honestly admit that their life and this world are purposeless. One meets hard-hit refugees who have lost everything, and eating away at their hearts now is a fearful despair. All the human things they relied on— their country, their leaders, their property, themselves—all these are overthrown. They can see only a mad, meaningless confusion.

Then there are the other heathen, the great bulk of them, who fear to face life squarely and flee from it. They try to forget the emptiness of their souls in liquor, sex, some bustling activity, or merely in the common round of routine: working, eating, sleeping, afraid to die, just going on existing, though existence is meaningless. How securely the devil has these people wrapped up in noise, bustle, and wheel horse routine so they are unconcerned about anything beyond their animal existence, their souls so shriveled that they are unaware of them.

Then there are some heathen who admit God. They will even claim to believe in God, but the God they believe in is a god of their own making, a god they can switch on and turn as required by their own comfort and convenience. The god they worship is really themselves. These are the heathen furthest from God, further than the fearful unthinking, who are in turn further from God than the despairing. To the despairing, God is often quite near.

These Greeks reared in man-centered heathenism had found no hope of salvation there. By the grace of God, they had come to know the Old Testament. Here they found true religion, not of fear nor of mere morality but in squarely facing up to God. God is central, He is the one certain fact, and only as we are tied onto that fact of God do we have any meaning or hope. Only with God is there life. They found also how we, by our sin, cut ourselves off from God, and a person cut off from God is dead. The wages of sin is death.

But God, instead of making an end of revolting people, who in sin try to put an end to God, gave promise of a way out of death. It was a way that led through death that could not be avoided. We are speaking here not of physical death but of spiritual death. Just as surely as taking poison gives your body over to physical death (your heart will stop beating), so surely sinning gives your soul over to death (you are cut off from God). The wages of sin is death, and God cannot contradict Himself. There is no way around this death. Yet so great was the love of God, though it cost Him dearly, He found the way by which this debt of death might be paid so we might be set free from death. There is no explanation to this except that God, in unspeakable love, saw that it must be so if we are to have life. Another must die in our place. Eve was told that a son of hers would conquer sin. The hope of life by another dying in our place, and so freeing us from sin's death, was set before the children of Israel in their sacrifices of lambs and goats. Sin means death. Humans sinned; therefore, death was coming to them. The only hope of being saved from that death was that another would die in their place. Lambs and goats were the prophetic substitute in the Old Testament. These sacrifices were pointing forward to the great substitutionary sacrifice for sin—the promise of God that He would send the Savior.

How much of this was grasped by these Greeks we cannot say. They probably shared with the Jewish people some hope that the Messiah would bring some sort of earthly deliverance and set up an earthly kingdom so they could partake in its earthly glories. Even the disciples on Maundy Thursday were still squabbling about who were going to be the big men when Christ was king.

Jesus' words to the Greeks, as ever with His words, exactly met their seeking and their need. He tells that He is the Messiah, then declares that the hour of His glory is come. What earthly glorious pictures those words must have called up in the minds of the disciples. They were flushed with the glory of the palms and hosannas of Palm Sunday. This, they thought, was the real Jesus, the royal Jesus. This was Jesus coming into His own. The kingdom was about to be established. The Greeks were rallying to Christ's cause. The crowd had acclaimed Him king, and now from His own lips the words, "The hour is come, that the Son of Man should be glorified" (John 12:23). But the glory of Jesus is unimaginably greater than any such earthly death-bound glory. Jesus knows how earthbound we are, how our hearts and hopes are imprisoned in the momentary, earthly things of food, drink, clothing, money, and vanity. He would free us from deathly slavery to these things, lift us above them, so we see their proper value and purpose. He would free us from the death that is in the worship of created things so we may have the life that is alone with Him, our Creator and Lord.

The word *life* is used in two ways in our text. First, the earthbound life of this world and, second, the life with God, the life everlasting. The man whose heart is set on the life in this world, we are told, is dead. Dead because he is debauched from God. He that loveth his life shall lose it. Jesus declared that He came that we might have life, life as He planned we should have it, connected to Him within His everlasting love and purpose. Sin cuts that life bond with God, so death is the consequence of sin. Only if that debt of death is paid by another can we be freed from death for life. Jesus, the promised Messiah, came to pay that debt of death. There could be no life for us if He did not die. It was not necessary for Jesus that He must die, but He died that we might be the living fruit of His death. This basic principle of salvation Jesus presents in a vivid fact of nature, life only from death: "Except a corn of wheat fall into the ground and die, it abideth alone: but if it die, it bringeth forth much fruit" (John 12:24).

The Greeks hadn't expected anything like this. The hour of Jesus' glory was to be the hour of His death, for He took our sins on Himself. Jesus suffered death for our sins, the death of being cut off from God. He was forsaken of God. He endured all the hell that was coming to you for your sins. Having suffered this death, He answered for sin. He achieved salvation. He cried, "It is finished." The victory over physical death had yet to be demonstrated, but the victory over sin's death was achieved. This was Jesus' glory—that through His death there might be freedom from death, that through His death there might be life, the full, assured, and cheerful life of those who are God's own.

This basic principle of "through death to life" is true not only of the work of Jesus, but it is also vital truth for you. Only if you die can you live. The life that Christ made possible is only yours if you go with Him through His death to life with Him. His dying must be your dying.

In the days when bridges were not so plentiful, there were strong men whose task it was to carry people across otherwise impassable rivers. That was the occupation of St. Christopher. He strapped people to his back and plunged in, bearing them through the water to the other side. Just so we are borne through death to life on the other side strapped to Christ. His going through death must be our going through death so we may arrive with Him to life.

Making our own the death of Christ is the action of faith, and this "through death to life" experience is ours in Baptism. It is most vividly shown in Baptism by immersion. We go down into the water. All that we are is drowned and dies in the water so what rises from the water is a new creature, made alive by being bound to Christ. In Baptism this bond of faith is created. We are bound to Christ and pass with Him through death to life. His dying is our dying, His life our life.

On Good Friday, when you see Christ dying on the cross, being cut off from God for sin, say, "That is my death for my sin." When Christ rises out of the whelming waters of death to life, say, "That is my rising to life." "I am crucified with Christ: nevertheless I live; yet not I, but Christ liveth in me: and the life which I now live in the flesh I live by the faith of the Son of God, who loved me, and gave Himself for me" (Galatians 2:20).

This passing through death to life with Christ is not something that happens once in the Christian's life at Baptism. Daily the Christian relives the Baptism experience of passing through death to life with Christ. St. Paul, our example, says, "I die daily." Every day is soil in which to plant the seed that is yourself. So hate everything that separates you from God, whether it be some earthly thing or some part of yourself. That must die. Everything that imprisons you in this worldly life must perish. If you love what you call your life—"my life is my own" sort of thing—then you have no part in the life that is eternal within the love of God. You are unplanted seed. But if you surrender this earthbound life, if you plant the seed, if you die, make an end of self, confess "Not I, but Christ," then you shall have life. Then I as a seed must die, cease to be what I am, so I may become new and alive and bearing much fruit.

What is this new full, fruitful life? It is being bound to Christ, serving Him, following Him so where He is, you are and where you live, He lives. By faith what Jesus did becomes yours. His dying is counted for your dying, His rising, your rising. Life is not what I have done, what I am doing, what I shall do. Not I, but Christ. What Christ has done is the glory of Christians. They show forth what Christ has done for them and now does in them. The life Christians live is the life of Christ. The life they live in the flesh is not anymore their own life but Christ's life in them. Their life and the life of Christ are so closely bound that their joys are Christ's joys and their sufferings are Christ's.

Oh, my friends, if we are not altogether enslaved in this worldly, deathly life, if we are not quite dead, detached from God, we do want to live with Christ so His life and our life may be joined. How miserably we fail. The very thought of Christ's life and my life being joined sounds absurd. Yet Jesus meant it to be so. He died to make it so. Let us, this Holy Week, go down with Jesus into death, repent, surrender all, plant the seed, lose our life and all that we are, and, like a seed, die. Christ can bring us up out of that death to fruitful life with Him, filled with His sort of glory. You will be dead so long as you refuse to die. No life without that death of total surrender. Not I, but Christ. "Dying and behold we live," and if living, then bearing much fruit. "For if we be dead with Him, we shall also live with Him: If we suffer, we shall also reign with Him" (2 Timothy 2:11–12).

AMEN.

Maundy Thursday

MARK 14:12–25

VALPARAISO UNIVERSITY (1974)

Like the disciples, we are drawn along by Jesus. There is nothing for us to do except follow Him, watch, and listen. Everything hangs on Him. When Jesus went ahead to Jerusalem, the disciples hung back because they were scared. What is He doing? Does Jesus want to get Himself killed? The fearful, faltering disciples Jesus draws on.

> Behold, we go up to Jerusalem; and the Son of Man shall be delivered unto the chief priests, and unto the scribes; and they shall condemn Him to death, and shall deliver Him to the Gentiles: and they shall mock Him, and shall scourge Him, and shall spit upon Him, and shall kill Him: and the third day He shall rise again. (Mark 10:33–34)

James and John thought of sitting on Jesus' right hand and on His left in the glory of His kingdom. No, said Jesus, that is not the way of My kingdom. "The Son of Man came not to be ministered unto, but to minister, and to give His life as a ransom for many" (Matthew 20:28). They were so blind. Jesus gave sight to the beggar Bartimaeus as He came into the land of Jericho. Then the dazzling hopes of Messiah king and the entry into Jerusalem with shouts of hosanna. A funny sort of king, nothing going for Him. A beggar king, says Martin Luther. Everybody that was anybody was out to get Jesus. The way they had things sorted out in their plans and power, He did not fit. He made them look silly. It was Him or them. What they were doing, what they had in mind was what mattered, so Jesus had to be gotten rid of. They did what they had to do to keep the action in their hands.

The disciples did nothing, just tagged along. When they did do something, it was usually wrong and made Jesus all that much more alone. Everything hangs on Him. Mark most vividly holds the spotlight on Jesus. That is where the action is. The disciples are there, too, but quite clearly that is not where the action is. They don't really know what is going on. Mary does a beautiful thing with her alabaster jar of ointment and Jesus says, "She is come aforehand to anoint My body to the burying" (Mark 14:8). That makes no sense because the death has to come before the anointing. But Jesus is anointed beforehand.

Then Jesus tells two of His disciples to find a man carrying a jar of water on his head, and follow him. Who ever saw a man carrying a jar of water on his head? Then there is a sort of password that brings them to a large upper room that is furnished and ready. What is going on? "And in the evening He cometh with the Twelve. And as they sat and did eat, Jesus said, 'Verily I say unto you. One of you which eateth with Me shall betray Me' " (14:17–18).

This statement shattered the disciples completely. Not only were they useless, but one of them would betray Jesus. In the Gospel of Mark no disciples are named at the Lord's Supper. It is all Jesus. Not one of the disciples is sure of himself. Mark tells it in a way that you know you are there. "And they began to be sorrowful, and to say unto Him one by one, 'Is it I?' And another said, 'Is it I?' " (14:19). Is it I? It could be. It has been. So much for us disciples and our contribution. But "the Son of Man indeed goeth, as it is written of Him" (14:21). What is going on is not just of this moment. It is the unfolding, the enacting of what the Scriptures are about, the promise of undoing the self-destruction we do with our sin.

The setting is a Passover with its ancient ritual, but there is no mention of the usual lamb, and some of what we are told never was in any Passover before. It goes in the ordinary way of the Passover celebration. "And as they did eat, Jesus took bread, and blessed, and brake it, and gave to them . . ." (14:22). Nothing extraordinary about that. The same exact thing happened in thousands and thousands of other Passover celebrations. But then something happened that had never happened before. Jesus said, "Take, eat; this is My body" (14:22). Then, continuing with the normal practice ". . . He took the cup, and when He had given thanks, He gave it to them: and they all drank of it" (14:23). This happened in thousands of Passover celebrations that year, and all the years before since the first Passover when the blood of the lamb saved them from death. But once again something happened that had never happened before. Jesus said, "This is My blood of the new testament, which is shed for many" (14:24). Jesus said that. Never before had such a thing happened, and to understand how outrageous it was, you have to be an Old Testament Israelite to appreciate the awesomeness of blood—sacred as life. Life and blood are one. To speak of drinking in any connection with blood was revolting.

Because this could not emerge from the matrix of the Passover, a certain methodology of biblical interpretation says that Jesus could not possibly have said this. The disciples only knew who Jesus really was after the resurrection. Before that they didn't know, and it seems He didn't either. These words must, therefore, have been inserted later, certainly post-Easter. Can you imagine anyone in Israel thinking up such outrageous words? We had a look at the disciples and can only say, "Not bloody likely." Some scholars say it must come from Greek religion. That won't wash either if you look closely at Greek religion and the role of blood. Here is "blood of the covenant," which is a quotation of the Old Testament (Exodus 24:8). The making of the first covenant with blood, blood of the burnt offering and the peace offering.

> Moses took the blood and threw it upon the people, and said, "Behold the blood of the covenant which the LORD has made with you in accordance with all these words." Then Moses and Aaron, Nadab, and Abihu, and seventy of the elders of Israel went up, and they saw the God of Israel; and there was under His feet as it were a pavement of sapphire stone, like the very heaven for clearness. And He did not lay His hand on the chief men of the people of Israel; they beheld God, and ate and drank. (Exodus 24:8–11 RSV)

This is a fellowship meal with the God of the covenant made with blood. Making such covenants is only God's doing.

Something like it had happened before as Jesus makes clear when He speaks of the blood of the covenant. The blood of which He speaks is His own blood, which is poured out for many. The "many" is from Isaiah 53:11, which we heard earlier when Jesus told what He had come to do: "to give His life a ransom for many" (Mark 10:45). To give His life and to pour out His blood are the same thing. "By His knowledge shall My righteous servant justify many; for He shall bear their iniquities" (Isaiah 53:11). "But He was wounded for our transgressions, He was bruised for our iniquities: the chastisement of our peace was upon Him; and with His stripes we are healed" (Isaiah 53:5). "The Son of Man indeed goeth as it is written of Him" (Mark 14:21).

As the bearer of our sins, Jesus dies. He dies the death for sin that was ours to die. He does it in our place. Body and blood separate are the sacrificed sin-bearer. Sin answered for can condemn us no more. We are forgiven. The sin that separates from God is taken from us and atoned for by Him. Jesus does it all and makes His disciples partakers of that sacrifice in restored fellowship with their Lord. His blood makes the new covenant in which we participate as we participate in that sacrifice and are given what it achieved as we are given His body to eat and His blood to drink.

It is Jesus who has done it all for us. He gives it all to us as He gives us His body to eat and His blood to drink. Look nowhere else, only to Him, not to any of our doing but only to His. We find ourselves among the disciples who can't figure out what is going on, who have no confidence in themselves, who can even see themselves as betraying their Lord. But they hear what the Lord says and receive what His words say He is giving them. It doesn't depend on them at all.

So come to His table, listening only to His words and receiving what He gives. All your doing doesn't count against you anymore. There is none of you, none of your doing outside of Jesus' forgiveness. Nothing can separate you from Him, for He has borne it all and answered for it in your place. The Lord invites you to His Table, family, and fellowship to share all His happy good. That is how much He loves you. And by this Meal the Lord brings you on your way to that glad feast that is the feast of the Lamb with all His saints.

Saints—that is you and me and all His disciples, the many accounted righteous, whose iniquities He bore, whose chastisement He took, those whom He makes whole by what He did as the sacrifice for sin and by what He gives us to share together at His Table.

AMEN.

Good Friday

MARK 15:33–47

LONDON (1957)

You have probably seen a single column on some tombstones that rises up, then is abruptly cut off. These columns symbolize the bitter tragedy of death. They stand there incomplete, supporting nothing, broken off. They declare that such is the life and death of us. We arise, only to be cut down with no lasting significance—incomplete. These columns express the grim hopelessness of us, whose whole lives are lived in bondage to death. Unwillingly, we move nearer each day to our graves, which cut us off and make an end. Such is our lot.

On Good Friday we gather outside the walls of Jerusalem on a little hill called Calvary to watch three of us die. These three have been tried and condemned as criminals, sentenced to be taken and hung until they die. Two of them have a pretty black past. One of these two admits as much, acknowledging they were getting what they deserved. But that was not true of the man on the center cross. Even one of the criminals on a cross next to Jesus knew that. How did he know? He couldn't have had much contact with Jesus, probably hadn't seen Him until they were thrown together by the soldiers. It is strange and striking how this criminal knew that Jesus wasn't one of his sort. He knew an innocent man when he saw one, and now this innocent man is put together with him, treated as one just like himself. They share the same execution together, brothers in death.

We know a good deal more about the man on the center cross than did the men on the crosses next to His. We have followed Jesus' life through this first half of the church year. We saw Him born just like one of us and grow into a man who worked as a carpenter until He was 30 years old. Jesus shared our whole life with us. He was our brother in everything, except that He did not sin. Jesus' life was in perfect harmony with God. He had no life apart from God. On Sunday we considered that saving will of God in obedience to which the whole life of Jesus was lived. When He faced His accusers, Jesus could ask, "Which of you convinceth Me of sin?" (John 8:46). If He did no wrong, then why did He die?

Some of us considered that question in the fifth of our Lenten services, and we saw the two levels on which that question must be answered. On the surface Jesus had to die because the leaders of the Jews hated Jesus, for He broke down their lines of defense against God. On the surface the treachery of Judas played a part, the cowardice of Pilate who didn't want to jeopardize his job, and the soldiers who brutally manhandled and crucified Jesus. But beneath the surface there was more, much more. We saw how Jesus stepped toward His enemies in the garden and compelled them to the final disclosure of themselves. Jesus had avoided death before that time. Then He went up to Jerusalem to face the basic and final issue of sin, and the representative sinners in church and state would have to face Him. Jesus knew what they had made of God's orders of church and state and would condemn Him. He showed them for what they were. But, most important, He deliberately went up to Jerusalem to be delivered into the hands of sinners and to be crucified to give His life as a ransom for many. Jesus' death did not overtake Him. He went to meet it. He said, "I lay down My life . . . No man taketh it from Me, but I lay it down of Myself. I have power to lay it down, and I have power to take it again" (John 10:17–18). Death did not cut Him down; it was the fulfillment of His whole mission.

Now the death of Jesus itself we must also see on two levels. There is the physical death by crucifixion. When a man is nailed to a cross and left hanging there, he dies. Thousands of men have died in the same brutal way. But beneath the physical death is the other death—the big death for sin. This is the death of the Lamb of God, the one without spot or blemish who takes our sin on Himself and takes its condemnation and punishment for us. It is the death of the Servant of God on whom God lays the iniquities of us all. Bearing those iniquities, guilty with our sin, Jesus is cast into that separation from God that is sin's consequence and curse. Jesus is forsaken of God. He bears our hell for us. Out of that death for sin comes the cry of utter dereliction, "My God, My God, why hast Thou forsaken Me?" (Mark 15:34). To the utter depth Jesus endures sin's separation from God. He bears it all. He comes through. He cries, and the Scripture is at pains to point out that He cries with a loud voice, "It is finished" (John 19:30). It is accomplished. The job has been done.

Sin—the thing that is wrong with us—has been answered for, and now it can no longer condemn us. Sin has spent itself against Jesus, and with the loud triumphant cry He claims the victory. Salvation is achieved. The death of sin we need no longer die.

That for which Jesus had come was almost done. One small item remained. It was now a small item because its power was broken. Jesus faced the death of the body. For us sinful people, this is dread horror, for we are separated from God by sin and face it alone. Jesus is in the dominion of sin, so He is in the dominion of death. "The sting of death is sin" (1 Corinthians 15:56), but when sin's bondage has been broken, death's bondage has also been broken. Jesus showed us this. He faced death without fear. He goes resolutely toward death. "Death I will be thy plagues" were the words penned by Hosea (13:14) and now accomplished by Jesus. He went straight at death, commending His spirit to God. This death was also of His choosing. This is clear from the fact that Jesus died extraordinarily soon. It astonished Pilate, who had considerable experience in such matters, and the Jews knew that if the crucified men were not to spoil their holy Sabbath they would have to be finished off. Pilate consented. Breaking their legs would speed things up, but when they came, they found one of the men already dead. Just to make sure a soldier ran his spear into Jesus' side.

Jesus came to go through our whole lot with us, which was completed by His sharing physical death with us. He is with us also in our body's dying. As these three men were made brothers in death, so we also. Jesus put Himself not only next to the two criminals there but also next to us and all rebels against God and thieves who have stolen from God. Jesus goes through it with us.

Jesus really died. Scripture emphasizes this by telling of His burial. In the Apostles' Creed we say not only that Jesus was crucified and died but also that He was buried. He really did die. Jesus' corpse was taken down from the cross by Joseph and Nicodemus, wrapped in a piece of linen, and put in a grave. Jesus was buried.

He was human all right, just like you and me. Whenever we put the body of a loved one down into a grave, we know Jesus has been there too. That makes all the difference, for in Jesus we see how God does things. On Sunday we saw how exaltation comes by way of humility, today that life comes by way of death. Jesus made this clear even before His death. He took a picture from God's creation:

> The hour is come, that the Son of Man should be glorified. Verily, verily, I say unto you, Except a corn of wheat fall into the ground and die, it abideth alone: but if it die, it bringeth

forth much fruit. He that loveth his life shall lose it; and he that hateth his life in this world shall keep it unto life eternal. (John 12:23–25)

Notice Jesus said His hour had come to be glorified. He referred to His death. As a seed only comes to fruition by first dying, so it was with the work of Jesus, and so it is with us in our coming to possess what the work of Jesus achieved.

Jesus did not love His life. He gave it willingly. Those who crucified Jesus—and every sinner is included in that number—loved their lives and sought to preserve and prosper them. It was because they saw Jesus as a threat to the lives they were making for themselves that they wanted to get rid of Him. Some had constructed religious lives for themselves that they thought commanded God's respect and reward. Men such as Pilate saw the whole basis of their lives in power and position challenged by Jesus. The men who lived by swords and staves saw their trusted weapons look foolish when Jesus, in Gethsemane, gave Himself into their hands. Men such as Judas, eager to use others to their own profit, saw what their money was worth. The soldier in charge of the crucifixion of Jesus saw all that for what it was worth as he watched Jesus die.

Jesus challenges every life that we would make for ourselves. If we want to preserve our lives and keep them the way we want them, then Jesus has to be gotten rid of. To set up one's own life apart from God is the essence of sin. Sinners intent on keeping their lives the way they want them are the crucifiers of Jesus. The crucifixion shows us what we must do if we would remain loyal to our sin and retain our lives intact.

The cross of Jesus grieves us not only because we are sorry for Him in His suffering but also because of what it says to us. To each sinner the cross shows, "This is what your sin means." We cannot dodge that accusation, for who of us has not tried to protect our lives from Jesus, keep them the way we want them, or at the very least put a leash on Jesus so He doesn't get at too much of our lives. We love our lives because we love ourselves and have taken on playing God's role. Such love twisted backward into ourselves destroys us like a starving animal eating its own flesh. In insisting on our lives, we destroy them. "He that loveth his life shall lose it." If we remain loyal to our sin, we are lost.

The only alternative is the way of Jesus who did not love His life but lost it for our sakes. This doesn't seem anymore promising than the way of sin. If I follow the way of sin, I can at least grab a bit for myself here and now. It is death both ways: either in our sin if we cling to it or with Jesus if we cling to Him. Jesus said, "Whosoever will come after Me, let him deny himself, and take up his cross, and follow Me" (Mark 8:34).

Jesus calls for the surrender of our lives, that we give them up as He gave up His, that we die. This means our crucifixion, and it is painful, for it means the death of ourselves as sinners, as those who seek to preserve their lives and keep them for themselves. Without this death, God cannot make anything out of us. He is a God who creates from nothing, who brings life out of death. Whatever life we insist on apart from God is contrary to Him, stands in His way, and must first be killed. When we are emptied of this life, we insist on, then God can make us alive with His life. God won't patch us up or give us a bit of supplementary assistance to make of ourselves what we want. He is not our apprentice, He is God. He planned what we should be, and when we went wrong, He had the astonishing patience and mercy to tackle the job of making us right again. Before He can put us right, all that is wrong with us has to be done away with, to perish, to die.

This death is what we call repentance. The recognition that what we are as sinners, and the life we would construct for ourselves, is all wrong and must be scrapped. This is the last thing that we, as sinners, want to see. We have to be brought to see it by the cross. The cross is the condemnation of us as sinners. It is our crucifixion. Are we in it? Or do we pull ourselves out of it, refuse to be crucified, refuse to die as sinners, and insist on maintaining our life as we want it. If we insist, God will let us, for He does not use force.

However, God would bring us to that death, to that participation with Jesus in His crucifixion, so as we stand beneath the cross today in our hearts we say, "As Jesus dies, I die too. Henceforth shall I know no life but that which comes from our dying together."

Jesus dies the big death for me. He bears the awful load of my sin for me. All that I am spared from is done by Him for me. Jesus answers for sin and so breaks sin's dominion, but all this becomes mine only as I die with Him, part company with my sin and the life that I would make for myself apart from Him.

Such repentance, such rejection, the crucifying of our flesh and all that is alien to God is alone the way by which we receive the cross of Christ to our salvation. Thus it is the only way we live with the saving cross of Jesus. St. Paul says we are daily crucified, for we daily are to die to sin. Thus the cross becomes the pattern of our lives, for daily we are to die to sin in contrition and repentance. The cross keeps us from consenting to sin and trying to construct a life independent of Jesus. We are to go to this death as willingly as Jesus went to the death of the cross. The path of life lies only through such dying. "Always bearing about in the body the dying of the Lord Jesus, that the life also of Jesus might be made manifest in our body" (2 Corinthians 4:10).

Jesus' death was the climax, the crowning glory. It did not appear so, but He committed Himself to God, the God who brings life out of death. So the death of our repentance, our parting company with sin, will seem to us as loss, but it is not so. For when we thus die, we cast ourselves on God, the God who brings life out of death—only out of Jesus' death. He died the big death for the sin that separates us from God. With our sin He suffered its forsakenness of God. Sin cannot again condemn us. "He died unto sin once: but in that He liveth, He liveth unto God. Likewise reckon ye also yourselves to be dead indeed unto sin, but alive unto God through Jesus Christ our Lord" (Romans 6:10–11). Thus the through-death-to-life given us in Baptism. The little death when our heart stops beating lies ahead. On our graves we will have no hopeless, cut-off columns but the cross of Jesus, His name and ours, by which He calls us to our Easter Day.

AMEN.

The Resurrection of Our Lord

MATTHEW 28:1–10

VALPARAISO UNIVERSITY (1981)

Jesus has done it; He is through. But Mary Magdalene and the other Mary didn't know yet. They were on their way to the grave, the same road we all travel. It was the same old story. They had hoped He was different. God was taking a hand, not the way people expected that God would take a hand, but they had met something in Jesus they had never met before. He had cared about the wreck of a woman that was Mary Magdalene, cleaned her up, and made her live again when she was all washed up. What about the other Mary? Who was she? Why did she so love Jesus?

All that was given to the women in Jesus was over. They came to weep out their grief at the grave and to do what their love might do for Jesus. He had done so much that it might not be the same old story. Jesus had lightened the darkness, made the women precious with His love, pushed back the things that oppress and undo us. Sin and guilt gave way as Jesus accepted and forgave them. Amid the powers that push us around, He had walked with a breathtaking freedom, the way it is to be alive, unchained, uncrumpled, not scared. Jesus had looked all His accusers in the eye, slave to none. But in the end, they closed in on Him. Jesus had defied them, and they got Him in the end. The end, the same end as for us all. Now the finality of the grave. The women went "to see the sepulchre" (Matthew 28:1). What is more real? What is there that you can be more sure of than the grave? Now you can be even more sure, for Jesus, in whom they had hoped, had come to it along with the rest of us. Crucified, dead, and buried. Was God not with Jesus? And if not with Jesus, then is God with anybody?

This was no way for God to take a hand, not the way of the cross, not according to what might reasonably be expected of God. He is not supposed to die, not any god we would think worth calling God. God is supposed to have lots of power that can lay anything low that He wants to, anything that stands in His way. Jesus was crucified, dead, and buried. Where was God in all that? What sort of a God?

That God was on the scene the Gospel declares with two earthquakes: Calvary earthquake and Easter earthquake, same God in action in both. That we might know what, in fact, is going on, God puts His words on it. His messenger says it, as at the beginning He put the words on Mary's unborn child. "And she shall bring forth a son, and thou shalt call His name Jesus: for He shall save His people from their sins" (Matthew 1:21). Angels were at Jesus' temptation and in Gethsemane. The angels strengthened Him. Jesus went on to Calvary, was forsaken of God as was our lot for our sins. He bore them, answered for them. Jesus cried, "It is finished." Now the Easter messenger sits on the stone as in victory, the stone that should close tight the grave. The angel sits on it and bids the women to no longer be afraid, for they are seeking Jesus who was crucified. To those who can't let go of Jesus even when He is dead, the message is given: "He is not here: for He is risen, as He said. Come, see the place where the Lord lay. And go quickly, and tell His disciples that He is risen from the dead; and, behold, He goeth before you into Galilee; there shall ye see Him: lo, I have told you" (Matthew 28:6–7).

The message gets the women going again. On their way to tell the disciples, Jesus meets them, and says, "All hail!" (Matthew 28:9). That seems like an everyday greeting, but when Jesus says it, it carries what it says: "Be glad. Rejoice." He who was crucified and now is risen can say it. Everyday thing transformed, so "Be glad. Rejoice!" Because Jesus was crucified and is now risen, His words draw the women out of all their fears. The fear that God had quit, the fear of slavery to sin and death, the fears of the same old story, that the world is just a big cemetery. Jesus said to the women, "Be not afraid" (Matthew 28:10). Again, the words are for doing. "Go tell My brethren that they go into Galilee, and there they see Me" (28:10). Galilee is Galilee of the Gentiles; therefore, on to Galilee and so to all nations the message of the crucified and risen Savior. The words of the messenger and of Jesus pick the women up, set them going, alive into doing the words and carrying the message.

So for you, too, Jesus' Easter words pick you up, pull you on, set you going into the living and doing of the words and the carrying of their message. In the living and the doing of His words, Jesus meets you with the message and gift of "Be glad. Rejoice." Go, tell, on your way! No more fear of living and of dying. You go now, you live now, you tell now: Jesus crucified for you and risen for you. That is now where you live, where that is so, in His kingdom. Therefore, "Do not be afraid." There is now nothing in all the world that you can be more sure of than Jesus crucified for you, risen for you. "Ain't no grave gonna hold this body down."

If you let go of Jesus, treat Him as dead, regard anything as more sure than He is, you are back in the prison of sin and death, the big cemetery, the same old story, on the way to the grave. Whenever there is anything that tempts you to despair, to conclude that God has quit, that He doesn't care, that it is all a bucket of ashes—between that and you stands the Lord Jesus, crucified for you and risen for you. Before they can destroy you, they have to destroy Him first, and they have already done their worst. This is not just head stuff, it is life stuff. You will know how sure, how true, how cheering, freeing, and enlivening those words are in the doing and the living and the telling of them.

Jesus lives, and by His words and Spirit He puts His death and His life into you. You are baptized. "Your life is hid with Christ in God" (Colossians 3:3). Go, tell, live that. There is angel's work to do. Jesus has done it, crucified and risen, but some don't know it yet, and some don't live it yet.

AMEN.

Second Sunday of Easter

QUASIMODOGENITI
JOHN 20:26–31

LUTHER-TYNDALE MEMORIAL CHURCH, LONDON (1964)

Thomas was the sort of chap who always expected the worst to happen. At the news of Lazarus's death, Jesus said He was going to Bethany, right into the hands of His keenest enemies, and Thomas shrugged his shoulders and said, "I suppose we had better go along and get ourselves killed as well." There is a sort of worldly wisdom in this way of looking at things. Expect the worst, and you will be prepared for it. If it doesn't happen, you will be pleasantly surprised. Before the Easter holidays, Thomas would say, "I expect it will rain the whole time." If the sun did peep through, he would be pleasantly surprised. If it rained all the time, he could have the satisfaction of saying, "Just what I expected."

That pessimistic thinking is behind the kind of comfort that points out that something could have been so much worse. Your leg is broken, and the Thomases stand beside your bed and observe, "You should be thankful you didn't break your neck driving the way you were. You could only expect to kill yourself." Because it is only your leg that is broken, cheer up and be grateful.

Now it must be admitted that the other extreme isn't any more sensible. The person that expects everything to be sugar and roses is in for some harsh shocks. At home and at school we are taught to be kind, honest, helpful, and truthful. We grow up feeling we can generally rely on others to do the same. Then we leave school and go out into the world. We get a job. Some are fortunate then; many are not. Some find that truthfulness is not regarded as important as making a sale—not, perhaps, a barefaced lie, but enough of a half-truth to work a fiddle, to cheat someone. Higher up, when the competition for promotion gets keener, it is the malicious hint that stabs one in the back. Where gambling with raffles is the done thing, foul jokes are a frequent source of laughter and taking God's name in vain the accepted style of talk. Many a young person reared amid kindness, honesty, helpfulness, and truthfulness is badly shaken up when he or she bumps into this sort of thing. So is it better to do as one father is said to have done in training his boy for the family hat business. He sold his son a hat—10 percent off—then hurried upstairs to the front window and waited for his son to go out into the street. As the boy stepped out, his father poured a pot of paint down over him and quite ruined his new hat. He waited, so his boy would see who had done it. When the boy rushed upstairs in a fury, his father said to him, "Sammy, my boy, never trust nobody." Isn't it more realistic and safer to expect the worst, like Thomas?

Have you noticed that when people draw pictures of what might be living on Mars, it is some hulking monster with hideous teeth and claws or some robot machine that stalks along with eerie flashing lights and destroys what comes against it with some fearful death ray. Why don't we imagine that there might be nice, kind, and good chaps on Mars? Why do we fear the unknown? Is that what experience has taught us?

Now the extraordinary thing is that no matter how bitter our experiences have been, we cannot accept that that is the way it ought to be. We feel that we have been wronged. We feel that we haven't been given a fair go. We resent and rebel against our misfortunes. In our lives we feel that things weren't intended to go wrong. We feel that our lives ought to mean something, our lives ought to be happy. This feeling could not really have been taught to us by experience. It must come from somewhere else. Yet we all have it. Without it, it would be impossible to know or say that something has gone wrong.

We hope for meaning and happiness in our lives. That is the way it ought to be. When it is not, we know something has gone wrong. We cannot surrender this hope, and one of the ways in which we try to protect it is by expecting the worst. Then it is possible things may turn out better than we expected. Hoping for what is good and expecting the worst are not alternatives but two sides of the same basic attitude, an attitude that tells us a lot about ourselves. When people say, "It is bound to rain the whole holiday," they are not saying that they want it to rain the whole holiday. They really want the sun to shine, but they seek to protect themselves against disappointment by expecting the worst. When Thomas set off with Jesus to Bethany, he wasn't particularly wanting to get himself killed. He expected the worst, then if it happened he could say, "I told you so," and if it didn't he could say, "Well, we are jolly lucky."

When the disciples told Thomas that they had seen the risen Jesus, it wasn't that he didn't want this to be true. Thomas wanted to protect himself against the disappointment that it might not be true. Thus he said, "I will not believe" (John 20:25). Thomas was prepared to face it not being true. He would expect the worst. Then if it didn't turn out that way, he would be in the position of being pleasantly surprised. So Thomas stuck to his attitude: "Except I shall see in His hands the print of the nails, and put my finger into the print of the nails, and thrust my hand into His side, I will not believe" (John 20:25).

That is what Thomas said, but deep down he was hoping that he would be wrong. For the next week, when the disciples were again gathered in the same place where Jesus had appeared to them, Thomas was there. If hope had died in him, if he were sure of disappointment, he would not have been there. Like most of us, Thomas couldn't quite give up hoping and slump to the conviction that it is all a bucket of ashes. There is more to us, more to life than meets the eye.

Thomas had made his statement, his defense against disappointment on the level of what his eyes could see. "Except I see in His hand the print of the nails, and put my finger into the print of the nails, and thrust my hand into His side, I will not believe." Then Jesus came and met Thomas on that level. The eyes of Thomas beheld the risen Jesus who said, "All right, Thomas, put your finger to My scars." Thomas didn't need to. He saw Jesus and that was enough. Then the astonishing thing happened. There burst from Thomas an acknowledgment far deeper than what his eyes could tell him. "My Lord and my God!" (John 20:28). As Augustine remarked, "He saw and touched a man and confessed God whom he did not see or touch."

Thomas was there, he was home, he got it, he believed. Jesus said to Thomas, "Be not faithless, but believing" (John 20:27). Jesus had pulled him through, taken hold of Thomas at the level of what his eyes could see and his fingers touch, and homed him in, fastened him to the central point and certainty. In Jesus, God had connected Thomas to Himself. That connection we call faith. Faith does not need to fool itself, faith is not captive to what meets the eye, faith does not need to protect itself against disappointment and despair by the pessimism of expecting the worst.

That pessimistic, worldly wisdom gives way in faith to a new realism that replaces always expecting the worst *and* always expecting sugar and roses. It does this because the center has changed. Those two sorts of expectations center in me. Their ultimate concern is me. But faith connects with the true and solid center that is God. God in Christ guarantees the expectation of victory, what the Gospel of John calls life—the real thing because it is connected with God, which replaces the death of disconnection from God.

Life and victory are ours because we are connected with and share the life and victory of Christ, and these are as solid and as certain as God in Christ. The meaning, the value, the good that are ours, are ours in Christ. They are no longer centered on that wobbling uncertainty of ourselves and what we can see and touch. The success of our lives is no longer judged according to these. No longer, "I am all right, Jack, because I am doing all right for myself, because I have a tidy bit put by, because I have a comfortable place to live, because I enjoy pretty good health, because we are getting a new television, because we are planning a better holiday than we have ever had before."

Now these may be blessings or the opposite depending on whether you see them as just tied on to you, you the center, you the number one, or whether they and all that you see and touch are connected with God in Christ. This is so not only because those things are not all that solid, certainly not solid enough to build a life on. Not simply because it may rain through your holiday, or your television set broke down, or your comfortable home seems unsatisfactory because someone else has a so much nicer one, or you may get run over tomorrow. While all this may be so, this can be recognized to be so even on the level of what you can see and touch. These considerations still have their center in you, which you must recognize is none too solid a center. Get "you" out of the center, dig through what you can see and touch, and have God in Christ at the center, and things are very different.

Then the things we can see and touch don't haphazardly float along, but they are connected with Christ and have their true value and lively purpose. This is true of the sunshine as of the rain, of vigorous health as of bereavement. A life dependent on what is seen and touched is fearfully breakable. A life connected with God in Christ nothing can shatter—not even sin, pain, and death—for such a life goes through these with Christ, and with Him there is a victorious way through. That is the meaning of Good Friday and Easter.

Jesus speaks His blessing on such lives, "Blessed are they that have not seen, and yet have believed" (John 20:29). Live no deeper than what you can see and touch and get for yourself, and your life, sooner or later, will fall to pieces. Live at the solid bottom level, live connected with Christ and you will have life indestructible. Jesus said, "I am come that they might have life, and that they might have it more abundantly" (John 10:10).

When you go home tonight, disconnect everything you can see and touch from yourself and see them connected with Christ. You will be amazed at what that means. They will then become yours in a fuller and happier way than ever before. Some things you will find can't be connected with Christ. These you will need to throw away. When you are connected with Christ, you won't want those things that contradict Him, nor will you want anything that is tied only to you and not connected with Him.

With everything—work, play, sleep, food, family, tears, laughter—with everything connected to Christ, not seen yet believed, you live solidly, happily, with that indestructible peace that the risen Lord gave His disciples, a peace that held through pain and persecution, gave courage to live and die for Christ, and put a song in their hearts and on their lips even when in prison. Easter declares that it works, that that is the way life and victory lie, for that is the way connected with the living and victorious Lord. That is the life of faith.

AMEN.

Third Sunday of Easter

1 JOHN 3:20

CONCORDIA SEMINARY (1993)

On yesterday's date in 1847 the Missouri Synod was organized in Chicago. In our constitution we read: "Where private confession is already going on there according to Article XI of the Augsburg Confession it is to continue. Where it is not going on the pastor is to work toward its introduction through teaching and instruction."

Confession is facing up to God with no fudging. Confessing is as He says it is: "You sinner." Yes, me—sinner. "Against Thee and Thee only have I sinned and done that which is evil in Thy sight." *Coram Deo*. If you need some help, there are the Christian questions and answers: "Do you believe that you are a sinner?" "Yes, I believe it. I am a sinner." "How do you know this?" "From the Ten Commandments, which I have not kept" (Luther's Small Catechism). If by question 20 you are still dodging or can't claim that you have the appropriate feelings, then just believe what the Lord says—Galatians 5 and 6, John 15 and 16, 1 John 2 and 5. If that doesn't do it, there is still the devil. Whose are you? "For if our heart condemn us, God is greater than our heart" (1 John 3:20). It is also with us in this way as He says it is.

Did you notice how the first dodge is cut off at the outset. The question was "Are you a sinner?" not "Have you done some sins?" To the latter we might respond, "Well, yes, I suppose I have. Nothing too spectacular this week, though I did get angry with my wife. All that money for a hat, well I ask you! Although it was Easter, and I must admit that the kids really do get on my nerves, and I know I should try to do better and spend some quality time working on our relationships." In this way we take over the matter of our not doing so well, sorting out our sins and doing something about them. It is a bit more comfortable than *coram Deo*. And it gives us some room to maneuver.

You may have noticed how some so-called confessions deal principally with the Second Table of the Law, where we suppose we have a better chance of calling the shots. *Time* magazine reports that people, while you can't say that they are seekers, are in the seeking mode. They are looking for places to get their needs met. Now you can't really say that you have needs. You may have perceptions or feelings, but even a baboon can have those. If you slip from the First Table to the Second Table of the Law, then there is no stopping. Slipping from *coram Deo*, we have slipped from the First Table, so we arrange things in a more domesticated, privatized, me-centered, my-family way in which we expect God to be of such help as we may feel we need.

Now it is no good just railing away at people. We are all in a society that knows no sure points of reference. Many live in the lonely prison of their own selves, and when there is nothing outside that you can be sure of, then there is nothing you can be sure of inside. Truth is subjective, irrational, relative. What is historical is relative, and there is nothing but what is historical. Wheel of fortune, grab something if you can, and that is how the cookie crumbles.

We recently heard Pilate ask, "What is truth?" At least Pilate still had the question, though he rejected the answer that was standing battered in front of him. But what of those for whom language has become incapable of truth-telling? Language, as it is fed to us by the manipulators and marketers, goes on with only a tenuous, tangential connection with fact. Secular schools and universities experience the same thing. Harvard still has the antiquated word *Veritas* with its shield. Just listen to how the language nowadays betrays us. Is it even our language? What happens to human words when our Lord takes to using them to get through to us?

Recently there has been some momentary interest in Woody Allen's difficulties with his relationships—if not typical, at least symptomatic. In reporting the case, the *Washington Post* quoted the 14-year-old Moses. Not *the* Moses—Moses Farrow Allen. "Everyone knows not to have an affair with your son's sister" were words that the *Washington Post* observed were not inscribed on stone tablets. It was written in a letter to somebody she once called "Dad." It stands in stark contrast to the rest of the bizarre trial being conducted in a dreary New York courtroom. Good and evil are now translated into appropriate and inappropriate. Right and wrong have become good and bad judgment. Woody Allen confessed, "I think I did make a mistake, an error in judgment."

Moral relativism cannot make a confession. Confession is *coram Deo* and has to do with sin, or better, with sinners. If you are not a sinner, why bother? Yet for all the glib moral relativism, there is still some law written in the heart in young Moses' letter, and it is there in the tables of stone of *the* Moses, the Ten Commandments, to which Luther's Small Catechism directs us. "And God spake all these words, saying, I am the LORD thy God . . . Thou shalt have no other gods before Me . . . Thou shalt not take the name of the LORD thy God in vain" (Exodus 20:1, 3, 7).

All human words are, by nature, law words. When the Lord uses them, it is natural for us to hear law words. That is right when He is using them to do a law job. But we draw a blank from our linguistic resources when He starts using our words to do a Gospel-delivering job, as is utterly so in Holy Absolution. For our words, as our words, that is utterly impossible.

Seminary is trying to stuff you full of God's words, when what is Law and when what is Gospel, so He can pull out of you—as He has promised to do—His words that He may have use of in the specific place with the specific persons, specifically sinners, that He may put you there for as His mouthpiece.

How can you get people to listen to the Lord? Let Him do the talking. Then you can ask when you are ordained, as the confessor does in the Small Catechism, "Do you believe that my forgiveness is God's forgiveness?" Then there is no doubt of the delivery.

AMEN.

Fourth Sunday of Easter

JOHN 16:16–23

VALPARAISO UNIVERSITY (1971)

Memento mori. Think on death. Learn how to die. This was a powerful theme in late medieval piety. Today's Gospel bids us to think on *life*. Learn how you are born. Death you can do by yourself, unlike birth. Another person gives birth to you, without your asking and without your doing. You are born. You are given life from another life. The pain that prompts your first breath is the pain of separation. Continuing in that way leads to the final separation of death, the final denial of what we are for, the final isolation and disconnection.

Today's Gospel tells of connection and of organic relatedness. What happens to Jesus is not one odd thing after another happening by chance, but each event is pregnant with the next. With Jesus, Calvary comes to birth in the resurrection, comes to birth in the sending of the Spirit, comes to birth in the new life when death shall be no more. Nor is all this of Jesus a floating disconnected sequence. He is born of the womb of Israel long pregnant with the promise, born of the womb of Mary by the quickening of the Holy Spirit, sharing humanity with us all, but purposefully as His genealogies proclaim. Son of promise, son of Abraham, son of Adam, the man sprouted from Israel's blasted stump, Rose of Sharon, fruit of a maiden's womb, little Mary's son, flesh of our flesh, bone of our bone, blood brother Immanuel.

The disciples didn't understand what Jesus was telling them. Jesus had spoken of His departure, His going away, His death, His going to the Father. They would not see Him. Then they would see Him. This made no sense. If we will see Him, how can He be going away? If Jesus is going away, how shall we see Him? It must be one or the other, but not both. Inescapable logic, a logic that works by separation and exclusion. A excludes B, B excludes A. *Tertium non datur.* No third possibility. The disciples operate with the same compelling logic as Aristotle's nanny. There is a third possibility that the disciples themselves name, but make no sense of, because they see only separated pieces. They have disconnected the clause "because I go to the Father," and disconnected it does not function, like a heart dissected out of a cadaver. In the same way much of our knowledge is dead and does not function. The disciples were imprisoned in their logic because they separated what belongs together. They disconnected into pieces what is living organic whole, and that spells death.

Jesus is what life is about—being born, new life, crying, breathing, moving, growing, changing, each step pregnant with the next. The signs between are not a mathematical plus, minus, separation, or exclusion, but an arrow. This leads on to this and the pull of the whole movement is in "going to the Father."

The disciples were so captive to their deadly dissection that they could not even ask Jesus what He meant. Jesus did this for them too. His answer did not dodge any of the evidence. Indeed, Jesus makes it heavier and deeper. Our estimates are mostly too simplistic and shallow. You will "weep and lament" (John 16:20) the howling, devastating grief of Good Friday. Total grief, not just the grief of the death of a man they loved.

The disciples could come to terms with that. They could think their way through that—Jesus ending as anyone ends. But Calvary's grief was far more than that. The numbed disciples on the way to Emmaus murmured, "But we trusted that it had been He which should have redeemed Israel" (Luke 24:21). They had thought that God was one who kept His promises. Their hopes were all shattered. Jesus had drawn them to stake their lives on Him, and now He was dead. Line across the page, and what did it add up to? Nothing. Nothing when God cannot be trusted, when God cannot be, at least not for them. The disciples had not imagined facing that nothing. Jesus points them forward to that death that is the final contradiction of us and God. Jesus goes under;

they go under. His is not a disconnected death. It is part of our death. Our death is then connected with His death. We are in it together.

What we are in on together, Jesus goes on to say, is a birth—birth when life is at stake. That the birth of new life should be at such a cost the Bible points to as a sign of our sin. How many women in the labor of childbirth have cried, "Never again!" "But as soon as she is delivered of the child, she remembereth no more the anguish, for joy that a man is born into the world" (John 16:21). The wonder of this new life that grew in her, implanted by the husband that is one flesh with her, their one flesh realized in the creation of this new life, flesh of flesh and bone of bone as they before of their parents and their parents, from God, who first created life and shares with us the joy and care of creating life and nurturing it, life always onward, moving, growing, changing, each stage pregnant with the next, on and on. We live in affirmation of life, in openness to life. We close life off and deny it when we come to a halt and slice it into pieces, when we cut ourselves off as an isolated, meaningless piece. There is no halt. We are carried along as isolated pieces of debris, or we are joined together with what life is about.

Jesus is what life is about. He is with us, and we are with Him, flesh of flesh, bone of bone. Jesus' death is the ultimate connection of us and God, for in Him we and God go together. Jesus points His disciples forward to that death as a birth of new life. No Good Friday, no Easter. Or following the arrow of the life that God lives and shares, if Good Friday, then Easter, and if Easter, then Pentecost, and if Pentecost, then on and on past our little death that we have already left behind at Calvary and received in exchange a birth.

Learn how to die? Rather, learn to live as one being born each day and through each stage, even when God has died, for in your Baptism you were incorporated into that death and into that resurrection. Living the life you were joined up with in Baptism, each new day a new person comes forth and arises who lives connected with Christ. Living in that connection is the life of faith, which is the gift of the Spirit, the Lord and giver of life. The Spirit gives us life as He gives us Christ, binding us in with Him through death and resurrection at Baptism, for we are not at Calvary or the empty tomb. Out of Good Friday came Easter, out of Easter came Pentecost. Life moves forward, not backward. Mary Magdalene wanted it backward, Jesus as He had been. But Jesus was now more for her, for He was going to the Father and was more than she could hold in her hands. All the more of Jesus could not be given the old way, that giving would be the Spirit's work.

Just before today's Gospel, Jesus said, "It is expedient for you that I go away: for if I go not away, the Comforter will not come unto you; but if I depart, I will send Him unto you" (John 16:7). Our advantage is always more of Jesus. Backward is less—not by reconstruction of some life of Jesus, not by nailing Him down by some historical proof, not by getting our hands on Him as Mary wanted to do, but by being born of water and the Spirit and going on being born as Jesus is always more.

"You will see Me," Jesus promised, for He promised that the Spirit would show Him to us and tie us in with Him. We see Jesus in His words, which are alive with the Spirit, for Jesus said, "It is the Spirit that quickeneth . . . the words that I speak unto you, they are Spirit, and they are life" (John 6:63). The words that the Spirit uses for giving life are the words of the apostles who were brought to birth through Calvary's death by the resurrection. Jesus prays not only for His apostles whom He sends into the world with His word and Spirit, "but for them also which shall believe in Me through their word; That they all may be one; as Thou, Father, art in Me, and I in Thee, that they also may be one in Us: that the world may believe that Thou has sent Me" (John 17:20–21). One, wholeness, together, connected, sent.

Jesus, His mission—that is what life is about, that is what we are joined into, His name on us with the water and the Spirit, born His child. He is with us, as food to our bodies and, more profoundly still, with bread and wine, His body and blood. We are incorporated, connected, together. Jesus is alive in us. We are alive with His life that is always forward and more.

We are not stray, inexplicable pieces but together with Christ, alive, in motion, sent to live and share the life of Christ, growing, changing, shaping ourselves to each person's need so we may have life and have it more abundantly, the joy that cannot be taken away. Remember your Baptism. Live your Baptism. You were born again, new life given. You are being born each day. Each day pregnant with the next, even the days that deny you and God, for we, too, are going to the Father. Quickened by the Spirit, we go with Christ who promised, "I will see you again, and your heart shall rejoice, and your joy no man taketh from you" (John 16:22). That is the dimension of life. That is what Jesus is about. Make a joyful noise to God!

AMEN.

Fifth Sunday of Easter

James 1:13–18

Cambridge (1967)

Do not err, my beloved brethren. Don't be tricked. There are some things you can rely on and some things you can't. One thing you can never rely on, one thing that will always deceive you, is sin. Sin pulls the great advertising deception, and what makes us suckers to such advertising is our own lust. We want to make ourselves big. We want people to envy us. We want to do ourselves good. That sets us up to be played for a fool.

The art of advertising consists largely in playing on our weaknesses, our lusts. Just check and see how many advertisements seek to take you in by subtle appeal to your pride or to some lust. "Smoke this particular cigarette, and you will really wow the girls, or this particular cigar will make you feel luxuriously upperclass." Then there is all the nonsense about the wondrous fluids you can squirt on yourself and smell bewitching. People must be fools to be taken in by such stuff, we are tempted to think, but the fact remains that such advertising works and pays. The appropriate way to treat people, then, would seem to be as fools. So don't blame the advertisers so much. They are only being realistic in the way they treat people.

Now not all advertising is false. The product may be a good product, but the advertising that sin does is always false both as to the technique of advertising and the product. Nevertheless, it works. It works because we are enticed and drawn away by our own lust, so we get hooked. The dishonest money we thought would do us so much good can only be kept by inflicting injury on our consciences and often inflicting injury on those who really love us. The adultery that promised to be such fun results in bitter personal damage. The drugs that promise happy experiences enslave and wreck a person. In the end, sin sits and laughs at us.

The question then is whether we ever learn our lesson: once bitten, twice shy. This means, however, that we acknowledge that we have been played for a fool, which is a difficult acknowledgment to make. Like mother Eve, we would rather make excuses and put the blame elsewhere. We are righteously indignant. Sin should have kept its promise and paid up. We have been cheated. Who is to blame? Not us. It must be whoever is behind it all. Like father Adam, we can blame God. If you can pin the blame on God, then you have certainly cleared yourself.

But that dodge simply won't work. God does not trick or entice into evil. Don't make that mistake. Do not err, my beloved brethren. The way sin operates is not the way God operates. We can't do business with God as we are tricked into doing business with sin. God does not trick us with the offer of a good deal as sin does. He does not make dazzling false promises. Not only is God no swindler, He is not a trader at all.

God is a giver. With a giver you can receive or reject, but you can't make a deal. And a deal is what we are always wanting to do, for when we are doing a deal, we can negotiate terms, calculate what we put into it and what we get out of it. Sin is always ready to play this game with us, for this is the way sin gets the advantage of us. James 1:5 says that the giver God does not try to get the advantage of us. That sort of thing is ruled out with Him, so we can't get the advantage of Him either. He doesn't play that game at all.

The game God plays is giving, and what a game and what giving! Every good thing comes from His giving hands. God simply loves to give, and we can never change Him into a trader no matter how hard we may try. There is no changing the giver God into any other kind of god. "Every good gift and every perfect gift is from above, and cometh down from the Father of lights, with whom is no variableness, neither shadow of turning" (James 1:17).

You can play all sorts of tricks with shadows. Remember how television lighting men made Sir Alec Douglas Hume look like a mudlark fresh out of its eggshell, and more recently, the district attorney of New Orleans was powerfully presented with half of his face in shadow? Then there is the concealment and peep sneaking technique of the fan dancer. Shadows can play all sorts of alluring tricks. But St. James was not thinking here so much of television lighting tricks as of the planets and stars.

From the shadowy deceptions of sin, God raises our eyes to the bright splendor of the heavens and the pure lights there. God is called their Father, their Creator. He made these clear lights, yet for all their bright splendor, He is more splendid and constant. As we look at planets and stars, they have their turnings, settings, and eclipses. Their light can fail us, but there is one who does not change or fail.

How do we know God, what He has done? God has brought us to life as His children. Life is always a gift. We can't make ourselves alive, as is shown in our natural birth. It is true of our birth, of our coming to life, as the children of God. God used our mother's bodies to give us the first kind of life. To give us life as His children, He uses the "word of truth." For most of us, this birth was by that Word joined with the water of Baptism. It was plainly all gift. Life as God's child begins as a gift, and it is gifts, gifts all the way. We live from the giving hand of God.

The greatest gifts are all given by the Word of God. The Word of God not only tells what these gifts are but also conveys them. When the word of forgiveness is spoken to you, forgiveness is given to you. When the Benediction is spoken to you, the blessing of God is given to you. In the sacraments, the Word is joined with extra means of conveying the gifts. It is then as if God takes your hand and presses His gift into it with the assurance, "Now you have really got it. Without a shadow of doubt, it is surely yours."

Jesus would be nothing for us if the Word of truth did not tell of Him and give Him to us. A silent movie of Calvary would be nothing more than a tragic piece of newsreel. The soundtrack of God's Word tells us what is going on there, what is achieved, and gives it to us with the words "for you."

Without the word of truth, the gifts would neither come to us nor would they be known as gifts. This latter is true of all the smaller and more obvious gifts that are listed in the explanation of the First Article in Luther's Small Catechism :

> I believe that God has made me and all creatures; that He has given me my body and soul, eyes, ears, and all my members, my reason and all my sense, and still takes care of them.
>
> He also gives me clothing and shoes, food and drink, house and home, wife and children, land, animals, and all I have. He richly and daily provides me with all that I need to support this body and life.

Such gifts of the First Article, of creation, are received by many without the Word of God as if they were not gifts at all. They just happened for some reason or other or for no reason at all. They are taken for granted the way a dog takes his tail for granted or (more foolish than the dog) the way some people suppose that their good eyesight, muscles, income, and looks are theirs because there is something special about them that calls for their being treated well. God's Word has to tell us so and make all these ours as gifts of God. Only then do they have their full size.

You may think that is not such a difficult job for the Word of God to do, and I suppose that is so because good eyesight, muscles, income, and looks are things that we naturally desire. We can be drawn to these by our own lust. When sin promises good things of this sort, we are apt to sin. If God can deliver the same goods, well, we are prepared to receive them from Him. People who take this position suppose that they are still in control of the negotiations, but, in fact, they are in a vulnerable position. If they do a deal with sin, they will be played for fools. If they think of doing a deal with God, they will find that God does not play that game. The idea of doing a deal with God can survive only as long as they get the things after which they lust. When they get things they don't want, those who hold to a negotiating position with God yell that He isn't playing the game according to the rules of doing a deal. Then they are likely to say, "If God does that to me, I am through with Him. He is not what God ought to be. I don't believe in Him. He doesn't exist."

Of course, the God whom we could do a deal with does not exist. The living God is the giver God. This we know from His word of truth that has made us His children. That gift and all the others the Word of God tells us of, and the Word of God makes them gifts to us from our giving Father God. This is true of your breakfast and your shoes, and not only of such obvious gifts but also of all the things that God gives us. Whatever He gives is a good gift from Him because His word of truth says so. God's Word settles it, not our judgment or our lust. It tells us all His gifts are good. He gives us His word that He is our Father.

"Father knows best" when spoken by earthly fathers does not always inspire confidence, but when spoken by the Father of our Lord Jesus Christ, it does. After Calvary we cannot doubt God's love. God does not give us any shady advertising talk. He tells us straight that He is going to make something of us, which will mean some sorrow and pain. God intends to kill what we are as sinners and make us new. "For whom the Lord loveth He chasteneth and scourgeth every son whom He receiveth" (Hebrews 12:6).

The Lord does not tempt or entice us as sin does, but He does test us. He tests whether we are the children of Himself, the giver God, or whether we have a god we have made up to serve our lusts. Affliction is such a test. When affliction cleanses us of trust in a false god and draws us closer to the living, giving Father God, then affliction is a good gift, for which we can come to thank Him. He cannot not be our Father. God is bound by His word.

As children of our Father God, we cannot be blown about by the winds of fortune or played for fools by the shadowy allurements of deceitful sin.

> Who shall separate us from the love of Christ? Shall tribulation, or distress, or persecution, or famine, or nakedness, or peril, or sword? As it is written, For Thy sake we are killed all the day long; we are accounted as sheep for the slaughter. Nay, in all these things we are more than conquerors through Him that loved us. For I am persuaded, that neither death, nor life, nor angels, nor principalities, nor powers, nor things present, nor things to come, nor height, nor depth, nor any other creature, shall be able to separate us from the love of God, which is in Christ Jesus our Lord. (Romans 8:37–39)

We can no more be destroyed than God can be made a liar. We belong to Him and are held to Him by His word of truth. We are the firstfruits. There is large promise in that. The first of the harvest was offered to God as token of the whole harvest, acknowledged as belonging to Him and as gift from Him.

To say firstfruits means there are more gifts to follow. With every gift, God pushes our hands wider open to receive a still larger gift. The bother with us is that we often hold our hands open just enough for little gifts in fear that if the gifts get too big they may overwhelm us. The gifts may begin to take us over, and we may not be able to manage them.

This is a genuine danger, for that is the way of gifts. You know how uneasy you get if somebody gives you lots of gifts—and rather big ones too. This uneasiness is born of our habit of doing deals. Before God it is completely out of place. We can only have such an uneasiness before God if we are still thinking of doing a deal with Him. That we nevertheless have such uneasiness is betrayed by our notions of not letting our religion go too far, not too much Word of God, not church every

Sunday, or not devotions every day. Some parts of our lives we simply must keep under our own control. To the extent that we still negotiate terms with God, we are setting ourselves up for a fearful crash. The God that can be negotiated with does not exist. If that is the one with whom we think we do business, our end is darkness.

As we live as the children of the Father of lights, the giver God, He will keep on pouring out His gifts, and they will overwhelm us more and more. The Epistle of James is mostly about what God's gifts do to us, how they work out in our lives. Nothing remote or beyond the bright blue sky about this. The gifts shape how you use your tongue, how you treat widows and orphans, the hungry, people with money, people you employ. James points out that if you think your religion is just a good deal you have done with God for yourself, you have had it.

But in James 1, we get the starting point: The giver God, from whom comes every good and every perfect gift, has made us His children with His word of truth. As God pours the gifts, with each fresh gift, He gives us another nudge, "Come on, join in My game. Help Me give My gifts away." God's children play the game their Father's way. To everybody else, to the deal-doers, it looks crazy, but, in fact, it is the best fun in all the world.

With hands held wide to Him for His gifts, we will be moved and shaped by those gifts forward from firstfruits to the final joyous harvest. When we shall "sing unto the LORD a new song; for He hath done marvelous things" (Psalm 98:1).

AMEN.

Sixth Sunday of Easter

JOHN 16:23

LONDON (1957)

It was only a little while before Jesus would leave His disciples. Soon they would see Him no more. The intimate personal contact would be broken. What a sad gap we have seen in the despair and fear of the disciples after the crucifixion. It seemed as if the bottom had fallen out of everything. The disciples had staked all on Jesus. They had given up their businesses and followed Him. Their lives had come to revolve around Him. Where Jesus went, they followed. The disciples' lives were given to Him. But when Jesus was gone, the heart was taken out of their lives. We know how our lives come to be meshed in with the lives of others. With those nearest us, we are like cogs meshed in movement together. When such a one goes from our lives, what a melancholy gap is left.

Jesus knows this feeling too. He was human like you and I, and He knew how far the disciples would be able to get along without Him on their own strength. So during the forty days between Easter and Ascension, He prepared them for His departure. The risen Christ did not fit back into the lives of the disciples as they had been living with Him previously. That is what Mary Magdalene wanted, but Jesus said, "Touch Me not." Before Calvary the disciples had leaned heavily on Him. Jesus had carried them as lambs, as children. Now He wanted them to stand upright like men and go forth into all the world with brave hearts and voice, proclaiming the crucified and risen Savior. The visible presence of Christ, which was as a hand holding them during their spiritual toddling, was soon to be withdrawn. Jesus was going on ahead, and He bade them, "Follow Me!" Through all their lives, they were to know that Jesus was leading them forward. "I am with you." The disciples walked in His steps. Following Christ, their journey was set from earth to heaven. They were to learn to walk by faith, not by sight.

Jesus knew the disciples' weaknesses and promised them that He would not leave them comfortless. Down to their weakness would come the strength of the Spirit of God. By His power, the living connection with Christ would be maintained and strengthened. Although the tangible contact with the visible Jesus would be gone, a deeper, more inward contact with God was thrown open to them. The disciples were granted the renewed privilege of prayer. They had prayed before, but now they were to learn to pray so prayer would be for them a mighty, strengthening contact with God. So far they had prayed with sight, now they were to pray with faith alone. To all disciples of Christ who walk by faith and not by sight is given this same privilege and promise.

Much ridicule is nowadays heaped on Christian prayer by the Christ-less, and they do it with a fine show of humility. They say, "Do you suppose that a puny individual like you can change the laws that govern the universe? Can you, who are so sadly shoved around by others, influence the course of this world or interrupt the chain of gigantic events? If there is a God, do you suppose that He is going to pay any attention to you?" Before the barrage of such contempt, Christians have sometimes weakened and backed down. They qualify and weaken the Lord's promise to match their own prayer experience so lacking in faith.

But this talk about unchangeable laws isn't nearly so impressive as it once seemed. The scientists aren't at all as cocksure about their unchangeable laws, and it isn't by our own power that we seek to achieve anything. If we stood alone in our own puny weakness, then we must certainly shudder at the thought of God and hide our faces before Him. In us there is no hope, and if in heaven there is no Father, then we certainly cannot pray. If we cannot pray, it is all up with us. But our text does not just speak of God. It speaks of the Father. That makes all the difference in the world, all the difference between life and death.

It is only because God has come to be our Father that we can pray to Him. Only because Christ has taken our sins on Himself and wiped them out by His victorious death can we stand before God, forgiven, His children in Christ. Only as we are bound to Christ can we come before God as His children, for then God sees us in Christ, wearing the garment of Christ's righteousness. This is the key to a living connection with God our Father. All contact, all prayer with Him must be in Christ, in the name of Jesus, that is, with faith in Him.

Prayer can only rise from faith in Christ. Apart from Christ and His atoning, redeeming work, God is no one's Father. It is delusive sentimentality to talk of the fatherhood of God and the brotherhood of man without Christ. Only in the acceptance, the clinging to, the giving of ourselves over to Christ is God our Father or anyone our true brother or sister. Faith in Christ is rejection of self and all we have to offer. "Nothing in my hand I bring, Simply to Thy cross I cling" (*The Lutheran Hymnal*, 376:3). Not I, but Christ. We come as beggars before God and have no right to ask anything. "We are neither worthy of the things for which we pray, nor have we deserved them, but we ask that He would give them all to us by grace, for we daily sin much and surely deserve nothing but punishment" (Luther's Small Catechism).

The perfect example of humble, selfless prayer is that sinner who, not venturing to go right into God's temple, bowed his head, beat on his breast and sighed, "God, be merciful to me a sinner." There was room for God in his empty heart. In the Pharisee there was no room. He felt no lack. He was making such a beautiful job of his life. His prayer was a summons to God to admire him. The publican went down to his house with a glad peace in his heart, justified. Jesus says so, as He does with the absolution, He bestows on penitent sinners by His use of the mouth He has put there to speak His forgiving words in His name. Our Amen speaks the prayer of faith in Jesus' name.

Praying "in Jesus' name" means to pray in the spirit, manner, and character of Jesus. Our prayers must be of the Jesus sort. Just as faith is created in our hearts by the Holy Spirit through the Word of God, so by the Word we are given guidance and example in the art of prayer. There we find our Lord in His life so rich in prayer. As we come to know Him better and are drawn closer to Him, our prayers will take on more of His character. We often take on the manners and speech of those with whom we associate. Traveling closer with Jesus, our prayers will be more and more pulled into the purposes for which Jesus gave Himself. In the name of Jesus is in the name of Him who is our Savior. Therefore, in the name of Jesus, we can ask nothing that is contrary to our salvation. Whatever would harm us or draw us away from our Savior is not in the name of Jesus.

Can we always know what is good or not good for building us up in stature for our salvation? Of course not. The confession that our heavenly Father knows better than we is basic to all rightful prayer. If you ask Christians, "Are you wiser than God?" they will, of course, say no, but if each of us will examine our prayer life, we will surely see how often we speak to God as if we know better than He. We become impatient and grumble when God doesn't jump to it and do as we tell Him. But someone will object, "Hasn't God promised to hear our prayer and give us everything for which we ask?" That is true, so long as it is asked in Jesus' name. As we might say, that is the catch. Is that just a loophole for God? Not so! God would not be our loving heavenly Father if He gave us everything that we wanted, just as those are pretty poor parents who give their children everything they want.

God loves us too much to give us everything we want. He draws a boundary around the things that He promises to give us in answer to our prayer. That boundary is His love. So often God's curse is His letting people have just what they want. That is the way people get to hell. God says, "Well, if you insist on cutting yourself off from Me and going full speed to hell, you shall have it your way." If we deliberately shut God out of our life, God finally says, "All right, you shall have it as you want it." Because God is our loving heavenly Father, He restricts His promise to those things that are for our good, which draw us close to our Savior, in whose name alone we pray aright. As our mind and wishes come more and more into line with our Father's mind and wishes, we shall more fully pray in the name of Jesus. As we learn to pray in the manner of Christ, we shall learn of Him to say, "Not my will, but Thine be done."

Yet even when our Father, out of love, refuses to give us that particular thing for which we may be foolishly asking, our prayer is not unanswered. The heart of our prayer is always granted us. Take the old example of little William asking Mother for a sharp knife. The heart of the child's request is that he may have fun playing with the knife. Mother refuses to give little William the knife, yet by doing that, she grants the heart of little William's prayer. Young William thought he would be happier playing with the knife. Mother knew he would be happier not playing with it. The happiness of William has been granted, though he may pout for an hour and think his mother most hard and unloving. So also our Father in heaven deals with us as His children, who so often ask for foolish and hurtful things.

It does not follow from this that we ought not to ask for particular things. We should have no desire about which we are ashamed to tell our Father. He is pleased with us when we speak to Him as dear children speak to their dear Father, even if it is about a new pair of shoes or the tomato plants, but always with the confession, "Lord, You know only too well what a foolish person I am and how apt I am to ask for hurtful and selfish things. To me it would seem that these things would be good for me and my neighbor, but I will leave it all up to You." Not my will, but Thine be done. We will learn to pray, "Lord, teach me to serve Thee with all I am and have" instead of a prayer that goes no further than "Lord, give me more money." In the perfect prayer our Savior taught us, there is only one petition for earthly things. We need them for a while and are glad and grateful for them, but the whole weight of prayer is in the things that last for good, that work our salvation, the things our Savior came to accomplish.

For these we can ask without condition. God has to grant them to us. He has promised, and God is faithful. Claiming Jesus' blood and merit, God has to forgive us our sins. That certainty is "in Jesus' name." We can hold God to His promise. That, however, means that we trust His promise. We may never complain of our prayer not being heard if we pray with a hit-or-miss attitude that says, "I don't know whether it will do any good, but I don't suppose it can do any harm either, so I may as well give it a go." This is insulting to God because not taking God at His word entertains the possibility that God is a liar. Thus all our prayers must be with confidence. We must take God at His word: "There hath not failed one word of all His good promise" (1 Kings 8:56). When we pray for our salvation for Jesus' sake, God has to give it to us. When we pray for earthly things, we tell our Father what we would like and are confident that He will give it to us. If it is for our good and He does not grant it just when and how we like, we know that He gives us what is better for us. The heart of our prayer, our sure good, is always granted. We confess, "Lord, Thou knowest best, and we trust Thy promise to hear our prayer."

When prayers seem unanswered, let us not first blame God but begin closer to home. Let us examine our prayers and see if we are not, perhaps, trying to order God around, telling Him just how and when He is supposed to do what we tell Him. Let us ask ourselves whether Jesus and all He stands for and wants to accomplish in us are at the heart of our prayer. If there is no Jesus in our prayer, then it is no prayer and we have no Father to hear us. How beautiful are our Collects that end "through Jesus Christ our Lord" in their recognition of this fact that without Jesus it is no prayer. Yet not in words mechanically added on for a prayer, but only in heart-filling faith and reliance in Christ do we pray aright in the name of Jesus.

Scripture abounds in examples of answered prayer, but there are also examples of what we would sometimes be tempted to call unanswered prayers. A Gentile Samaritan woman prayed to Jesus for her daughter. Jesus said it wasn't fit to take the children's bread and cast it to dogs. Her prayer's answer came later to that conquering, humble faith that clutched Jesus' words and cried, "Truth, Lord: yet the dogs eat of the crumbs which fall from their master's table" (Matthew 15:27). Mary begged Jesus to do something for the embarrassed host when the wine gave out at Cana's wedding. Jesus replied that He had His own good time. When Lazarus lay dying, his distressed sisters sent to their best friend for help. Jesus tarried and Lazarus died. St. Paul was afflicted with a thorn in the flesh and prayed three times to be cured of it. God did not take away that thorn, but He built Paul up to bear it. Monica prayed forty years for her son gone to the dogs.

Ambrose comforted her that a son of so many prayers could not be lost. And her son was finally gripped by Christ and became the great man of God, Augustine.

If God seems to tarry, let faith cling fast. We are given the example of the widow who kept troubling the godless judge until he gave her justice just to get rid of her pestering. Jesus says we can surely expect better treatment than that from our Father in heaven.

> Or what man is there of you, whom if his son ask bread, will he give him a stone? Or if he ask a fish, will he give him a serpent? If ye then, being evil, know how to give good gifts unto your children, how much more shall your Father which is in heaven give good things to them that ask Him? (Matthew 7:9–11)

Today we have only considered prayer as asking, but it is infinitely more. Prayer is, first, an act of worship. We open ourselves to God. Guided by His Word, we point ourselves in His direction. Prayer is an answer to God's word of saving, life-giving love in Christ. In prayer we make reply to Him, giving Him back our love, our adoration, our praise, our loyalty, our lives. As we pray we are in contact with God our Father through Christ, and therein we are made strong as His children. The more we pray, the stronger we are. We can only breathe out as often as we breathe in. Prayer is the heartbeat of the Christian life. As we are alive in Christ, we pray.

AMEN.

The Ascension of Our Lord

LUKE 24:50–53

CAMBRIDGE (1965)

We have followed the life of Jesus this first half of the church year from the wrinkly, red infant on the straw in the stable to the baby receiving the homage of the Wise Men. We have followed Him from the boy in the temple to the man to whom John the Baptist pointed, "Behold the Lamb of God, which taketh away the sin of the world" (John 1:29). Then, baptized of John in the Jordan, the Spirit came down on Jesus and we heard the Father's voice, "This is My beloved Son, in whom I am well pleased; hear ye Him" (Matthew 17:5). Tempted in the wilderness, Jesus held to God's high-saving purpose. In Lent we followed as Jesus moved to the fulfillment of that purpose: Palm Sunday, Maundy Thursday, Good Friday, and Easter. All this that He might bless us.

We are not told what words Jesus spoke in blessing. We do not need them because we have only to look and we shall know. In the hands that He raised in blessing we can read the meaning and blessing of Jesus. These are the hands that pushed at Mary's breast in all our human littleness and frailty. These hands learned to hold a pen and write the words of Scripture that Jesus knew so well by the time He was 12 years old. These hands worked with hammer and saw, sharing and blessing our work with us. These are the hands that touched the eyes of the blind and the tongue of the dumb, the hands that had taken hold of the pale cold hand of the little girl and given her back alive to her wondering father and mother. We read so often of these hands that Jesus stretched them out, touched, or grasped with that personal, individual love and help that marks the healings of Jesus. He did not heal people by the dozens lumped together, but was there for each one that needed Him as His hands took hold of each one. We recall that moving scene when, after a full and busy day, Jesus went far into the night, helping and healing. St. Luke records, "Now when the sun was setting, all they that had any sick with divers diseases brought them unto Him; and He laid His hands on every one of them, and healed them" (4:40).

These are the hands that gathered the little children into His arms to hug them and bless them. These are the hands that gripped Peter when he looked away from Jesus and began to sink. These are the hands that broke the blessed bread and gave them His body to eat. These are the hands that Thomas held and conquered all his doubt. All this the ascension hands of Jesus say, and we have not yet mentioned the biggest thing of all, for in those hands we see the print of the nails. That jagged scar tells us the full size of the blessing and how it was won for us. This is what the artist says when painting the scar in the hands of Jesus as a cross. It is a big blessing indeed that cost that.

All our wrong, our sins, Jesus took on Himself and bore the punishment for them. He was forsaken as we had coming to us, so we might not be forsaken of God but forgiven, and because of what Jesus did for us there on the cross, be made alive again as the children of God. Because

Jesus' hands were stretched out on the cross, they are today stretched out in blessing on His disciples. The one who ascends and blesses has the marks of the cross in His hands. No cross, no blessing. That is why the sign of the cross is made with the blessing. That is what Jesus means to us at His ascension: life and blessing won and given.

Now I should like to add one thing that Jesus' ascension does not mean. It does not mean that He has gone away. Before Jesus ascended, He promised that wherever we may be He is with us. The difference is that after the ascension, Jesus does not show us Himself anymore, or at least not until the next time, which will be the end of the world or when we die, whichever comes first. And it is a jolly good thing, too, for suppose Jesus had gone on showing Himself as He did before His resurrection. Where would He be this evening? In America or in New Guinea? We would say, "If He is there, then He is not here." But because Jesus has ascended, His people in America and New Guinea and in this room know that He is with them. He has promised it. How Jesus can manage it we cannot figure out, and what tells us that we can't and that it is silly to try is the bright cloud that took Jesus out of the disciples' sight.

This wasn't an ordinary cloud. We have seen this cloud before at the transfiguration, and in the Old Testament there was the bright cloud that stood above the two angels on the ark of the covenant, the bright cloud that led Israel on their journey to the Promised Land. That cloud was the guarantee of the presence of God. So at the ascension a cloud is used to mark Jesus' entry to the realm of God, which we can neither understand nor measure with our present little thoughts and limited experience. We can't push our little measuring tapes into that cloud and say how things have to go on there. They go on as God says, and that is the way with Jesus now.

Jesus didn't travel thousands of miles like a space rocket. He rose up a little way above the earth and a cloud received Him out of their sight. All that was gone was the sight of Jesus. The cloud means that He is no longer within our ordinary limits. Jesus is now present and does things in the whole range of God's way of being present and doing things while remaining a man, but a man fulfilled and glorified. We confess this when we say that "He sitteth on the right hand of God the Father Almighty." The right hand is not some particular place as we think of, but the exercise of the whole power of God, which is now in the hands of Jesus.

So the ascension does not mean that Jesus has gone away. Quite the opposite. He is with us now even more powerfully than when men saw Him. We live, then, in the presence of our ascended, ever-present Lord. Because He is with us, we cannot be destroyed. Jesus has made the way to victory for us. He leads us that way, gives us strength and courage for it, and finally brings us to the bright cloud of heaven. We go on, then, from the ascension as did the first disciples "with great joy" (Luke 24:52).

Amen.

Seventh Sunday of Easter

Luke 24:44–49

Valparaiso University (1970, the year kinsey hall caught fire)

We came close to three events last week: Kinsey, Kent, and Cambodia. There is a legend that it was a toss-up whether Valparaiso University would be carried on by the Lutherans or the Klansmen. The Lutherans won out, and the Klansmen have since gone underground. But they are still there. By "there" we usually mean "in the town," but there is a little klansman in the heart of each one of us. In the night he got control of someone's heart. It happened on Ascension Day in the morning, while it was dark, on the green of Old Campus. It wasn't a burning cross but a burning building.

One person is enough to do that. We each have a shuddering potential for evil. I speak of human hands starting the fire. This seems most likely, though one must allow the possibility of accident or spontaneous combustion, just as one must allow the possibility that Mr. Nixon might have made a wise decision. There are few things we can be quite certain about. It seemed to me there were people burning too. Some of Albert Huegli, his colleagues, and the musicians was being burned up. Let us not make a too facile decision between human and material things. If I snatch from you something that is precious to you and trample on it, I am trampling on you. A faculty wife stood guard over a rescued pile of papers. A pile of papers? Yes. Ten years of a man's music work. Then a student's thesis was announced not burned. The harpsichord was safe. The organs damaged but not ruined. Through the hideous smoke came bright bursts of thankfulness. No one, I think, looked on the fire and found it good. Yet if we had spotted the person who started the fire, the little klansman in the heart of each of us would have cried, "Lynch that person!"

When we are deeply stirred, we want to do something. It was good to get into a line and work together moving things out of the smoking building. The fraternity brother's cup of coffee was like Jesus' cup of cold water. We wanted to speak our revulsion at the insanity and wanted to save as much as we could for tomorrow. We wanted to say it in a way that matters, say it with action.

We do not begin to probe the fire, I feel, if we see it as intended to attack Albert Huegli or this university. It may have been a brainwashed anarchist or, perhaps, someone driven mad by the appalling follies inflicted by people captive to an often inhuman system, someone who felt that something must be done. The bitter turmoil of our frustration burst out there in blind destructive folly. One folly does not overcome another. By such a folly we are taken over by folly. Even worse than being unable to do anything is to do something stupid and destructive. That puts us on the side of what we oppose. It was a paralyzing eruption of irrational destruction. What can we say?

There are times when any of our own words are too cheap. Then it is good to say together words that we have from Christ. We needed to get our bearings, and it was Ascension Day. There was hold, resource, and direction. In the Chapel of the Resurrection there was a man screaming, crazed by acid. He came, finally, to kneel at the high altar, moaning out his mangled heart to Christ. Then he went away, not to come back to us. He may have written himself off, but Christ has not nor may we. There are worse fires than those that burn out buildings. Fires burning out people are burning among us every day. The Ascension Day sermon said the things that are said on Ascension Day, but they were said for us this Ascension Day. Then the choir rang out *Et Resurrexit*. That really connected. We prayed. We were blessed. In the evening the cry was heard, "Not Kinsey, but Kent and Cambodia. Do not ask us to stop. We have our holy cause and must press on," which at that stage sounded rather like the priest and the Levite.

Remember the words of our Ascension Day Lord: "Ye shall be witnesses unto Me both in Jerusalem, and in all Judea, and in Samaria, and unto the uttermost part of the earth" (Acts 1:8). If we forget that, we may find ourselves making outraged holy statements about apartheid in South Africa while doing nothing about how a black man may be treated in Valparaiso. Or we may be so fired-up righteous in the Cambodian cause that we break off communication with a roommate. We may not stay in Jerusalem and make that the limit of our care. Our Lord points on to Judea and Samaria and to the ends of the earth, but we may not go on to them shirking and bypassing what our care is here.

Our Lord bids His disciples to stay awhile in Jerusalem so they may be equipped to go into all Judea and Samaria and to the ends of the earth. The enabling equipment is in Christ's promise in the Gospel for this Sunday between Ascension and Pentecost. Jesus says some hard lines: being cut off, killed. "You have to be ready to face it as My disciples, and you won't be seeing Me around much longer." He was crucified, dead, and buried. The third day He rose again and ascended. Then the Counselor would come. He would not come before that. His work is to convey what Christ achieved, so Christ must achieve that first. Then the kerygma or, more fully, the Gospel, the liberating Good News. It is that that the Counselor would bring us to fasten on, on Christ. We frustrate His work if we pay too much attention to Him. Whether we call Him Comforter, Counselor, Paraclete, Holy Spirit, or Holy Ghost does not matter to Him so much as that we have hold of Christ. He is God at work through the lowly means of words, water, wine, and bread to bring home to us Christ and His gifts and set them aflame in our lives. Holy fire. But that is next Sunday's lesson.

In today's Gospel we have the promise for the days when we no longer see Jesus. There is a personal organic wholeness to what Jesus ties together. The Spirit comes from the Father and from Jesus and bears witness of Him, and we are drawn into that witnessing as we receive Christ and are with Him. If we are with Jesus, then we have conflict with all that is antichrist, and the supreme antichrist is the one who operates in the name of God. It is in the church that we have the opportunity to be the supreme antichrist. This we do when we displace Christ with our own notions; when we say, "Thus says the Lord," when the Lord has not spoken; when we put God's name on our own wishes, plans, and programs, then unchurch those who disagree with us. "What sort of a Christian are you if you burn your draft card?" "What sort of a Christian are you if you are willing to fight in Cambodia?"

Jesus does not promise that the Spirit will give us little messages to settle our questions. We are not slaves but children, and we grow in stature as we wrestle our way through. The Spirit brings Christ alive in us and brings us resources to live out His forgiveness and His love. Christ's forgiveness and love take a different and unique shape in each person. There are some cantankerous, dim-witted, too clever by half, ostentatious, fanatic, complacent people. I can tell you what is wrong, what each needs to do, what is the score. When I do that, I am making a mocking imitation of God. God, in Christ, does not deal with us on the basis of our score. He loves the whole mangy lot of us, and we are stuck with the whole mangy lot when we are with Christ.

Again this morning Christ's forgiveness wipes us clean and we go to live out that forgiveness with one another. We shall not then be able to write someone off as a lost cause. If we think others are misguided or evading their responsibility, we will tell them so, debate, and seek to persuade back and forth, but as they are Christ's child and I am Christ's child, I cannot cast others aside without at the same time denying Christ. We may each live out our loyalty to Christ in a different way, embrace one another as brothers and sisters for Christ's sake. There are not the resources for that in me, or in others, but only in Christ, the Brother of us all. Christ's body and blood go into you and into me. Thus we are bound together. With such resources we live together. No other fact is larger than that.

First in Jerusalem, then also in all Judea and Samaria and to the ends of the earth. Kinsey, Kent, Cambodia. At whatever point we see our task for living out our loyalty to Christ—in conflict with evil, sharing suffering, healing bodies and lives—we are His witnesses. With Him and unafraid, we are bold to act, bold to prepare to act, even when things may look as if they are crashing down on us. Without panic we may even go into God's world that we have marred and cheerfully plant an apple tree.

AMEN.

The Day of Pentecost

Matthew 10:16–23

Concordia Seminary (1986)

Matthew 10 is sort of the disciples' vicarage assignment, their first go at it. They get a pretty precise briefing, though they are not yet ordained apostles to all the nations. On this assignment, they go not to all the nations but to the lost sheep of the house of Israel. There are twelve disciples, all named. The Lord has His Twelve. Things do not slip out of our Lord's hands or dribble through His fingers.

On Sunday we heard of Pentecost, the Twelve—Peter standing with the Eleven. He is the voice of the Lord's Twelve, the Lord's voice. His text is from Joel: "Whoever shall call on the name of the Lord shall be delivered" (2:32). Those who do are baptized. But that is ahead of our text where the Twelve are sent only to "the lost sheep of the house of Israel" (Matthew 10:6).

Vicarage is not yet the lot. The disciples are not yet given to baptize. They are to preach, and the message is the same one John the Baptist proclaimed when he spoke of Jesus: "The kingdom of heaven is at hand" (Matthew 3:2). The message that the disciples are to preach is given to them. It is not their production. If they get hauled into court and are scared of what will happen to them and what they should say, they are to forget about thinking something up and simply say what is given to them: the message of Jesus. That goes with the Holy Spirit who will be speaking through them.

Today's Gospel strengthens the disciples for the task. It will be tough because it is a task in the Lord's name. But because it is a task in the Lord's name, they cannot be destroyed. If the disciples put their trust anywhere else than in the Lord's name, they will surely come unstuck. "What shall I say?" is no excuse. Neither trust in themselves nor in anybody else will see them through. Jesus wipes out any such ground of confidence. You can take it from Him. Not your own family—they may want you dead for being given over into the service of the Lord's name. They may insist on being put ahead of Him. They may see Him as the enemy of what they plan and desire.

Jesus puts it straight. He doesn't want you to come unstuck. He doesn't prettify anything. You will never be able to say this is worse than Jesus led me to expect. In the worst possible scenario, there will be nothing for sure except His name, His promise, and His Spirit. Then when your confidence is nowhere else than in these, your strength will be the strength of His name, His promise, His Spirit. The scenario Jesus sketches for the disciples sounds rather different than yours. Their mission was a frightful failure. Your failure might look like splendid success. The wolves you will meet will be mostly those in sheep's clothing. You will need to spot them—"wise as serpents, and harmless as doves" (Matthew 10:16)—not "wolf bite wolf." You don't stand much chance of being dragged before governors and kings. You may even be invited to Rotary or the country club. Having a cleric around adds a certain something to the tone of things. But he had best not speak out of turn. The world will seek to domesticate you to its ways. And the ladies exclaim, "Oh, I simply must tell you about our new vicar. He is such a perfect pet."

The pyramids were visited by the blind Argentinian writer Jorge Luis Borges. As he went from the mighty pyramid, he stooped and picked up a handful of sand. A little further on he dribbled the sand to the ground and felt that he was changing the desert by moving the sand. Whether building a pyramid or picking up a handful of sand—one seems to last a bit longer than the other—do I dare disturb the universe? Remember that your days are in the name of the Lord. Your times are in His hands. The Lord has His timetable. He has His Twelve. He runs the timetable. He has told us so, but in such a way that we can't figure it out so as to work prediction or control. "Ye shall not have gone over the cities of Israel, till the Son of Man be come" (Matthew 10:23). Schweitzer, you recall, said Jesus was mistaken.

You will be tempted to say the same when you are up against it and nothing seems to work, modifying the Sahara. It is at that point that you may receive the gift of today's Gospel, having had the theology of glory knocked out of you "for My name's sake." In Christ crucified is true theology and knowledge of God. "He is worth calling a theologian who sees the visible and posterior things of God through suffering and the cross." His humanity, weakness, and foolishness. It is enough for the disciple to be like his teacher and a servant like his master. So have no fear.

Borges confesses that, thanks to his blindness, he came into the treasure house of Anglo-Saxon literature and much poetry by heart.

When the day's a blank and you see nothing, a handful of sand from here to there, work through the Hebrew of next Sunday's Old Testament lesson. Read Dostoyevsky. Go to school with the lilies or a child or some battered old Christian. It is only your first go. You won't disturb the universe. That is not what you are for. Jesus sent the disciples, we are told, because He had compassion. By way of them people should know the compassion of Jesus. In His foolishness He may have such use even of you, for His compassion's sake, for His name's sake, for His Israel. His peace goes with you.

AMEN.

The Holy Trinity

ROMANS 11:33–36

LONDON (1955)

What is God like? If somebody asked you this question, your first answer would probably not be the Athanasian Creed. At first glance, that creed looks as if it were intended to show how mysterious God is. It is not easygoing, that Athanasian Creed, and you could hardly expect it to be, for it speaks of the Holy Trinity. It speaks of God as He is in Himself, and we cannot hope to grasp or understand that. We are not big or smart enough for that. It is supreme arrogance to suppose that we can. "For who hath known the mind of the Lord?" (Romans 11:34). No one can claim that, for God is unsearchable and is way past understanding. He dwelleth in a light that no one can approach.

Isaiah tells of God as sitting on the circle of the earth, and the inhabitants are as grasshoppers. When you hold a grasshopper enclosed in your hand, you may wonder what the grasshopper understands of our nature. Two things, perhaps, the grasshopper realizes: first, our power that holds him fast, and second, the fear that we can crush and destroy him. That is all the grasshopper in your hand can know of our nature. How much more can we, in the hand of God, know about the nature of God? The power of God is unmistakable. The Scripture says, "Lift up your eyes on high, and behold who hath created these things, that bringeth out their host by number: He calleth them all by names by the greatness of His might, for that He is strong in power" (Isaiah 40:26). This knowledge of the power of God is coupled with the fear that God may crush and destroy us. When people and nations, with their pride and power, crumble to dust, when earthquakes, floods, and hurricanes destroy, we are filled with a dread before God before whom "the nations are as a drop of a bucket, and are counted as the small dust of the balance: behold, He taketh up the isles as a very little thing.... All nations before Him are as nothing; and they are counted to Him as less than nothing, and vanity" (Isaiah 40:15–17).

If this is sure of all nations, what of one little person pushed along in the crowd? Our little lives are constantly under threat, and we expend ourselves trying to safeguard our lives and prop them up. For primitive heathen, gods are identified as the threat. For modern heathen, the threat does not have a name but remains, calling in question the efforts to make something of our lives. Yet we are driven by an "ought": We ought to make something of our lives. We have a conscience, a knowledge of right and wrong. We are answerable, and if there is a God, we have every reason to be afraid of Him.

We see this fear working itself out in the endeavors of the heathen to escape the threat of their gods. They do everything to win them over. Such heathen are not so far gone as those other heathen who would stifle the thought of the nameless fear, deny that they are answerable, and reject the name of the God who threatens to punish all those who transgress His commandments. Whether it be the fear of running away from God or the fear of the frantic efforts to earn God's favor, the fear remains a dread fear, for they remain uncertain and cannot be sure, for they do not know God.

When filled with dread and fear of the unsearchable Almighty, we know that we are guilty before God. To us is given a conscience, a knowledge of right and wrong and a sense of responsibility. We are answerable to our Maker, and we know that we are guilty. Justly we have every reason to be afraid of God. Just take a look at yourself and what God expects of you.

How should the grasshopper in your hand come to know our nature? Only if we would become a grasshopper and show it, expressing in terms of a grasshopper what we are like. So to the question what God is like, the first and immediate answer is Jesus of Nazareth. Here was a man who claimed to be God, said things that only God can say, did things that only God can do, and accepted worship that belongs only to God. Some called Jesus a blasphemer, which was near the truth. The only other possibility was that here actually was God, God confronting people as a man. Here was God expressed in human terms, which is what the Scripture says of Jesus. He is called the Word, that is, the active statement, the expression, the revelation of God. He who was God from all eternity now shows Himself in human terms to us. "And the Word was made flesh, and dwelt among us" (John 1:14). God was seen and heard and touched. To know Jesus is to know God. Here is the answer to the question what God is like. We beheld His glory, the glory as of the only-begotten of the Father full of grace and truth, and the height of that glory was the cross. God became a man, went to the cross, and the agony of the hell that is sin's punishment. Jesus died for the ungodly. He died for those afraid of God and fleeing from God. He died for sinners. He died for you and for me.

There is no greater love imaginable, and that, my friends, is what God is like, abundant in mercy. God loves you. There is nothing lovable to God in you and me as sinners, yet He loved us so much that He died so our sin might be set aside, forgiven, and we may be made God's own. When sin, which puts us wrong with God, is answered for and forgiven, our guilt and dread fear before God is gone. Forgiven, we are no longer afraid of God. We come to know Him as Father because of what Jesus did for us.

Jesus gives the answer to the question of what God is like in His prophetic office. He shows us God is holy and just, merciful and forgiving. By His priestly work as our replacement, Jesus answers for our sins. Because of His atonement on the cross, our sins can no more drag us fearfully from God but are forgiven, and we, washed white in the blood of the Lamb, stand before God as His glad children and call Him "Abba, Father."

Through Jesus, God is our Father. Jesus is the way. "No man cometh unto the Father, but by Me" (John 14:6). There is no other way to the Father. Outside of Jesus, God is no one's Father. The only Father is the Father of our Lord Jesus Christ. The Fatherhood of God is not based on the First Article. God is not your Father because He is your Creator. Even rejected as Father, He remains your Creator and your Judge from whom there is no escape. The Father has only forgiven children. When His forgiveness is rejected, it is replaced by the judgment spoken inescapably on rebellious sinners, who are still His creatures. Here applies that fearful word of Scripture: Can the clay vessel answer back to the potter? As clay vessels, as His creatures, we have no claim on God, for we are what the Scripture calls "marred vessels." "And the vessel that he made of clay was marred in the hand of the potter" (Jeremiah 15:4). We are sinners. There is no way around our sin. It is there. It makes us guilty and rejectionable before God. Only if sin be forgiven is the honest thought of God anything but dread fear, so only through Christ and His cross is God our Father. He is the way; no man comes to the Father but by the Son.

There is no Father for us but the Father of our Lord Jesus Christ. First, God is Father because He is the Father of Jesus Christ, and that is the recognition that Jesus Christ is the Son of the Father. Does Jesus look like the Son of the Father? Not really. Born in beggarly conditions, cruelly kicked about, not a penny in His pocket, not even a furnished room, and despised by everybody respectable. Then He was executed as the lowest criminal. Son of God? Not likely.

No one can be talked into calling the crucified carpenter the Son of God. Some, of course, will call Jesus a son of God (even the number one Son of God) but not "the only-begotten Son of the Father." To protect themselves against who He really is, such folk tell sweet fairy stories about a dear old indulgent grandfatherish God who doesn't mind having His whiskers pulled and really wouldn't hurt a fly. Such notions are far removed from the facts of sin, from the God who is a consuming fire and the God who is the Father of our Lord Jesus Christ.

That Jesus is the Son of God is nonsense to our human understanding. We can't see it. Of what use, then, is a Father and a way to the Father through the Son if our whole nature and reason see it as nonsense. No use at all if we are left to ourselves. But the God who died for us to make us His children knew that, too, and promised not to leave us comfortless.

When Peter made his great confession, Jesus said, "Blessed art thou, Simon Bar Jonah: for flesh and blood hath not revealed it unto thee, but My Father which is in heaven" (Matthew 16:17). This work of revealing Jesus as the Son of God, and in Him to know God as Father, is not especially a work of the Father but of the Holy Spirit, the Comforter. The Scripture says, "No man can say that Jesus is the Lord, but by the Holy Ghost" (1 Corinthians 12:3). It is the work of the Holy Spirit to bring us to know Jesus so we may recognize Him as the Son of God, our only Savior from sin, and, therefore, as the way to the Father. The Holy Spirit shows us the Son through the Scriptures, which are also His workmanship. He spoke by the prophets. It was He who got hold of certain men and brought them to point to Christ and tell what God was up to in His redeeming work. Through that word of Scripture, written and spoken, the Holy Spirit is active, getting at people, getting them to know Christ, and through Him making them the children of the Father. The Holy Spirit does not point to Himself. He gets behind us or in us through the Gospel and swings us round so we see Jesus for what He is, Son of the Father and our Savior. "I believe that I cannot by my own reason or strength believe in Jesus Christ . . . but the Holy Spirit has called me by the Gospel . . . and kept me in the true faith" (Luther's Small Catechism). That is the one true faith that holds to God in Christ, reconciling the world to Himself, not imputing their trespasses to them, that is, bringing forgiven sinners to the Father. "Behold, what manner of love the Father has bestowed upon us, that we should be called the sons of God" (1 John 3:1).

Have you noticed how in all that we have said of the Holy Trinity we have spoken of what God does? He is the living God and is known best by His actions—above all, His redeeming action in Christ. It is in His actions that God has revealed Himself as a three-personed God, and we confess the mystery of the Holy Trinity most fully when we speak of His actions. We can't make much sense of the relationship. For that reason the Apostles' Creed is the greatest of the three ecumenical creeds, for it declares quite simply what the triune God does: creates, redeems, sanctifies. God rings through most clearly in these great saving verbs.

The Nicene and the Athanasian Creeds became necessary when people began to say things about God that called into question what God does. So it was that when Arius maintained that the Son is not eternal but a creature of the Father, the whole redeeming work of Christ was called into question. For if He who redeemed us is not altogether God, then His death is only a man's death, and there is no forgiveness and salvation accomplished for us. It was Athanasius who saw this most clearly and heroically defended the truth of Christ's deity at the Council of Nicaea in the year A.D. 325. In the creed drawn up as a result of that council, we have that glorious confession of "Jesus Christ, the only-begotten Son of God . . . being of one substance with the Father, by whom all things were made."

Some 100 years later the church had to defend the truth of God, for people were doubting the humanity of Christ or making Him subordinate to the Father. The whole matter of the relationship of the persons of the Holy Trinity was also called into question. The creed we confess on Trinity Sunday, like so many things in the church, just grew into use and was called the Athanasian Creed in honor of the great defender of the deity of Christ at Nicaea. Because of its so careful statement of the doctrine of the Holy Trinity, we confess it on this, the Feast of the Holy Trinity. It is not merely a list of facts about God. However, when we confess these creeds, we may not suppose that we have got God solved, searched, found out, or that we have understood the mystery of the Holy Trinity. We have said what it has pleased God to show us of Himself. This we must say clearly, but no less and no more. God is bigger than both our understanding and His revelation of Himself to us. We understand the mystery of the Holy Trinity as little as grasshoppers. We are often baffled by God. We don't see it, we don't understand, but it is folly and arrogance to suppose we can attempt to work God out, to take Him to pieces and try to see how He works. "For who hath known the mind of the Lord?" (Romans 11:34).

But, my friends, we are not in utter and fearful ignorance, for while God has not shown us all of Himself (why would He?) and we can't fathom what He has told us, yet He has shown us Himself and all we need to know for our salvation. There is mercy and forgiveness for sinners, and how astonishingly clearly we see this, for He became a man to accomplish our salvation for us and arrange its sure delivery to us. God has put Himself within our grasp. He has expressed Himself in Jesus of Nazareth. He has chosen to be available to us through things of our human world, through words, water, bread, and wine. Within the means of grace, God makes Himself known to us, He imparts Himself and His salvation to us. There He would be found. It is folly to look elsewhere, though it pinches our pride to think of receiving God through a book, water, wine, and bread. Such pride is born of the thought that we can find God elsewhere and of ourselves. We cannot tell God who He is. God tells us.

God is only found by His disclosing Himself. We cannot come to Him. He comes to us, all the way. He is made known to us in reading and hearing His Word and in the Holy Sacraments. He shows us what He is like and bestows on us what Christ achieved. O God, show us ever Thyself and Thy salvation. This we pray for Thy triune name's sake, for we pray to the Father through the Son by the Holy Spirit.

AMEN.

Second Sunday after Pentecost

GALATIANS 1:1–10

CONCORDIA SEMINARY (1998)

The Galatians had it told to them straight and solid, no beating about the bush—there is good news and there is bad news. First, the good news. It is an apostle talking; therefore, it is not just his two bits' worth from men but through Jesus Christ and God the Father who raised Him from the dead. You can't get anything more solid than that.

So what follows? What comes of that? Churches are what comes from that. Not some isolated human specimens but joined together in church. The Galatians know who is being addressed, and to them another lot of foundational core data is given in the greeting: *Grace* is the first bestowing word. And with grace comes peace—the real thing—from God the Father and our Lord Jesus Christ. And what comes from Jesus Christ? He is the one who gave Himself for our sins to deliver us from the present age, according to the will of God and the Father to whom be glory for ever and ever. Amen.

Got that? You can't get any more Good News than that. But what follows, not going on in the Good News, the Gospel, that has been displaced by something called "another gospel." How can you tell the difference? By Christ. Another gospel has another Christ—not the one the apostle has just recalled the Galatians to, the one they have deserted. The apostle won't let them stop short of facing up to Christ. Knocking Paul out does not get them clear of Christ, the one they are replacing with another Christ.

Now that is something they are unwilling to admit. Nobody is challenging Christ. Oh dear, no. The problem is only in what more needs to be said about Christ. That can always be improved, expanded, interpreted relevant to our questions and problems, worked into our program. There must be something that we can show for it, and that best be what God expects and demands, like circumcision.

No one admits to adjusting Christ. "It's the Gospel we're working on." The apostle won't let them get away with that. Adjusted Gospel is adjusted Christ. And for an adjusted Gospel, you don't really finally need Christ. The apostle goes on to make that quite clear. Can you talk about a Gospel if Jesus had not been crucified? Then the stumbling block of the cross has been removed. Then Christ died to no purpose. The only Christ who is your Savior is the one crucified. The death He died there for your sins is your death for your sins. He did it in your place.

> I am crucified with Christ: nevertheless I live; yet not I, but Christ liveth in me: and the life which I now live in the flesh I live by the faith of the Son of God, who loved me, and gave Himself for me. I do not frustrate the grace of God: for if righteousness come by the law, then Christ is dead in vain. (Galatians 2:20–21)

To pervert the Gospel of Christ is to nullify the grace of God. Then Christ died to no purpose.

If that is the Christ you are talking about, then you have fallen away from grace. There can't be much worse bad news than that. It is the rejection, the opposite, of the Good News. The Good News was all about what Christ has done. They have turned away from Him to something else, something that they call "gospel," running it still under Christ's name. Tricky business.

That is bad enough, but there is still worse bad news that targets those who have been preaching another gospel. They get the straight curse. The preachers of another gospel do not come straight out against Christ. The apostle says, "Watch out—they are not straightforward." He gives some clues to help us recognize what is going on. "They make much of you"—persuasive talkers. What are they working you toward? They may indeed say lots of nice things in praise of Christ. Then comes the hook: "Oh, how I love Jesus, oh, how I love Jesus." Then if you want to make sure of Christ, there is something you better see to, you better work on. Christ plus something more. That "something more" that is added to Christ is clearly from people. This is quite clear when it is referenced to humans, evidenced by humans. The history of the church tells of the unapostolic succession of things added to Christ as "Christ clinchers," evidences that can show that Christ really works.

Look at us. Or, worse still, look at me. There is every variety of such infringement of Christ. Spot your own special one. What is it you look for to make Christ for sure? The preachers of another gospel in the churches of Galatia were thumping circumcision. Christ is great.

We don't deny all the good things that Paul has been telling you about Him, but if you want to be sure it is okay with you before God, you jolly well better be circumcised, for that is undoubtedly commanded by God. So they had God and His Law on their side—it is in the Bible.

The preachers nowadays who preach another gospel, what are they thumping as additions to Christ to make sure that it is okay with you before God? If He is blessing you, why is that? If you want to be sure of God's blessing, what is it you had better be doing? Are you tithing? Do you have more than one pair of shoes? Are you happy? Don't you want to be happy? Here is how to make it happen with Jesus. Let me tell you about me and my Jesus.

Faith plus obedience is not faith alone. It is not Christ alone. The apostle makes it clear that another gospel is not the Gospel at all. And what is not the Gospel is then clearly recognizable as the Law. And if that is how you want it with God, there is no bad news worse than that. There is Good News and there is bad news. Which is for you? Get it straight and clear. Read further in Galatians, all the way through until everything you add to Christ to make Him sure has been stripped away and you have nothing left to be sure of but only our Lord Jesus Christ who gave Himself for us and to deliver us from the present evil age according to the will of God the Father to whom be glory forever and ever. Amen.

No, not yet *Amen*. Be sure to read through chapters 5 and 6. There Paul seems to have three goes at ending the letter, like some sermons you may have heard. We are not saved by imitation of Paul but only by the message delivering Christ. That is the Gospel, which Paul was made an apostle by the Lord to proclaim. Sometime you too. Cast out the slave. You were baptized into Christ. Christ has set us free. Stand fast, and do not submit again to a yoke of slavery. If I was still pleasing men, I should not be a servant of Christ.

AMEN.

Third Sunday after Pentecost

LUKE 14:15–24

ZION ACADEMY (1996)

The Lord loves a banquet. He is happiest when His people are gathered at the table with Him. The Lord delights in giving out good things—ordinary, everyday things, and things far beyond the ordinary. It has always been that way. When He created the world, God was so pleased with it that He couldn't keep it for Himself and simply had to share it with some who would delight in it with Him. And there is always more—more than we could ever imagine. The solar system is quite a lot, more than enough, we would likely say. Then the Lord flings out the galaxies and nebulae and more beyond that. No two of anything the same, and on one tiny particular speck He puts water. "And God said, Let the waters bring forth abundantly the moving creature that hath life, and fowl that may fly above the earth in the open firmament of heaven" (Genesis 1:20).

Half a dozen different birds would surely be enough, perhaps a dozen kinds of fish. But no, we have some of the craziest looking fish. Some from deep down in the darkest depths of the sea we have only recently got pictures of. Only the Lord knew they were there all this time, but now we have cameras that can take pictures of them and we can wonder at them. "Why on earth did God make something like that?"

Why on earth did the Lord make something like you? There is only one like you—ever has been, ever will be. The Lord multiplies His delight. He doesn't have the same delight in any hundred of the same. He has a different delight in each unique one of us, and He invites us into delighting with Him in each one.

But we are so bent in on ourselves; we are what first engages our attention. There is no delight in that. That is the opposite of what we are created for, so we rebel against that fact as evidenced by our envious complaints: "Why does he have a quicker brain than I do?" "Why am I so fat? Just look at her lovely, wispy figure." "Why should I have to get on now with only one lung?" "Why can't I be like those beautiful people? rich people? aerobic people?" Even if people get what they envy others for, they are even more miserable because it didn't make them happy the way they thought it would. Measuring ourselves against others is the opposite of our delighting in what a unique mixture of things each one of us is.

The delight of each thing in paradise for its own uniqueness we are told of because each thing has its own name. The naming is the delighting in, the receipt as gift of each one—the way Durer receives a unique hare and squirrel and blade of grass. This one received, depicted, held up to the Lord. "Look, I have received this hare just as You have made it and given it to me to enjoy." And Durer doesn't just delight in that hare by himself; he draws us into enjoying it with him and the Lord. But sin said, "No, I won't have it that way. Unless I can say it is mine, without You in the picture, no thanks." After all, that is what it is like to be God, isn't it? Having everything for yourself and not having to thank anybody for it. Mine, that is how I want it. This is the way we are tempted to think about God; this is how we would like to be, if we were God, and we can only be like that if we get rid of Him as such a God. So rebel along with Satan, who thought that being God meant, above all, being number one, having the lot—mine.

That is the death of delight. Delight doesn't happen in you by yourself. It happens outside yourself: the hare, the squirrel, the blade of grass, the child in Zion Academy. Each one unique, named with baptismal identity, named with the name the Lord put on him or her with the water. That is who they are, as they are to Him, each one. Each with unique DNA, uniquely located. You are born where you were born: one father, one mother. The uniqueness that holds beyond all others is the uniqueness given you at your Baptism.

So far we have been mostly in the First Article, extolling the way the Lord does creation, but we couldn't be sure of things just that way. What clinched our Lord's delight in each one of us was His baptizing us. He says you are one of Mine, yes, you. My name I put on you with the water. You are the only one like you, so you can have delight in all My gifts to you as I delight in your crinkly ears, gray hair, funny belly button, and eyes that speak like nobody else's. But that is going on in the Third Article with the life of faith, life lived as nothing but given to, but there wouldn't be any of that without the Second Article. If you say Second Article in Zion Academy, they will know what that is, recite it from the catechism, and if they know it, there is a chance they may be glad of it—someday.

The Second Article delights in Jesus. In Luke 14, He is on His way to Jerusalem, to Zion. Jesus tells of a banquet. It is an old picture of how the Lord delights to dish out His good things, drawing us into the enjoyment and delight of them with Him. "Thou preparest a table before me . . . my cup runneth over" (Psalm 23:5). "They shall be abundantly satisfied with the fatness of Thy house; and Thou shalt make them drink of the river of Thy pleasures" (Psalm 36:8).

Who wouldn't want to be there? One of those who sat at the table with Jesus exclaimed, "Blessed is he who shall eat bread in the kingdom of God." Now you couldn't say it better than that, but Jesus won't let it rest just saying the pious words, especially if the piety pushes things off to some other time and place—"No, not now. Later." Jesus cares more for that man than to leave him with only his okay-for-Sunday-morning talk of the kingdom of God as if it were some far-off thing and not there where Jesus is kinging it as He speaks and gives out His gifts.

The Lord has been working as the sort of Lord He really is for a long time. Those to whom He first spoke today's parable have a long history of His dealing with them as His people, of His inviting them to His banquet. First, the advance invitation, which they accepted, then the second, "Come, for all is now ready." With our Lord's parables, they can't say it both ways at the same time: The way it goes as He wants it to go, or the way it goes wrong. Today's parable tells how things went wrong with the Lord's invitation to His great banquet. They had agreed to come, then some things more important claimed their attention—perhaps another time when they could fit the Lord in.

The first people invited may have assumed they had an invitation to the banquet coming to them. Of course they would be invited; they were among those who couldn't not be invited, and thinking that way, they added up whether to go to the banquet or whether to attend to something more important. Measuring things up that way destroys a gift. The Lord turns away from those who scorn His gifts. He won't stop giving out His good things, and Jesus tells them of His giving to those to whom His gifts are clearly nothing but gifts, to those who would never suppose they had such good things coming to them.

The way of today's parable is the negative way, how it goes when it doesn't go the way the Lord wants it to go. Because it is a gift, it is rejectable. This may be seen in those in Israel who time and again rejected the Lord who has Himself a people only in the gift-giving way. We are in the middle of Luke; Jesus is moving steadily toward His ultimate rejection. Jesus has warned:

> O Jerusalem, Jerusalem, which killest the prophets, and stonest them that are sent unto thee; how often would I have gathered thy children together, as a hen doth gather her brood under her wings, and ye would not! Behold, your house is left unto you desolate: and verily I say unto you, Ye shall not see Me, until the time come when ye shall say, Blessed is He that cometh in the name of the Lord. (Luke 13:34–35)

When will the Lord come? The Lord comes to Zion, to Jerusalem, with His words He speaks to you. This parable warns and calls us to repentance—all our taking Him for granted, all our fitting Him in to second, third, last place, or finally no place (that is, hell), subordinate to our priorities. Are you surprised at all that He has given you here at Zion? Not surprising at all, what we have coming to us, we are Zion Church, we are.

To the repentant, the Good News is that the Lord does not give up. He won't let Himself be made into a god we can manage with our measurements. He goes on being the Lord who won't stop giving, won't stop inviting to His banquet. The Lord's banquet is extolled in the psalms sung in the assembly, where His words and His Sacraments give out the gifts. "They shall be abundantly satisfied with the fatness of Thy house" (Psalm 36:8).

As part of the house you have here at school, as was the way with the temple of old in Zion, where Jesus attended when He went up to Zion as a boy of 12. Couldn't keep Him away. Zion Church, Zion Academy, two things? No, not really, the gifts given in the assembly through our Lord's Word and Sacraments live on and grow into the lives of our children, now and on through all life's days, on to the final fulfillment of those gifts in the ultimate festivities of the banquet beyond measure. He would like you to be there.

All goes well when everybody involved remembers in whose house the banquet goes on and the gifts the Lord has, each one there for the giving of: liturgy, singing and gym, arithmetic and prayers—the way the parts of the body work together, as St. Paul says—Christ's body. But today it is not body but banquet, a great load of good things to be identified, named, enjoyed. What gifts are you there for?

In our Lord's great household, there are lots of people doing lots of things that all go into the celebration of the great banquet, so many things to be seen to, so many gifts to have, each its own delight. We thought earlier of each child uniquely delighted in Zion Academy, also learning the names of things in our Lord's astonishing creation, in heaven and on earth, our own bodies, what makes us tick, what enlivens us together in music and song, and in Zion Academy what it means to live our lives in the way of delight in our Lord's gifts, the life of faith, the life we are made alive with at our Baptisms, and that life nurtured, nourished, and exercised in the whole range of the way the life of faith is lived. That takes learning, schooling, practicing. So Zion Academy, but Zion Academy and all connected together from the Lord. Zion Academy not a separate thing from the church, the church not a separate thing from the academy. So you have called Pastor Brondos to be pastor and headmaster. Is he for church, or is he for academy? You have said here at Zion that church and academy are not alternatives. It is the gifts of the Lord so many, each unique, that you would delight in to the full.

"To the full" sounds like a banquet, only with ordinary banquets, we reach a point where we say, "I couldn't eat another mouthful." Our Lord's banquet is no ordinary banquet. At His banquet the more you eat, the more you can eat, the greater delight in His gifts, some you can't even imagine. "Open thy mouth wide, and I will fill it" (Psalm 81:10), says the Lord. All the great things of His banquet will be thus delighted in and relished as His gifts when first comes, "O LORD, open Thou my lips; and my mouth shall shew forth Thy praise" (Psalm 51:15).

Liturgy and botany and arithmetic, languages and music, how to sing, how to speak, how to think: "Think the things that are right, and by Your merciful guiding accomplish them." The Lord's banquet has ordinary things and things far beyond the ordinary, the gifts flowing from the generous hands of the man who gave a great banquet, who gives a great banquet, and sent His servant to those who had been invited: "Come, for all is now ready."

AMEN.

Fourth Sunday after Pentecost

Luke 15:1–7

London (1954)

Last Sunday Jesus was with respectable people—rich, religious, honored people. It was a fine house and a sumptuous supper. When Jesus was invited, He went. He did not despise or scorn those people because they were rich. Jesus did not come just for the sake of the poor or just for the sake of the rich. How much money a person had was not the important thing. He had come for all, not for all vaguely and in general but because each single man, woman, and child needed Him.

The people Jesus had supper with last Sunday did not feel that they had need of Him because they felt quite sure of themselves. They lived decent lives. They were prominent in the church. They were leaders among God's chosen people. They had the Scriptures, the Law and promises of God. They were the seed of Abraham on whom God must surely look with satisfaction. When Jesus came their way, they were interested in what He had to say. People were talking about this man from Nazareth. They wanted to look Him over, to confirm their views and prejudices, their opinions of themselves. Jesus would be, perhaps, useful for their purposes, or they would have to take Him to pieces and set Him straight according to their way of thinking. But whether He came or not, whether He made interesting conversation or was merely an opinionated and boring son of a Nazarene carpenter didn't concern them deeply and certainly wouldn't make any difference to them. That there might be need of a change in themselves, that they might need or be deeply influenced by Him was far from their thinking. That Jesus might be their Lord they didn't even consider.

To these people Jesus spoke some hard words. Jesus does not allow Himself to be considered in this detached and condescending way. Jesus forces us to face up to God. When we confront Christ, we must say either yes or no to God, and God can't be taken in just a little dose.

Jesus' hosts last Sunday felt they did not need God or acted as if they had God in their pockets. When God came to them in Christ and called them to Himself, they all, with one consent, began to make excuses. Other things were more important to them. They wanted to keep their lives and interests intact. They were well satisfied with themselves and their lives. They felt no need. Therefore, from Jesus they received nothing—nothing but rejection. Of His supper they did not taste.

Today Jesus is the guest with a different set of people. These are the riffraff, the poor, the despised. The sort of people you wouldn't want to be associated with if you valued what people might say. Their lives hadn't turned out so well. They had failed of respectability and success and had given themselves to all manner of loose living to fill up their hollow, sinful lives. When Jesus visited them, He didn't have to tell them that they had gone astray and wandered far from God. They knew that quite well. Their trouble was that they doubted whether God would have any use for them. They saw their need and looked to Jesus.

When Jesus received them and went to have supper with them in their home, the respectable people complained. "How can this man be a man of God if He associates with that sort of people?" They were anxious about the cause of God—their sort of God. It was unhallowing God's name for a man who claimed to speak for God to be mixed up with such disreputable people. God's business was with the good people, the decent and respectable, with people like themselves.

How completely they misunderstood God's business Jesus shows in the parable of the lost sheep. God's business is bringing and keeping lost sheep close to Himself that they may be forgiven and have the achievement and joy that God wants them to have. Jesus came to give all that to us. When some said that they didn't need Him, Jesus turned to others who knew their need. It was not that He approved of their sin but that they needed Him so badly. Last Sunday it was the poor, the lame, and the blind that received the fellowship and food of Christ. Today it is the lost sheep.

Now a sheep is the most helpless and foolish of all animals—*Schafskopf* ("mutton head"). Sheep need constant care, watching, and protection. By themselves they are an easy prey. All is well with them only when they stay close together within the shepherd's care. They can't get along alone. So when Jesus calls us sheep, He is saying some basic things about us. We should cling together close to the Shepherd. But the big point of today's parable is about the sheep that goes wrong and gets lost.

If you have ever heard the bleating of a lamb that is separated from the flock and lost, you will know how pitiful its plight is. Its peril and need are great, and to this need a good shepherd makes ready response. A hireling will, of course, not worry much, for what is a single sheep here or there among so many? A hireling thinks only of the less or more of his own advantage. The shepherd to whom the sheep belong has quite another feeling. He does not think numerically but individually. When one sheep goes astray and is in danger, he leaves the ninety and nine and goes after the one that is lost until he finds it.

This is not a more or less in Jesus' love for any particular sheep. He does not love the ninety and nine the less because He leaves them and goes in search of the one that is lost. He would do the same for each one of them. A good mother loves all her children, but when one of them gets sick, then she gives all her attention to that child, worries and cares for it so the sick child may soon be better again. This does not mean that she has ceased to love her other children, but the one child is sick and needs her special love and care. As it is with a good mother, so it is with a good shepherd. Special need calls for special care. All this we have experienced.

The lost sheep is, first, me. Most of us have been with the flock since infancy, with the community of God's people among whom alone is our safety and welfare. You can't be a member of the flock in isolation. A sheep that is separated from the flock is a lost sheep. There are times when we have gone our own way, deserted the flock and the shepherd. Left to ourselves we would perish, drugged and poisoned by the noxious weeds of the world, a prey of that lion who walketh about seeking whom he may devour, and torn by the sharp teeth of fear and uncertainty.

But the Good Shepherd would not let us perish. He came after us, patiently and lovingly, and carried us back on His shoulders to the flock. On our wounds and injuries Jesus poured the balm of forgiveness, and for our hunger He gave the food of His Word and the fellowship of His family. If we are in the flock today, we must confess it is because Jesus has so often come after us and carried us back.

When we stray, we know that it is we who stray; when we are brought back, we know it is He who has brought us back. It is of the Lord's mercy that we can call ourselves "His" today and hereafter. Here is our reliance and our certainty, not in our respectability or decent lives or anything of us. It is only in the unfailing mercy of our Shepherd, so patient and so good.

To be in the flock means to be guided by the Shepherd, to follow His bidding and example, and that means sharing His concern for the lost sheep. We may not, like the Pharisees, ignore the lost sheep and write them off as not good enough, not fit to be associated with Christ and ourselves. Nor may we, like the prodigal's elder brother, resent the special effort for the lost son and claim that if anybody is to be bothered, it must be me.

We know ourselves to have been so often lost sheep. We know what it means to be a lost sheep, to be found, and to be borne back to the flock on the shoulders of the Shepherd. We want other lost sheep to know that too. We do not have to look far to find lost sheep. Within the circle of our own family and friends we find them. Near us there are many wandering, lost from the Shepherd and the flock. There was one person who recently told the visitors, "We have seen people from your church go past on their way to church for years and years, but nobody ever invited us to come."

When we go after the lost sheep and seek them out, we show Jesus what it means to us that He has sought us out and brought us back to the fold. In doing this we are promised a share in the angels' joy. This joy is God's goal for us. Joy is never in isolation. Separate from Christ and His flock this joy is lost to us. His joy is in us knit together, sharing the angels' joy over lost people brought to life in Christ. This joy is ours in giving our lives to the Good Shepherd who gave His life for the sheep.

AMEN.

Fifth Sunday after Pentecost

LUKE 6:41–42

HOLDEN VILLAGE (1971)

Why do we laugh at Charlie Chaplin? He is the little man paddling along with the sad face who is always being bumped into, tripped up, pushed around, and always getting the short end of the stick. He is the little man battling a world that keeps knocking him down. We see ourselves and identify with him, we recognize the wrongness of it all. Our hearts go out to him. But first we laugh, we laugh and laugh. Then we may feel like crying. It is so close to being true.

When Jesus gives us the ridiculous picture of a speck in one man's eye and a log in our own that we do not notice because we are so intent on spotting the speck in the other man's eye, we laugh, too, if we have not altogether lost the freshness of vision of a child. But after the chuckle at the comic picture, we recognize it is too close to being true to be only funny, and if we feel like crying, let it be a brimming flood, for it is a log that has to be washed away. Some logs not even Railroad Creek seems to be able to budge.

The kick in the tail of Jesus' story is to self-knowledge and so repentance. The first item of business is the log in your own eye. After that is removed, you may be able to help your neighbor with the speck in his or her eye. The first sins to be acknowledged are your own, not somebody else's. We often do a better job confessing other people's sins and pointing them out: their lack of love, their pride, their prejudice, their lack of understanding. Against such a dark backdrop our own virtues shine the more sharply. We are not like those benighted people. We are then a matter for admiration by others and God. And we can do it so piously: "I thank You, God, that I am not as other people are."

Our log is not only so large but also so near to us that it blocks our vision and we do not even see it. Jesus is the one who gives sight to the blind. He reaches out His hand to our log and pulls it out. "This must go. I want you to see." Jesus takes the logs out of our eyes. He drags them to Calvary, and on the timber that blinds and kills, He is killed. Jesus dies for our sins, and the wood we have supplied becomes, by His death, a declaration of that sin's forgiveness.

When the logs from our eyes have been through Calvary, we see. We see Jesus on the cross supplied by us, for us. We see ourselves as forgiven sinners. Then, when we bump into another sinner, we are able to help, for love comes sideways. We know the things that contradict Christ and the pain and ruin they work. We want each person we meet to be freed of them, and we are there to help him or her.

Most specks in our eyes hurt like hell, yet we can't get them out by ourselves. Often we can't even see them. As a boy, when there was a speck in my eye—gouging around my eyeball like those rocks in the glaciers that Floyd has been talking to us about—I would go to my father. He would take a handkerchief—it had to be a clean and lamb white handkerchief—and press a corner to a point. Then he would take hold of the eyelashes and pull back the lid. "Hold still. Don't flinch." Then in would come the enormous whiteness and out would come the dirt. Happy eye, and such relief was like forgiveness. My mother was not good at it because she was too afraid of hurting me. As for my brother, well, when he put drops in my eyes, he made it a fiendish exercise in high altitude bombing. I wasn't blessed with a sister; only heaven knows what she would have been like.

Holden is not only great for glorious mountains but also for getting splinters in your hands and elsewhere. At Holden you bump into people you don't feel fit to be in with. You just feel shabby in comparison with them. They get splinters, too, but who are you to help them get rid of their splinters? If you love them, you will. If you love them, you will cut any self-regarding humility fandango and just deal straight and clean with them. "Let me help you get that splinter out. Hold still. Don't flinch. There it is. See it?" We throw it away.

Your willingness to help will not always be appreciated. People get used to splinters, carry them around, forget them, or sometimes even boast of them. "Look at the size of the splinter I have." So it is usually easier to pretend not to notice. You will get along much more smoothly if you let them slide past you and stroke their ego as they go. Why risk a superficially satisfactory relationship? Risk it is, and it is bound to turn out bad if you come to them down from above and not sideways, or better still from below. Love comes as a servant, there for that person. Love cannot not care. Love takes the risk of losing esteem, of being the easygoing good person. Love grows through these risks, through possible resentment to the possibility of being for the other something more, something for his or her good.

Perhaps your best friend is someone you got mad at when he or she made you aware of how you were putting people down, blocking off love, or hurting someone. We often do that unaware, and it is helpful to be made aware of it. It may hurt, but how else will we get rid of the things that damage and block the flow of love? My real friends do not tell me what a wonderful chap I am. They are not such fools. I know they want my good. A true friend levels with you.

Scripture bids us to thank God for the person who hits us straight in the face with the truth, and that is not just about spraying the right brand of stuff into our armpits as the way to happiness. There are things, though, that do hinder happiness, all the things we do to block happiness or hurt others. A friend will help us see them and help us get rid of them. Before you can thank God for such a friend, you must have embraced Him, and you will be growing then toward being such a friend.

But for heaven's sake, don't go round hunting for specks in people's eyes. You have some logs to confess, logs to be pulled out and dragged to Calvary. Cleansed and forgiven, you may then see as a servant sees, as a burden-bearing Savior sees. Lord, take from us, though it hurts, all that blinds us and hinders the flow of Your love.

AMEN.

Sixth Sunday after Pentecost

LUKE 21:25–38

CONCORDIA SEMINARY (1984)

You know that summer is near or summer is here. Can you be sure? Well, not yet anyway, at least not last week. St. Louis has a foul summer. If it is not foul, it is not summer, or it is not St. Louis. *Tertium non datur*. It is St. Louis, and so it is not summer. Actually, it must be the jet stream that is out of whack. Aristotle, who was at the cutting edge of natural science, had explanations for almost everything. But he didn't know about the jet stream.

Martin Luther didn't know about the jet stream either. What Luther knew about was faith. That is Jesus, for sure. Luther observed that there was no lack of people who had explanations for all the spectacular things in this apocalyptic passage, Luke 21. There were plausible explanations and natural explanations, even without knowing about the jet stream. Confronted by these explanations, we can get into a hassle with them, attempting some better explanations, or even come up with some reliable calculations, and miss the whole point—faith. Jesus.

There is a lot of heavy stuff in Luke 21 before we come to today's Gospel, today's Good News. The fig tree is good news. Consider how the fig tree grows, gaunt in winter, all its leaves stripped off, stark, bare branches, quite dead, finished. Not so. Around Nisan, fresh leaves come alive, sprout, and grow. On the old branches, the first figs fall.

Later, on the new growth, there comes a further crop of fruit. Now before we slip into any calculations or alluring allegory, we need to be reminded that the fig tree was a parable, a disclosure of Jesus, with a point of comparison: "As surely as the fig tree puts forth leaves, so surely summer is near. So surely Jesus is bringing His work to completion." In our Gospel, that work is called the kingdom of God. All that belongs to the kingdom of God will surely be accomplished.

During the generation contemporary with Jesus and during this generation, while there are still Jews, all things will be accomplished for the kingdom of God. Jesus still yearns to be their Messiah until the end. Yet Messiah's work was soon to be accomplished that same week. After the death, resurrection, and ascension of Jesus and the sending of His Spirit, the next and last big thing will be the Son of Man coming in a cloud with power and great glory in summer's full harvest.

We live in the time between. The parable of the fig tree tells of Jesus of whom we can be sure. Anything that suggests we cannot be sure of Him, that there has been some slip-up, that perhaps His promises cannot be trusted, is a contradiction of the message of the parable of the fig tree. If you can't be quite sure of Jesus, then the temptation is to attempt some faithless shoring up. If we can get a handle on the signs, then we may show that Jesus is actually not off course or behind on the timetable. Or we give our readings of what is going on: With the proliferation of nuclear warheads, any day some fool may press the button and we would be wiped out. But we here will have worked out a way in which the Lord might be able to manage the end of the world. "The heavens being on fire shall be dissolved, and the elements shall melt with fervent heat" (2 Peter 3:12). Now we have the bombs to do it. Or if the world won't be fried by the sun getting too hot, it will be frozen by the sun cooling off.

The old liberal theology was buried in the mud of the trenches of the first World War. A secularized kingdom of God was not in the cards. And utopian Marxism gives way to *Realpolitik*. Not much of a future, not much hope, so grab what you can, while you can. World pessimism has had a considerable run, and there are signs of a swing to optimism. America has turned around. Reagan is in the White House, all is right with the world. But the Democrats tell us what a hash Reagan's made of it, on the brink of disaster. The politicians, as they give their readings, will occasionally make a respectful reference to God, sometimes even linking Him with their promises, usually with a pluralistic vagueness. All of this can be so in the forefront of our thinking that we quite forget about the fig tree, about "fig tree" Jesus. As surely as the new leaves mean summer is near, so surely Jesus is doing His work through it all, bringing to completion the kingdom of God.

Where is the kingdom of God? The kingdom of God is where Jesus is king. Where I live is where Jesus is king, say the faithful. The message of the fig tree and of the signs is given only to faith. That is sure Jesus. All our past He has taken on Himself. All our future is His sure gift, as the fig tree says. So we have a present, a Jesus present. No absent Jesus, no delaying Jesus, but present Jesus, for we are given His words that tell of Him and bestow what they say by the working of His Spirit. Heaven and earth and all the evidences they may supply are not so sure as His words.

Summer school is extra time for new growth in Jesus' words in us, even if we can't be quite sure that it is really summer. For those who have heard the message of the parable of the fig tree, for those who live in the present sure of Jesus, sure of His words, as sure as He is sure, there is no time to escape into fluctuating optimisms and pessimisms. There is simply not enough time to do the things that are ours to do where He is king.

The ways of Jesus' kingship are given us through His sure words. For they are more sure than anything or everything in heaven and earth. We close our eyes to nothing. Only faith can have the courage to face it all without blinking, without suppressing or inflating any of the evidence. A spade is a spade and Jesus is a fig tree Jesus. Hence, the watchfulness, the sober realism, the bottom-of-it-all confidence that it is the Son of Man before whom we stand, the Son of Man of whom Daniel speaks, the Son of Man who gave His life as a ransom for many, the Son of Man who was lifted up and who cried, "It is accomplished." That fact holds through it all. The one who sits on the throne to judge is the same one enthroned on the cross. Jesus' dominion is an everlasting dominion that shall not pass away, and His kingdom is one that shall not be destroyed. The tree bears its fruit. The fig tree and vine give their full yield.

Is that where you live? Is that where you do summer school? The answer is not from ourselves or from our calculation, but only from Christ, from His words. So let us pray in His name and build our lives and our prayers on His words.

Amen.

Seventh Sunday after Pentecost

MATTHEW 11:25–30

HOLDEN VILLAGE (1978)

If being a Christian is something that makes you groan, you have almost certainly got it wrong. Burdens are for groaning under, and burdens are what Jesus is talking about in our Gospel. If you have burdens, then it is to you that Jesus calls: "Come unto Me, all ye that labour and are heavy laden, and I will give you rest. Take My yoke upon you, and learn of Me" (Matthew 11:28–29).

Yoke is a word used of the Law. The burden of the Law Jesus had Himself shown the heaviness of in those parts of the Sermon on the Mount that make quite clear we cannot bear it no matter how hard we try, and only in the trying, only in laboring at it, do we know the heavy load, a load we cannot bear. We cannot qualify for God's favor by our performance in keeping His commandments. We are sinners.

Jesus bids us in these Gospel words to come to Him and bring our heavy load, give over all that laboring to justify ourselves, all that yoke of the Law, to Him. He relieves us of all that. What we cannot bear, Jesus bears for us. He carries that yoke for us, fulfills the Law for us. Its condemnation on our sin He bears for us, for on Him is laid the burden of the iniquity of us all. The death for sin Jesus dies in our place. The forsakenness of God, which is for our sin, He takes in our place, for He is the sin-bearer for us all, the Lamb of God who takes away the sin of the world.

Then Jesus gives us His yoke. It is a happy exchange: Jesus, I am your sin; You are my righteousness. Our yoke of sin He takes and bears for us, then gives us His yoke. What a yoke, though! Never such a yoke as this, really no yoke at all, as is shown by the paradox of its opposite canceling it out. Yoke easy, burden light. What is light is no burden, and what is easy is no yoke. We know how this is from the cross. It is dread death for sin, forsakenness of God, that is ours, that is His, that is ours. Jesus gives His cross to us and with it forgiveness, acceptance. God is our Father as surely as Jesus is His Son who exchanges yokes with us, and the yoke that is ours from Him is easy. The whole heart's ease and happy freedom of one of Christ's own is in that "easy" that Jesus lays on us. It is how you feel when the heavy pack comes off and you take off your heavy boots and your feet can't believe the ease and the lightness of walking. That is in the word *light* when Jesus says, "My burden is light," a word that has in it quick, nimble, capering, as when we say of some who dance that they are light of foot.

That is our Jesus on our Holden altar. Dancing Jesus, light of foot, down on one foot, and the other up toward the next part of the dance. And what does He have that He is about to throw us from His right hand? A ball, an apple, or a donut? And decking Jesus' left, a cloth. Is it a serape or a towel? It could be either, depending on what is next in the dance. It could be a shroud, but from Him it wouldn't be a shroud anymore, but something for going to the big dance in, or to lay aside at the door.

With this Jesus you can't predict, demand, force, or commandeer. The Law can do that, but no Law can hold captive the One who is gentle and lowly of heart. He is free; He has taken all that the old Law could do to crush Him. That yoke is not there for Jesus, or for us for whom He bore that yoke. We move in contradiction of Him when we crawl back under that yoke as if it is still ours to bear in the pride of our doing it, not He, and the more we groan, the more proof of our doing it. Far too sadly much of Christian piety is in the dreary and groaning contradiction of this word of Jesus and of His cross that is ours, too, our life and our joy. What would have destroyed us is dealt with at Calvary by Jesus. Whatever comes now in laughter and in tears, we are in it together with Jesus. What is with Him is not for groaning. To those who don't know Jesus, it may appear we have an awful heavy load. For us it is what He happens to have us into with Him. Listen to Luther and hear the singing nevertheless:

> The world looks upon it as heavy and more than we can bear, but it is not, for we have one with us who is a good companion, as the saying goes, "The singing goes great when you have a good companion." Two can carry a burden easily, that would be too much for one.

With the Jesus yoke, we can only be crushed if He gets crushed too. He has been there, and on from Calvary no more yoke of Law, of sin, of sin's death, but forgiveness, life with Him, dance with Him, singing with Him. Not by might or by power but Jesus, the gentle and lowly of heart, is Lord of the dance. He bids us join in, learn of Him, and dance free. The yoke He gives in exchange is easy, and His burden light.

AMEN.

Eighth Sunday after Pentecost

1 Corinthians 10:13b

London (1955)

The Iroquois had a custom for a young boy. When it was time for him to be made a man and to be numbered with the braves, he was put through some hard training. One of the things intended to make a man out of the boy was the requirement that he spend a night camped alone deep in the forest. In some small clearing, he would build his little fire and watch and wait through the eerie night. From the surrounding darkness came the weird noises of the forest and the cries of the wild animals. The gleam of threatening, furtive eyes out of the blackness might fill the lad with fear, but if he got scared and ran home to mother, he was disgraced. He was not yet a man. If he bravely held his ground, then he was clearly growing into a man.

It seems cruel and rash to expose a boy to danger and risk his life like this, but it really wasn't. High up in a tree near the boy sat his father with his bow ready. His father was watching over him all the time. The lad was quite safe, and it was making a man of him. This was the boy's temptation. He was put to the test. The temptation would show what sort of a lad he was, and the temptation would change him. If, in fright, he fled from the forest, he was more cowardly than before, but if he bravely held his ground, he had grown into more of a man and could be numbered with the braves.

God is interested in who we are and in changing us into braver, bigger people for Him so He exercises our faith. Thus for Adam and Eve, God put the tree of the knowledge of good and evil in Eden and told our parents that they were not to eat of it. Each time they passed that tree, they showed whose and who they were and became changed. Each time they said no to the tree, they said yes to God. They showed that they were His and loyal to His word. Each affirmation of their being God's children made them bigger and stronger in their loyalty and love toward God.

The Scripture also tells how God tempted Abraham and what a fearful temptation that was! Isaac was given to Abraham in his old age, and God promised that from him would come a great nation and blessing. Now God told Abraham to sacrifice Isaac. What of the promise and what of the killing? We cannot imagine the anguish that must have torn at the heart of Abraham as he went up Mount Moriah with his boy. The lad said, "Behold the fire and the wood: but where is the lamb for a burnt offering?" (Genesis 11:7). Abraham said, "God will provide Himself a lamb" (11:8). God! Despite the arguments of his heart and his reason, Abraham stuck to God. God had said so, and so it must be. In this temptation Abraham showed who he was—a faithful man of God. When he came down from Mount Moriah, he was a bigger and stronger man of God.

Here we have two instances of how God, dealing directly with His children, tempted them. The Scripture tells also of the devil's tempting. Satan, cast out by God because of his rebellion, set himself to destroy all that God designed of happiness and beauty. In serpent's form he came to Eve and tempted her (Genesis 3:1–6). Temptation here again showed who they were and changed them. Adam and Eve were disloyal to God, their Father. They became sinners, guilty and scared of God. If Eve had stood her ground, remained faithful to God, said no to the devil and yes to God, she would have been a bigger and stronger child of God. But she said yes to Satan and cursed and crippled herself. In temptation there is always this either/or, plus or minus, growth or decay, blessing or curse.

The two sides of temptation we see clearly in the case of Job—Satan bent on destruction, God bent on blessing, all in one and the same temptation. God permitted Satan first to ravage Job's property, then to ravage Job's body. It is a moving history. There were the temptations of the so-called comforters and of Job's wife. There was the sin of Job in cursing the day of his birth, but ultimately, in the depth of his desolation, the faithful man cried, "Though He slay me, yet will I trust in Him" (Job 13:15). Job knew that his Redeemer was not dead but was the living God who would bring him through. Out of his fearful temptations, Job had grown a bigger and stronger man of God. The blessing of God was on him.

We should pause here to consider the question of responsibility. Why does God tempt or permit temptation? Is God to be blamed for the resulting curse and damage? A ghastly thought! God cannot be blamed. He is never responsible for evil. His purpose is to bless His children. To bless, God allows the risk of temptation, but it is a calculated risk. Our text is His promise that He will never allow a temptation "beyond what we are able." Therefore, if we sin when tempted, we cannot blame God. We are responsible. It could have been a blessing for us. That is what God wanted it to be, but we rejected the blessing in consenting to sin. The temptation that curses is never the will of God. This is the temptation of which the Small Catechism speaks when it says, "God tempts no one." And Scripture says, "Let no man say when he is tempted, I am tempted of God: for God cannot be tempted with evil, neither tempteth He any man: But every man is tempted when he is drawn away of his own lust, and enticed" (James 1:13–14).

The temptation that curses is the temptation of Satan. So he tempted Eve, intending her misery, and so he tempted Job. But here we see the wonder of God, beyond our understanding, that He uses Satan and would make even the evil-intentioned temptations of Satan serve His purpose. God would turn the temptations of Satan to the blessing of His children. God would have us grow. God could destroy Satan by His almighty power, but He wants us to grow into such men and women so we are able to get the victory over the evil one. He does not want us to stop growing; therefore, He does not stop temptations coming to us. Despite themselves and what they want to achieve, the devil, the world, and our flesh are made to serve the purpose of God.

The world, as the Scriptures and the catechism speak of it in this connection, is not the creation as such, not the trees, the stars, the birds, or my fingernails, but everything about us that strives to drag us away from God. The pride and power of this world are such temptations. A Brother of ours was presented with this temptation when He was taken by Satan to a high mountain and shown all the kingdoms of the world and all their glory and all their power. Most potent among the temptations of the world is the love of money. Money can be an instrument of blessing, but to many it signifies pride and power. It becomes a god in which they put their trust, and in its acquisition, people think their lives complete when others judge the success of their lives by the amount of money they have, or they suppose they will be happy and solve all their problems if they would win the pools. Of those who fall to this temptation of the world and set their hearts on money, the Scripture says:

> But they that will be rich fall into temptation and a snare, and into many foolish and hurtful lusts, which drown men in destruction and perdition. For the love of money is the root of

all evil: which while some coveted after, they have erred from the faith and pierced themselves through with many sorrows. (1 Timothy 6:9–10)

Another great source of temptation is the enemy within the camp, the fifth column agent of the world and the devil. This is the flesh of which we heard last week, the part of us that does not acknowledge Christ as Lord but pulls away from Him. The flesh, the old man, is a most persuasive tempter. He is part of us and presents his temptations as in our own interest. The flesh always argues in favor of putting me first. Whenever we have the opportunity to reach out and help another person, to share with them what we have, the flesh immediately questions, "Why bother about him? What is he to you? Why don't you just take care of yourself—nobody else will."

From the flesh come so many temptations to selfishness, which is the denial of love, which is the denial of Christ. Each temptation from the devil, the world, and our flesh is intended for our harm. Each would put us wrong with God. Each would have us say something untrue to God and treat Him as a different sort of God than He is.

Remember that when Satan tempted Eve, his first endeavor was to make her doubt God. He tried to make her not quite sure of God and of what He said. The satanic suggestion was, "Yea, hath God said?" (Genesis 3:1). When Satan makes us unsure of God, he has more than half won the victory. To Job came the temptation to think that God was a deserter. Job's wife wondered why he would stick to a god who allowed him to suffer like this? "Curse God, and die" (Job 2:9). But Job was sure of God in the end. Abraham was sure of God. One stands amazed at the faith of the man. God was contradicting Himself. God against God. God had spoken the promise of a son to Abraham whom he was now told to sacrifice. That was it. Abraham knew God was faithful, that is, God is true, true to His promises. He cannot become another sort of God. What He says stands firm.

Eve sinned because she did not hold God to be faithful. She distrusted God. She thought of God as different from the God who had spoken to her. Temptation to evil is always deceitful, not only toward God but also about what it promises. The luring promises of the devil, the world, and our flesh are always lies. The devil lied to Eve. She did not become as God; she destroyed her happiness. The advantage or the happiness that the tempting devil, world, and flesh hold out to us always turn to ashes in our mouths. They are goods peddled by rogues.

When we fail in temptation, we call God unfaithful, untrue, and we take as truth the lies of the devil, the world, and our flesh. When we fall, we can neither blame God nor the devil, as Eve did, nor the world nor our flesh. There was a way of escape, but we refused it and consented to sin.

Such experience of temptation humbles us to confess our sins and plead for forgiveness for Jesus' sake. We are also instructed. We know ourselves more honestly, and we are prompted to abandon the folly of trusting the promises of the devil, the world, and our flesh. When they have played us for a sucker, we are to learn a bit more sense. Once bitten, twice shy.

Temptation teaches us the frailty of our own wisdom and strength. The resources of our strength are not in ourselves but in our faithful God and in His Word. Thus our Brother overcame temptation with the mighty weapon of God's Word. Three times Satan was overthrown with the victorious, "It is written." The same weapon is placed into our hands. We must know it and use it. Opposite this deceitfulness we have the faithfulness of God. The guarantee of His Word is His character. We know His character because He has shown us most clearly in Christ.

And we are baptized. There we were pledged to God, and God was pledged to us. He can't break His Word and desert us. In Baptism, the Old Man was so put down that there is never again in him such strength as can of itself overthrow the New Man. Last Sunday we had our Holy Communion. There Christ came to dwell in us, and with Christ came the strength of the Holy Spirit. With such strength, which is the strength of God, we cannot be overthrown. God is true, and no temptation can harm us if we be but true to God.

God wants us to be much blessed; therefore, He will allow much temptation. The stronger the faith, the greater temptation He can allow, and the greater the blessing of growth He would make ours. Our faith is likely not yet strong enough for God to allow so great a temptation as came to Abraham and Job. We would not be able to bear it. But such temptation as we can bear, He would lead us through, growing from strength to strength. Sickness; bereavement; the bitter heartlessness of people; the lying, flashy promises of the devil, the world, and our flesh will all try to make us doubt God and drag us from Him. God will hide Himself high in a tree, but He will be there nonetheless, watching over us, our faithful Father.

When we are tempted, we can show God that we are His brave children and by His Spirit's strength be made bigger and stronger, "more than conquerors through Him who loved us" (Romans 8:37), even Christ, our living Redeemer and Lord. When you struggle with temptation, fasten all your thoughts and hearts on Jesus. Hang on to Him, and He will pull you through.

Amen.

Ninth Sunday after Pentecost

Matthew 7:16b–18

London (1954)

In ancient Greek theater the actors would put on masks to hide the actor and portray the character. Nowadays they are more skilled with powder, cream, and paint, but the actor still puts on another face. What is underneath is to be concealed; what is on the outside is to represent another sort of person.

Most of us do the same sort of acting everyday. We change our face or part we play according to the differing situations in which we find ourselves. We go off to business in the morning with our business face. When we come home, we change our face again. With various people we have various faces. With some we may be stern and cold, with others jovial and warm. With one set of friends we may enjoy the doubtful joke and give our tongue license. With another set we feel unsure and strive to impress as being better than we are. With another set we may be most pious and demure. Through all these changes of face, we feel that we are the same self, just dressed up differently. For the sake of getting along better and protecting ourselves from possible hurt, we have disconnected our outside from our inside. We manipulate and change our outside to suit our need.

The roots of all these masks are fear, pride, and greed. In dealing with some people, we feel unsure of ourselves, afraid they will write us off, so we put on a face that will cover our ill at ease feeling and make an impression. This is closely connected with pride. We want to be accepted and win the approval of certain people, so we present ourselves as better than we are. In greed we seek some advantage for ourselves. Somebody is useful to us socially or commercially, so we put on a special face for them so we may use them for our purposes.

We usually see all this more clearly in others than in ourselves. How we feel hurt when someone has been particularly kind and helpful to us and we have grown to like this person. Then we discover that it is all a face this person has put on to serve his or her own advantage. In our dealings with other people, we expect that their outside should correspond to their inside. We look for sincerity.

In school I was told that the word *sincere* originally meant "without wax." It was common practice when selling statues and such things to fill in the cracks and holes with wax so the statue would look in perfect condition, so it would appear something different from what it really was. Therefore, it was necessary for the honest tradesmen to guarantee that their statues were without wax, that is, sincere, what they appeared to be.

We resent other people covering things up, waxing them over, and appearing to be what they are not. All the while we are often busy with wax on our own outside. What we condemn in others, we must condemn in ourselves. It is not only to be condemned, but this disconnection of the outside from the inside is sheer foolishness in the light of today's text. A tree and its fruits are of the same kind. Do people gather grapes of thorns or figs of thistles? The Bible speaks of us as a unit, one thing. Therefore, to divide us up, to attempt to disconnect one part of us from another is to attempt something contrary to God and to our nature. Every false view of a person is in some way a disruption of the design of God.

There were those who divided us into the material part and the spiritual part. The material part of us is bad; the spiritual part is good. The root of our trouble is that the good spiritual part, the divine spark, is imprisoned in the bad material part, the body. Therefore, salvation is in liberating the spiritual part from the material part. This takes one of two forms. Either we starve and weaken our bodies to remove the hateful bonds from the spiritual part or we disassociate ourselves from our body; what happens in the body doesn't really matter and we give free rein to lusts until it wears itself out and is done for. Both of these were found in Colossi and Corinth, and both we find today where, on the one hand, you have people making regulations about food and fasting, and on the other, those who use their bodies in fornication and think that this is only a matter of their bodies and not their real selves.

In this dividing up of a person the body is despised. Nowadays it is rather the spiritual part that is ignored and denied. We are regarded as complex and highly developed animals, the product of a chance chain of evolution, and any religious or moral feelings, sense of guilt are explained away in physical terms. In the former case we had to be freed from our bodies, in this case we are to be freed from our souls. Some part of us must be destroyed.

The more subtle slicing apart of a person we saw earlier in the disconnection of a person's outside from the inside, where we use our words and actions as masks, as our diplomatic representatives, as something different from what is inside. We find this works pretty well. People are taken in by our outside and cannot see what is inside. We even take ourselves in. When we have successfully played a certain role, we congratulate ourselves and begin to suppose that is the sort of person that we really are.

We can fool others, we can fool ourselves, but there is one whom we cannot fool. Under the eye of God, how pitiful are our various faces and pretenses, yet being successful on the level of others and ourselves, we are tempted to try the same thing with God. He should deal only with the outside too. Many with the name *Christian* think it is enough to have a respectable outside. The obvious example are those who think that essential Christianity is giving up smoking and never touching alcohol. Tidy up a few things on the outside and God will be satisfied. The same thing (a bit more subtle) is in those who say, "I don't steal. I live a clean life, take care of my family. I am decent and respectable. I think so, my neighbors think so, and God must think so also." However, "The Lord seeth not as man seeth; for man looketh on the outward appearance, but the Lord looketh on the heart" (1 Samuel 16:7).

No outward appearance, sham, or pretense will deceive our Lord. He goes right to the center; we cannot shut Him out. We may disconnect our outside from our inside to keep our inside intact and to ourselves. We may make our inside as a walled city from which we send out diplomatic missions. From this center we may plan, manipulate strategy, and negotiate without exposing ourselves to attack. But all such defenses are useless before God. We cannot keep Him at a distance, negotiate with Him with a part of ourselves. God pierces through to the center, to headquarters, to the control center, your heart, your soul. He will not be impeded, fiddling about on the outskirts of your city. A concession to Him here or there is not enough; God wants all or nothing.

To God, we are a unit, one whole thing. God does not deal with pieces of us; we are all one bundle to Him. That is the way He made us; that is the way He wants us; that is the way He deals with us. God sees through all our outward appearances, our endeavors to shut Him out and to be in control ourselves. He sees our trying to keep Him at a distance, do without Him, get rid of Him. He sees it all. "For the LORD searcheth all hearts, and understandeth all the imaginations of the thoughts" (1 Chronicles 28:9). "Can any hide himself in secret places that I shall not see him?" (Jeremiah 23:24).

Under the eye of God, all our outward appearances are crushed. St. Paul says, "God accepteth no man's person" (Galatians 2:6), and the word for person is that for the Greek actor's mask. The faces we put on and the different roles we play crumble, and we are naked. Before God we are not what we appear to be, we are just what we are and that is what He calls us, we are sinners. The wonder of God is that He loves sinners and would rescue us from our sin. He would put us together, every part of us, unify us, so we become one whole thing that He can call His child.

To do this, God sent His Son. Jesus was a whole, complete man. There was no division or deceit in Him. Inside and outside He was the same. Here was the new man that came to make us new like Himself. To remove the divisions in ourselves, to make us whole, Jesus took our sin on Himself. He suffered for that sin and was forsaken of God as we should have been forsaken of God, had God left us in our sin. Jesus died in my place for my sin. He rose again victorious, the first of the new men whom God would create through Him. Through Jesus, I can become like Him; through Him I am forgiven every sin; through Him I am made whole and can stand before God as His child.

When we are no longer afraid of God, when we no longer try to hide from God or give Him only a piece of ourselves, we shall have joy in knowing that His eye is on us and that He is pleased to call us His. When we are no longer afraid of God, then surely we shall fear no one. No one can make us feel unsure, put us on the defensive, and drive us to put on some false face. When we know that we become God's children through Christ alone, we cannot convert something better or in pride strive to construct an outward appearance that will impress others and make us out better than we are, better than being

God's children. That would be to regard the favor of people more important than the favor of God. Greed also shall have no part in us, for in place of making some pretense to serve our own advantage, we shall sincerely be to others what we are, what Christ has made us, His children, new and whole.

This is not some theory spun in the air but is the secret of personal health for each of us. A divided city cannot stand. The unhappiness and collapse of many people is in their being divided in themselves. One part of them pulls against another part and the tension breaks them. The man who plays husband to his wife and lover to another woman is in constant fear of the two parts clashing and destroying each other. So also a man who is one thing in one part of himself and something different in another part of himself is in danger of such clash and destruction.

Christ came not only to bring peace between us and God but also peace to the conflicting parts of our own selves and to heal the divisions there. Christ came to put us together, to make us whole. To make us whole He goes straight to the heart of us, strips away all falsehood and sham, shows the sin, and forgives the sin. By His Spirit we are born again, made new. Christ ties us all together, unites all parts of us into one healthy whole. He makes us good trees. "Every good tree bringeth forth good fruit" (Matthew 7:17). It cannot produce anything else if it is a good tree. The tree and the fruit are one. When the love of Christ is alive in our inside, it will be active in our outside. There is a constant connection between what we are and what we do. Our actions are never cut off or independent of our central selves. Each action states what we are, good tree or thistle. Nor is this something complete or finished. We are constantly becoming a better tree or a worse tree. Every action we do marks a change. Each action means we have become more like an angel or more like a devil. We are what we do. By our fruits we are known.

You cannot make a thorn tree into an apple tree by hanging some apples from its boughs. A complete change of tree is necessary. You cannot become one of Christ's new people, one and whole, by patching on some good features to your outside and tidying up the exterior. A complete change is necessary. God can make that change. We see it in Christ. It becomes an actuality in you when God pierces through to your heart, uncovers, cleanses, forgives, and restores you to the whole health and vigor He means you to have in Christ. Do not hide from Him behind some outward appearance.

Think of the outward appearance of the baby about to be baptized. We can't get beyond the outward appearance, but God can. He goes to the heart of this child as He goes to your heart. You didn't do anything to bring Him in and neither does this child. But God goes in. He takes hold of this child's heart and puts it right, forgives, and makes it alive by the power of His Spirit in the water and the Word.

What is inside must be vitally connected to what is outside. Here is the task of parents and godparents. As the child becomes able to express himself or herself, yours is to nurture and train the expression of the faith that is created in the child this morning. You would have him or her grow into a good tree. A good tree grows strong and bears good fruit only as it is rightly watered and nourished. Such nourishment must be for the whole of the child, not just some part.

If you do nothing but read the Bible to the child all day, he or she will soon be bodily weak and sick. If you give the child ever so carefully just the right bodily foods and neglect to show and speak the love of Christ, you will soon have a robust little devil on your hands. The child needs not only physical nourishment and not only spiritual nourishment but both so he or she may be not some pieces of a person but whole and complete.

This morning we have been nourished here by the Word of God. It is not only our souls that are nourished, not only some part of us, but we have been nourished. Soon you will sit down to Sunday dinners. It is not only your body that is nourished, but we are nourished. Each is a gift of God that we may be whole and healthy and bear good fruit. When we see ourselves not as parts or pieces but as one whole thing—thus dealt with by God who sees our sin, forgives our sin for Christ's sake, and makes us one like Christ—then our divisions are healed and we are truly joined together, sincerely in ourselves for we are with God in Christ. We "shall be as a tree planted by the waters, and that spreadeth out her roots by the river, and shall not see when heat cometh, but her leaf shall be green; and shall not be careful in the year of drought, neither shall cease from yielding fruit" (Jeremiah 17:8).

AMEN.

Tenth Sunday after Pentecost

Ephesians 4:1–16

Concordia Seminary (1997)

Many Ephesians felt as if they were random bits and pieces, floating around the universe. Amid all this chaos they were helpless and often quite desperate. Of what possible use to them was an apostle? Paul was just a traveling teacher. There were plenty of teachers around Ephesus, peddling their nostrums—some very high-sounding ones—to lift you up into the light, out of *anagbe*, the dark, meaningless necessity. But more utterly useless than any of these was an apostle who was sitting in prison. Paul could do nothing except write a letter, send them some words.

"To the saints which are at Ephesus, and to the faithful in Christ Jesus" (Ephesians 1:1). High-sounding talk is only worth something if tied in with the God and Father of our Lord Jesus Christ, in whom we have redemption through His blood, the forgiveness of sins. You can't get much more located and specific than that blood and what it won for us and the words that carry that to us. The first part of the letter is loaded with Christ—in Him, through Him, and to Him—to pull everything together in Him. Chapter 4 begins the second part of the letter, really getting down to earth, speaking of the Ephesians being chosen before the foundation of the world and joined with Christ and how that plays out in their everyday, down-to-earth lives. They are no longer jangling, isolated bits and pieces but holy people joined together, not as swallowed up but as each one precious with the gift of how Christ joins them in, each one unique, Christ-gifted, His way. Love never repeats itself.

The apostle rings in Psalm 68 with the kicker, "He gave gifts unto men." Where does God do that? Can we determine the place? If no place, then no gift. Gift to us happens at a place and at a time. For a gift to be given, there needs to be not only a time and a place but also a gift. And there is gift when there is someone who gives the gift and someone to whom the gift is given. These three.

We have just heard that it is the Lord who gave gifts to men. Now we are told of His giving the gift of those whom He sends, puts there for His giving out His gifts, specifically, apostles, prophets, evangelists, pastors, and teachers, all doing the same thing, yet each with a title that indicates some specificity in the Lord's use of them for His giving out His gifts. The apostle goes on to tell of three such uses the Lord has with these gifts for His giving out His gifts.

There are more than three. And you can find a good summary in Articles V, XIV, and XXVIII of the Augsburg Confession. But why these three? First, because these are the three about which the Ephesian saints—Christ-believers—especially needed to hear. Part 1 delivered a load of Christ Jesus. Part 2 was working at ground level. It is Christ Jesus who gathers things together, things in heaven and things on earth, things within each person, things in them, together in Christ. How that can run off the tracks, go awry, is shown by the admonitions: "With all lowliness and meekness, with longsuffering, forbearing one another in love" (Ephesians 4:2).

"Run off the tracks" is not the apostle's way of saying it. He speaks of the body. There are things in the saints that are not as they should be. Broken, twisted, dislocated. What a doctor does with bones, setting them right, is the first good thing they need to know as gift intended by the Lord, which He gives by way of the gifts to them of apostles, prophets, evangelists, pastors, and teachers.

They are there for the work of the ministry, not for their own sake, as is implied by the word *work*, which here and in some other places is used in a way that makes it perfectly clear that the Lord is the one who is doing the work, which He does through those whom He has put there for His doing it. This we confess when we confess the holy ministry as *instrumentum secundum* and the means of grace as *instrumenta prima*.

The third thing the Lord achieves through His gifts to the church—apostles, prophets, evangelists, pastors, and teachers—is the edifying, the fitting them together into a building. Not jangling bits and pieces but parts put together in a building, or, more livingly, together in a body. Not just any body, but Christ's body. We do not assemble the parts to make a body, then put a head on it and say, "That is Christ's body." What can be rejoiced in as in no other body is that it is Christ's body. It is the body it is because it is His body. Whether we speak of the saints—the Christ-believers—or those saints whom He has given to the saints for surely located giving out of His gifts—the apostles, prophets, evangelists, pastors, and teachers—we can only speak in the way we are taught to do in the apostle's letter to the Ephesians: "In Him, through Him, to Him." Then there are no more jangling bits and pieces just floating around, bumping into each other, power games bigger and smaller, me against you, us against them. Brothers and sisters speaking the truth in love. We are to grow up in every way into Him who is the head, into Christ, from whom the whole body, joined and knit together by every joint with which it is supplied, when each part is working properly, makes bodily growth unto the edifying of itself, in love.

Amen.

Eleventh Sunday after Pentecost

Matthew 14:13–21

Valparaiso University (1981)

Five thousand people—that is more than the whole university put together. When our Lord gives out, He gives it out bountifully. He is one who loves to give out good things. The Lord made more than 5,000 stomachs full and feeling good, ready to move on, and 12 baskets full of more than enough.

You come into a university of more than enough. There are whole chunks of this university that you will never be inside of or may only get a glimpse of. The nurses way over on LaPorte Avenue are in danger of being so deeply involved in the things that nurses need to know about that they may not get to enjoy the good things of the music school. Those who live in the more remote regions of Mound Street may not get to the probing and entertaining things given by the drama school. One advisor last year, who shall remain nameless, gave the advice, "Take your general education classes pass/fail. Only the grades you get in accounting matter." Your major matters, but a university is for more than just one thing. Not only bread but also fish. Lots of them, "both small and great." "Delight yourself in fatness." As freshmen, you will have the opportunity to taste a lot of things. Something you have not yet considered may get more of your wheels humming than anything you have been into before. Enjoy the freedom of having a go at one thing and another, and you will happily settle into what engages most of you most fruitfully. Some of you may know that already; some may still be uncertain. Eat hearty and be filled, and even then there will be lots left over.

This Chapel of the Resurrection is really a bit more than what might be calculated to be enough.

> ... this immense
> And glorious Work of fine intelligence!
> Give all thou canst; high Heaven rejects the lore
> Of nicely-calculated less or more;
> So deemed the man who fashioned for the sense
> These lofty pillars, spread that branching roof
> Self-poised, and scooped into ten thousand cells,
> Where light and shade repose, where music dwells
> Lingering—and wandering on as loth to die;
> Like thoughts whose very sweetness yieldeth proof
> That they were born for immortality. (William Wordsworth, *Inside King's College Chapel*, Ecclesiastical Sonnet XLIII)

Here is where your songs and prayers and praise can soar out together with a thousand others. Here is where you can come alone and lay it all out before God, get things a bit clearer, ready to move on. Or you can talk it all out with someone that is here for you.

From time to time Jesus needed a lonely place to be by Himself. Not the crowding in of pressures, but space to breathe in a quietness for deep refreshment. Take time to go through your house, open the windows, air out the rooms, clean away the clutter and the mess. Each of us is a large mansion with many rooms. Some rooms are for everyday and all kinds of people. Some rooms are for working in together, some for play, some more private rooms for special friends, and a suite of rooms only for that person who will be your husband or wife. A room, too, for the fruitful uses of solitude where you are alone and not alone. Not even your best friend knows all your rooms. There is more to you than anyone knows, than even you know yourself. Discover the ways of living in more and more of the rooms. Move the furniture around, add some pieces, paint the walls, hang a picture, practice hospitality and the pleasures of eating together that are more than the food, but the food too.

The disciples knew the people needed food. It was good of them to worry about that, so they suggested that Jesus tell them, "That is all there is for today. Time to go home now and get a bite to eat." That is the sensible thing to do. But Jesus does not live within the boundary of the sensible thing to do. No sense at all in His telling His disciples, "You give them something to eat." So the disciples started counting. Five loaves and two fish divided by 5,000 plus—why, they won't all even get a lick. It won't work. Jesus asks the disciples to give Him the loaves and the fish. He invites them to sit down on the grass in order (in Israel that meant in families). Then, as if they are all His family, Jesus says grace, blessing God as the one from whose bountiful hands come bread and fish. Then Jesus starts giving food out. He had asked His disciples to give them something to eat, and now they are doing it. From Jesus' hands the bread and the fish kept coming till the last and the biggest stomach was full. They all ate and were satisfied. They didn't need to cram, for there was lots left over.

Now neither you nor your parents are the Messiah, the Shepherd of Israel. That is why the Gospel mentions the grass. John, who is always playing the overtones, says, "Now there was much grass in the place" (John 6:10). Today's Gospel tells that it all happened on the shore of Galilee, thus "beside the still waters" (Psalm 23:2). "The LORD is my shepherd; I shall not want. He maketh me to lie down in green pastures; He leadeth me beside the still waters. He restoreth my soul" (Psalm 23:1–3).

The heart of any slice of the Gospel is the Jesus it gives. John, you recall, goes on to tell of eating Jesus. Faith is receiving the gift of Jesus. He is the whole lot more, the more that is beyond even the full 12 baskets left over. As the 5,000 and more went home, pondering what had happened, the light was to go on. "Hey, that Jesus, He is something else. Green pastures, still waters, food when there was none, and us all sitting down in families around Him just like our forefathers around the tabernacle. He is the one, the Messiah, the Shepherd of Israel."

Why didn't Jesus just say that to the crowds directly instead of feeding them and letting them wander off home, wondering about what had happened? Some got it right away. Some got it years later: "He is it, what all the promises were about." Some never got it. Jesus does not coerce. His way is the way of gifts, of bounty, of always more. That is the way of His love. Jesus does not pull out a scale and weigh out three ounces of bread and $1^{1}/_{4}$ ounces of fish. "That is enough for you. Move on, eat it, go away." He keeps on giving, so all thought of calculation of what is your just portion is left behind and you have Him going on giving, more and more left over.

That is Jesus. The point of the Gospel is not that you dash off and have a go at feeding 5,000 people. That is Jesus' stuff. The disciples put together all they have got and give it into Jesus' hands. In John they pool their money. They have 200 denarii, which is not quite enough, as many realize when doing the Parents' Financial Statement. But here you are. You made it somehow to school. But don't let that be what is the size of Valpo for you, what you pay for. The best of Valpo is something you cannot pay for. If you insist on what you pay for, you may get only that. There are some things that you get here not because you have paid for them, but because they are given to you. Let it all be gift, your bread and fish and 200 denarii into the hands of Jesus. Then, from His hands, gifts that grow more and more beyond any little calculation of what is owed to you or what is enough. He doesn't stop at what is enough.

Jesus' hands, from which you receive it all as gift, now bear the marks of Calvary. Calvary happened so you would not receive what is your due. Calvary was where Jesus was for you with a love that did not count the cost. Jesus poured out His life for you there. He shed His blood. The blood that is given to us to drink at His table where our Good Shepherd, who has given His life for the sheep, prepares a table before us in the presence of our enemies.

There are enemies here, too, that will seek to bring you into falsehood and bondage, take you over, use you, wreck you, toss you. You will face it all from Jesus' table where He has given the body He gave for you and blood He shed for you. His body and blood will enliven you to brave truthfulness and to walk the way of your pouring out your life, spending it as one prompted and shaped by His love. There is that spending now in the way we live and work and play together here, and later that spending of our lives for which we are here to be equipped. In that being equipped we do much counting, measuring, calculating, weighing up the evidence for different sides of the argument, learning to think straight and clear and honest, deepening our sensitivities to the heart's fears and anxieties, joys and beauty.

All of that is much and already bounty, yet by best calculation that, too, is not enough. But put it into the hands of our Lord, then from Him to us as gift and by us carried as gift to others, we shall know the astonishment and joy of disciples beyond any calculation of enough. The Lord is my shepherd; I shall not want.

Here Jesus gathers us to feed us with Himself. "I am that bread of life" (John 6:48). "I am the good shepherd: the good shepherd giveth his life for the sheep" (John 10:11). "I am come that they might have life, and that they might have it more abundantly" (John 10:10). Eat and be filled, and there is always more—more Jesus than you have so far calculated, imagined, delighted in. From Him, then, receive happy, growing, deep-down days that pull you forward to the always more He would give you. "Thou openest Thine hand, and satisfiest the desire of every living thing" (Psalm 145:16).

AMEN.

Twelfth Sunday after Pentecost

LUKE 18:9–14

LONDON (1954)

"Get in the queue and look English" is the advice that has been aptly given to foreigners in this country. People here in England are much schooled in the practice of queueing. It is not only a national habit but also a national pride. We are thankful that we are not as impatient as other nations are or as those Frenchmen, who plunge into a mad scramble and jostle the moment the bus draws up. No, in England we queue with decency and dignity. We even queue more times in the week than is necessary.

From all this queueing we learn a lot. There is the crime of jumping the queue and the wretchedness of having stood in the wrong queue. When you have gone to a government office to get some permit or license, how often have you stood in the wrong queue? You are timid about asking questions and don't want to appear foolish, so you stand doggedly in line until, after an hour or so, it comes your turn and you are told that you can't get what you want. You are in the wrong queue. You must go somewhere else and start over again.

In coming to the church many people get into the wrong queue. Recently several men came to me, as a representative of the church, and wanted money. Some seven or eight years ago they had gotten some money from the church, and now they were hard pushed again, so they came back. They regarded the church as a simple milch cow. Of God and their stand before Him they had no thought, so they had no thought of how the church might really help them. Work was hard, money was short, so they would try the church. They got into the wrong queue.

Then there are those in the church queue who, in very English style, queue without really knowing the reason why. Their families have put them in the queue. It is a good habit, so they decently go on queueing. They meet their friends and relatives in the same queue. There they can attend to lots of things. They are not upset if they lose their place in the queue. They are not in any hurry for their turn. They can always come back later. They drop in and out of the queue. Such people seldom get to the head of the queue and come to the person in control face to face.

Others queue at the church for political or social ends. They use the church to support their program or their class. The church should make a declaration about private property or nationalization. It should declare itself for increased pensions. It should approve foreign policy and bless all our nation's war endeavors. Those who would put the church into their service are in the wrong queue.

Today's Gospel shows us two examples of queueing. The Pharisee was, first, a queue-jumper. He strode past everybody else and took up the front position. The Pharisee had priority. He had a better claim to attention than anybody else. He produced his credentials. Onto God's desk he laid out his papers, which were proof and evidence of his rights and claims. The Pharisee knew his way around and knew that politeness usually pays, so he politely thanked God. It was only politeness, of course, because he hadn't received anything from God. Thankfulness is the response to a gift, and to accept a gift is to admit help or need of somebody else. The Pharisee wasn't going to weaken his case that way. In himself was everything that was necessary to secure his claims. He didn't need any help. He trusted in himself, yet it was nice to be polite, so he thanked God.

As the Pharisee stood at God's desk, he looked around at the other people waiting in the office and found them a pretty sorry lot. He spotted the man who had made money swindling the farmers. Then there was the man who couldn't get anybody to work for him. The Pharisee looked sternly at an untidy little child's noise and even more sternly at the mother, for everybody knew what had happened there. As the Pharisee looked around, he didn't see anybody that he could admire. There was nobody there like himself. This made him feel comfortable and pleased. It enhanced his chances.

Most of us, for our contentment, find it necessary to see somebody else as less than ourselves, something of a different class or color. We are more pleased with the car we drive when we see that it is better than somebody else's. When things go wrong in our lives, we console ourselves with the consideration that others are worse off than we are. No matter how depraved we are, we can still name somebody more depraved than us, somebody we can look down on. We crave some excellence in ourselves that raises us above others. This superiority is then emphasized. If we have powerful muscles, this is what we assert, and we scorn weaker and smaller people. The person with the quick mind will make fun of the dull, muscular ox. If someone is musically talented, he or she will tend to regard unmusical people as pitiably less than himself or herself. When we feel inferior to anybody in some point, we quickly discover some other point in which we are clearly superior. Although so and so may be more well-liked than we are, we make more money. Although they have more splendid children, they can't get about as much as we do. Theoretical communism, perfect equality, will never work, for we would be utterly miserable if we could not find somebody less than ourselves, somebody to look down on, somebody to make us more pleased with ourselves.

The Pharisee had no difficulty in finding people less than himself, so he felt fine. He listed his superiorities. He fasted twice a week while most ordinary people fasted once a week, at most. This extra fasting the Pharisees did to atone for the sins of the people. The common people were such dreadful sinners that the Pharisees who didn't have much, or any, sin to atone for fasted for the sake of other people's sins. And these other people should realize how sinful they were in comparison with the Pharisees. Therefore, it was the custom on Tuesdays and Thursdays to do this fasting with special public prayers and services. Tuesdays and Thursdays were market days, and everybody would be in Jerusalem to see those pious Pharisees who were fasting for the sins of the rest of the people.

The Pharisees acted similarly with the tithe. The Law of God required a tenth of one's produce or income. Many farmers and traders did not give the required tenth. To point out this sin, the Pharisees had the habit of giving not only a tenth of their own produce and income but also a tenth of what they bought. When they bought flour or sheep, for example, the Pharisees knew they were likely buying untithed goods. To have no part in this robbing of the Lord, the Pharisees tithed such purchases also. This cost them a lot. We know that one's money is usually the last thing to come under the control of the love of Christ. So you see, these Pharisees did have a lot to show for themselves. We must be careful not to despise the Pharisees. They lived clean, decent, useful lives. They were exhibited a keen responsibility for the welfare of their people. They did their utmost to fulfill the Law of God.

Before we despise them, we should compare their exemplary lives with our own. How many of us are ready to give 10 percent twice to the Lord? Nor may we assert our superiority by saying that they had good works that don't count; we have faith, faith counts. This is a favorite way with lazy Lutherans. We see others doing so much for missions at home and abroad, being so much more useful in the community, and we say, "Yes, that is true, but we Lutherans have the pure Gospel. We are justified by faith alone and not by works." We thank God that we are not as others are: Roman Catholics who pray to Mary, Anglicans who muddle the Gospel, Methodists who make such a fuss about pacifism and temperance, or even communists. We rightly divide the Law from the Gospel; we distinguish correctly between justification and sanctification; and we can point out everybody else's errors.

No, my friends, we may not condemn that Pharisee. We must learn to recognize and condemn *this* Pharisee. This Pharisee is the hardest one of all to recognize, for a Pharisee is always looking at other people or, rather, looking down on other people and seeing them as less than himself. Having sized them up as less than himself, the Pharisee measures himself according to other people and finds himself bigger and better than they.

This is not even the height of Phariseeism. That is in people taking the Law of God and using it for their self-glorification and in the observance of an externally understood law, strutting before God and expecting Him to agree with their good opinion of themselves. God becomes a mere adjunct to one's self-admiration. Such people are at the furthest remove from God, for between themselves and the living, personal, holy God they have put the Law of God, itself transformed into a set of rules according to which they can pronounce favorable judgment on themselves, glorify themselves, trust in their own rightness, and despise others.

My dear friends, there is a Pharisee in us all. How often do we look at other people and find them inferior to ourselves? How much of our Christianity is thought of as being a nice, decent person whom others can admire? How much of our thanks to God is not based on indebtedness for what He has given to us but on what we are showing Him? Such self-regarding thanksgiving and morality block us off from God, from looking upward to Him and seeing ourselves alone in His presence. What does that say of us?

There was someone there that day who knew that he stood in the presence of God, the personal, living, holy God. And he was afraid. He didn't dare go right into the church. That was for the good people, the people who had tamed God and gotten Him under their control. This man knew he didn't belong in the church, so he stayed outside. He didn't think that he knew how to pray. He lacked the fine phrases and outward gestures. He didn't fold his hands or close his eyes. He just blurted out the truth about himself, the truth about himself in the presence of God. He was a sinner. Mercy was his only hope. He cried to God.

The true realization of sin does not come as we compare ourselves with other people. It comes in the presence of God, the living, personal, holy God. When we stand before God with every deceit and pretense stripped off, we see what we amount to. God Himself is the standard by which He judges. And it is He that judges. "Ye shall be holy: for I the Lord your God am holy" (Leviticus 19:2). We are not the least bit the way He is, that is, we are sinners. As long as we look at ourselves in comparison with other people's performances, we shall not know what we are. The recognition of what we are comes only when we look up to God and stand before Him alone.

The original language of the text reads "God be merciful to me a sinner" (Luke 18:13). The publican feels that other people may be all right; he does not judge them or look at them. He stands alone before God. It is between him and God. When one confronts God, one is a sinner. As sinners we have no rights before God. Our lot is desperate.

If you have ever seen a refugee waiting in a passport queue with papers that aren't quite straight, hoping for freedom and another chance at life, you will have seen fear and desperation. His or her only hope is that the official can be fooled. When you step before God, there is no hope in trying fool Him. Your faulty papers cannot establish your right to freedom and a new life. When you face God, no papers, recommendations, or references will help you. You stand there as what you are. You know that He knows what you are; you also know what you are. If you try to do a deal or pull anything else, your chances are ruined. Just as when you offer money to the official to help you along as you apply for some doubtful license or visa. If he happens to be an honest man, you are done for. God's an honest man, and you cannot bribe Him. You cannot do a deal with God. You cannot buy God off. Anything you get from God is a gift. If you claim your rights and deserts from God, you will get them, and that will be the end of you.

The Pharisee claimed his rights. He spoke for God and gave the verdict. He declared himself righteous. He didn't need God. He did admirably without God. Therefore, he went down to his house without God. The publican knew all his rights were forfeited. He gave God the right to condemn and reject him. He was a sinner and needed God. Only by the mercy of God could he stand. He cried to God for mercy. He returned to his house having received mercy. He returned with God. The publican was in the right queue. This queue is marked "for sinners only."

Not that sin recommends one to God—quite the reverse. Our Lord neither condemns the exemplary life of the Pharisee nor does He commend the disreputable life of the publican. The crucial point is that the Pharisee negotiates with God, does a deal, calculates, and tells God the answer. God is expected merely to nod approval. God has no choice but to accept and admire this splendid man. The publican surrenders every claim and calculation. The decision rests with God. He gives God the right to condemn him; hence God has the possibility of showing mercy. Mercy is only possible when you surrender yourself into the hands and decision of God. Where there is not God's mercy, there is only hell.

The Pharisee did not surrender himself into the hands and decision of God; the publican did. The publican went down to his house justified. He was given mercy; he was forgiven. Now he was God's free, glad, and grateful man. You who have come to church this morning must ask yourselves, In which queue do I stand? Remember that in the Church of the Nativity in Bethlehem the entrance door is small and low. It is only possible to get in on your knees.

AMEN.

Thirteenth Sunday after Pentecost

Luke 12:49–53

Valparaiso University (1980)

Have a baptismal beginning of your Valpo days. That means beginning with Jesus: His baptism, your Baptism, your new life at Valpo. In today's Gospel Jesus speaks of His baptism. "I have a baptism to be baptized with" (Luke 12:50). When Jesus was baptized in the Jordan by John, the name was put on Him and with that name who He is and what He is for—His work. "And the Holy Ghost descended in a bodily shape like a dove upon Him, and a voice came from heaven, which said, Thou art My beloved Son; in Thee I am well pleased" (Luke 3:22). The words are from Isaiah, which tells of the Suffering Servant: "Behold My servant, whom I uphold, Mine elect, in whom My soul delighteth; I have put My spirit upon Him: He shall bring forth judgment to the Gentiles" (42:1).

Justice here is righteousness, which is the opposite of sin. John called sinners to repentance and baptism. Jesus was baptized with the baptism for sinners. He is sinner in solidarity with us, not with His own sins but with ours. Jesus takes our sin on Himself as Isaiah says of the Suffering Servant: "He hath poured out His soul unto death: and He was numbered with the transgressors; and yet He bare the sin of many . . ."(Isaiah 53:12). Sin is denial of God, setting us apart from and against God. To depart from God is to go to death—big death. "The wages of sin is death" (Romans 6:23). When Jesus takes over our sin, He takes on our death for sin. His baptism puts Him to that death.

Today's Gospel is from that part of Luke called the Travel Section. Jesus has set His face to go to Jerusalem, to His death, to the cross, to His baptism carried to completion. "I have a baptism to be baptized with; and how am I straitened till it be accomplished" (Luke 12:50). In that "straitened" is Jesus being torn within Himself? Here is a glimpse of the shuddering and agony of Gethsemane. Jesus is for real, for human real. He knows what it will cost, and He goes toward it. He goes on for you, bearing your sin, so much He loves you, so much you are worth to Him.

By love consumed, that is Jesus. The hell coming to you for your sin

He goes to, bearing your sin. He is forsaken of God in your place, and the fire of hell does not destroy Him. Instead of that fire for you He kindles another. "I am come to send fire on the earth" (Luke 12:49). "To cast fire" is a liberal translation of a Semitic idiom that means to kindle fire. Not as Zeus, then, flinging his thunderbolts down from some heavenly Olympus. The gods of natural religion are produced by man's sense of guilt and powerlessness and meaninglessness. Natural religion produces gods to supply these needs, ways of getting around such gods, of buying into their power and meaning, of buying off their judgment.

Jesus is not like that. He joins us in our powerlessness, our meaninglessness. He takes on our guilt and sin, and inside the pile of all that He kindles a fire, a fire of redeeming love that consumes Him. Kindling a fire is laborious business, especially if you don't have a lighter or matches. At first, it seems that it is not burning at all, but inside the pile, it is beginning to burn. Hidden under the hard wood of the cross, the fire is kindled. From the ashes of Calvary, Jesus' risen body has the light of Easter, and the fire is given out on Pentecost Day to burn in His witnesses. The wind of the Spirit brings the fire to bright flame in Jesus' disciples, and they are to carry that fire through all the world. It came to you at your Baptism, when God's name was put on you with the water, and with that name the action of the Holy Spirit kindles the fire of faith. There was no evidence then that it was burning, and since then, too, there have been doubts whether or not it had died.

Everybody has a different idea how a fire should be laid and lit and tended. The Jesus fire, the Calvary fire, the Easter fire, the Pentecost fire is *His* fire, *His* baptismal fire that is kindled in you at your Baptism. His baptism was for us all, and you are given that baptism at your Baptism. In Baptism, Jesus' death for sin is your death for sin, what you were, alien to God, is drowned and you are raised a new creature, His, with His name on you. "Know ye not, that so many of us as were baptized into Jesus Christ were baptized into His death? Therefore we are buried with Him by baptism into death: that like as Christ was raised up from the dead by the glory of the Father, even so we also should walk in newness of life" (Romans 6:3–4).

Now you are walking into your new days at Valpo. Who it is that walks, you know from your Baptism. What life lives in you, you know from your Baptism. Your newness of life, how now at Valpo? What is your name? There will be much exchanging of names these days as you begin at Valpo. Go gently with those names. When we are given someone's name, that person has given us something of himself or herself. We can use the name as a handle for getting hold of people, to grasp, to manipulate, to crunch. Or we can use the name to say, "Hey, you are somebody," a person I would be glad to get to know, a person with whom there are things to share.

The way we use one another's names is best and happiest when it is "in the name" we all share, the name that was named on us at our Baptism. To forget that name is peril to ourselves and to how we are toward one another. To deal with people as if the Lord had not put His name on them, as if they were not God's, is murderous sin. To deal with someone as having the Lord's name on him or her, as His, is happy recognition of what that person is worth, of how that person is loved, of how that person is to be loved—according to the name put on that person at his or her Baptism.

When in the Nicene Creed we acknowledge "one Baptism for the forgiveness of sins," we are not only saying that Baptism is unrepeatable, we are acknowledging that each of us has the same Baptism. There is only one into which we are all baptized, Jesus' baptism, His death, and His resurrection. The Calvary connection is given "for the forgiveness of sins." That is the one for-the-forgiveness-of-sins Baptism, Jesus' baptism, the only one.

Being all in together in that Baptism, we are all together in that forgiveness. "For as many of you as have been baptized into Christ have put on Christ. There is neither Jew nor Greek, there is neither bond nor free, there is neither male nor female: for ye are all one in Christ Jesus" (Galatians 3:27–28). The oneness may not be denied or divided on grounds of race, social status, or sex. When any factor in us is regarded as predominant over the Jesus' baptism factor, that oneness is turned to division.

Whose you are is fact number one, whose name is on you from your Baptism. Either you are glad of that name or you are ashamed of it. There are those who confess Jesus' name and those who deny His name, and the division between them is as between the living and the dead. Jesus is the truth point, the point of division that can cut through families, the point of division that can cut through a university. In this university there are those who confess Christ and there are those who deny Christ, and you will be on one side of that division or the other.

Besides fire as statement of life, there is fire as hell and judgment. If you deny Christ and insist on going to hell, God is not going to compel you to go the other way with a gun in your ribs. The salvation way is the Calvary way, the way of love. What a love, tearing Jesus' heart, we have caught a glimpse of in that word *constrained*. What Jesus says in today's Gospel He says on the way to Calvary. There He bears the sins of many, the same "many" that He speaks to us of at His Supper, at His Table. There at Calvary the fire is kindled on the earth, for you at your Baptism, His baptism. Live your Valpo days in that one Baptism's forgiveness, confidence, and lively, sharing joy.

AMEN.

Fourteenth Sunday after Pentecost

GALATIANS 3:15–22

LONDON (1955)

Humans are unhappy when they do not have what they want. Their search for happiness is a striving to get what they want. If they get what they want, then that brings a new set of wants that must, in turn, be pursued, and so on and so on in a restless circle of wanting and getting and wanting again and getting more and wanting. In this there is no content, no happiness. The whole direction of grasping, wanting, getting is the reverse of the way in which happiness lies.

The secret of happiness is in God. He has nothing to get; He has only everything to give. In giving away His gifts, God has His happiness. Here is the true happiness that lives not in getting but in giving. So He might give, God needed those to whom He could make His gifts. There must be somebody to receive them. Therefore, God created us. He designed us as the recipients of His gifts. Thus God would fulfill His happiness. This happiness was not for Himself alone but for His creatures whom He created and equipped for similar giving, for similar happiness. So He created the complementariness of husband and wife and the way of sex. God designed the giving of themselves to each other, the one flesh, the shared happy life of mutual giving. This giving, which is the action of love, is never static but ever growing. The more that is given, the more there is to give, the greater the happiness.

Therefore, God ordained that children should come from the giving of husband and wife to each other. In children are opportunities for further giving, for further happiness. Marriage, family, and society place us amid many provocations to giving, that is, to happiness. There is God's design. There is God's happiness that He wanted to share with us. All He asked of His creatures was that they should receive His gifts from Him, allow themselves to be given to, and find their happiness as He finds it in giving.

The ruination of all this happiness is our proud refusal to be given to by God and our selfish refusal to give. When we twisted ourselves around from giving and set ourselves to get, our happiness was destroyed. No more the happy, quiet mind and contentment. No more the joy in the gifts and the giving. Now the fretful, coveting, grumbling restlessness of grasping, wanting, getting, and wanting. God could have said, "They don't want My gifts. They don't want Me. All right, finished!" Instead of wrath's destruction, our sin drew from God higher and greater giving. St. Augustine audaciously exclaims, "O happy guilt that drew from God such a gift."

God could not restore our innocence. We had made ourselves into sinners, but He gave the promise that a son of Eve would arise who would rescue and restore us to God's happiness. This promise is the whole point of the Old Testament. It was repeated to Abraham. "Now to Abraham and his seed were the promises made" (Galatians 3:16). God made a promise, and this in itself was a restoration of His dealing with us as a giver. His promise was purely gift. All God expected of Abraham was that he receive the promise, that is, believe God. That is all you can do with a promise—accept it. That is the way God wants to deal with us. He wants us to receive His gifts. Abraham was happy to receive God's gifts, and God was happy with Abraham.

But all this was too good. In sin people had so turned from God and giving that they dealt with others to get from them what they wanted. Man was set against man, each striving to get for himself what he wanted, and happiness was driven far away. However, this is not the most dire destruction of happiness. People also dealt with God in such a way as to get from God what they wanted. They would not be given to by God. No, what they got they would get by themselves. They insisted that if they got anything from God it was not a gift but had been earned. They would do their bit and claim their reward.

Therefore, it was necessary for God to show people what their wages were. If they refused God's gifts and demanded what was owed to them, God would tell them plainly what was owed. Four hundred and thirty years after the patriarchs—how patient God was in waiting for us to accept His gifts—He gave the Law through Moses. The Law plainly set forth what God requires. As for wages, if people kept the Law, all right; but if they did not keep it perfectly, they would be done for with God. God said, "If you want to be left to yourselves to do it, then left to yourselves you shall be."

"Thou shalt love the Lord thy God with all thy heart, and with all thy soul, and with all thy strength, and with all thy mind: and thy neighbour as thyself" (Luke 10:27). The Law demands the giving of love, which is the opposite of what we are bent on getting for ourselves. It is God's judgment and condemnation of every motive in us that is contrary to God's way of giving. Looking at what God requires, then looking at ourselves, we may see how we have become the opposite of what God wants us to be. As the Scriptures say, "By the Law is the knowledge of sin" (Romans 3:20). No one can make a claim for oneself on the basis of the Law. "The scripture hath concluded all under sin" (Galatians 3:22). God gave the Law to drive people from the folly of trusting in themselves. He would bring them to recognize the suicide of rejecting God's way. He would bring them to despair of themselves so that emptied of proud self-getting they might be open once again to receive His gifts.

But now came the supreme folly. People took hold of the Law by which God would crush them to the realization that they cannot get His favor by their own endeavors and said, "We will do it. We will show God what splendid people we are and claim our reward." It is against this wresting of the Law from its chief function that St. Paul is contending. People took the Law as disannulling, as replacing God's way of promise and gift, as if God provided another way, a way in which they could earn God's favor. They would transform the gracious, giving God into a spectator who should applaud their achievements.

Two Sundays ago we heard what Jesus had to say about those who trusted in their own righteousness. He told of the two men who went up to the temple to pray. The Pharisee had no need of God or any of His gifts. God was there only to admire and reward him. In the Galatian church this same spirit was abroad. There were Jews who were willing to accept Jesus as the Messiah, but they clung to the Law and insisted that by their performance of it they were doing their bit to earn God's favor—not gift, but wages. Confronted by this suicidal folly, Paul cries out, "O foolish Galatians, who hath bewitched you, that ye should not obey the truth, before whose eyes Jesus Christ hath been evidently set forth, crucified among you" (Galatians 3:1).

In Christ it is all clear. He is the fulfillment of the promises, and He sets aside the condemnation of the Law. God's promises cannot be repeated or replaced. The Law that uncovers sin and condemns Christ put Himself under with us. He was "made of a woman, made under the Law" (Galatians 4:4). What we could not do, Christ did for us. He kept the Law in our place, and He endured its condemnation on our sin. Christ took our sins on Himself and on Calvary bore their condemnation in our place. He was made a curse for us, so He redeemed us from the curse and condemnation of the Law. Christ has done it all.

To insist on our merits is to rob Christ of doing it all for us. If we can do it, then Christ died unnecessarily, in vain. Paul would bring home to us the peril of diminishing or rejecting the completeness of Christ's redemption, for if our reliance is not completely in Christ, then it is in ourselves and it is all up with us. If we are unwilling to receive all as a gift from God and would claim our due, then we shall receive the wages we claim, which is being left to ourselves by God, which is hell.

God has not given two ways of salvation—one of gift and promise and another of our getting achievements by the works of the Law. That is to make the Law contradict the gift-giving promises. God gives only the one way to His favor, which is the way of His giving and our receiving. His giving what we do not deserve is His grace. Our receiving what He gives is faith. God's way is the way of gracious giving and the only response to that is our receiving, our faith. That is what alone makes God happy; that is what alone makes us happy.

The gift God gives is, above all, His Son. Here is the height of giving. For those who rebelled and refused His gifts, God gave His Son to die and rise again so to us He might give the forgiveness achieved by Christ's atoning death and the risen triumphant life victorious over sin, death, and hell. From all the wretched unrest of getting and wanting and getting and wanting again, we have been made free. We are God's own, living from the gift of His hand. From our glad and grateful hearts we sing, "Thanks be to God for His unspeakable gift!" There it is. Is it yours? Do you receive it, that is, do you believe?

In speaking of this unutterable gift of God in Christ, Martin Luther describes the two sorts of people who reject and spurn this gift. He calls them dogs and swine. The swine hear of this gift of complete forgiveness in Christ and say, "Well, if forgiveness is so cheap, let us sin to our flesh's fill, and we can always get this free gift of forgiveness." What a filthy abuse of God's gift this is! Christ died that all might be forgiven, might be freed of sin. Some make this a cushion for abounding in sin. Those people consent to sin, relying on forgiveness.

The dogs are those who rend the Law of God from its purpose and make of it a way of their own achievement by which they claim God's favor. They even add to the Law. They make extra rules so they may appear extra righteous. They fast twice in the week. They make rules about days and meats and forbid to marry as the Scripture records. These Christ confronted in the Pharisees, Paul in the Judaizers, Luther in the sale of indulgences, and we, we confront them at every turn. Talk religion with people who boast that they are Christians. They say: "God made the world. I recognize a Supreme Being. I live a clean life and try to do the decent thing. It is all right with me." Such heathens are trusting in their own achievements before God. They would justify themselves by the deeds of the Law. They claim their desserts, and that is what they will get. And ourselves? Are we among those who permit this or that sin, relying on Christ's cheap forgiveness? Are we among those who look to our own efforts and think how we must impress God and win His favor?

The Law is then to perform its true function of showing us our sin and what we really deserve so we may be emptied of self and its rebellious getting and earning, emptied to receive God's gifts. This is not the end of the restoration but the beginning. God wants more happiness for us than only that between us and Him, though that is the number one happiness and runs through every happiness. We are happy indeed to know that God does not condemn and cast us off as we deserve. We are no longer bargaining with God, no longer scared of Him. He has given us to be His children who love now from the resources of His gifts.

When God can give, He is happy. When we are given to by God so unimaginably abundantly, we are happy. Being made happy with God's giving, we multiply our happiness when we also give. The opportunities are plentiful in spouse, family, friend, and others knocked about beside the road. Our enemies provide the opportunities of purest giving, for then it is not so easily mixed with getting. As God's happiness increases, as His giving increases, so does ours. For this purpose God gives us abundance of gifts so we may have joy in giving them further.

God's gifts always grow; they grow by being given away. If they are not given, they wither and die. This is, above all, true of the Gospel. God, you see, is not greedy of His happiness. He did not insist on having all the joy of giving it away. God gave it into our hands. Just think of that! When you have given Christ away to somebody, then is Christ more richly and powerfully yours.

We are, perhaps, not so willing to agree when it comes to some of God's other gifts, our work and business and money, for here the emphasis is so strongly on getting. These things, however, we must see in the light of their purpose. If we work hard, strive to increase our wages or business to get for ourselves, then we are only breeding further restless wanting and getting and wanting. If we work and earn so we may have more to give for God, for friends, family, and others, then happy is our work. Our work is worship, for it is performed in God's way of doing things.

The increase of happiness' treasures is by giving, not by getting. As the loaves and fishes were multiplied by being given away, so all the gifts of God are multiplied by being given away. It is far happier to give than to receive. God knows that, and He wants us happily to know it too.

Amen.

Fifteenth Sunday after Pentecost

Luke 14:1, 7–14

Valparaiso University (1977)

We have a disappointing sort of Gospel today. "Don't make a social ass of yourself" is a piece of wisdom we hardly need Jesus to tell us. We have heard the worldly wisdom of the Book of Proverbs: "Do not put yourself forward in the king's presence or stand in the place of the great; for it is better to be told, 'Come up here,' than to be put lower in the presence of the prince" (25:6–7 RSV). You would expect that Jesus could do better than that. Well, actually, He does. You must never let Him go until He does. As Jacob would not let the angel go until he gave a blessing, so we may not let Jesus go until He gives us some Gospel.

There is some strong Gospel in the part that the lectionary committee snipped out, but it is important for what is going on. Here is how it goes:

> One Sabbath when He went to dine at the house of a ruler who belonged to the Pharisees, they were watching Him. And behold, there was a man before Him who had dropsy. And Jesus spoke to the lawyers and Pharisees, saying, "Is it lawful to heal on the Sabbath, or not?" But they were silent. Then He took him and healed him, and let him go. And He said to them, "Which of you, having an ass or an ox that has fallen into a well, will not immediately pull him out on a sabbath day?" And they could not reply to this. (Luke 14:1–6 RSV)

Now that is Jesus for you. He accepts an invitation from a man who is certainly no friend of His. "They were watching Him." But Jesus just carries on being Himself. There is a man in need, so Jesus is there for that man. Won't the others be there for this man too? Isn't it all right to help him and make him glad? It is the Sabbath. But they were silent. The day God appointed for rejoicing in all the goodness of His good gifts they had made into a performance. They jacked up the requirements that served to show how much more than splendidly they were doing and also furnished a more exacting standard for comparing themselves with others and finding themselves superior.

There is no point in being superior if you don't get recognition for it. Jesus goes on to tell of the way He observed of claiming and showing off such superiority. It is not very American. The egalitarian "You all just come now and sit down anywhere" does not enable you to tell, by where someone is sitting, how high or low he or she is respected in contrast with someone else. If you are interested in that sort of thing, you have to watch for other signals to ascertain this, but in our text, where you sat gave your place in the order of honor.

Jesus saw what was going on and talks about it, it seems, on the level of prudential etiquette, which nobody is likely to disagree with much. It is risky to push yourself too far forward because you may be shoved back. Better to go low and you will have a good chance of being advanced "in the presence of all who sit at table with you" (Luke 14:10 RSV). Jesus is up to something more than what lies on the surface. He leads His hearers to the point where humility becomes the instrument for self-advancement.

Jesus has a disconcerting way of peeling off our pious pretenses and disclosing their phoniness. Humility is a game you cannot win. Try and you will end up doing its opposite. Truly humble people never mention humility as a virtue in themselves. They are otherwise engaged. Those who draw attention to it in themselves or how frightfully hard they are striving to be humble are almost certainly phonies, the opposite of humble.

The Harper Study Bible states in the footnote that this passage is a lesson on humility given by Jesus. That is to get only the husk, not the kernel. We have been warned against this by being told that Jesus was telling a parable. A parable casts its statement alongside the intended message, the kernel. The parable does its job in bringing that message, that kernel. Parables are a way of doing this so you are not hit over the head with it or looking down the barrel of a .45. That is not Jesus' Gospel way at all.

The parable is about a marriage feast, which is a traditional way of telling of the Lord's love for His bride, His people. The feast is a celebration of that love, and the bringing on of the feast is the Messiah's work. Here Jesus is telling about it—what contradicts it and that it is bestowed not according to our calculations of first and last, or high and low, but only of His bounty. Those who are surprised by God's bounty are the truly humble who are not prompted by calculation of their own advancement or reward.

There are all sorts of rewards, all sorts of good things given, but if you target yourself at them as at humility, you will end up with the opposite. The rewards business is God's business, and Jesus is in the running of it. He runs it the opposite of our calculation. "Every one who exalts himself will be humbled, and he who humbles himself will be exalted" (Luke 14:11 RSV).

So it is with one another. How can I put this Bill or this Mary to my use? Advancement is turned around to what good and happiness can I be or do or share with Bill and Mary and the whole rum bunch? Then the fabrications may fall away, the futile rivalries, the phony pieties, the fiddling of people, the falsifying of people into quotients of usefulness and advantage, and the Phariseeizings of fake humility.

Be on your guard against the tempter should anyone ever tell you how humble you are getting to be. Give him only a mocking laugh. The one thing that the devil just can't stand is to be laughed at, as

Martin Luther observes. Keep your laughter ready for any pretensions at virtue—particularly humility. If you become absorbed in taking your humility seriously, it is Satan who would have you be in dead earnest, sweating to show how you are notching it up. Then you will be a pain not only to yourself but also to those who have to live with you and also to God who wants us to be a happiness for one another and for Him.

God dishes it out beyond our calculations of our advantage and reward. These deny His way and so deny also the counterpart of gift that is faith, receiving His gifts. Faith lives in giving on the gifts as gifts, that is, without calculation of return, of how I can get the better or the use of others. Life is to be a feast of good things, so live it that way.

"But when you give a feast, invite the poor, the maimed, the lame, the blind, and you will be blessed, because they cannot repay you" (Luke 14:13–14 RSV). Jesus doesn't blame His host for having friends to dinner. Some of our happiest times are feasting with our friends, and Jesus got a bad name for being part of such feasting. But on this Sabbath, contrary to the pieties of the surface appearance, it was not a gathering of friends. They were jealous of where one another sat. Jesus was not invited as a friend but to give them an opportunity to size up how He might be used.

Even before Jesus shows the deceitfulness and hypocrisy attending the performance of humility, how it was with them was shown by how the man with dropsy is welcomed. The traditional show of piety was to have the door open for the stranger and the poor, which was fine, so long as some fool of a stranger or person in need didn't take this seriously and actually come in. You could then, of course, stare him down. That would make him feel uncomfortable in various ways so he would go away and not do such a presumptuous thing again. Giving him some food at the bottom place or in the corner could also hasten his departure.

The Jesus contrast is all around us in the Gospels. A summary of the Gospel is that Jesus is the friend of sinners and eats with them. Jesus feasts with Zacchaeus and his crowd, with Matthew and the pretty rum bunch that gathered there, bringing their need with them, or to show Him how much they loved Him and wanted to be close to Him. The happiness of being at the table with Jesus is the now of that feast to which we are all invited. He really means it when He has His door open. You may doubt your worthiness and you may hesitate when you see how some of those with Him look at you, but you cannot doubt Jesus and His invitation.

Top-seat people such as "Abraham, Isaac, and Jacob and all the prophets" will be moving over for those who come from all over the place, as we were told in last Sunday's Gospel. "And they shall come from the east, and from the west, and from the north, and from the south, and shall sit down in the kingdom of God. And, behold, there are last which shall be first, and there are first which shall be last" (Luke 13:29–30). We hear this echoing in Jesus' summarizing words today: "For every one who exalts himself will be humbled, and he who humbles himself will be exalted" (Luke 14:11 RSV). There is dread warning in these words and promises of our Lord's incalculable bounty. God grant His Spirit to work the truth of these words in us to repentance and faith, toward lives freed for the feasting with Him, of being for one another, enjoying one another without calculation of what use or advantage we may get out of them. Such love forgets about trying to be humble, about showing off an honor above others. Our place and who we are and what we are worth does not depend on any of that but is given to us by our Lord, who is the Jesus He is, who is the Gospel He is for us today and at the resurrection.

AMEN.

Sixteenth Sunday after Pentecost

MATTHEW 6:28

LONDON (1954)

There are two ways of looking at the world. To many people, the world is a collection of things that are real and exist in themselves. A tree is a tree, coal is coal, and water is water. To get hold of as many of these things as possible and use them for their pleasure is the way many exhaust their lives. Intoxicated with the world, they strive to acquire and to exploit. Alternating with this intoxication is a great anxiety about not getting enough of the things of the world or of being cheated out of making the most of them. Such anxiety breeds despair or greater greed. This first attitude of the world is not a happy thing.

The other way of looking at the world is to recognize it as God's creation. This means that the right meaning and use of the world are found only in reference to God. What is God saying and doing in His creation? It is He who is active here and behind it. His action, His dealing, His utterance are expressed in His creation. What does He say there? God says many things. We are directed to what the heavens declare and what the earth shows forth. We are to be instructed by the ant, the bee, and the spider. In all things, from the greatest to the smallest, there is message of God. Often the greatest messages of God come through the smallest things.

In today's Gospel we are asked to learn what the lilies say. The lilies of our text are neither those large, splendid white lilies that we know by that name nor the Easter lilies. These lilies don't grow in Galilee. The lily of our text is a tiny flower that grows among the grass in the field. This tiny flower we are to consider but not as a passive contemplation or poetic nature mysticism. We are to learn from the lily the way we are to grow, to live, and to die. Go to school with lilies, and be taught by them.

The first lesson of the lily is that it grows as a creature of God. It is God that made and designed the lily. To say that the lily grows is not as true as to say that God grows the lily. Its existence derives from Him. Not by its own achievement but by the action of God is it a lily. Therefore, the lily can do no more than wait on God and grow as He gives strength. The design is of God; therefore, the lily accepts what God wants to make it. The lily does not try to grow into a tree. It cannot add one cubit to its stature; it would be a lily. Its fulfillment is in growing into what God wants it to be. All this is in the hand of God; therefore, the lily is not impatient. There is no hurry, no fluster, for its time is in the hand of God and time belongs to God. God is never in a hurry. Slowly, steadily, and quietly God grows the lily. God's great works are done in a deep quiet, hidden surely. Thus His work is done in the leaven, the mustard seed, and in the heart of us.

God worked this way in Mary's baby born in a stable in Bethlehem. His was a quiet, hidden growing. Thirty years in quietness Jesus grew amid the lilies of Galilee. The boy at school, the boy at play, the young man in the carpenter's shop. This was the Son of God growing into the manhood in which God's greatest work was to be done on a cross.

When we fluster and become all heated up in impatience and are so fretfully busy, trying to be bigger than we are, let us remember the lily. When we try to be something bigger than God designed, we are attempting the impossible. We can become something different from God's design, but that will always be something less—pitifully less.

Our design, our time, our existence is from the hand of our Creator. We grow from Him.

The lily not only grows from God, it lives to God. One day Martin Luther was overwhelmed by the fantastic variety of birds in God's creation. With a smile he wondered whether anybody had tried to calculate how much it must cost God to feed and keep them all with grain at such a price. A few standard types of bird would surely be more economical. Perhaps the king of France, with his great wealth and taxes, might conceivably be able to meet the cost of feeding the sparrows, but what then of the ravens, jackdaws, crows, canaries, wrens, finches, and a thousand other kinds? Yet God knows each one of them, and no sparrow dies except when it is God's time for him to die.

In the vast endless desert of central Australia, you might ride a hundred miles and see no one, yet high overhead a thousand parrots fly, waiting for the troublesome person to be gone. You might say that they are useless or even pests, but God keeps them. Their mother makes an egg within her body, and having laid it, she knows that she must regularly turn it over. By a miracle, from the glob in the shell comes a bird. It becomes a beautifully feathered bird, big brother to the budgerigar. It flies out its life over the desert and dies. Why? The only place we can find a reason is in God. God has delight in His creatures, the whole innumerable host of them. He made them for Himself. Their life has meaning in being lived to Him.

When we live our lives to God, we call them lives of faith. The only other way is the life of anxiety and worrying. This is what the Bible calls "taking thought." There is insecurity and fear before what life requires, fear in facing up to the basic questions of life or fear in trying to hide from them. This insecurity drives us to grasp hold of some things of this world and try to possess them, find some security, permanence, and value for our lives. Such effort is vain, as vain as trying to add one cubit to their stature. We are designed to live to God; to twist our lives to something else means present failure and final ruin. The lily is fulfilled in living to God. It knows no anxious toiling for security, no spinning, no storing up in barns or banks. The particular care with which our Gospel deals is the care for clothing: "Wherewithal shall we be clothed?" (Matthew 6:31). The lily does not worry. It does not spin. It receives the garment of its beauty as a gift from God.

Now our text is not to be understood as an admonition against work. The lesson of the lily is not that we should sit down and do nothing and expect God to drop us down a suit of clothes from the sky. The whole life of Jesus was hard work. He gave His disciples work to do, work that would call for their utmost effort. In this people are worse off than the lilies. They fulfill their Creator's design, but humans rebelled against that design, against God. They sinned and bear the curse of sin. Work that should be happy, creative achievement has by sin become toil, arduous and burdensome. The curse of sin is on work: "In the sweat of thy face shalt thou eat bread, till thou return unto the ground" (Genesis 3:19). Jesus Himself was worse off than the animals. "The foxes have holes . . . " (Matthew 8:20). We cannot expect better than Jesus' lot, for on us the curse rests justly.

But we do not toil as the heathen, the Gentiles, do. Their toil is with anxiety. They take thought, saying, "What shall we eat? or, What shall we drink? or, Wherewithal shall we be clothed?" (Matthew 6:31). The difference is at the heart of us, whether we think that we are our own makers, live by our own hand, or whether we know that God is our maker and that we live from His hand and live to Him.

How can we know this? How does God set up His rule in our hearts? The kingdom of God comes to us by the righteousness of God. God's righteousness is God's judgment on us whereby He calls us just and counts us righteous for Christ's sake. God forgives our sin for Jesus' sake. He restores us to Himself. God puts us on the rails again and heads us toward our goal, the fulfillment of our design that we should henceforth live to Him, trusting Him and not ourselves. Thus as the lily is fulfilled by God, so we may be fulfilled as the children of God. In this trust is the end of anxiety and that cheerful confidence within the love and care of God. He who sent His Son to die for us knows our needs and promises that for whatever He intends us to achieve, He will give the strength. Hence not anxiety but faith.

There is one more lesson from the lily. The lily that "to-day is, and to-morrow is cast into the oven" (Matthew 6:30). We love the beauty of a flower, but so soon it wilts away. Beside the goldfinch and the lamb are the tiger and the octopus. The Scripture is far too realistic to encourage a romantic jungle nature worship, for all creatures are subject to death. Nature in itself is tragedy.

> The weariness, the fever, and the fret
> Here, where men sit and hear each other groan;
> Where palsy shakes a few, sad, last gray hairs,
> Where youth grows pale, and specter-thin, and dies;

Where but to think is to be full of sorrow
And leaden-eyed despairs,
Where Beauty cannot keep her lustrous eyes,
Or new Love pine at them beyond tomorrow. (John Keats, *Ode to a Nightingale*)

To me the meanest flower that blows can give
Thoughts that do often lie too deep for tears. (William Wordsworth, *Intimations of Immortality from Recollections of Early Childhood*)

Nature is tragedy not only for those who exclude God from nature but also is felt by our Lord Himself. St. Paul speaks of nature made subject to vanity, groaning in pain. For the corruption, the decay, the tragedy of all creatures now subject to death, St. Paul unrelentingly blames man who sins. The creation is now a world gone wrong because of sin. We, my friends, are partners with Adam in bringing vanity on all creatures. If we think this strange, it is because we do not realize the dread horror and consequence of sin. "The wages of sin is death" (Romans 6:23).

Sin brought the world into such a cursed mess that only the Son of God could rescue it. This He did by becoming part of our sin-cursed world, making Himself our brother and subject to the curse. Jesus staked Himself with us. If He is crushed by the curse, there is no hope. If He overcomes the curse, then death cannot have its way with us. The fate of Christ and the fate of me are one. I can only be destroyed by death if Christ can be destroyed by death. Christ did die, but He rose again. His resurrection means my resurrection and also that of the lily. When I come to die, I can now die as the lily dies, quietly and without complaint.

The tragedy is abolished. Death does not destroy. That God is sure of this we see in the way He deals with the lily. Lavishly He clothes each little lily with beauty. It lives its little day to God and dies, but it is not a wasted life. God delights in its beauty and the lily fulfills itself in His design. In the face of the lily's death, God makes mockery of death and feasts the flower with beauty.

So God makes mockery of our death with all the abounding gifts of beauty and strength that He showers on us. Our life is in His hand. The whole of our life is in God's hand, even to old age. The lessening of strength in old age is to us, therefore, not just the pathetic relic of a vigorous youth that we miserably covet. The flower, indeed, is gone, the plant shrivels, but soon the seed will fall into the ground. From that seed comes the resurrection, a new life untouched by sin, entirely free of every anxiety, for it is a life entirely to God. We are one with the lilies not only in that we must die but also in that we are the creatures of God, fellow creatures with Christ. Our Lord takes our brother creature, the lily, and bids us learn how to grow, to live, and to die. Therefore, consider God's lilies.

AMEN.

Seventeenth Sunday after Pentecost

JAMES 2:1–5, 8–10, 14–18

CONCORDIA SEMINARY (1991)

It is always a bit risky and a little suspicious to cut snippets out of the lectionary. What could it be in James 2:6–7 that they don't want us to hear? We never had that in the traditional lectionary. The snippeting came with the three-year lectionary from Rome and also the troubling of the lections from James. If there is any book that it is hazardous to play snippets with, it is James. That is a long story, and you can be grateful that the next lecture begins at 10:15 this morning.

It is the last verse that sums it up. If you are running with something that won't go into the summary, then clearly you have got that something wrong. So also the other way around. Or as the body apart from the spirit is dead, so faith without works is dead. We are given away by recognizing what is dead. If there is no breathing going on, the body is dead. If there are no works going on, faith is dead. Works are to faith as breathing is to the body.

One may go on to clarify by contrast with the ways of getting it wrong. Most of these we are defended against with the recognition that James is written very Hebrew-mindedly. We have seen that with the word *spirit*—what goes in and out of your lungs and gives evidence that you are not dead. Such physicality of spirit is matched by physicality of body, which is matched by physicality of faith. What is faith that is not located in some body? Is that body breathing or not breathing? There can be no breathing where there are no lungs. But there may be lungs where there is no breathing. Dead lungs.

Now here is a way of talking about faith that we are not good at. We are much better doing it more spiritually and more inwardly, more invisibly, more abstractly. Now we can handle that. Indeed, we are good at it. We can say, "Faith is a heart that gives us an invisible church." That leaves us, then, to be deciding about the visible one—and here is the latest program to make it work. That line of thought is most un-Hebrew-minded. We can learn from Augustine about external, internal, lower, and higher levels: the more upward, the more spiritual; the less physical, the nearer to God.

Only Jesus has these elements in balance. He is true God and true man. He is both spiritual and physical. In Jesus faith and works are in equipoise. He died on the cross for our sins—His body lifted up from the earth on a tree that was rooted in the earth. He rose from the dead for our justification—a glorified body with flesh and bones that walked on the ground, then ascended into heaven.

When Lutherans slip from being Lutherans, they slip back into what they were just before, that is, Augustinians—sanctification in the way of the Law. There are always two ways of going wrong, each way of going wrong and its opposite. To do no more than contradict what is wrong is to make the same error in reverse. Thus "it is all works and faith has nothing to do with it" is contradicted by "it is all faith and works have nothing to do with it." Neither James nor Paul says either of these. Nor do they do fractions to a compromise: part faith, part works.

No. It is all Jesus. The source for what is said in James 2 is found in James 2:1: "My brethren, have not the faith of our Lord Jesus Christ, the Lord of glory, with respect of persons." It is from Him that it all flows as gift. James 1:5: παρὰ τοῦ διδόντο" θεοῦ πᾶσιν ἁπλῶ". The giving God loves dishing out the good things, ἁπλῶ". No bottom line.

Before such a God, cutting out snippets, the refusal of any gift, won't do. Oh, I will take this. This will be enough but not that. Thanks. No thanks. Faith, okay, but I will leave the works—at least for today but perhaps tomorrow. We go wrong when we play one thing against another. Because we can only do that in forgetfulness of the fact that both are gifts to us, and as gifts they run in the way of the Gospel, which does not come in the way of snippets, of fractions, or of levels.

You have faith? How come? The Lord forgave me all my sins. I am baptized. You have works? How come? The Lord gave them with His enlivening gifts. So if someone says, "I have works. Look at what I have done. God should be pleased with me," such a one you will deliver into the hands of Paul. If someone says, "I have faith. I can say the Small Catechism forward and the books of the Bible backward," such a one you will deliver into the hands of James.

But before any of that, there is the repentance that James calls for to us proud Lutherans, who can go on and on about faith while knifing one another, who do big praying, talking mostly about ourselves as the Law-fluid gathers in our lungs. They are most surely dead who are unaware that they are dead, that they are not breathing anymore. You only notice your breathing when there is something wrong with it. *Kyrie eleison.*

AMEN.

Eighteenth Sunday after Pentecost

GENESIS 8:18–22; GALATIANS 3:26–28; MARK 10:2–9

VALPARAISO UNIVERSITY (1971)

Noah survived. Shall we survive? How long shall we survive? Where will you be ten or twenty years from now? Is that a question you can face, or do you turn away from it? It is enough to get through today, survive one day at a time. For some of you it seems doubtful whether you will survive this semester, plowed under by the grade point and a lost scholarship. Statistically we may expect several of you to be killed on the highway. One of us was recently slain in the street. All around us are the forecasts of decay and doom: cities, pollution, oppression, violence, ravaged resources, the pile of bombs, and the war that won't go away. More fearful still, the counterpart of these inside people, people so eaten away inside or so polluted that they can only be said to survive in some no longer human way. In such a world a cheerful man, for Berthold Brecht, is a man whom no one has yet told. The facts will kill his cheerfulness and give him a realism that only hopes to survive a little longer.

When hope reaches only to survival, survival becomes the justification of what we do, as when a student cheats to survive or as when a professor fakes it. You, too, may have spoken with soldiers returning from Vietnam. When you are horrified by what they relate about what happened there and what they did, you, too, may have heard the justification, "If I had not done it, I would not have survived." What would be the point of getting killed? Death is robbed of dignity and significance. It achieves nothing. At the end of the day, it is only a body count, if that. The antihuman, antilife forces are at work not only over there but also in our own country, society, cities, towns, and hearts. We can often see such things more readily at a distance, then hopefully we are better able to recognize them closer to home. The walls of Attica prison do not have prisoners only on one side. We, too, are victims of the pressures that diminish and destroy what is living and human. If we are helpless, then our only hope is that we may survive for a while. There are no possibilities in nonsurvival. Not to go under is then victory. The hero is not the one who dies but the one who survives.

Such a hero is our contemporary, Alexander Solzhenitsyn. Astonishingly, he has survived the Russian Front, eight years in Stalin's camps, cancer, and suppression as a nonperson unfit for the Nobel Prize. His books tell of the heroism of survival. Shukhov, the simple-hearted hero of *One Day in the Life of Ivan Denisovich*, is this kind of man. He has been unjustly imprisoned and has lived years of days in subzero weather without decent clothing or a warm place to sleep, rising each day before the sun to twelve hours of heavy labor on a starvation diet. He steers his life through sickness and exhaustion, through the random cruelty of camp procedures and the betrayal of fellow prisoners ready to sell their souls or another's life for a few ounces of bread. Yet he is not broken, he is not turned into a jackal.

In Darwinian survival, the jackals survive as do the cannibals who have the power and skill to use up their fellow creatures. Solzhenitsyn says no to the jackals and the cannibals. Such survival is human suicide, a fate worse than death. Death is only the penultimate enemy, but keeping that enemy at bay can itself be an heroic achievement of human survival. Although the jackals prevail, there are rare examples of those who have it in them to survive without human suicide, such as the Englishwoman Margaret Henderson, who survived years of imprisonment by the Hungarian secret police on her resources of courage and wit. She said she would have been lost if she had allowed herself to be drawn into their world. She disconcerted her interrogators with all sorts of amusing and ingenious devices. She kept her sanity through weeks of darkness, recalling all the characters in Dickens that she could possibly remember. Such a woman is a candle in a dark world. She was old and did not fear death, which was the worst thing her captors could do to her. But she could do worse to herself, which she did not do. She did not commit suicide. She survived while most don't.

We honor the noble human. We may not turn away from such rare examples and look for another way because we know ourselves weaker than they. God is not honored by being invoked for the benefit of the bottom 99 percent of us. We must follow what is human to its highest reach, as in thought we push the counterargument to its maximum cogency. At that point we may recognize the critical inadequacy or at least the contrast.

Solzhenitsyn's survivor is not only a superman; what he preserves is himself. That man has life and is free who spends it, who gives his life away. As our Lord said, he has life who loses it. Here is the central question of the location of life. This is illuminated by Martin Luther's statement that a Christian does not live inside but outside oneself, for one lives in Christ by faith and in one's neighbor by love. Survival is not enough. If I keep myself alive, even if I do it without human suicide, it is not enough if I do it only for my own sake and if I keep myself alive only with a life that goes on in me.

The interrogators work on the principle that we all have a weak point that they have to find to break us. This is difficult to deny, and we do have techniques in pharmacy and neurology for breaking people. If my life goes on only in me and I am broken, then my life is broken. But if my life is outside myself, has its source and foundation outside of me, then it is not broken, though I may be broken. What am I? This skin full of tubes, bones, nerves, brain, blood, or the one who lives in Christ by faith and my neighbor by love? In heaven we shall be so happy, so alive, that we shall be unaware of ourselves. We catch a glimpse of this when we love someone, particularly in the marriage-size love of today's Gospel.

Noah was a good man. He must have been strong to build his ridiculous ark to the accompaniment of the mockery of friends and neighbors. Noah had his strength from the word of the Lord and in doing it.

The situation is clear in the covenant with Noah. No Noah factors are adduced as foundation or guarantee of the covenant. "The imagination of man's heart is evil from his youth" (Genesis 8:21). The covenant rests entirely on God. His promise is as reliable as He is, and this not in some mistakenly conceived "spiritual" realm but in the world of sun and season and rain—never again quite so much. The covenant embraces the birds, animals, ants, fish, and plants.

> My heart leaps up when I behold
> A rainbow in the sky:
> So was it when my life began,
> So is it now I am a man,
> So be it when I shall grow old
> Or let me die!
> (William Wordsworth, *My Heart Leaps Up When I Behold*)

But more. The Bible says the rainbow will remind God to keep His promise. In the Chester miracle play God says, "The string is turned toward you and toward me is bent the bow." God stakes His life on the promise. That is an extraordinary way of talking about God. The point is brilliantly clear. He is as good as His Word. We live our lives, no matter what, under the rainbow of God's lively promise. That is more than survival. The life with which He made us alive at Baptism He will bring to flowing fulfillment. It is a gift, so we have the option of suicide, but He cannot fail, cannot deny His name that was named on us, without ceasing to be God.

> For ye are all the children of God by faith in Christ Jesus. For as many of you as have been baptized into Christ have put on Christ. There is neither Jew nor Greek, there is neither bond nor free, there is neither male nor female: for ye are all one in Christ Jesus. And if ye be Christ's, then are ye Abraham's seed, and heirs according to the promise. (Galatians 3:26–29)

We are prisms for God's lively light. Prisms need cleaning, and they are just lumps of stuff without light. Come, receive the body and blood of Christ given and shed for you on Calvary, our rainbow's end and beginning.

AMEN.

Nineteenth Sunday after Pentecost

EPHESIANS 5:19

LONDON (1955)

Music is one of the happiest gifts of God, as Martin Luther said. In music we sometimes feel that we have caught a glimpse of a higher reality, an echo of celestial music. Music seems to capture some of the happy harmony that is with God. It is one of the best images of heaven's joy, and there is much music in Scripture. From the jubilant glory of God's creative work "when the morning stars sang together, and all the sons of God shouted for joy" (Job 38:7) to the glad rejoicing of all God's children come safely home: "And they sing the Song of Moses the servant of God, and the song of the Lamb, Saying, Great and marvelous are Thy works, Lord God Almighty; just and true are Thy ways, Thou King of saints" (Revelation 15:3). From beginning to end, through it all plays the music of God.

Yet how can we say such a thing when around us we hear harsh and jarring discords, screaming confusion of noise, and the heartrending, monotonous drone of paltry, empty lives? What has happened to the music that a loving Father gave His children? We hear the jingling of pride, the strident cries of hate, the sickly swooning of lust. Music that began in heaven, accompanied the mighty creation, and was the melodious language of Paradise has been much seduced and perverted. The charms of music are used to adorn what is unclean and to serve pathetic human pride. Clearly something has gone dreadfully wrong.

The nature of music requires that it is to be heard and responded to. God's music was the theme of love played to His children. Their part was to receive that love and return it back to God played on the harp strings of a happy heart. In the giving and returning of love was the glad harmony that was God's melodious purpose in making you and me. Our happiness is in loving and being loved. Each one's life was to be a variation played on the theme of love given out by God. The music of Paradise was a response to the melody of God's love.

Then comes the jangling catastrophe of sin. Humans turned away from God and shut out God's theme of love. God strikes up a theme of His own: "All glory be to man in Me." But the harp of our hearts was not made for that sort of music, and the noise it now makes is a sorry tune. The first known song after the fall is the boastful cry of Lamech, "I have slain a man to my wounding, and a young man to my hurt. If Cain shall be avenged sevenfold, truly Lamech is seventy and sevenfold" (Genesis 4:23–24). That is what we made of the harmony that was given out by God. Yet even in this perverted music, there remains a power and a charm. The music that we manufacture for ourselves, apart from God, does help one go to war more cheerfully, enables one to show lust. It can stir one to proud scorn of all lesser people not born of a most excellent breed. God gave us music, teaching us to play the happiest of all melodies, and this is what we have made of it.

The music that we were designed to play was a glad response to the love of God. Such happy music is possible only so long as God's theme of love is heard. When people close their ears and hearts to this melody of God, they are compelled to hear a different tune from God. This is the holy anger of a blasphemed God against His creatures who try to do away with Him and treat Him as if He did not exist. This wrathful music to strike terror into the rebellious hearts of humans was heard in the Old Testament, but its whole purpose was to lead back to the theme of love.

God did not destroy rebellious people as they deserved. Despite their turning themselves away from Him to their own destruction, He found a way by which the harmony might be restored. It was the way of love, love that would not let us die, Love that would die that we might be recovered for the happy harmony that is God's plan for us. The first statement of that theme of redeeming love was heard in Eden. It was repeated to the patriarchs. Thus the symphony of God's plan played on, sometimes in most fearful terror as people clashed against God in rebellion. But this theme of redeeming love was ever recurring, growing clearer until that love reached its climax and was worked out in the life, death, and resurrection of Christ. By Him was made possible our return to God our Father. In Christ was fully declared the redeeming love of God. All they that truly hear that love of God in Christ are enabled by that love to play the music in their hearts and lives for which they were created, that happiest music that rises in response to the melody of God's love.

Have you heard Christ's love? Has it awakened your heart to responding love? If so, your eager question will be, "How may I express the joy that is mine in knowing that through Christ I am God's forgiven and loved child?" Our text tells one of the many ways by which people in Christ express the love that grips and empowers them. It is in psalms and hymns and spiritual songs, singing and making melody in their heart to the Lord. The song of the new person in Christ is, above all else, a song of faith, faith that hears, receives, and lays hold of the promises of God—faith that clings to Christ. It is a song of trust whose complete reliance is in Christ. Because it is in Christ, it is a song of certain hope and assured joy. Our text says our singing is to the Lord.

The best hymns are those that direct us to the Lord, fasten us to Him, and extol His saving name, hymns that rejoice in the saving truths of Scripture. Inferior hymns are those that are preoccupied with ourselves, hymns of sentimentality and mawkish self-pity. We are to look at ourselves in the light of God's truth so we may see ourselves honestly for what we are. But in ourselves we do not find the reason for happy song. Whenever we look at ourselves, it must be with penitence.

Our singing is to be to the Lord, and if we are mentioned, it must be in relationship to Him. The tragedy of us not in happy relation to God is matter not for song but for tears. So also earthly things come into our Godward song only as they are related to Him, only as they proclaim His glory. Anything can bounce back the happy melody, as we read in Isaiah: "The mountains and the hills shall break forth before You into singing, and all the trees of the field shall clap their hands" (Isaiah 55:12). If the trees of the field are carried away with joy in the Lord, what song shall be on the lips of those whom God has raised from dark death to the radiant life that is in Christ?

From hearts that have deeply experienced the love of God there have risen songs of joyous adoration. We have the Song of Moses, the abounding treasury of psalms, the Song of Mary and of Zechariah, and Paul's hymn of love. The hymn writers have put into words and music what we feel and know but cannot express. To us in these hymns is given strength and joy to worship God. How mightily God's children through the ages have been strengthened by hymns. Think of the heroic martyrs, raising their songs of praise even to the lions' teeth. Paul and Silas cheerfully sang hymns in the dark dungeon of Philippi. When Luther was despondent, confronting the lowering difficulties before him, he would take his lute and sing. Then he would have strength again to face his arduous work. "Music," Luther said, "drives the devil away."

How often have we not been comforted by a hymn that has grown into our hearts? One finds Christians whose years have been spent close to God comforting and strengthening themselves with a hymn that was taught to them in childhood. The years have taught them to treasure those precious words, for by them they have been consoled and strengthened in days of difficulty and doubt.

There is not only strength for us on our road to God our Father, but in our hymns there is also a mighty proclamation of the salvation that is in Christ. How many people have not been drawn to Jesus by the songs of the church? How many have come face-to-face with Christ in a hymn for the first time? We who have known Jesus through the years, how often are we not drawn closer to our Savior, given a deeper understanding of God's love and plan for us, in our precious hymns? When we come to tell others of the faith by which we live, so often a hymn expresses best of all what we know and feel about Jesus.

Then, too, think of the victories won by hymns for the recovered Gospel in the Reformation. Whole provinces were won over by the stirring hymns that proclaimed Christ. When next we thank God for the blessings of the Reformation, we should remember that one of the great blessings was that the congregation was given the hymns. Prior to the Reformation, the congregation had little part in the service. A great screen across the church shut them off. The priests did the business with God. The Reformation recovered Scripture's truth that there are not higher and lower ranks in God's family but that we are all brothers and sisters together before God our Father.

This fellowship is one of the greatest things expressed in our congregational singing. When we as a congregation sing to the Lord, we do not sing as individuals, but the voice of each of us is blended into the one voice of God's family, giving glad answer to our Maker's message of love. As our combined song of adoring love rises to our Father, we are knit more closely in the bonds of fellowship in Christ. In this expression of God's family's joy, there is no place for the jarring notes of selfish pride and vanity that mar the harmony of the fellowship of God's people. As our voices are taken up into the united voice of the church, we are a part of that body whose head is Christ. When we sing together, our fellowship is not only with all who worship in this church but also with the whole body of Christ that is not limited by place or time.

The hymns we sing have risen from the lips and hearts of God's people through the ages. Some of the hymns we sing have been gladly rising up to God through fifteen centuries. And some psalms date back to the time of Moses. The lips that first muttered their joyous praise now raise a far happier song around the throne of the Lamb, yet as we sing the same hymns, we are one with them. We are not divided. We are all one body. When we sing a hymn that was a favorite of someone we loved who has gone ahead, how deeply are we joined with them!

Nor does place sever the fellowship that is expressed in our hymns. The silly lines that we draw on maps and kill one another for do not divide our fellowship in Christ. Our hymns are from many nations and many tongues. The hymns that we sing this day are also rising to our Father from the four corners of the earth. Not only are our individual voices blended into one voice that rises from this church, but the voice of this congregation is also blended with the voice of an Indian church, with the voice of a company of black brothers in New Guinea, with the voices of all the saints of God under heaven. Think of that mighty voice giving answer to God for His love in Christ. In that universal anthem of praise you have a part.

If we did nothing but sing hymns at church, what true children of God could sink so low as to say that they couldn't be bothered to take their place in that glad anthem sung by the one voice of God's family of every land and every time? When we consider the joyous privilege that is ours in our singing here together, surely we must despise our negligence and lukewarm feelings. How often do we not sing a hymn with as much praise to God as a gramophone could render? At the end of a hymn ask yourself, "What have I been singing about?" Instead of raising happy heart and voice to God, we have gone through it with empty hearts, wondering how many more verses are left.

Our text notes especially that our heart must be in our singing, otherwise we might as well stay at home to sleep. How Jesus hated hypocrisy. His hardest words were for those people who drew nigh to Him with their mouths and honored Him with their lips but whose hearts were far from Him. Let us not insult the Lord Jesus with singing that is empty lip service. The secret of success is in the parallel to our text in Colossians, which begins: "Let the word of Christ dwell in you richly" (Colossians 3:16).

Our singing to God is ever a response, an answer. We can only answer truly if we have first truly listened. Just as the choir must first carefully study the notes of the music before it can sing, so we can only fitly sing to God if, first, we have taken in and possessed the Word of

Christ. Just as the choir sings best when it has the music by heart, so we sing best to the Lord when His saving truths have dwelt richly in our hearts. When we have been eager to take in the Word of Christ and have truly heard the melodies that God has set down for us, then our song will be from our hearts, hearts in whom the love and power of Christ reverberate.

Finally, if there is such joyous faith and strengthening fellowship in the singing of the church in her time of strife and suffering, what surpassing joy must there be in the song of the church in her triumph. May we, in the meantime, devote ourselves to choir practice for heaven, rehearsing the melodies that have been given to us by God so we may be trained to take our places in the choir of heaven when our voices, with a joy now unutterable, will blend with the voice of the angels about the throne of Christ.

Amen.

Twentieth Sunday after Pentecost

Matthew 21:33–45

Valparaiso University (1975)

Today's Gospel belongs in Holy Week. Chapter 21 begins with the entry into Jerusalem, the cleansing of the temple, and the barren fig tree. "Who do You think You are anyway?" the chief priest and elders asked Jesus. Then comes the parable of the two sons and today's parable of the wicked tenants in the vineyard. Next Sunday is the parable of the marriage feast. The marriage feast and vineyard go together. Today's Old Testament lesson begins with a love song that turns the beloved into a vineyard.

> ... the voice of mirth and the voice of gladness, the voice of the bridegroom and the voice of the bride, the voices of those who sing, as they bring thank offerings to the house of the Lord: "Give thanks to the Lord of hosts, for the Lord is good, for His steadfast love endures forever!" (Jeremiah 33:11 rsv)

It was time for the Feast of Tabernacles, camping out, picnicking, glad for all the wilderness they had been brought through, and it was also a vintage Oktoberfest.

The parable tells of everything possible being done for a time of wine and mirth, a vineyard planted, a hedge set around it, a winepress dug, and a tower built to watch against marauders. Then the householder made his first mistake: He let the vineyard out to tenants. He would have spared himself all the subsequent trouble if he had kept the vineyard for himself, its grapes and wine, its mirth and gladness. Then he does another silly thing. He goes to another country. Everybody knows that if you want things taken care of the way you want, you stay right there and keep watch. You certainly can't depend on an honor code. The owner of the vineyard goes away to another country. What does he expect? Crazy man, he expects the tenants will be so glad of the fruits of the vineyard that they will be happy to give him his portion and everyone will celebrate together. "Not bloody likely" is the response of the tenants. They figure that anything they give away is so much less for them, and why should they? Who can make them? A householder in another country isn't going to be able to do much about it. "The tenants took his servants and beat one, killed another, and stoned another" (Matthew 21:35 RSV).

The householder doesn't seem to understand. "Again he sent other servants, more than the first; and they did the same to them" (Matthew 21:36 RSV). The next statement knocks out whatever credibility may still be left in the story: "He sent his son to them, saying, 'They will respect my son'" (Matthew 21:37 RSV). Not these tenants; they have a keen eye for the big chance. The absentee householder is obviously not someone you have to worry about, and if they get rid of the son, then no more problems. The vineyard will be theirs for keeps. So they do it. "They took him and cast him out of the vineyard, and killed him" (Matthew 21:39 RSV).

Then comes the big theological question. "When the owner of the vineyard comes, what will he do to those tenants?" Obviously the owner will clobber them. Wouldn't you? Martin Luther says: "As you believe, so you have." If you treat God as one who is interested in getting things out of you, depriving you of good things, as if anything He gets means less for you, one who demands His rights and pays back evil for evil, then that is the God you have. If you treat God as one who can't be trusted to care for your good, if you treat Him as a threat, as an enemy, then that is the God you have. The evil you think of God, you will receive from Him. People's evil toward God returns on them in judgment. There is nothing capricious about God's judgment. It acknowledges what is the fact with a person and deals with him or her accordingly. Κακοὺ" κακῶ" ἀπολέσει is the Greek. You know about cacophony. *The Jerusalem Bible* brilliantly translates, "These wretches He will bring to a wretched end." What they are is matched by their end. What they are is what they believe to be the case with themselves and with God. They expect God to act as they would—self-interestedly and retributively. As you believe, so you have. In Matthew those who answer Jesus' question speak judgment on themselves. In Mark our Lord speaks the judgment. Both are true. Judgment on whom? On the wretched Pharisees, of course. "When the chief priests and the Pharisees heard His parables, they perceived that He was speaking about them. But when they tried to arrest Him, they feared the multitudes, because they held Him to be a prophet" (Matthew 21:45–46).

The multitudes do not get the parable either. They get it less than the chief priests and Pharisees. The chief priests and Pharisees get the point so clearly they want to kill Jesus. The multitudes held Jesus to be a prophet. They could handle a prophet. That was the category into which they put Jesus, but a category impossible to contain Him if they really heard the parable. "Really hearing" is what faith does; what is really heard creates faith. "Yes, that is how it is. That is God's way, His way with me too." His incredible generosity again and again. Giving things over into our hands, God's giving that makes not less but more. So that we may share His delight in giving, sharing, celebrating, mirth, and gladness—His lifestyle.

We don't have to be under judgment. Not what we give makes less for us, but there is always more to give. Not what I deserve, not unless I insist on it. If we insist on what we deserve, God will give us that. If we treat Him as threat and enemy, then that is what He will be. But that is not what God wants. He wants vineyard, fruit, wine, and the joy of harvest, "Here's to you" and "Here's to you." The flow for one another back and forth. That is love. That is life. You don't have to ruin it, grubbing, grasping, grouching. God has put us in a vineyard, and we know what a vineyard is for.

A couple of days later Jesus said, "I will not drink henceforth of this fruit of the vine, until that day when I drink it new with you in My Father's kingdom" (Matthew 26:29). That makes the kingdom of God sound rather hedonistic. Actually, it is the reverse of hedonism, for the hedonist uses for his own pleasure, grabs, devours, and destroys. The hedonist has self at the center and has a narrow range: the things that give me pleasure.

The total range of Jesus is shown by His way with wine. At Cana the astonishing bounty of His wedding gift, that the voice of mirth and the voice of gladness might ring on in celebration. And in the Upper Room, when Jesus spoke of drinking the fruit of the vine in the kingdom of God, He gave them wine. "This cup is the new testament in My blood, which is shed for you" (Luke 22:20). Jesus' blood poured out is the death He dies in our place for our sins. That is the ultimate incredibility of Jesus' love for us. What we had coming to us for our sins He took in our place. Because our sins are answered for, they can condemn us no more, but we are forgiven, restored to fellowship with God, at His table, now and in the fullness of His kingdom.

"For as often as ye eat this bread, and drink this cup, ye do shew the Lord's death till He come" (1 Corinthians 11:26). Jesus' death, the ultimate horror of all history, for your sins. If you can face that, then there is nothing you cannot face, nothing you have to shut out or pretend isn't there in all the hideous, twisted evil that we can see about us. There is no misery that goes deeper than the cross. The Crucified One is there and deeper down still. Everything that would destroy us Jesus has faced, and it did not destroy Him nor does it destroy those who are His. "Until He comes," when He will drink again of the fruit of the vine in His kingdom. But He is not one to drink by Himself. To His disciples He says, "That ye may eat and drink at My table in My kingdom" (Luke 22:30). Wine of the vineyard for the blood of Jesus' death for our sins. Wine of the vineyard for the marriage feast, His bride, His people, the voice of mirth and the voice of gladness, the voice of the bridegroom and the voice of the bride.

You, in the vineyard, how goes the digging, the watering, the weeding? What of the harvest, the fruit, the wine? The joy of harvest, how do you live toward it? How goes it with the wine? Happy gift, making glad and large the heart, convivial cheer and good times together, rejoicing in God's bounty. Or is it huddled hedonist sipping, a cowardly escape from the things you don't want to face, abuse of brain to blot out thinking, a way of getting someone usable, obliteration of moral perception, giggling fool or grunting flump? Some of this, I imagine, went on at Cana and at Valpo too. Why a vineyard? To ask that question is to put ourselves in the position of instructing God, and many philosophers and theologians have attempted to bring Him into line with how they think God ought to behave. The God they make is the God they have.

Are you living in a vineyard or a house of constraint? The answer is given when you tell of God, your creed, by what your life is lived. Jesus did not fit with the Pharisees' idea of God. Thus to preserve God as they wanted to keep Him, they were planning to kill Jesus. They called Jesus a winebibber, and when His disciples were told to sober up because God's business is grim business, Jesus said, "Can the children of the bridechamber mourn, as long as the bridegroom is with them? but the days will come, when the bridegroom is taken away from them, and then shall they fast" (Matthew 9:15). Then He spoke of new wine that burst old wineskins.

Jesus gives days of fast—"gone to another country"—and days of festivity, drought, and plenty. This Lord of the vineyard would have us live not some fearing narrow slice but the whole range that takes in the lot, from direst death to high happiness, because He frees us from the sin of denying His bounty and His vineyard ways. With wine Jesus gives us His blood to drink, poured out for our sins. Deepest repentance, then, and highest joy, proclaiming His death until He comes to drink of the fruit of the vine with us at His table in His kingdom, vineyard's harvest home.

Don't try and kill Jesus with unbelief, insisting on another sort of God. He is the only one, and He is a vineyard God. You can insist that He be a God who gives you hell, but He doesn't really want to. God wants the joy of harvest and calls on us to play our part in furnishing fruit and wine for the festivity.

> ... the voice of mirth and the voice of gladness, the voice of the bridegroom and the voice of the bride, the voices of those who sing, as they bring thank offerings to the house of the LORD: "Give thanks to the LORD of hosts, for the LORD is good, for His steadfast love endures forever!" (Jeremiah 33:11 RSV)

To Him be happy times of loving thanks and praise, now and forever.
AMEN.

Twenty-first Sunday after Pentecost

EPHESIANS 5:15, 17

LONDON (1956)

Never before have we had so much knowledge. We send radio messages to the moon and fly round the earth in a couple days. We sit at home and see things that are happening miles away. We hear people who are speaking on the other side of the world. We eat butter from New Zealand and wear cloth made from wool. We can be cremated for five guineas, killed by a motorcar, and our city destroyed in a minute. Knowledge, vast and astounding indeed, but also rather frightening, for knowledge is only an instrument, a means, a tool. Behind knowledge are always the questions "For what purpose?" "How shall we use all this?" He who has and practices the right answer to these questions is wise. Wisdom is the execution of what is right and good. Knowledge is not wisdom. We all studied mathematics at school. This knowledge can be used for making a builder's blueprint, doing our accounts, making an atomic bomb, or working out a particularly brilliant permutation for the football pools. The same figures are used for each, but all these uses are not equally wise. Possessing the knowledge does not determine whether our use of it will be sensible or silly, good or evil. Behind knowledge lies the question of purpose.

"For myself" or "for me and mine" are the answers of most people. Their principle is "I want to be happy." They seek to capture happiness with all their knowledge and skill. But, my friends, nobody who hunts for happiness ever finds it. The moment you make happiness your goal, you have lost all chance of achieving it. Happiness is always a byproduct. It is the byproduct of love in action. The two who marry happily do not marry to be happy but because they love each other. I can't explain why, but that is the way it works. So to have "my happiness" as basic principle is not wise. Take, for example, the shrewd man we heard of last Sunday. He had done extremely well for himself. He had everything he wanted, or so he thought. "Soul . . . take thine ease, eat, drink, and be merry," said he (Luke 12:19). But God said to him, "Thou fool, this night thy soul shall be required of thee: then whose shall those things be, which thou hast provided?" (Luke 12:20). Not very wise, was he? Yet most people live in the same folly as that seemingly successful gentleman. But we must not be taken in by appearances. We are expected to walk circumspectly. That means keep your eyes open, see clearly, and don't be fooled.

To say that something is expected of us—and we all acknowledge that—means that we are responsible to somebody, that we are not lords and masters of ourselves, that we belong to something or somebody larger than ourselves. The person to whom we and the whole business belongs is God. The question of wisdom, the "what for" question, can be solved only in connection with God. When it comes to this basic problem—"What is behind it all, the meaning, the purpose? What are we for? What are we to do?"—we must look beyond ourselves. We are the problem. The solution must come from elsewhere, from above.

In His mercy, God has shown us His meaning and purpose. We see this in the way He made this universe. In wisdom God has made it all. He has spoken to us through His prophets and told us what we are here for. Above all, God has revealed Himself to us in Jesus. For in Jesus, God's Son has become a man. Here is God expressed in human terms. Jesus is called the Word because He tells of God and reveals the truth and wisdom of God. If ever we are in doubt or perplexity, we have only to look to Jesus. Here is the most complete revelation of the wisdom of God. However, because this wisdom is God's wisdom, it is often more than we can grasp or understand. That is natural, for our minds are rather too small to grasp and understand God. If we could understand God and His wisdom fully, we wouldn't have any need of God because we would be equal with Him.

But now are we creatures made by God, and in making us, He had His purpose. This was a wise purpose and, above all, a purpose of love. He designed us to be His children, reflecting the wisdom, joy, and love that are from Him. Sin wrecked this. Yet God did not give up His purpose. His great love found a way of surmounting sin. In this we see the supreme wisdom and love of God, a wisdom so great, so far above our understanding, that it just doesn't make sense to us. The Son of God became a man, and as a substitute for each of us, He was obedient to God's holy Law for man. Taking our sins on Himself, He died the just death for our sin of being forsaken of God. Just as a king shows his complete sovereignty in pardoning rather than in punishing, so God is supreme wisdom and love in this death of the Son of God for our salvation. Such love and wisdom are too high for us. To us this is utterly unbelievable. It is foolishness—the folly of the cross, as the Scriptures call it. But the folly of God is greater than the wisdom of us.

> For after that in the wisdom of God the world by wisdom knew not God, it pleased God by the foolishness of preaching to save them that believe. For the Jews require a sign, and the Greeks seek after wisdom: but we preach Christ crucified, unto the Jews a stumbling block, and unto the Greeks foolishness; But unto them that are called, both Jews and Greeks, Christ the power of God, and the wisdom of God. Because the foolishness of God is wiser than men; and the weakness of God is stronger than men. (1 Corinthians 1:21–25)

There it is: through Christ, the wisdom and the strength, making us the children of God. We can't hope to understand. With overflowing hearts we can only say, "Yea, Lord, I believe." The wisdom of God needs no explanations. God does not explain. He decides, acts, and does. You can't cross-examine or argue with God. You can't tell God that He has done things wrong, that He is a fool. Even if the acknowledgment of God's wisdom means to acknowledge that apart from Him you are a fool. If we have gotten so far as to confess that God is wiser than we, we are well on the way. Most people, on the other hand, think they are wiser than God and have no need for Him. They despise His Word and His wisdom. They neither read their Bibles nor go to church. But here we are, my brothers and sisters, in church. The folly of the cross is for us the highest wisdom. It means life and salvation. But God's wisdom is not something theoretical. It has to be lived. Wisdom proves itself in practice. Our text calls on us to practice the wisdom of God that is ours through Christ in our daily walk of life. The meaning and the purpose of us that is revealed in Christ are to guide our every thought and decision.

We are told to be wide awake, alert, with our eyes keenly open, so we may know what is really going on. Fools get taken in. They are deceived by appearances. They don't see further than earthly things. They are so taken up by the goings-on in this world that they think they are the final and real things. They don't see further. They seek to get happiness in earthly things, and in getting they are miserable. They are genuine fools. They strive for one thing and get the opposite.

Don't be fools, says God. See everything for what it is worth. Use everything for its proper purpose. Use it wisely, and that means according to the will of God as we know it in Christ. The constant question of the Christian is "What would Jesus have me do?" Whatever your eye falls on, always ask, "What does God mean this for?" When you take a slice of bread in your hand, ask, "What does God mean this for?" Knowing that God gave it to you for your pleasure and strength, you will eat it wisely. When you look at your hands, ask, "What does God mean these for?" So also your tools, your wages, your shoes, your hat. What does God mean these for? Understanding what the will of God is, you will use them wisely. If we walk in the light of God's wisdom, we shall not stumble. Our lives will not be wasted in vanity or folly, for we shall not be duped or deceived. Living by the wisdom of God for His purposes and with cheerful confidence, our lives will be meaningful and worthwhile. This is all summed up in the exquisitely beautiful collect that we prayed, as it has been prayed by God's children for more than 1,000 years, when we asked for a "quiet mind," a mind free from deceptions and doubt, free from anxiety and fear, for it is a mind that through faith has received pardon and peace, a mind illumined by the wisdom of God.

Such a mind had William Tyndale, the anniversary of whose martyrdom was yesterday. He saw clearly what God meant him for, and he did it heroically with a quiet mind. From his cell he wrote the following words to one of those in control of his prison.

> I beg your lordship, and that by the Lord Jesus that if I am to remain here through the winter, you will request the warden to have the kindness to send me, from the goods of mine which he has, a warmer cap; for I suffer greatly from cold in the head. My overcoat is worn out; my shirts are also worn out. He has a woollen shirt, if he will be good enough to send it. And I ask to be allowed to have a lamp in the evening. But most of all I beg and beseech your clemency to be urgent with the warden that he will kindly permit me to have the Hebrew Bible, Hebrew grammar, and Hebrew dictionary, that I may pass the time in that study. . . . But if any other decision has been taken concerning me, to be carried out before winter, I will be patient, abiding the will of God, to the glory of the grace of my Lord Jesus Christ; whose Spirit I pray may ever direct your heart.
>
> Signed W. Tyndale

How wise was his use of cap and candles, Bible and knowledge. Soon after came the sixth of October when he was strangled and burned, but he did not lose his quiet mind. He had lived wisely, doing the will of God.

Every Christian, at the end of a day of honest toil, may happily thank God with a quiet mind for the privilege of having worked in the service of God and others, doing the will of God. Ours in Christ are the wisdom and strength of God. Our text calls on us to live by that strength and that wisdom. When we catch ourselves fretting and fussing about little earthly things, we are to stop and have a proper look at those things and see clearly what their true value is and what God means them for. When our temper gets short, we should stop and see clearly that there is no wisdom in that, for God's Book says, "Anger resteth in the bosom of fools" (Ecclesiastes 7:9) and "It is an honour for a man to cease from strife: but every fool will be meddling" (Proverbs 20:3).

All along our journey through this world, we have the Word and wisdom of God to check and guide us. Directed by God's wisdom we shall move toward the fulfillment of His happy purpose for us—that we should be His sons and daughters, holy, happy, driven by love. To try to be something else, something different from what He has designed us for, is bound to end in wretchedness. It is the height of folly. It is not wise to use an eggbeater to peel potatoes. The eggbeater has its proper purpose. So have we our proper purpose. The purpose God gave before He made this world and us. The purpose that is realized in us through Christ "in whom we have redemption through His blood, the forgiveness of sin, according to the riches of His grace" (Ephesians 1:7). For God has allowed us to know the secret of His plan, and it is this: He purposes in His sovereign will that all human history shall have its purpose in Christ, that everything that exists in heaven and earth shall find its perfection and fulfillment in Him.

AMEN.

Twenty-second Sunday after Pentecost

Luke 18:1–8

Valparaiso University (1980)

"Do not lose heart." So who is losing heart? I know there are some who were losing heart this last week. There are others, I know, who were having an enjoyable week, for whom Valpo Days are some of the best days so far. The Engineers' Day banquet and much laughter, the Chapel Workers' Party, the seniors' interviews that show a stirring range of opportunity, deeply rewarding days of studying and hard thinking, days of friendship and fun, bright days with a crisp nip in the air that quickens your step, and fall colors that take your breath away, if you will pause a while and be open to the vivid splendor of autumn's beauty.

How does today's Gospel speak to us all, to those who this last week were slipping toward despair and to those for whom this last week was a jolly good one? Today's Gospel speaks deeper than the shallow worldly wisdom of having to take the rough with the smooth, sometimes up and sometimes down. Today's Gospel speaks of the bedrock of our lives. It speaks of judgment and the life of faith, of our being given to and of our holding God to being such a God who loves to give.

Last Sunday nine lepers got what they wanted from Jesus, and that was all they got of Jesus. One leper returned and was given overwhelmingly more. "Now he was a Samaritan" (Luke 17:16). Today a widow, a nobody, a woman with nothing and what little she has has been ripped off. Yet she does not despair, does not lose heart, for faith is alive in her. She won't not be given to. A true daughter of Israel, she wrestles or rather pounds. "To strike below the eye" is the original meaning of the pugilistic term used, which is so pallidly translated as "she will wear me out" (Luke 18:5). She keeps pounding away. Her life was in the judge's hands, and she will not let Jesus off giving judgment. Judgment was to be the work of the Son of Man. Jesus speaks strangely of the Son of Man in the third person, as if the Son of Man might be someone else. Who is this Son of Man, the one who comes to judge, the one who looks for faith when He comes?

Just before, Jesus had been speaking of wishing "to see one of the days of the Son of Man" (Luke 17:22). Some will say, "Lo, here," while others will be saying, "Lo, there." They said to him, "Where, Lord?" He would not give them a place or a time. 9:30 A.M., March 21, Mount of Olives, 2003. How debilitating of faith that would be, for faith has no other final certainty than in God and His judgment. We know that we all face judgment, and even those who deny this still go on seeking to justify themselves. Listen to the ingenious defenses and pitiful excuses.

Jesus says the Day of Judgment will be like lightning from which nothing is hid. No point in trying to grab hold of anything then.

> On that day, let him who is on the housetop, with his goods in the house, not come down to take them away; and likewise let him who is in the field not turn back. Remember Lot's wife. Whoever seeks to gain his life will lose it, but whoever loses his life will preserve it. I tell you, in that night there will be two in one bed; one will be taken and the other left. There will be two women grinding together; one will be taken and the other left. (Luke 17:31–35 RSV)

The two in bed, the two grinding together, you or I could not judge between them. Yet one will be taken and the other left. Only God knows how it really is with each one. What He looks for is faith.

Then, so we do not think of faith as some virtue or quality or achievement that we can claim credit or reward for, Jesus tells of a widow, destitute, but who keeps pounding the judge until he gives judgment. So we are to keep on praying to the Judge to give judgment on us. We may shudder at that judgment when we look at what we have done with what God has given us already, at how we block His gifts, want only little gifts, won't let His gifts have their way with us, treat Him as a paymaster, or even as an enemy. That is unfaith, unfaith that denies God, unfaith that will not be given to, that seeks its own life despite God. "Whoever seeks to gain His life will lose it" (Luke 17:33). Of all such unfaith we are called on to repent and to claim God's judgment. We are in His hands. There is no escape. We cannot pull ourselves away from Him to commandeer and secure our lives away from Him. Our lives are lost to God, and how will He deal with us, how will He judge?

Not the way of the judge who did not want to be troubled. The one who is our judge is so troubled that He goes to Calvary for us.

The judgment on our sin was done at Calvary. It can no more bring us to condemnation. Thence forgiveness, thence how God is toward us. The one who was on the cross for us will be our judge. He is the Son of Man. "When the Son of Man comes." When is that? The final judgment. When we stand before God, then it will be clear how tenderly, how generously He has brought us on our way through those dark times when everything went wrong, and we and our lives seemed widowed, worthless. God's delaying, His seeming not to care, will then be seen as part of His wanting our good, readying us for larger gifts, the wholeness and fullness of our good, our salvation.

The word *delay* in our Gospel is the word of God's forbearance. He patiently and lovingly bears with us, with our faltering and little faith, that treats God as if He were a piecemeal Savior, a part-time Lord. His forbearance, His delaying, His seeming not to care is part of His nurturing us toward the bigger and much more He wants to give us. You see, He really loves us, more than we can expect. Expectations that would lay our calculated demands on God, He wants to clean out of us, and that may take some painful scouring. Those expectations are all too small, like those of the nine lepers who wanted no more of Jesus, were closed to His giving more, which is unbelief.

Two women grinding together, two women studying together. "The one will be taken, the other left." When the Son of Man comes, will He find faith on earth? In the reading room of the library, in classroom, in bed, on the playing field, in the frat house, under the trees decked these days in their breathtakingly beautiful color? "On earth" is where we are. If heaven is some place far away, and God is there, what use is that? No matter how kindly we would like to think of His being disposed toward us, there are times when it seems the opposite of that.

What staggered people about Jesus was that He forgave sins on earth (Luke 5:24). How He deals with us is how it is with us before God, and that is on earth. Jesus deals with you here on earth as His words of forgiveness are spoken to you, giving what they say. He deals with you here on earth as He gives you His body to eat and His blood to drink. And with all that He gives His judgment.

Judgment now on earth. The later judgment only makes perfectly clear how it is with you: faith or unfaith, Jesus or no Jesus. Jesus is the Son of Man, or do you look for another, make up one of your own, or be your own son of man, your own judge? "When the Son of Man cometh, shall He find faith on the earth?" (Luke 18:8). The life of faith is a life of prayer, hanging on to the Son of Man as your judge and not letting Him get out of being such a judge for you.

Jesus would have us pray in the words of Martin Luther's explanation of the Third Petition of the Lord's Prayer: "Your will be done on earth as in heaven. What does this mean? The good and gracious will of God is done even without our prayer, but we pray in this petition that it may be done among us also." On earth. "It is your Father's good pleasure to give you the kingdom" (Luke 12:32)—where Jesus is your king and your judge. That is His good and gracious will. When you cling to that, that good and gracious will that is yours in Jesus, He cannot cut you off nor does He want to. By Jesus' forbearance, His delaying, He wants only that you would grow strong in faith, in openness to His giving, to the always more from Him, for He means to make you whole. Then you will be really and truly human, and that is more than you can now imagine. So hang in there with faith alive.

Today's Gospel gives birth and growth of faith with the recognition that the Son of Man is Jesus, the one on His way to Jerusalem for you. He is your judge. Don't ever let Him not be such a judge for you. The judgment at Calvary, here on earth, is the bedrock certainty of our lives that holds through the dark days and deepens the days of delight. Our days are the days of the Son of Man.

AMEN.

Twenty-third Sunday after Pentecost

COLLECT AND COLOSSIANS 1:9–10

LONDON (1955)

At the end of a day it is interesting to realize just how many decisions you have made, how often your actions were the result of deliberate and considered choice. It is amazing how much of our lives go on by force of habit. We can almost stand outside ourselves and watch ourselves going through our daily routines. A man gets up, puts on his clothes, shaves, has breakfast, looks at the paper, kisses his wife good-bye, and goes to work. Should he happen to pause round 9:15, he may suddenly think, "Well, here I am," and for the first time that day become aware of himself as a conscious person, capable of decision and choice. It is comfortable to be wrapped up in habit and routine. It avoids the difficulty of making decisions. The head of a firm goes gray making decisions while the workers go unconcerned through their routine of work. How nice to have everything arranged and decided for us, but how empty and how dangerous it is to abdicate ourselves.

In affairs of this world, we do have the power of free will. We can choose whether to go by the Underground or by bus, whether to have carrots or sprouts for dinner. You can choose to be a bricklayer or a baker, to vote Labor, Liberal, or Conservative. Yet even in decisions about earthly things, we have our perplexities and distressing worries. We feel the lack of some guiding principle, and, worst of all, we don't know enough. Because of our ignorance, we don't know the right choice to make.

What, then, of the things of the higher reality? How do we make our decisions in the realm of spiritual things? How shall we choose with regard to God? Ignorance is what makes our earthly decisions so vexing, and when it comes to spiritual things, our plight is even more pitiful. We are unable to figure God out. There is no way by which we can get at Him or get a hold of Him. By looking at the world about us, we may deduce that someone almighty and most wise created the earth. Within ourselves we see planted a law of right and wrong and that we are meant to belong to something greater than ourselves to which we are responsible.

So natural knowledge doesn't help us much. We cannot climb up to God and secure a knowledge of Him by moral striving, mysticism, or reason. We cannot capture God. God, as He is known to us, is holy and all-powerful. Therefore, He is feared, for we are puny and faulty and know that we are unholy, guilty before God. All natural religions are the expression of this fear. They are an effort to buy off God, to soften God, to bribe Him over to our side. The only decision that we can make about such a God is to fear or to hate. We cannot get a hold of God. God is God the Creator, the holy God, and we are the created things, weak and guilty by our sin. God is only really known as He reveals Himself. If we are to get to know Him, He must descend to us and tell us of Himself. Because God went to the trouble of making us, He is interested in us. Apart from God's interest in us, we have no significance, so God made Himself known to us. He has spoken. We have His Word. Does this revealed knowledge of God enable us to make a decision?

God, as He revealed Himself to us, is a holy God who loves what is good and hates and punishes what is evil. This makes sense to us and agrees with our natural knowledge. But, then, in God's revelation of Himself there comes the utterly unreasonable. We learn of a God who loves us, though hateful in our sin, who loved us so incredibly much that He sent His Son to become one of us. Taking our sin and guilt on Himself, Christ died for our sin where we should have died. In Christ there is now offered forgiveness full and free. In Christ we can stand before God as His loved and happy children.

To us, as we are by nature, this doesn't make a scrap of sense. It is not fair. It is not reasonable. There must be some catch. We can't believe it. The only decision we are capable of making, confronted by God's revelation, is a negative one. This is what is meant when we say that we have no free will in spiritual matters. We are incapable of choosing God as He has revealed Himself. It is just all too much for us.

Scripture is quite explicit on this point. "But the natural man receiveth not the things of the Spirit of God: for they are foolishness unto him: neither can he know them" (1 Corinthians 2:14). We are spoken of as being dead, spiritual corpses. Even worse than being dead toward God is that we are in willful opposition to Him. "The carnal mind is enmity against God" (Romans 8:7). This enmity against God is an act of our will. We are responsible for our rejection of God, for no one is compelled to reject God.

This is our sad plight. We are incapable of choosing God, for God is not within our grasp. God, of course, knows all this. He did not have the way of rescue achieved and proclaimed just to make us more wretched as if He were like the Greek gods, like the grapes of Tantalus, grapes that were lowered, then snatched back when grasped at by the tormented wretch. The love of Jesus, which took Him to the cross, moved Him also to send the Holy Spirit so we might be won to the acceptance of Christ and all that Christ achieved for us.

This is the miracle of conversion by the gracious working of God the Holy Spirit. He creates faith in us through the Gospel, that is, He brings us to our hold on Jesus. Our coming to faith is not an act of our free will. Yet it is not by compulsion; we may resist. Our conversion is the miracle of creative love. God's love in Christ awakens us to a responding love. Love cannot be compelled or directed. Love begets love, and there is no greater love than the love of God in Christ.

"Therefore if any man be in Christ, he is a new creature" (2 Corinthians 5:17). This radical change is called being born again or, as Ezekiel says, taking out our heart of stone and giving us a heart of flesh. It is a conversion, that is, we are turned around, the whole direction of our lives is reversed. Without Christ we were heading away from God to utter ruin. In Christ we are turned around, and our course is set toward God and the life that is with Him. God's will, God's plan for us, is being realized in us.

It is God's plan that we should be His children, belonging to Him and rejoicing in His love and strength. The fulfillment of that plan of God is the only thing that we can ever successfully be. A monkey was designed to be a monkey. It may resemble or mimic a human, but it can never be a human just as we may resemble or mimic a monkey, pig, or fox, but we can never be one. We were planned to be God's children. When we try to be something else, we only achieve some pitiful clowning and the end is ruin.

What beauty there is in the bud of a rosebush becoming a rose. It has fulfilled the will of God. So we fulfill the will of God as we become His children. Our becoming God's children is a double becoming. There is our entry into God's family by faith in Christ. When we put on Christ, we stand before God as His forgiven, holy children. We are His children, for we are in Christ. This is justification. It is utterly complete, for it is altogether of Christ. But we are not yet completely as God would have us be in ourselves. The flesh still clings to us. We still falter and stumble and fall. We frustrate the will of God in sin, following our own perverse will. There is division in us, the pull toward God and the pull toward sin and death.

Knowing how our rebellions against God's will grieve our Father, our hearts are crushed in sorrowing repentance. We look to Jesus as our only hope. We pray God may forgive us and grant us strength to conquer sin and grow ever more and more His children. This growing, this becoming, is an unending process that lasts until our dying day. When we come to death, our prayer will still be, "O God, my sin is great, forgive me for Jesus' sake and make me more Thy child."

Every day we are to grow more like what God would want us to be. For this is the will of God, even your sanctification. How may this growth in holiness, this fuller realization of God's will in us, go forward? The basic requirement laid down in our text is knowledge—knowledge of God's will. We cannot fulfill God's plan in our lives unless we know what that plan is. There can only be right action where there is right knowledge. God sets forth His plan for us in His Word. There is God's plan in which the simplest child may know what God's will is for him or her. There the profoundest Christian may never cease to find new treasures and a higher glory.

If we are sincere about being God's children, we will eagerly study His will. In the Bible we see God's will worked out in the lives of His wayward saints. We also see how it may go so tragically wrong when men despise it. Through and behind it all is God's great plan of salvation, His will to make you completely, joyously His.

To neglect your church, your prayer, your Bible study, your devotions, is to tell God that you have no desire to grow, to become more and more His child, that you are satisfied with being a weak and shaky Christian, and that you have had as much as you want from Him. How perilously such a person is slipping away from God. Everything that is not in accord with God's will is given over to death and the power of darkness.

But, my friends, if we cling to Christ and His Word, growing daily in the will of God, striving to bring our lives into harmony with that will, what strength is ours, what then can harm us? When we are given over into the will of God, nothing can destroy, no more than God and His will can be destroyed. The unshakeable strength of the will of God is in us, though the world turn upside down. "And the world passeth away, and the lust thereof: but he that doeth the will of God abideth for ever" (1 John 2:17). God has set you in the paths of sonship, and His unbreakable promise is that He will never leave you or forsake you. Jesus died that God's will might be accomplished in you. He prays for you,

> Father, I will that they also, whom Thou hast given Me, be with Me where I am; that they may behold My glory, which Thou has given Me: for Thou lovest Me before the foundation of the world.... I have declared unto them Thy name ... that the love wherewith Thou hast loved Me may be in them, and I in them. (John 17:24–26)

Can our hearts contain such blessedness? We were slaves to sin. In Christ we are made free, new creatures. God's will is the only will that is truly free, and as our wills come into harmony with His will, they partake of that freedom. In your own earthly family what happiness there is in the harmony of wills and what heartache when the will of a son is set against the will of a father, or the will of a wife against her husband. Such wretchedness there is when a human will rebels against another human will, but what words of horror shall describe the rebellion of a human will against the will of God.

Happy harmony with the will of God can only be achieved in loss of self, for that is the way of love, and love is the way of God. Jesus has shown us that way. He prayed, "Not My will, but Thine, be done" (Luke 22:42). If we truly pray, "Thy will be done," we will eagerly go to the Word to be filled with the knowledge of the will of God in all wisdom and spiritual understanding. Increasing in knowledge, we shall walk more worthy of the Lord being fruitful in every good work.

St. Paul writes, "And be not conformed to this world: but be ye transformed by the renewing of your mind, that ye may prove what is that good, and acceptable, and perfect, will of God" (Romans 12:2). As we get to be well-versed in God's will for us, decisions even in earthly things will not be so irksome. We shall have resources by which to decide all things. This is not in an external set of regulations but by the inward impulse of the love of Christ. Our decisions must be worthy of people who are God's people and our only wretchedness is in rebelling against God's will.

AMEN.

Twenty-fourth Sunday after Pentecost

1 THESSALONIANS 4:13–18; MATTHEW 25:1–13

VALPARAISO UNIVERSITY

Last Wednesday, for 53 minutes, photographs were taken of our sister planet Venus, then the camera died. There was nothing living there, just rocks. One scientist commented that the images would force a rethinking of the theories about Venus because instead of sand, the pictures revealed jagged, sharp-edged rocks. Dr. Carl Sagan said that the perception of color on Venus would be of a "deep, red gloom."

The more we learn about the universe the more preposterous it becomes that we are here looking at it. This is the reverse of the former preposterousness drawn from the work of Copernicus that was used to belittle us. When our earth is seen as a tiny speck in an inconceivably immense universe, how preposterous for us to suppose we have anything in the way of significance, ourselves of the same atomic material. We are a fleeting agglomeration of propagating atoms, each specimen soon dispersed again into the dust from which it came, and the whole class of such phenomena have only a precarious continuity. A few degrees of wobble in the earth's axis, a shower of meteors, an ozone upset, and they will be snuffed out, leaving rocks or sand or ice. Where on earth could anybody have gotten the idea that we have any significance?

"Man, proud man, dressed in a little brief authority, plays such fantastic tricks before high heaven as make the angels weep" (*Measure for Measure*, 2.2.117). If no "high heaven" and "no angels," then no "fantastic tricks." No "proud man," no man. Shakespeare speaks of men and women and the astonishing world that each one is—all the wonder and horror that goes on between them.

> What a piece of work is man! How noble in reason! How infinite in faculty! In form and moving how express and admirable! In action how like an angel! In apprehension how like a god! The beauty of the world! The paragon of animals! And yet to me, what is this quintessence of dust? (*Hamlet*, Act II, Scene 2)

How like an angel, how like a god. No god, no angel—only dust.

> Imperious Caesar, dead and turned to clay, might stop a hole to keep the wind away. (*Hamlet*, Act V, Scene 1)

Yet more preposterous still that dust and clay should mock themselves. There is nothing funny or tragic about dust and clay. Yet there is about this quintessence of dust, even among the most avowedly materialist of such quintessence.

When the first Russian astronaut was orbiting the earth, he reported back to headquarters that he couldn't see any God. When he later visited London, he received an enormous welcome. Questions were asked in Parliament, expressing uneasiness at a Russian so captivating the hearts of the people. To these questions, Prime Minister Macmillan replied that we ought not to be too upset; instead consider the fuss if the Russians would have sent the dog. Ponder, too, that quintessence of dust who made up the story that tells of Kruschev drawing the astronaut aside after the official reception and saying, "Now, I have heard all you had to say here today, and it was well said, but tell me honestly and without any fear of punishment, is it true that, in fact, you found no God up there?" The astronaut replied, "No, I found no God." Whereupon Kruschev sighed, "That is what I was afraid of, but don't tell anybody." Later, when the astronaut visited Rome, the pope asked the same question and was given the same response. This story suggests how utterly preposterous it is to posit a controllable location for God and, on that basis, one way or another, deny His existence.

This implies no disrespect toward the pope. The story could also be told using the archbishop of Canterbury, or the president of The Lutheran Church—Missouri Synod. Yet your capacity to be disrespectful let no one rob you of, for it is part of the funny and the tragic that remain indestructibly characteristic of the quintessence of dust we call human. What forbids you to grin is an idol.

What could be more preposterous than this little living earth and on it our little lives? There is nothing like it, as far as we know, in all the universe. The earth may not be the center, the sun may not be the center of the universe. What difference does Copernicus make to them or they to Copernicus? The jagged rocks of Venus are about as jagged today as they were in Copernicus's time and as dumb. For the stones that cry out, you must go to Jerusalem, and they speak when the words are not heard, which cry, "Blessed be the King that cometh in the name of the Lord: peace in heaven, and glory in the highest" (Luke 19:38). "Highest heaven." Where? Riding on a donkey, and a few years earlier, "wrapped in swaddling clothes," and in a couple of days after today's Gospel, "hanging on a cross."

Here is the ultimate preposterousness. Those who exclude God with their presuppositions have no other explanation than to say that people make up their gods. This can accommodate much of the data but not all of it. The data that does not fit the hypothesis is usually particularly significant. Tertullian is reported to have said, "I believe because it is absurd." We would be led astray by this if we would set up absurdity as the ultimate criterion or, for that matter, reason, or what is emotionally satisfying. We cannot logically think: "What is absurd is true. God is absurd. Therefore, God is true. What is reasonable is true. God is reasonable. Therefore, God is true. What is emotionally satisfying is true. God is emotionally satisfying. Therefore, God is true." What comes at point two or three in a syllogism is not God. We may not give reasons for God and so give Him His clearance to exist. So to do better by Tertullian: "I believe, and I recognize that I could never have brought myself to think of God the way He really is, as He is in Jesus of Nazareth, in the manger, on the donkey, and on the cross." Such a king, in the name of the Lord. This one, highest heaven, peace and glory. Hidden in Him who weeps over Jerusalem and who tarries with His consummation so they all fall asleep. At the time He has appointed He comes—at midnight, as bridegroom and as judge. The lamp of faith lights the way into the festivity. Those without that light remain in darkness. A lamp lives from the oil that is put into it.

Those whom we have buried this last year we have buried in the confidence that they had with them their flasks of oil with their lamps. Now why should they get there ahead of us? In Thessalonica they were thinking that the faithful departed would only come in second place. They were so gung-ho about the Lord's return. Some were so excited about Jesus and His coming again that they gave up doing their work. In their adventist enthusiasm, they felt sorry about those who had died before He did return. Would they be left behind or even left out?

The apostle begins, "But I would not have you to be ignorant, brethren," (1 Thessalonians 4:13), which is his way of saying, "Now, please settle down and let these facts sink in." Fact number one is Jesus. Jesus died and rose again. That makes all the difference. Okay, got that? Well, He didn't need to do all that for Himself, did He? He did all that for you. Right? Right. "Even so," says the apostle. The consequences are drawn from Jesus' death and resurrection. Those who have fallen asleep did so "through Jesus." *Through* is a preposition of agent and instrumentality. Jesus gives them a Jesus' death. So you don't need to be full of worry about them. If theirs is such a "through Jesus" death, then it is not death that finally wipes out or separates from Him. If anything they are closer in than you are. The way by which they tunnel through is the Jesus tunnel. Whether they are already through into the light, the apostle does not say. We reckon with two points of time and get into puzzles of the day of our death and Resurrection Day. Don't get lost doing puzzles. Hear the clear word of the apostle.

What he says he draws from Jesus, His death and resurrection for us, His drawing us through death that is His kind of death. Through Jesus, with Him. And there is a word of the Lord that says where there is such falling asleep through Jesus, such with Him, there isn't any being left behind or coming in second.

Have you got that? Through Jesus, with Him. Then you won't go wrong. This calls for a bursting shout of triumph, and for that the apostle uses the spectacular, and to our ears rather curious, language of apocalyptic.

> For the Lord Himself will descend from heaven with a cry of command, with the archangel's call, and with the sound of the trumpet of God. And the dead in Christ will rise first; then we who are alive, who are left, shall be caught up together with them in the clouds to meet the Lord in the air; so shall we always be with the Lord. Therefore comfort one another with these words. (1 Thessalonians 4:16–18 RSV)

Marvelous, but first words: Jesus died and rose again. The one who is coming is the one who has come. Last words: always with the Lord. Shouldn't we have a shout of triumph? Of course, but we must let the apostle's language be the sort of language that it is and not try to make it into something else. This happens when people fasten on to "the air." What is this air? Where is this air? Gets a bit thin up there. (Greek contemporaries of Paul thought of air as what is between the earth and the moon. Then came purer ether. The further from our earth, the purer, the nearer the ultimate point of reference, pure spirit. The Jews did not have an airy realm for demons. They were expected to know Psalm 139, and from Genesis 1 the creation was demythologized for them.) Or the clouds. (Kittel 1.165 n 3. See Daniel 7:13; Matthew 17:5; 24:30; 26:64; Exodus 13:21; 40:34.) Are they cirrus, cumulus, or strato-cumulo-nimbus? They will have to be pretty big clouds, won't they? If you calculate a square foot per person and multiply by whatever figure you have to multiply by, will there be room? Then we are back again with the silly astronaut who didn't find God on the path of his orbit around our little earth or with Hal Lindsey and his "rapture" and "two separate events," which is what some Thessalonians had gotten into.

It is a constant temptation of little faith to try to calculate God's scenario. If we can figure out the when and the where, then we have God tied up with our calculations. We can predict where and when He is going to jump. How He may or may not jump. When we have God figured out, then He is really redundant, or at least a possible embarrassment to the way we have taken things in hand and are running them, as in the story that the astronaut did find God.

Will your dog be with you in heaven? Remember Martin Luther's letter to his little son Hans, telling of all the fun of playmates and ponies and such an orchard in heaven? We are all little Hanses before the words that tell of the fruition of God's promises that are theirs who fall asleep through Jesus. With Him God will bring them together with those who haven't died to be with the Lord always.

You too? Absurd, isn't it? Let our Lord do His absurdity of loving you, little you, a speck on a speck of the universe, without cooking up your own absurdities. And this Lord, who will bring you through death as His death, can be relied on to make the necessary arrangements for what we cannot calculate or even say or think. We are given some happy hints, but the center, the heart of it all, we do know and rejoice in. Next Sunday's Epistle says, "God has not destined us for wrath" (1 Thessalonians 5:9 RSV). If you want a day of wrath, you can have it if you insist. Nobody gets whipped in.

God has not destined us for wrath, but to obtain salvation through our Lord Jesus Christ, who died for us, so whether we wake or sleep we might live with Him. Through Jesus, with Him, with the Lord always. "Comfort one another with these words" (1 Thessalonians 4:18).

AMEN.

Twenty-fifth Sunday after Pentecost

MATTHEW 25:14–30

VALPARAISO UNIVERSITY (1978)

God is obviously no egalitarian. There is no equality in five, two, and one talent. And a talent is a hefty chunk of money. He is not at all cautious in the way He dishes out the stuff, then, quite foolishly, goes off with a "Now, you carry on." I know undergraduates who wish their parents treated them that way. There was one who found that on her corridor she was the only one whose mother had not insisted that, going to Valpo, she must go on the pill. That daughter wrote a beautiful letter to her mother: "Thanks for trusting me." Something terrific was going on and growing between that mother and that daughter.

Trusting is risky. It is much safer and shrewder to trust nobody. Then you can't be disappointed when you are let down or betrayed. If you defend something that way, someday you will look for it and it won't be there or it won't really be worth much at all in the end. Our beginning is when God shares His talent for creating with a man who begets and a woman who conceives. They become a father and a mother, and we become a son or a daughter. Father and mother are given to do our Father God's caring for us and nurturing us into persons, that is, loving us.

Parents are apt to say we love all our children equally, but we must be aware of what is good in saying that and what is bad. We may start all our children off with piano lessons. To keep them all at it equally can be tyranny. Perhaps only one has been given that particular talent. Our talk of talents and being talented derives from today's Gospel, though many have forgotten who it is who gives the talents, so they fall short of entering into God's joy.

You have entered into Valpo, which may not be quite the same as entering into joy, but a most vital gift in coming to university is the opportunity to test your talent, identify it, then multiply it. On Parents' Weekend we are reminded of what is come to us through our parents, who have been God's deputies for us. This morning we again acknowledge our Lord as the astonishing giver of gifts and talents. They are His, and He entrusts them to us to use and to enjoy, and gladly to show what all we make and do with them, our worship, and He has a whole lot more up His sleeve that we grow toward by using and enjoying the present ones now.

God loves to pour it out without calculation, equalization, or quantification. Such bounty is hard to bear for shriveled sinners who won't be given to but who insist on taking over and getting control. Part of controlling is a measuring of quantities that is based on comparison of sizes. Instead of receiving gifts from Him, I measure what I have as my own. If it is more than somebody else's, I am pleased and proud. That is why it is so important to have some people around who are clearly, by some yardstick or other, inferior to me. Or the yardstick we use may show that we have received a raw deal, whereupon we may flump or move on quickly to point out whose fault it is: parents', God's. "He is a hard man." If you make Him into a hard man who infringes your rights, who demands what He has the right to demand, then that is how you will get it from Him. You will get your rights. We make God our enemy when we clutch what we have as our own for ourselves. Then He is a threat to us. Others are, too, against whom we must protect ourselves and what we have. That is the way of losing even what we do have and finally ourselves too.

But that is not what God wants; He wants to be pouring out some more. Faith is receiving His gifts—not receiving the Giver from the gifts but the gifts from the Giver. Because these gifts are from Him, they are for our good, and not because we lay on them and Him some yardstick we have constructed. With whatever yardstick we are using, we may then pronounce the measurement satisfactory or unsatisfactory. No yardstick can cope with five, two, and one. So much the worse for the foolish yardstick.

On Friday at a party, I found that two men whom I have always thought of as my friends were still wearing those impossible, old-fashioned trousers that have no cuffs at all. In some cultures a big bottom is an embarrassment; in others it is a thing of beauty, enormously admired. Measuring and comparing are not the ways of love. You are not loved because you are like or unlike somebody else. You are loved. Why on earth God should love somebody like you or me is a question that has its answer only in Him. We can't work out the five, two, and one. We do know that they are all from God, and His love we cannot doubt, for it is the love that went through Calvary for each one of us. He has only one just like you. You are irreplaceable. He has none for swaps. Envying and trying to duplicate somebody else runs counter to His love. That is true even of trying to duplicate Jesus. God doesn't want a whole lot of little Jesuses. He has one of those; one is enough. He wants one *you*.

Five, two, and one are then not so much a lot, less, and little, but each one different. *Vive la difference*. Each person has a different taste, resonance, and color and can give a unique delight. So we are persons by being thus loved by God, and so by Him we are enabled to be there for one another. The picture of the body says it. The joined togetherness of being for one another. Love says it best; we are given also humility and subordination: "I am here for your sake." Shinbone can't say to the kneecap, "I can be a kneecap too" or "You don't matter." We can't even say to the apparently useless appendix: "A rabbit has a better one than I have." Bully for the rabbit, and bully for the one who gave him the better appendix. Besides I am not really all that dead keen on eating grass, and if He wanted me to, He would have given me a better appendix.

The differences matter to God. He can then love each one in a different way with a different delight. His whether you are a Jew or a Greek, slave or free, male or female. St. Paul says none of these differences may be asserted as a ground for doubting or denying anyone's being His. Paul is not propounding some sort of egalitarianism. The differences are a part of the particularization of His love. No one of us is the same as any other to our Lord. This fact is not much served by bringing in egalitarian talk and saying we are all equal to God. We are not. If there is any useful meaning in this statement, it is hidden in His love for us, and His way of loving us is with a differentiating love: five, two, and one.

This semester at Wednesday Feature we have had pastors from Namibia, Papua New Guinea, and Tanzania. The more you know them, the more different they are. They and their people are in danger of being undifferentiated, homogenized, shaped to more marketable patterns. The fact that they are Christ's men is their resource against this. We, too, may take a cool and courageous look at the attempts to standardize and equalize us. All that conformity to patterns, models, fashions we do not surrender to. We may play along with the legal fictions that are for the good of society, but our personing, our differentiation, is from Him who gives five, two, and one.

At Christmas each member of the family may get a pair of socks. A family is a little country with a realm of justice and useful fictions of equality, but that gift is most delightful that is just perfect for Jim and only Jim. When he has it all put together and holds it up, or wants you to come and share his delight in working it, you know what the next gift for him might be. Then you also know something of the joy spoken of in today's Gospel. My wife has a friend to whom she is always giving some other crazy kind of turtle. I had an unforgettable classmate who would turn around and draw funny faces and things in my book and another whose laughter is the happiest sound I have ever heard.

Gifts, gifts, gifts, not so much bigger and smaller but all different and uniquely precious—Milton and his blindness, one sparrow, one hair on your head—precious to God and so precious to us, too, to whom He gives them over. He gives so many, so we can share His joy of giving for using and sharing together. Enter into the joy of our Lord. To Him be all our joyful praise through happy, giving, sharing days.

AMEN.

Twenty-sixth Sunday after Pentecost

EXODUS 32:1–20

CONCORDIA SEMINARY (1990)

Countdown to the end—the third to the last Sunday in the church year. The horrendous Gospel has its counterpart in the horrendous Old Testament Lesson. "Lo, here is the Christ!" Aaron

> ... made a molten calf; and they said, "These are your gods, O Israel, [note the plural *gods*] who brought you up out of the land of Egypt!" [They still know to say the right phrases.] When Aaron saw this, he built an altar before it; and Aaron made proclamation and said, "Tomorrow shall be a feast to the LORD." And they rose up early on the morrow, and offered burnt offerings and brought peace offerings; [How much more correctly religious can you get?] And the people sat down to eat and drink, and rose up to play. (Exodus 32:4–6 RSV)

When the Lord is replaced by an idol, no matter how much you pretend that it is still the Lord, the idol takes over. Here Baal takes over. Nowadays, it is pluralized Baals. This third to the last week in the church year we do well (in view of the end) to recognize what replacements we are putting in place of the Lord, though we still call them by His name and go through the liturgy as if it were still in His name. "Be not deceived; God is not mocked" (Galatians 6:7). When you pray about the call you may be given or already have, is it to the Lord you pray, or have you slipped in some golden calf in His place?

When we come to the Lord's Table by way of the Small Catechism, as it admonishes us to do, we are called to examine our lives according to the Ten Commandments. "By the law is the knowledge of sin" (Romans 3:20). Note the singular. Sins in the plural don't usually cause us too much bother, least of all when we make a parade of confessing them. Identifying sins is not all that difficult. The real job is probing the sins until you identify the idols in whose service you have done them. Who or what did you put in place of the Lord? To break any of the commandments, you have to first break the First Commandment. "Thou shalt have no other gods before Me" (Exodus 20:3)—one Lord, one sin, the root and total of all sins. "Against Thee, Thee only, have I sinned, and done this evil in Thy sight" (Psalm 51:4), that is, *coram Deo*. At Sinai they went on as if *coram Deo*. They had the right phrases. They even used God's name, but they had slipped in a replacement, so they gave themselves to Baal and also to Baalim.

There are no excuses. They are fit only to be damned, and damned they are in their sin. Is there any hope? If there is any hope at all, it can only be in the Lord. Moses pleaded, "Remember Abraham, Isaac, and Israel, Thy servants, to whom Thou swarest by Thine own self" (Exodus 32:13). He clings to the promises and glimpses a way. He offers to die in place of the people. "Blot me, I pray Thee, out of Thy book which Thou hast written" (Exodus 32:32)—book of the covenant, blood of the covenant (Exodus 24:7–8). One greater than Moses, like unto him, was blotted out. He poured out His blood. "The LORD hath laid on Him the iniquity of us all" (Isaiah 53:6)—yours too. His name is Jesus, for He saves His people from their sins. From Jesus' atoning sacrifice He gives us His body to eat and His blood to drink, given and shed for you for the forgiveness of your sins.

Repent then, drinking the bitter cup of your ground-up idols. That will empty you out, and into that emptiness God gives His gifts. As surely as you eat His body and drink His blood, you are in and are held by His covenant, His testament. My forgiven people, says the Lord. They ate and drank with God and were not wiped out (Exodus 21:11).

AMEN.

The Circumcision of Our Lord

NUMBERS 6:22–27

VALPARAISO UNIVERSITY (JANUARY 1, 1978)

Today the name of Jesus is put on Mary's child, and we would put that same name on the new year that we begin. To put a name on something declares whose it is and who cares for it. You put your name on a book so everybody may know the book is yours. The mark of a name is branded onto cattle so everybody may know whose they are. The Hebrew word translated as "name" probably comes from a word meaning "to brand or to mark."

Thus the Lord put His name on Israel. They were His people, marked, called by His name. This was done again and again when they gathered to worship God. The priests, the sons of Aaron, the Levites, were to put God's name on the people. "And they shall put My name upon the children of Israel; and I will bless them" (Numbers 6:27). Our text gives the words of the blessing that puts the Lord's name on them. Three times His name is named. Each time His name is named on them, blessings are drawn out of His name and given to them.

The Lord's name is full of blessing, and in ownership that fullness is unpacked and extolled. Thus it is as in the liturgy: "Our help is in the name of the Lord who made heaven and earth." With these, we lay claim to what is there for us in the name of the Lord that is named, for God's name tells of God toward us. He has given us His name, His personal name, which conveys Him with all He has said and done and promised. We acknowledge God as Creator who made heaven and earth. He made us; we are His. But we have turned away from Him and become other than what He made us for. We cannot achieve that happiness and health that is peace (*shalom*), which we have shown by trying to make it on our own apart from Him and against Him. The help needed is not in us but in the Lord, that is, in His name, which tells who He is and what He is like. Our help is in the name of the Lord. When He tells us who He is, we know and tell who we are. This is the point of personal truth. His name puts Him true, and we respond with the truth about us. "I said I will confess my transgressions unto the Lord." Not just "I will confess my transgressions," but "I will confess my transgressions unto the Lord." Before Him, we name His name, and there no untruth or deceit can stand. We name His name and lay claim to what is in His name for us—the forgiveness of the iniquity of our sin. That forgiveness is given us in the name of the Lord. The man who has been given this to do speaks and bestows this forgiveness in the name of the Lord whose name He names on us. We know, then, whose people we are. We rejoice that we belong to Christ, for by His name we know Him and all that He is for us. Our worship, then, rejoices in and extols all that.

For Israel, God's name had in it all that He had done for them. When Abraham called on the name of the Lord, that name had in it God's call and promise to him that changed everything for Abraham, who he was and what he was. Everything was bound on the name of the Lord, who promised to make Abraham's name great, that is, one from whom would come blessing. This was declared by Abram's name being changed to *Abraham*, father of many peoples. What Abraham was for was in his name. In such usage, name and person go together and this, above all, of God. He cannot be other than His name. So His people call on His name. He cannot desert His name and become another sort of God than His name says and promises. Worship and prayer grow out of the name of God. That is why our prayer best begins with naming God and drawing out of His name something that He cannot find in anything of ourselves.

God does not have to be there for us because we need Him, or because we have some sense of dependence or inadequacy, or even some so-called religious experience. We do not have direct experience of God. We could not stand it. "Thou canst not see My face: for there shall no man see Me, and live" (Exodus 33:20). Mercifully God deals with us indirectly, immediately, by way of things of our creaturely world that He takes into His use for dealing with us, making Himself known to us, and bestowing His gifts. Above all He gives us His name—into our words for us. These words convey Him to us. We know Him through His name. We do not know God directly; we know His name. His name is Him for us. Outside of His name He cannot be known. Attempts to know Him apart from His name only project our fears and desires and seek to find our help in ourselves and not in the name of the Lord, which He has given us, which He has put on us, which makes us His.

Sin is the opposite of this. Most crassly we say, "I am not His. I belong to me." Or we supply God with a name, and we say who He is and what He is for. We put our name on God in rejection of His name on us. When we repudiate His name, He deals with us in accordance with that fact. When Israel suffered the judgment of God on her rejection of Him, the prophet cried out for Israel that they had had become as if God were never their Lord, as if His name had never been named on them.

Such a cry does not echo to death in the dark void of despair, for it is still a cry to God. There are times when everything contradicts that God is there for us. What He is putting us through seems the opposite of His name. Then we have only His name to cling to, and in that name the promise, "For whosoever shall call upon the name of the Lord shall be saved" (Romans 10:13). The Lord is committed to His name and its promise. He cannot wriggle out of it. He has put His name on us, and in that name we call on Him. "Our help is in the name of the LORD" (Psalm 124:8). In that name is blessing, everything that He would give us for our good. He promises, "In all places where I record My name I will come unto thee, and I will bless thee" (Exodus 20:24).

The Lord causes His name to be remembered when His name is named on us with the Benediction. The Benediction bestows what it says as surely as it puts the name of the Lord on us. He is for us the God He is according to His name. We are His. In our being His, we are who we are. Our identity, who we are, derives from Him. Hence the Christian custom of naming the child at Baptism. Who this child is derives from its being the Lord's, from the name being named on it with the water.

How is this child to be named? Johanna Anastasia. A girl. Wonderful! We say "sugar and spice and everything nice." When I was born, they said, "A boy. Ugh." Johanna, gift of God, happily received by Patrick and Jeanette, who bring her for the name of God to be named on her with the water, as our Lord has bidden us do. She is, then, surely His, and with His name, He is committed to care for her as one for whom Christ's death for sin is her death for sin and whose rising is her rising "to newness of life," as her name says—Anastasia, "resurrection's child."

And this on the day we celebrate the naming of Mary's child eight days after His birth, as the Jews counted. He is circumcised. On His body is cut the mark that He belongs to Israel, belongs in the covenant and the promise that the Lord gave Israel. He is an Israelite—*the* Israelite—for the name by which He is named gathers into itself all the good that God has promised His people. He will save them from all that has gone wrong with them, from all that puts them wrong with God. His name is Jesus, "for He shall save His people from their sins" (Matthew 1:21).

Who Jesus is and what He is for is all in His name. To save us from our sins, He bore them "in His own body on the tree" (1 Peter 2:24). He suffered for the forsakenness of God that was ours for our desertion of the name of God. Yet in that forsakenness, He called on the name of God. He held to that name and to the name of Jesus, to what was His to do to save us. He gave His life in place of ours. His blood was shed for us.

Tombstones nowadays have little more on them than a name. What is in all these names only God knows. But now and then there is a known name there. What is in that name, we may know much of—a person we knew, we loved, we shared life with. We know who they were, what they did, things they said—all this pours out of their name. We are still living things into our names named on us at our Baptism and that does not yet appear on a tombstone. Another year has gone into our names, and we are given another year.

The name our parents put on us at Baptism is not the primary name there put on us, for there the Lord put His name on us. His life, identity, person-bestowing name overflows into our empty one. That life is blessed that enjoys this flow from His name into ours. His name is the first, the giving name; our name is second and receiving. Our sin is the contradiction of this. Those who strive to build a Babel tower cry, "Let us make us a name" (Genesis 11:4). To Abram the Lord said, "I will bless thee, and make thy name great; and thou shalt be a blessing" (Genesis 12:2), and the Lord gave him a new name. In that name was what God had in mind for Abraham. We are promised a new name when what God has in mind for us is completed.

He whose name is Jesus says to His own:

> For thou hast a little strength, and hast kept My word, and hast not denied My name . . . I will write upon him the name of My God, and the name of the city of My God, which is new Jerusalem, which cometh down out of heaven from My God: and I will write upon him My new name. (Revelation 3:8, 12)

What is all in that bounty of names only our Father God knows. Meanwhile, we rejoice today in the name of Jesus and all that we have already received of what is in that name. With all that, and more to come as it flows into our names, we enter the new year in the strong and saving name of Jesus.

AMEN.

The Confession of St. Peter

MATTHEW 16:13–23

CONCORDIA SEMINARY (JANUARY 18, 1999)

There was no indulgence for Peter. Jesus exorcised him: "Get thee behind Me, Satan" (Matthew 16:23). Our Lord certainly does not beat about the bush. What had Peter done to get pushed away like that? The confession of St. Peter can hardly be improved on. It was given to him from the highest possible source. Jesus says, "Flesh and blood hath not revealed it unto thee, but My Father which is in heaven" (Matthew 16:17). We can't get a more solid confession than that. It is so solid that Jesus says that is what He will build His church on, playing with Peter's name.

Peter confessed what was given him to confess. What went wrong was by his subordinating that to the way he figured things out and how they ought to go. He subordinated the Christ, the Son of the Living God, to his definition of the Christ and also of the Living God. Peter worked these words His way to what worked for him. How Jesus works His words and does His words, how Jesus does the Christ-the-Son-of-the-Living-God, He tells with His prediction of the passion. That destroys the Christ-the-Son-of-the-Living-God as confessed by Peter. Peter's confession, given him to confess, he denied. Peter would not let Jesus be Christ His way. He would lay on Jesus the sort of Christ he wanted Him to be.

Now the Gospels make it clear that Peter was a pretty emotional chap, great on gut reactions. By his emotions he usually got things wrong. He certainly loved Jesus. Was it love for Jesus that prompted Peter to protest against Jesus having such a hard time ahead? The demands of love can get things terribly wrong. Law wrong. Not love, but faith. Faith has nothing to point to of itself, not even how much love it has going. Faith has nothing to say about itself but only what it is given, given as the Lord gives His gifts with His words that are His to do and to give what they say. Peter would not let Jesus be such a Christ, such a Son of the Living God. He attempted to take control of the words given him to confess. Peter would stop Jesus doing them His way.

Recently up the Jordan at Jesus' baptism, the name Servant/Son was placed on Jesus by the one whom He here recalls, "My Father which is in heaven." Suffering Servant/Son is taken up by Satan at the temptations in ways that offer alternative ways of His doing His name, non-Calvary, theology of glory ways. Satan speaks again at Calvary. "If Thou be the Son of God, come down from the cross" (Matthew 27:40). Peter speaks for Satan even with a heart full of love: "This shall not be unto Thee" (Matthew 16:22).

You can confess, saying all the right words, with a heart full of love for an alternative Christ and be the mouthpiece of Satan. Seminary attempts to fill you with all the right words, and you are daily tempted to take them over, run them the way you figure they ought to run. They aren't your words to run as you may wish to make them run. They are Christ's words, and He runs them as the Christ, the Son of the Living God, who goes to Calvary, identified as the Suffering Servant who makes Himself a sacrifice for sin. Yours, too—all of them. Even your satanic attempts to commandeer Him. That, too, and especially that, He would bring you to repentance of.

Jesus turned and looked at Peter, and Peter went out and wept bitterly. "Feed My lambs, pastor My sheep, feed My sheep." You cannot be a bigger sinner than Peter with his satanic Christology. Nevertheless, Jesus did not give up on Peter. "Simon, Simon, behold Satan hath desired to have you, that he may sift you as wheat: But I have prayed for thee, that thy faith fail not: and when thou art converted, strengthen thy brethren" (Luke 22:31–32). Have you ever thought of Jesus praying for you like that? You might ask Him.

The good news is not in some Peter, mighty hero of faith, prince of the church, number one pope. That is all law stuff. Rather, Peter, greatest possible sinner, who had such a Savior, who was the biggest sinner of us all, for He had the lot and He answered for the lot at Calvary. Such is Christ the Son of the Living God. Then there are the chummiest words that we hear from Jesus spoken to Peter: "How about taxes? What do you think? We are sons and are free, but we will pay it anyhow." And Jesus arranged for the shekel for the tax for us. That is where it is at for the two of them—together. There is something special with Jesus and Peter and with you too. He doesn't do us by numbers. You, sinner, repentant, forgiven, for Christ's sake, for Calvary's sake, here, today.

AMEN.

St. Timothy, Pastor and Confessor

JOHN 21:15–17

CONCORDIA SEMINARY (JANUARY 24, 1992)

When they had finished breakfast, Jesus said to Simon Peter, "Simon, son of John, do you love Me more than these?" He said to Him, "Yes, Lord; You know that I love You." He said to him, "Feed My lambs." A second time He said to him, "Simon, son of John, do you love Me?" He said to Him, "Yes, Lord; You know that I love You." He said to him, "Tend My sheep." He said to him the third time, "Simon, son of John, do you love Me?" Peter was grieved because He said to him the third time, "Do you love Me?" And he said to Him, "Lord, You know everything; You know that I love You." Jesus said to him, "Feed My sheep." (John 21:15–17 RSV)

So where is St. Timothy in all the foregoing? It is also just as hard to spot the man in Article V of the Augsburg Confession. Nothing of St. Timothy in the lessons. But I didn't pick them. Nothing of St. Timothy in the lessons; everything of St. Timothy in the lessons. Everything that matters. Everything that he is there for. Everything that he was put there for at his ordination by the Lord with His words and the hands of the presbyterium into the apostolic ministry. Same one as Paul. As Paul put it, "Till I come, give attendance to reading, to exhortation, to doctrine. Neglect not the gift that is in thee, which was given thee by prophecy, with the laying on of the hands of the presbytery"

(1 Timothy 4:13–14). They are the verbs a pastor is given to do. They don't happen unless he is there doing them. They are his office. This office has a number of names, and each name says it with some particular facet. The name in today's Scriptures is "pastor," "shepherd." It is one of the numerous names that belonged to Jesus that He gives to the apostolic ministry, so the names give a Jesus location. Where He is present in His words with the mouth He has put there for the saying of them, there is the saying and hearing of His words and there is the church.

The words are what feed the sheep. This feeding is the big verb for pastors. So those who may be called by the Shepherd to be pastors are filled up with the words of the Lord at seminary. At ordination a load of the Lord's words are read onto and into the ordinand. The words are in there for the Holy Spirit's use as Jesus promised that His Spirit would bring them out as may be needed. A pastor is not left to try and think up some of his own. A pastor's feeding the sheep is then Jesus feeding the sheep. Jesus' feeding the sheep goes on where the pastor is feeding the sheep. They hear the Shepherd's voice. The shepherd is Jesus. The shepherd is pastor. Separate those and we are done for. Fit only for the dunghill. Augsburg Confession XXVIII says it.

Ezekiel 34 is even more devastating. The words of the Lord that He gave to His prophet Ezekiel to say for Him.

> The word of the LORD came to me, "Son of Man, prophesy against the shepherds of Israel, prophesy and say to them, even to the shepherds, 'Thus says the LORD God: Ho, shepherds of Israel who have been feeding yourselves! Should not shepherds feed the sheep? You eat the fat . . . but you do not feed the sheep.' "(Ezekiel 34:1–3)

"My sheep," says the Lord. The rejected shepherds have been saying, "My sheep, my people, my members, my church" and have been acting as if that were indeed the case. Then comes our Old Testament reading where it appears that the Lord, having written off the unfaithful shepherds, takes over the work of shepherd and does it Himself. He is doing the good shepherding Himself. "I will be the shepherd of My sheep." True. But if you look more closely, you see that He is doing it by the mouth of His prophet who speaks the words that carry the Lord's shepherding. Similarly in Augsburg Confession Article V. After confessing the Office of the Holy Ministry, instituted by the Lord for the delivery of the salvation gifts confessed in Article IV, our attention is no longer directed to the ministers but to the means of grace, which have been put there so the men who occupy the office can give them out. Thus we are left in no doubt that it is the Lord Himself who is doing what the pastor has been put there to be His mouth and His hand for.

As the Large Catechism observes, we see in Holy Baptism a man's hands, but it is the Lord Himself who is doing it. In contrast with this we have the consumerist church growth people clericalizing by directing our attention to the man. You must sell yourself before you can sell your product. So the salesman puts himself forward, with sort of the Johnny Carson entry, and having established a relationship with himself may go on into something concocted to work the people toward the manipulated result, which may help to meet the mission board's quota and so avoid a budget cut.

One newly ordained pastor was told by the branch office that he had five years to meet the quota and, if not, then he would get the ax. Ezekiel speaks to this situation. The Law part speaks to the pastors who put themselves in the way. The Gospel part speaks of the Lord Himself doing it with no attention paid to the prophet through whom He is doing it. Separate the prophet, the pastor, as an independent item, and he is done for and will be no more use than his own doing it, which will then not be the Lord's doing it and will not last. Only the Lord's doing it lasts, lasts to unfailing glory. This, too, the Chief Shepherd shares with those whom He puts in His place for feeding the sheep.

Hear the words given to Peter to speak, words brought out of him by the Holy Spirit, so bestowing what they say and working their gifts in those into whom they are said, as they are read into you there at your ordination:

> Feed the flock of God which is among you, taking the oversight thereof, not by constraint, but willingly; not for filthy lucre, but of a ready mind; Neither as being lords over God's heritage, but being examples to the flock. And when the chief Shepherd shall appear, ye shall receive a crown of glory that fadeth not away. (1 Peter 5:2–4)

Did we forget about St. Timothy? No, we have been where he is all the time. Where the Lord put him, reading of Scripture, preaching, teaching. Where the Lord may put you, for the preaching of His words,

for the giving out of His gifts to His people, where there is salvation delivered for your hearers and for you—crowns of unfading glory.
AMEN.

Polycarp, Bishop and Martyr

REVELATION 2:8–11

COUNCIL OF PRESIDENTS (FEBRUARY 23, 1978)

"Eighty and six years am I his servant and he never did me any wrong. How can I blaspheme my King who saved me?" (*Martyrdom of Polycarp*, 9.3). Polycarp, whom we celebrate today, offered these words, and they have been ringing through the centuries of the church and now here, too, among those given particular responsibility and care for the good of those of Christ's people indicated by The Lutheran Church—Missouri Synod. For Polycarp, it was the church in Smyrna. He was likely there when the letter that is our text arrived from John. Polycarp's martyrdom lives through its promise's fulfillment. He would be the messenger of the Good News, the angel of the church in Smyrna. Polycarp's title is not because of him but because of the message he is entrusted with. The words of that message are not his but are of "the First and the Last, which was dead, and is alive" (Revelation 2:8). It is the Lord who speaks, "I know."

When you have confronted problems and perplexities and sought the ways forward that may best serve Christ and His people, you have need to hear the Lord say, "I know." In our uncertainties and the mess that we often make of things, we are to know quite surely that our Lord knows, not just with a knowledge that has the facts straight. That is a knowledge that may prompt our repentance. But the knowledge that is His kind of knowing, personal, pulling to Himself, and prompting us along with Him to share in what He has in mind to do. The Lord knows what we have to face: enemies from the outside and from within, the temptation to doubt Him. Even the worst of it the Lord uses as a way to bless us, to test, to cleanse, to have no other reliance than in Him. He is the Lord; He numbers the days. Ten days, a short time, and a specific time, that He specifies.

Polycarp spoke of the short time it would take the fire to kill him, by which he would escape the unending fire that would be his if he denied Christ. The heroic martyrs may seem to have had it clearer and easier than we do. Polycarp was asked to curse Christ by saying *anathema Christos*. There it is full and clear. Our temptations to deny Christ, to put other things ahead of Him, come in subtler ways, even in ways that suggest we would thereby be doing Christ service.

How can we know? Our Lord says, "I know thy works, and tribulation, and poverty, (but thou art rich)" (Revelation 2:9). Martin Luther's final words say it also: "We are beggars that is true." We are rich because He says so, because He makes us so, even when we can see only our poverty. Bengel comments, "Count up your spiritual pennies. They won't add up to much." Not our pennies, but the Lord's riches given us. The one who died and came to life says, "I know," and further commits Himself with His promise, "I shall give."

Whether it is 86 years that Christ is lived with and from, the First and the Last who died and came to life, or through the particular number of years that He has measured for you, He is faithful. He knows. He gives. Behold in Christ and from Him the confidence unto death—the little death that a little fire can do, the big death, the second death of the big fire that shall not hurt us, for in Christ we are more than conquerors.

> Nay, in all these things we are more than conquerors through Him that loved us. For I am persuaded, that neither death, nor life, nor angels, nor principalities, nor powers, nor things present, nor things to come, nor height, nor depth, nor any other creature, shall be able to separate us from the love of God, which is in Christ Jesus our Lord. (Romans 8:37–39)

As members of the Smyrnian church, rich in their treasuring the words of our Lord as is The Lutheran Church—Missouri Synod, as they remembered and told of Polycarp's martyrdom, they said, "We can never forsake Christ who suffered for the salvation of those who are being saved in the whole world, nor can we worship any other" (*Martyrdom of Polycarp*, 17.2). With them and Polycarp, we say,

AMEN.

St. Matthias, Apostle

ACTS 1:15–26

Concordia Seminary (February 24, 1995)

Why all the fuss about Matthias? The Acts of the Apostles opens with the big event of the ascension. The next big event is Pentecost. In between is a call meeting. With a short list of two candidates, they prayed, the Lord decided, and it was Matthias. We never hear of him again. Why bother about Matthias? Actually, we do hear of him again. On the day of Pentecost there stand the Twelve—Peter, standing with the Eleven. Peter preached a sermon. Peter plus eleven equals twelve. Similarly, Matthew 28:11, to whom the apostolic mandate is given, twelve minus Judas equals eleven. That eleven plus Matthias equals twelve. Are you still with me?

The Lord is going to have His Twelve. You can't do anything more Yahwehish than that. Luke 6 tells us that Jesus prayed all night, and when it was day, He called His disciples and chose from them twelve, whom He named apostles. Of the Twelve thus ordained—it can be done without the hands bit, as Dr. Walther observed—we are told their names. No one is left in doubt who is ordained. The last name is Judas Iscariot. Twelve minus Judas equals eleven. Eleven plus Matthias is twelve. The Lord has His Twelve. He does not get stuck at eleven, He has Himself a people, an Israel, a Twelve. All clear. Carry on.

The mandate for the Twelve is carried out on Pentecost Day. There is the apostolic ministry. There is teaching. There is baptizing. There disciples have thus been made. Getting close to three thousand. Isn't that just the way we push statistics? Unlike our Lord's counting, we may miss somebody. On Pentecost Day, there is no doubt there are Twelve. There is no doubt there is church. Those giving out the gifts and those to whom the gifts are given. Without both, no gifting (Augsburg Confession V).

How many did Matthias baptize? The apostle Paul would not let us get stuck with that question. Christ is the one, Christ crucified, by whose cross the gifts were achieved, and He is the one who gives them out by use of the instruments He has put there for His giving them out. If you wanted your child baptized, Pastor Paul sent you along to one of the other pastors. Baptizing is not in his *missa canonica*, his call in the specifying sense (Augsburg Confession XXVIII, 8, *iuxta vocationum*).

What is important is that, as the Large Catechism notices, the baptizing is done by the Lord by His use of the instrument He put there for His doing it. That belongs in our celebration of St. Matthias today. St. Matthias does best for us in pointing us to Jesus, the Twelve-er. It is Jesus' show, and what He is into is having Himself augmentingly a Twelve, an Israel, His own people, His apostolic church, as we confess every Sunday.

It is Luke who delivers this Twelve/Israel most fully. We can only hope that Theophilus had enough schooling to catch on. How cross-cultural can you get? Matthias, as his name would indicate, was an honest-to-goodness Jew, "gift of Jehovah." These would have no problem in getting all of this talk of the Twelve. But after Pentecost the Twelve are not heard of again in the Acts of the Apostles, except when they appoint seven men to take care of the distribution to the needy so they can stick to what the Lord put them there for. That they disappear is really not surprising because, as apostles, they went. Where they all went we are not told. We are told how the Word of the Lord grew and how it traveled—*per pedes apostolorum*, beautiful feet— to the center of the world and on to the uttermost parts of the world. More apostles were made—Paul, Barnabas, Timothy, Titus. From the start no one doubted that it was the Lord who made them that. The Lord's mandate ran beyond the reach of the first apostles, the Twelve ones. What uttermost part of the earth Matthias went to we are not told, but we do know what he did there or, better, what the Lord did there by His use of Matthias: teach, and baptize and so make disciples and have Himself a people.

The "there" to which this year's candidates will go we shall (God-willing) hear on call night. They may go, and we may never hear of them or see them again until the joyful Twelve-ing of which Revelation tells us. The Lord surely has His Twelve. The Twelve can't hold it all, so twelve times twelve. If not before, see you there. And St. Matthias too. And those whom you and he baptized and taught, whom the Lord baptized and taught. His name on them, a 144,000. He has us counted. He can't forget you. Don't forget St. Matthias. You can be sure our Lord hasn't mislaid him.

AMEN.

The Nativity of St. John the Baptist

Luke 1:57–80

Holden Village (June 24, 1971)

I had first thought of preaching about the uses of a dreary day and of receiving such a day as a gift of God. I could preach how we are pulled to Him not only when the sun shines brilliant in the splendor of the mountains but also through days of cold and rain. I could preach how God's holding of us in His loving hands is all the time—through cold and through sunshine, through sunny days and through days of darkness. That would be relevant, but there is another wholeness of Christian living to which we should think about today. We are not just an isolated little group of people at Holden Village, but part of God's people through the centuries and around the world. It is in the company of Christ's people that we have our place, our identity, and our task. Around the world today millions of Christian people, as they have done for centuries, are remembering that today is six months before Christmas Eve and our Savior's birth. Christians are also remembering the birth of John the Baptist, our brother in the company of God's people in which he also has his place, identity, and task.

Two boys are born at the beginning of the Gospel according to St. Luke, one born six months before the other. Because their mothers are cousins, artists have often pictured the boys playing together, but they grew up in opposite parts of the land: Mary's boy up north in Galilee and Elizabeth's son in the hill country of Judea. One grew up in the home of a carpenter, the other in the home of a priest, a more comfortable and cultured home.

The hill country and the wilderness saw John grow to mature manhood. Like Elijah before him in the wilderness, John knew the winds and storms and quaking of the earth. His still, small voice was the message of his parents telling him of the work that he had to do, his role in God's dealing with His people. We are not told about John's long years of training and preparation, of setting and equipping himself for his task.

John's father had sung of God's dealing with Israel, of the promises to Abraham, the promise of deliverance, of bringing to completion what God has in mind to achieve in this world. So John was not a young man without history and without identity. He knew he belonged in the people of God and had his part to play. Then, when the time came for John to do what he had to do, he burst suddenly on the scene—a gaunt, startling figure with hair and clothes that declared what he was for. John had the garment of camel's hair and leather belt of a prophet, of an Elijah. The word of the Lord came to John, the son of Zechariah, in the wilderness, and he went into all the region about the Jordan, preaching a baptism of repentance for the forgiveness of sins. As it is written:

> The voice of one crying in the wilderness, Prepare ye the way of the Lord, make His paths straight. Every valley shall be filled, and every mountain and hill shall be brought low; And the crooked shall be made straight, and the rough ways shall be made smooth; And all flesh shall see the salvation of God. Then said he to the multitude that came forth to be baptized of him, O generation of vipers, who hath warned you to flee from the wrath to come? Bring forth therefore fruits worthy of repentance, and begin not to say within yourselves, We have Abraham to our father: for I say unto you, That God is able of these stones to raise up children unto Abraham. And now also the axe is laid unto the root of the trees: every tree therefore which bringeth not forth good fruit is hewn down, and cast into the fire.
>
> And the people asked him, saying, What shall we do then? He answereth and saith unto them, He that hath two coats, let him impart to him that hath none; and he that hath meat, let him do likewise. Then came also publicans to be baptized, and said unto him, Master, what shall we do? And he said unto them, Exact no more than that which is appointed you. And the soldiers likewise demanded of him, saying, And what shall we do? And he said unto them, Do violence to no man, neither accuse any falsely; and be content with your wages.
>
> And as the people were in expectation, and all men mused in their hearts of John, whether he were the Christ, or not; John answered, saying unto them all, I indeed baptize you with water; but one mightier than I cometh, the latchet of whose shoes I am not worthy to unloose: He shall baptize you with the Holy Ghost and with fire: Whose fan is in His hand, and He will

thoroughly purge His floor, and will gather the wheat into His garner; but the chaff He will burn with fire unquenchable.

And many other things in his exhortation preached he unto the people. But Herod the tetrarch, being reproved by him for Herodias his brother Philip's wife, and for all the evils which Herod had done, Added yet this above all, that he shut up John in prison. (Luke 3:4–20)

Sudden, swift, devastating, dramatic—then John's life was all over. Prison and execution, John's head cut off at the request of a strip dancer, daughter of a marriage-breaking mother, and by a half-drunk princeling. In prison, John wondered whether it was all a mistake. But he did not just slump there and go to pieces with complaints that he deserved a better deal. He reached for an answer where, if there was an answer, it alone could be found. John sent to Jesus with the questions, Are you for real? Are you the one?

The answer that John got from Jesus was nothing that he did not already know. He was given no special word, experience, or demonstration. His disciples came back reporting that Jesus only said, "Go and shew John again those things which ye do hear and see: The blind receive their sight, and the lame walk, lepers are cleansed, and the deaf hear, the dead are raised up, and the poor have the gospel preached to them. And blessed is he, whosoever shall not be offended in Me" (Matthew 11:4–6).

This last was John's temptation. Jesus was doing His work His way, which did not seem to fit the way John thought things should be done. Crowds had flocked to John, then they had left him and gone to Jesus. John's message was the stern denunciation of sin, and Jesus was associating with doubtful and unlikely people, not the sort of people you would think of in connection with the kingdom of God.

John was faced with the question: Jesus' way or the way I think things should go? He had already given answer with words. John had said, "He must increase, but I must decrease" (John 3:30), and now he was faced with living it out. He answers his own question with his life. Against John's doubts and uncertainties he lays his head on the block, and with his death he confesses with ultimate clarity, "Yes, you are the one. Your way, not mine."

We see in John the Baptist how Christ's people lay their lives on the line, refusing to serve their advantage by accommodating to the

Salomes, Herodias, and Herods of this world, refusing to make popularity and success the measure of their lives. In John, we see the faith that holds through death, which is Christ's gift.

If we use the lives of God's great heroes only as examples, we end in discouragement. The comparison crushes us to wonder what is the use or hope of a feeble Christian like me. John the Baptist is most for us when we hear and heed his message—a message of repentance and, above all, a message that points to Christ. Follow the hand and the words of John as he points to Jesus. "Behold the Lamb of God, which taketh away the sin of the world" (John 1:29). So your sin and mine, all our failures, our doubting God's plans and promises, our insistence on our own way instead of His.

Christ answers for our sins, the Lamb slain for our forgiveness, our liberation, our being included in God's company of people among whom we know who we are and what we are for. He associates with such unlikely people as you and me, and with us He would do His work in the world. Forgiveness, acceptance, liberation from all our slaveries, life that is shaped and shines with His love, even in prison and through dreary days.

So we thank God for John the Baptist. We thank God for all who this day are thanking and praising God with us in New York and New Guinea, in Holden Village, for each other, and through and above it all giving thanks for Christ, who has joined us to Himself and to one another with a love that holds through death itself, for Him whose birth we shall celebrate, God willing, six months from tonight, whose coming John the Baptist heralds. John, who serves us still, as he points to the Lamb of God who takes away the sins of the world.

AMEN.

St. Peter and St. Paul, Apostles

MATTHEW 16:13–20

HOLDEN VILLAGE (JUNE 29, 1971)

June 29 is another saint's day, and not just one but two of the biggest saints: Peter and Paul. Early Christian artists put Peter on one side of

Jesus and Paul on the other. It is, however, a bit much to commemorate both Paul and Peter in one day. It is more than we can handle. Because Paul is traditionally a great Lutheran hero, let us do just Peter.

Of all the Twelve, Peter appears the most warm, vivid, and human. It is easy to love this man—spontaneous, impetuous, ardent, all the way with Jesus, getting things frightfully wrong, failing wretchedly, then pulled back into the big action. Oddly enough, Peter is not there where the action first begins. So his brother Andrew goes and gets him. "We have found the Messiah" (John 1:41). Peter is ready for this. Jesus says, "Thou art Simon the son of Jona: thou shalt be call Cephas [Peter], which is by interpretation, A stone" (John 1:42). Jesus gives him a new name—not really a statement of fact but a promise and a gift. Peter would be given the Rock that would strengthen him with the rock faith that would carry him through to the final victory. Along the way it is made quite clear that the rock strength does not come from him but is a gift—Christ for him.

Christ is for Peter from top to bottom. From the mighty words of Messiah, what Israel was all about, from the promise of the new name, Jesus goes with Peter into the everyday world of his home where there is a problem with his mother-in-law. What is ailing her Jesus heals, and she puts the kettle on for a nice cup of tea. Jesus comes into the world of Peter's job, too, and tells him what to do—imagine a carpenter telling a fisherman how to fish (like one of us telling Al or Will how to catch trout in Hart Lake). But Peter listens. "We have been doing it the right way all night and caught nothing, but if You say so, okay." Then he is staggered by the catch. This is too much for Peter. He confronts a generosity that does not make sense either according to how you catch fish or his deserving. This simply bursts Peter's way of understanding, and without that, he can't figure out what he is in for with this man. No man has ever done this to him before. He blurts out, "Depart from me, for I am a sinful man, O Lord." "Don't be scared," says Jesus, "I've got fishing for you to do that you never dreamt of. From now on you are to catch men for Me."

With Peter we see the wonder of Jesus' way with a man—all His warmth and His humor—the nickname, fixing his mother-in-law, then the big joke about paying taxes together. Jesus asks Peter like you ask a buddy, "What are we to do about our taxes? We are in this together." Jesus had called Peter away from his source of income to be a son of the kingdom, God's kingdom, and enslaved no more to any of the kingdoms of this world. "Do the kings of this world take taxes from their sons or from others?" "From others," replies Peter. Then Jesus, playing with the words, says, "Then the sons are free." What a miracle! These two Galilean friends are together as kings and lords of the world, subject to no power or prince. Lord of all things, they are, therefore, free to serve. They pull their weight for the little kingdoms of this world; they will pay their taxes as free men. "Go catch a fish and the money it brings in its mouth will pay our taxes." Fantastic! What freedom these two friends share (Matthew 17:24–27).

There is another joke when Jesus again plays with the words, this time with Simon's gift name, Peter (*Petros*), which means rock (*petra*). It is the big question, "Whom do men say that I the Son of man am? And they said, Some say that Thou art John the Baptist: some, Elijah; and others Jeremiah, or one of the prophets." Then He probes to their hearts, "But whom say ye that I am?" (Matthew 16:13–15). What was churning inside their wondering, doubting, hoping, Peter gets it out for them bold and clear. He could sound so brave. "Thou art the Christ, the Son of the living God" (Matthew 16:16). Peter had understood. "Blessed art thou Simon Bar-Jona," says Jesus, using Peter's old name.

> For flesh and blood hath not revealed it unto thee, but My Father which is in heaven. And I say also unto thee, That thou art Peter, and upon this rock I will build My church; and the gates of hell shall not prevail against it. And I will give unto thee the keys of the kingdom of heaven. (Matthew 16:17–19)

Then Jesus brings them close to this rock, the mighty rock whose strength and power are the opposite of what this world honors as strength and power, for this is the mystery of love's power and victory that suffers and goes all the way to death and through it. This bursts all Peter's way of figuring things out. This is not his kind of Christ at all. And Peter says so. Never! With all the vehemence of his love for Jesus and all his getting it wrong. Jesus gives it to him straight, "Get thee behind Me, Satan: thou art an offence unto Me: for thou savourest not the things that be of God, but those that be of men" (Matthew 16:23). From the summit of the great rock confession, Peter is flattened by Christ, to whom he had put the temptation of Satan to do the things the world's way and make Himself big and, of course, His followers along with Him.

The rock way is the cross way. That is the way of victory and liberation. The giving way of love. Anyone who tries to serve oneself, make oneself big and secure, is done for. The way of life is only the Christ-given life. No matter how much money we may make, no matter how big we may make ourselves or defend ourselves against God in the God spot we have taken over, we are lost, for we have blocked and destroyed our lives in which the living flow is outward, the giving way, the longing way, all the way, always on, forward, without termination. Sin offers terminations. "At this level, this size, you will be able to say, 'I have made it. I have what I want.'" The offer is a lie, the opposite of life, the termination is death. Jesus rescues us from termination, from the mortal terminations, the levels, the size of self or achievement by which we would secure ourselves against every threat—even the threat of God, for this is deception, the no to life, with termination death.

As Jesus entered Peter's home and work and brought with Him opportunities to serve, so He enters Peter's death, the death of us all that we determine with our no to love, to life, to God. The prison of our mortal constructions, our ways of figuring things out, our ways of making ourselves big, defensed, and secure, our termination, our death. He enters them all. Jesus dies our death for us, the death that terminates the loving, giving life that flows from generous God. He bears our separation from God. Jesus suffers our hell, but hell and death cannot hold Him, for He never said yes to them. He did not sin. The sinless one takes what was coming to us by our sin. Jesus takes sin's claim on us and suffers it through. For on Him sin had no claim. Because of Jesus' taking it, sin can no more make claim on us. We are liberated from its claim and dominion, its death that we willed with our sin.

The smile that Jesus shared with Peter over the little kingdoms of this world He shares with us over all that would destroy us: sin, death, Satan, and hell. From their dominion we are free, kings, priests, a holy nation, God's own people in the life that is always onward and more, without end. The rock of certainty is Christ. Even in our last glimpse of Peter, we see him still getting things wrong. He wanted to check out what our Lord had in store for John. Jesus gives him a friend's straight answer, "That is not your business. Your business is discipleship. Follow Me." Peter followed. Jesus had told him of the death with which he would glorify God.

Tradition tells that Peter never heard a cock crow without tears and that when they came to crucify him he asked for the upside down way of doing it, for he was not worthy to be crucified as his Lord in His crucifixion, the rock, the Cavalry rock against which little Nero, nor sin nor death, nor the gates of hell can prevail. Peter confessed the Rock. He often slipped from the Rock, but the Rock carried him through. Lord Jesus, rock us too.

Amen.

The Visitation

Luke 1:39–56

Holden Village (May 31, 1971)

Little Mary is pregnant with Jesus, has no husband, perhaps her mother is dead, and she is an orphan. To whom can she turn? She goes to her cousin, who is also expecting, a much older woman who can help. The evangelist does not tell us that Elizabeth had been reading Dr. Spock and wondering how that fit in with her own mother's "Spare the rod and spoil the child," but we get the picture: two women getting together to talk about having a baby, the caring and things that needed to be done. Womanly hearts flow out to these two women with a warmth of shared feeling and understanding that men cannot grasp. Good, helpful Joseph would really not be much help at all. Mary needed Elizabeth, the older woman, to help her and tell her so many things. Mary had need, and a kind of desperation, for she went with haste. How was she going to handle her situation that would set the tongues wagging? She wanted to be a good mother and know all the things that needed to be done for her child.

At Mary's coming, Elizabeth was thrilled when her child began a lusty kicking in her womb. She was glad to God as she was joining Him in the creation of life and someone more to be loved, her child, and to his mother's joy was given more. It was given to Elizabeth to know that her little cousin's baby was something more. Her young cousin was mother of all mothers of all the world. In Mary, through her womanhood, the Lord was coming.

Blessed art thou among women, and blessed is the fruit of thy womb. And whence is this to me, that the mother of my Lord should come to me? For, lo, as soon as the voice of thy salutation sounded in mine ears, the babe leaped in my womb for joy. And blessed is she that believed: for there shall be a performance of those things which were told her from the Lord. (Luke 1:42–45)

Elizabeth agrees with Martin Luther in recognizing the greatest miracle in all this. There is the miracle of the angel's message to Mary, the miracle that God should love us who waste and destroy His world, each other, and ourselves in rebellion and disobedience against Him. That God should love us so much that He joins us in our world to get under the burden of the misery we have made, as one of us, to free us, love us love's way all the way to the bottom, and chooses a maiden, whom no one thought of any importance, to be His way to join and rescue us, born of a virgin. Then there is the most staggering miracle of all—that Mary believed it. She was given to, she received beyond thought and imagination, and simply acknowledged the gift. "Behold the handmaid of the Lord." Here is the miracle of faith. Into her nothingness the gift, the nonentity of Mary becomes "the mother of my Lord."

Mary's response is not, "Yes, that is me. Just think what it does for my self-image." Hers is the song of faith that tells giver God what an astonishing God He is with all of herself. "My soul doth magnify the Lord, And my spirit hath rejoiced in God my Savior" (Luke 1:46–47). We call it Mary's song, but it isn't something that she just whipped up for the occasion. It is some Scripture she had learned by heart at Sunday school, so she is equipped for some solid praise. It is mostly Hannah's song of praise to God for the son that was given to her, Samuel, whom she gave back to the Lord's service. Leah's song is in it too. So Mary's song is a piece with the song of all grateful mothers for the gift of a child created with them. Yet Mary is mother number one. Blessed is she among women, for the fruit of her womb is my Lord.

So there is a size of joy and gift in Mary's song above all others. As mother she has the part of God to play for her child, and her child is God Incarnate. God hidden in child and boy like other children, whom she must nurse and teach to pray and help Him learn the commandments and the promises. The Fourth Commandment says, "Honour thy father and thy mother" (Exodus 20:12). This is honor that belongs only to God, and this honor He shares with parents who have the part of God for their children as His deputies in creating and nurturing their children's life.

The role of motherhood, and a mother's love, like all the other loves we have been studying this week, needs another love running along with it, the love of the First Commandment. God's love and love of Him are always first and largest. For only as all our loves are tied in with God's love do they have their health, vitality, and happiness. In this way, too, a mother's love is kept from shriveling or growing hazardously oversize. We are told of two occasions when Mary had to learn this. At Cana she gave Jesus a prod, "Aren't You going to do something about it?" Jesus says, "What I am to be doing is not something that you have the management of." Mary took it and magnificently and humbly she tells the servants, "Whatever He tells you to do, do it."

On another occasion Jesus was with His disciples and preaching. Mary sent a message summoning Him to come to her. Jesus did not go but proclaimed a relationship with Himself that is deeper and larger than mother and child, into which the relationship of mother and child is to be included and find its maturing and fulfilling place. Mary, too, had to learn discipleship. It was not easy. Yet in the hour of her utmost grief, a sword through her heart, she knew that being Jesus' mother was not something to be cast aside. Jesus appointed John to do the son's part for her that He could not do because of what was His to do by cross and resurrection for her and for us all. Tenderly from the cross, "Woman, behold thy son! . . . Behold thy mother!" (John 19:26–27).

All our loves have their full meaning, maturing, and fulfillment within His strong, saving, forgiving love to a happiness unimaginable but toward which all our love and happiness are to point and pull us as they are held within His love.

Let us pray:

For mothers, God, we thank You, for Hannah, for Leah, for Elizabeth, and for our own mother.

As mothers, we thank You, God Creator, that You use us, sharing with us the joy of creation, giving us children to love and care for with You. Forgive us when we play God without You and forget that we are Your deputies and disciples.

Dear Lord, bless all mothers everywhere.

We thank You for Mary and Your being born of her to become one of us, travel our way with us, and bear the burden of our sins to Calvary.

Keep all our loves within Your forgiving and life-giving love. We thank You also for all the mothers' sons who are not called on to wage war, and be the strength of all mothers whose sons are killed. Frustrate the designs of all evil, and bless the efforts of all those who serve peace and justice among us. Grant us peace and, above all, Thy peace.

Amen.

St. Mary Magdalene

Luke 22:14–23

Concordia Seminary (July 22, 1987)

It is Wednesday in the week of Pentecost 6, July 22, Mary Magdalene's Day. Yet the Gospel appointed today puts us at the first full moon after the spring equinox—Passover. Why bother with what day it is? They all look the same to me. And aren't we going to be rising above things temporal to things eternal to escape our boring, temporal location here? Nothing of the sort, says our Lord in today's Gospel. He is quite specifically and uniquely located. The evangelist has quite circumstantially told of the Passover preparation in the appointed place, the Upper Room, within the city limits of Jerusalem. The disciples went and found it as He had told them, and they prepared the Passover. They do not choose the place—He does. Clearly Jesus is running things. Thus nothing is by chance or by their ideas and projections. How wrong these are, the evangelists never tire of telling us.

Then *the* hour came, and not just any hour, *the* hour, *the Lord's* hour. Without specific time and place, nothing can happen for us. That is where we are. And Jesus graciously appoints the place and the time where He will be with us. More specifically, He will be with us at table—reclining at table, which is a feature of free men celebrating Passover. Not slaves, but ransomed free men. And it was thought that you were clearly not slaves but free when you did not serve but someone else served you. Jesus rejects such a notion: "I am among you as He that serveth" (Luke 22:27).

In John we are told of Jesus' washing their feet and Peter's objection. They can't stand a servant Jesus. That doesn't fit in with their plans. They want a Jesus who enables them to play it big. This is told to us at the end of today's Gospel: "And there was also a strife among them, which of them should be accounted the greatest" (Luke 22:24). Following today's Gospel, Jesus rejects such leadership notions. Not leaders but servants is how it is with those who are His. Who is greater? One who sits at table or one who serves? Is it not the one who sits at table? But Jesus is among you as one who serves. A disciple is not greater than his master. The impulse to be great pushes upward and away from where Jesus is at, here at the table. He has given them the place and the time. They are here with Jesus at table at Passover time.

Jesus speaks, "With desire have I desired to eat this passover with you before I suffer" (Luke 22:15). It is Passover, but such a Passover as there never has been before. This Passover is linked with His Passion. Because it is such a Passover, Jesus points to the fulfillment of all Passovers. "For I say unto you, I will not any more eat thereof, until it be fulfilled in the kingdom of God" (Luke 22:16). What is happening here is linked with the fulfillment of the kingdom of God. This rings in everything that has been said about the kingdom of God in the Gospel. It belongs to the poor, those who are only giveable to.

Most of what is said in Luke about the kingdom of God is dread warning to those who think it belongs to them, something they do or decide about. In today's Gospel everything is centered in Jesus, what He says, what He does. He took a cup and gave thanks. Both of these are participles. The main verb is "He said." The one who takes the cup and says the prayer is the head of the family. Jesus thus embraces the disciples as His family and more. They are the apostles, and in Luke that is clearly the Twelve. Jesus is having Himself an Israel. He is doing the Passover liturgy. Jesus does it as if it belongs to Him. He gives them a cup to drink. Jesus has His cup to drink. He prays about it in Gethsemane and drinks it at Calvary.

"Divide it among yourselves" (Luke 22:17). They do not here drink each from his own cup according to Passover custom, but from a cup Jesus gives them to drink from. And it comes with the promise of when He will drink with them again in the fulfillment of what is going on here: "For I say unto you, I will not drink of the fruit of the vine, until the kingdom of God shall come" (Luke 22:18). So Jesus is going to do that. He has promised to. With whom? With those to whom Jesus here gives the promise and those to whom they, the apostles, give it.

Now, indescribably more, Jesus took bread and said the prayer, broke the bread, and gave it to them. Nothing unusual about all of that. That happened at every Passover, at every meal. Only this time it is Jesus, and He says what had never been said before, what it takes Jesus to say. Of the bread He said, "This is My body." What Jesus gave them to eat He said was His body. That this is theirs only as His gift is repeated: "This is My body which is given for you" (Luke 22:19). Only in Luke are we told "this gift." The "for you" is sacrifice language, which is clearly shown by Jesus' speaking of blood. To speak of body and blood separately is to speak of a sacrifice. So the "given" refers to the sacrifice, to Calvary. Yet it speaks of what is happening here. From the sacrifice, the body and the blood, they are given to eat and to drink now as He gives them.

This does not fit with what we know of time and place. But it is the Lord Jesus who says it, so it is as He says. We have only His words for it, but they are His words. We may not subject His words to what we know of time and place. He does not burst our locatedness at a particular time and place. That is where we are created to be. And Jesus is there for us—nowhere else. Thus He is there for them at Passover in the Upper Room. Jesus gives them His body to eat and His blood to drink.

Thus also according to Jesus' bidding, here this morning, Wednesday in Pentecost 6, Mary Magdalene's Day, the so-many-eth day of summer school, we are at this table here this morning, eating and drinking, remembering Him who gave, who gives for us His body and blood to eat and to drink. Jesus is the giver, and you are given to by Him, according to His bidding, and the instrumentality of His apostolic ministry. Those who serve Jesus' serving, speaking His words and giving out His gifts, are His instrumentality for His Divine Service. The glory of this service is given only to servants and may not be infringed by anyone presuming to play the leader. None of our doing, only His, this giving. We are only given to. And as those who have been given to, we go from His table as those into whom He has given His body and blood, which bring us on our way through this specific day and each one of our specific days to the fulfillment of what happens here this morning, when it is fulfilled in the kingdom of God, which He will celebrate with us and all into whom He has given as gift His body and His blood. That makes all the difference how we live the rest of this day and each one of our days.

Another day nearer to the fulfillment of His Passover's promise at His table. As surely as today at His table He gives us His body to eat and His blood to drink, given and shed for you.

AMEN.

Formula of Concord

1 TIMOTHY 6

CENTRAL LUTHERAN, MINNEAPOLIS, MINNESOTA (JULY 24, 1977)

It really is frightfully deadening to live in a family that never has a good row. You may have noticed that you hardly ever have a good row with someone you don't care about. We have the oil of politeness for sliding past the people we don't want to bother with, but if we care, there will probably be some rows. Your child is going to the devil. There is a spouse who is drinking too much or never wants to have any fun. You have it out with them because you love them, want their good, and want to have happy times together. You are ready, if it has to be, to have a row about what is blocking things. Doesn't it make you sick at silver wedding anniversaries to hear, "There has never been an angry word between us." Liar! Or what a boring time they must have had.

Even cousins can have a good row. Yesterday's *Minneapolis Star* told of one cousin telling another cousin what he thought of his synod. Then there was all that funny business about those notorious fleas. That can sink to the level of "You have got more fleas than I have," "I like my fleas," "My fleas are fatter than your fleas," or they might end up doing something together about all those fleas. There is never a lack of fleas—though, of course, there may be more in a dusty Texas town than super-clean Minneapolis and almost-as-clean St. Paul. Fleas are not something to cherish. Two years ago in New Guinea, a man summed it up for the whole network of extended family bonds and responsibilities: "My people never lack someone to pick the fleas out of our hair." In the mutuality is the caring. We can usually do a better job with somebody else's fleas than with our own.

They had worse than fleas in the sixteenth century. Martin Luther, who was not slow to call a flea a flea or even a bloody flea, was succeeded mid-century by the much more polite and compromising Philipp Melanchthon. Melanchthon gave an uncertain sound: "You could say that, but on the other hand, you could say the other thing too. Perhaps we can do just a tiny bit for our salvation." In reaction against this latter comment, Matthias Flacius cried, "No, not one bit," but he said it in a way that implied that what is wrong with us is that we are human instead of saying what is wrong with us is that we are sinners. Nikolaus von Amsdorf thought to make the fact that we are saved by faith alone more sure by saying that good works are not only not required for salvation, as Georg Major said, but are detrimental. Some said that the Law of God has no useful role in our living of the Christian life. As is usually the case, the final focus of dissension was Christ and His Supper. If not agreed here, then not agreed, but if agreed here, then there is nothing that cannot be dealt with.

They worked at it for thirty years and came finally to the Formula of Concord. Through much pain, they helped one another through to this confession, to which our pastors pledge themselves at their ordination and which we all would do well to study, for we are all responsible for what our pastors preach and teach and for what we each confess.

The word *confession* comes to us from Latin. What went into this Latin word from the Greek was *homologeo*, which means "to say the same thing." First is what God says. If He didn't speak, we would be in a mess, though we are tempted to diminish that a bit so we have more room for some of our own ideas. To confess is to say back to God what He has said to us. Then what we say is as sure as God is sure. "You are a sinner." "I am a sinner." "You are forgiven for Christ's sake." "For Christ's sake I am forgiven." To confess the creeds is to say back to Him what a God He is, as He has shown Himself to be in His Word.

In the Epistle today, the apostle recalls for Timothy the good confession made at his Baptism, at his ordination. The heart of that confession is Christ and His confession. He said and did the same thing: the Christ, the crucified. When confessing, you lay your life on the line. Sometimes it might be better if you didn't just say the creed and it is not just some inside-you, cozy-me-and-Jesus thing. Not to be hidden, you make your confession for all to hear and to see, publicly, corporately. As it is with your confession, so it is with you before God. Jesus said, "Whosoever therefore shall confess Me before men, him will I confess also before My Father which is in heaven. But whosoever shall deny Me before men, him will I also deny before My Father which is in heaven" (Matthew 10:32–33).

Who Timothy is, what his life is about, is put in the "good confession" before men and also first before God. From that good confession, who he is and the commitment of his life, so also with the confessors of the Formula of Concord. They acknowledge themselves to be confessing "publicly before God and all mankind." What they see at stake is God's honor and our salvation. They confess, that is, say the same thing, disavowing new and different doctrines. The fullness of the Gospel they are committed to for Christ's sake and for sinners' sake.

> We desire such harmony as will not violate God's honor, that will not detract anything from the divine truth of the Holy Gospel, that will not give place to the smallest error, but will lead the poor sinner to true and sincere repentance, raise him or her up through faith, strengthen in new obedience, and thus justify and save him or her forever through the sole merit of Christ. (Solid Declaration XI, 96)

The ground of confidence in such confession is nothing other than the Word of God. In this confidence they stand before God and before men "with intrepid hearts," confessing the same as has been said by God in His Word.

But there have always been those unwilling to say the same thing, as our Lord Himself has warned us. If anyone says to you, "Lo, here is the Christ!" or "There He is!" do not believe it. For false Christ's and false prophets will arise and show great signs and wonders to lead astray even the elect. Lo, I have told you beforehand. And the apostle is quoted in the Formula: "Even if an angel from heaven should preach to you a Gospel contrary to that which we preach to you, let him be accursed."

Hear paragraph two of the Solid Declaration:

> Since in ancient times the true Christian doctrine as it was correctly and soundly understood was drawn together out of God's Word in brief articles or chapters against the aberrations of her-

etics, we further pledge allegiance to the three universal creeds, the Apostles', the Nicene, and the Athanasian, as the glorious confessions of the faith—succinct, Christian, and based upon the Word of God—in which all those heresies which at that time had arisen within the Christian Church are clearly and solidly refuted.

The horror of heresy is making Christ less and other than He is. It is from the Christ He is that our salvation comes. The Gospels report many attempts to make Him into another sort of Christ. The Gospels tell of Him as the one who goes to Calvary for us. Christ's temptation was to turn aside from the way of the cross, and when Peter does not want such a Christ, he is identified with Satan. In Mark, the one faith-confession of Christ comes when He hangs dead on the cross. There He is most the Christ He is for us. So Paul defines the Gospel as the message of the cross. "We preach Christ crucified" (1 Corinthians 1:23). And Luther states, "The cross alone is our theology." That is how God is toward us.

Is not Christ crucified, then, the touchstone of all doctrines? The Formula of Concord says, "The Holy Scriptures remain the only judge, rule and norm according to which as the only touchstone all doctrines should and must be understood and judged as good or evil, right or wrong." This, however, is a spurious alternative. The only Christ that is given us is the Christ in Scripture, and whether we are rightly understanding the Scriptures is shown by whether we are confessing this Christ and Him crucified.

Then we are kept from making Him into a different Christ, another Moses, an example to emulate to make ourselves acceptable to God, or a glory Christ whose power we may usefully get in on. So the Gospel may be nothing but the Gospel, so Christ may be our Savior by His cross, the Formula of Concord extols the distinction between Law and Gospel as "an especially brilliant light which serves the purpose that the Word of God may be rightly divided and the writings of the Holy prophets and apostles may be explained and understood correctly."

> The content of the Gospel is this, that the Son of God, Christ our Lord, Himself assumed and bore the curse of the law and expiated and paid for all our sins, that through Him alone we re-enter the good graces of God, obtain forgiveness of sins through faith, and freed from death and all the punishments

of sin, and are saved eternally. For everything which comforts and which offers the mercy and grace of God to transgressors of the laws strictly speaking is, and is called, the Gospel, a good and joyful message that God wills not to punish sinners but to forgive them for Christ's sake. (Solid Declaration V, 20)

Such declarations are the best of the Formula of Concord, and when the Formula goes on and on and on about one thing and another, it is from such statements that we can understand why it goes on and on. It goes on and on not just about one thing and another but to extol Christ in all the fullness of His Saviorhood and to reject any diminution of Him "in accordance with the pure, infallible and unalterable Word of God."

He who speaks that word is committed to keep that word. He committed His life to keeping that word, the crucified, "Jesus of Nazareth, Mary's Son, born of a human being." "No God apart from this man," says the Formula, for only in Him is God surely our Savior. To divide Christ into human and divine, earthly and heavenly, Jesus of history and Christ of faith, is to rob us of the Savior He is for us. Nor may such a division be made the reason for denying that He gives us His body to eat and His blood to drink as His words clearly say. Eating and drinking are done with our mouths. Christ does and gives as He says whether we believe it or not. There is no ground of confidence in us, only in Him.

Isn't this all pretty obvious? Yet because it was denied, it had to be confessed. It is not obvious that the new liturgy pays too much attention to the Formula of Concord. Two statements of the drinking have been removed from the Words of Institution: our Lord's bidding us to drink and "as often as you drink it" has been omitted, and we are encouraged to pay attention to other things.

The work is now done of confessing. It is not enough at such a celebration as this just to shout "hurrah" for the Formula of Concord. A Lutheran sermon calls to repentance and preaches faith, that is, Christ, the Christ who alone is our Savior as He is given us in the Scriptures, from which "the basic and mutual agreement" we celebrate today. Hear the Solid Declaration:

> We have reached a basic and mutual agreement that we shall at all times make a sharp distinction between needless and unprofitable contentions (which, since they destroy rather than edify,

should never be allowed to disturb the church) and necessary controversy (dissension concerning articles of the Creed or the chief parts of our Christian doctrine, when the contrary error must be refuted in order to preserve the truth).

Disavowing disputatiousness and indifference, the confessors face the scandal of dissension. There are bad rows as well as good rows, and they are often painfully muddled.

Some will doubt if the pure doctrine can coexist among us with such division, while others will not know which of the contending parties they should support. After all, these controversies are not, as some may think, mere misunderstandings or contentions about words, with one party talking past the other so the strife reflects a mere semantic problem of little or no consequence. We are bound to expound controverted articles according to God's Word and proven documents so everyone of Christian understanding may see what agrees with the Word of God and the Christian Augsburg Confession.

As in Corinth and Laodicea so with us too. If there was a time when Peter was called Satan and the pope the antichrist, may not we also qualify? We are not saved by proudly waving the Formula of Concord but only by the Christ of "that word of his that alone brings salvation." We join with the confessors of the Formula of Concord and affirm the apostolic faith: "By the help of God's grace we, too, intend to persist in this confession until our blessed end and to appear before the judgment seat of our Lord Jesus Christ with joyful and fearless hearts and consciences."

AMEN.

St. James the Elder, Apostle

ACTS 11:27–12:3

CONCORDIA SEMINARY (JULY 25, 1996)

James and John. It is always James and John, never John and James. I know what that is like. I had an older brother. Whenever we were referred to, it was always Keith and Norman Nagel, never Norman and Keith Nagel. Besides, he was always better at everything—"Get out of the way. I will do it." You can't imagine how that blighted my tender little psyche, to grow up in the shadow of such a brother. It was much more often my brother that I wanted to kill than my father. The advantage was that when something had been going on that ought not to have been going on, he got the first and bigger blame. "You are older, Keith. You should know better," our parents would say. And I, innocently led astray, could not disagree with that.

Now that is not how it goes with Jesus. To Him James and John came with their plan, their career projection. They were in it together. They both wanted the same thing, or, actually, not quite the same thing. If they had both wanted exactly the same thing, they might not, perhaps, have been so brotherly in cahoots. These two wanted two things, one for each, equal shares. As my fair parents were apt to say to settle a dispute about the bigger slice, "Share and share alike." So two seats in Jesus' glory—one on Jesus' right hand and one on His left, one for James, one for John.

Again, that is not how it goes with Jesus. Jesus never gives any two of us the same. He has His only-one-like-it way with each one of us. There isn't anybody else whom Jesus loves in the same way He loves you. He would draw James and John and you and me into rejoicing in that only-one-like-it way. Jesus would free them from doing things by sizes on each other—Who is bigger? Who comes first? James and John, or John and James?

Because they are in the same family, James and John agreed to see to it that, as brothers, they would get a place at least equally as good or, perhaps not better, but why not both of us better than the others? Not on your life, say the others, similarly far from the way of Jesus. His way is the opposite of all the foregoing. Unimprisoned is Jesus in who is first, who is bigger. He is so free of all that, that He does it by giving Himself away, His life poured out as a ransom for many.

Are you in for that too? Jesus asks the disciples. Because He asks them and Him whom they are answering, they say astonishingly, "We are able." With Jesus, if you are that far in, you are in for more than you could ever imagine. Jesus says it to them, but how much did James and John grasp? Or through all their days, were there not days when they saw more fully what Jesus freed them into when He said, "Ye shall indeed drink of the cup that I drink of; and with the baptism that I am baptized withal shall ye be baptized" (Mark 10:39)? So don't be worrying about the two top spots. There will be two who come to that, but not by chance or by the way you have been asking for it. Those who heard the Gospel read in church know how it turned out with those two on the cross. Same place, two places, not the same, not equal. One died cursing. The other heard Jesus say to him, "Today shalt thou be with Me in paradise" (Luke 23:43).

What of James and John? They didn't get the two places they had asked for or that they hadn't asked for. They got places better than they could imagine and not the same. Jesus doesn't answer our prayers, giving us the same as somebody else. It is a risky business, praying. You will get more than you ask for. The prayers in His name, the prayers He has promised to answer in His way in His name.

When Peter asked Jesus how it would be with John after Jesus had told Peter how it would go with him, Jesus said, "You can leave John to Me. I will see to that too. You have been a great plunger in following your impulses. When I have brought you to your end, your death will be a gift from Me, a death that will glorify God." It was the same yet not the same with James. James did die first by way of Herod Agrippa's sword. Now James and John join hands once more above, before the Conqueror's throne. Thus God grants prayer, but in His love He makes times and ways His own. Happy Saint James' Day. We ponder the Jesus way with each one of us, the life of faith all the way and always beyond our prayers.

Amen.

Holy Cross Day

JOHN 12:20–33

Concordia Seminary (September 14, 1992)

Crux sola est nostra theologia. The cross alone is our theology. These are the words of Doctor Luther and, too, of every Lutheran sermon. If the cross is not in the sermon, it is not a Lutheran sermon. Or if you take the cross out of the sermon, and it can get along just as well without it, it is not a Lutheran sermon. As Lutherans we preach Christ crucified: "For I determined not to know anything among you, save Jesus Christ, and Him crucified" (1 Corinthians 2:2). Still more Lutheran—"I am crucified with Christ: nevertheless I live; yet not I, but Christ liveth in me: and the life which I now live in the flesh I live by the faith of the Son of God, who loved me, and gave Himself for me" (Galatians 2:20).

The Small Catechism bids us to begin each day and to end each day with the sign of the holy cross. Thus each day is set to be lived in our Baptism, which incorporated us with the death and resurrection of Jesus. At Baptism the cross, the abbreviated name of God, was done on us. Where His name is, there is the Lord. Where His *doxa* is, there is the Lord. His *doxa*, His *chavod*, locates Him.

The Lord is, of course, everywhere. But is He there for you? Is He anywhere for you? Today's Gospel says yes. Jesus says there is a place where I am there for you. The cross is the *doxa* point, and it has time/location—"under Pontius Pilate," we say. Jesus said, "The hour is come, that the Son of man should be glorified . . . . but for this cause came I unto this hour" (John 12:23–27). This is an enthronement word, and His throne is the cross. That is the *doxa* point. "Turn to Me and be saved, all the ends of the earth, for I am God and there is no other." There is God. There for you, and not only for you but also for everyone. Or, better still, for everyone and also for you. No "just me and Jesus." Yet "for all men" can fly past us, as can the "for you"—the delivery—done by the means of grace.

As Doctor Luther says, "The Gospel is not Christ." The Gospel is the proclamation of Christ. The proclamation of Christ is the proclamation of the cross, the proclamation of the cross for you. Thus the delivery of the cross and with it all that was there achieved for you that day long ago. We are not back there. Nor need we attempt to get back there with some sort of getting contemporary with it.

Our Lord is not back there today, but here, where He is having His words spoken, the words that deliver Him. Doctor Luther said if you want your sins forgiven, don't go to Calvary. There forgiveness was won for you, but there it is not given out. You go to the Lord's Supper. There forgiveness is not won for you, but there it is given out. The Lord's Supper has always a specific place and time. For there to be a delivery to us, it cannot be otherwise. We go on only as we are located at a particular place and time. The Lord has appointed the place and time for the delivery of His gifts, means of grace, *externum verbum*. And so gifts, that is, from Him to you by way of located words, water, wine, and bread.

So here we are in the liturgy at Concordia Seminary on September

14. September 14 is neither September 13 nor September 15. Is it just another day? Never! The Lord has gathered us here in His name. He speaks His words to us by the mouth that He has put there for His use in speaking His words. God speaks them into this day. If that does not make it special, what would? Each day into which He speaks His words to us is a particular day. What and where are you today? Is that important? Must be, if our Lord thinks it is worth speaking His words into it, His words that deliver what they say for you today, September 14.

For all of today's specificity, the specificity of our Lord's located words and the specificity of your day today do not isolate this September 14 from all other September 14s. "And I, if I be lifted up from the earth, will draw all men unto Me" (John 12:32). The cross is the central and focal point of all days, rejoiced in by all who rejoice that Christ has drawn them to be His, to be His servants, who follow Him each of their days under the sign of the holy cross.

So it is a sort of Sherlock Holmes hunt to follow the liturgiologists as they track down why September 14 is Holy Cross Day. You can't have a Holy Cross Day without a particular day. And there is no particular day without its specific this and that, its particular peculiarities, none of which is a matter of indifference to our Lord. How particular things were in the early seventh century. It certainly looked as if the church was done for. Princes and prelates and even some theologians were playing power games in the name of Christ. Evil empires, first one, then another from the south went on destroying churches. It was in the year A.D. 614 that the Persian King Chosroes II conquered Jerusalem and took away what was regarded as the true cross. The Emperor Heraclitus defeated him and brought the cross back to Jerusalem on September 14, in the year of our Lord 629. Or it may be that September 14 came to be the day for celebrating this event because it was the day of the discovery of the true cross by St. Helena and its placement in the Church of the Holy Sepulchre in A.D. 335.

To be uncertain about which day does not mean that there was no day. Nothing happens except on a particular day at a particular time. The temptation to our piety is to slip away from such locatedness, as we observe in those walking past this place at 9:30 today. If we examine the piety of Heraclitus, we may find a few things wrong with that. Best begin with ourselves. There is no hope for any of us apart from the cross. Where is that? At a place identified by the cross and where the means of grace are going on for you, here, now, September 14,

Holy Cross Day—its gifts blessings for Heraclitus, Helena, and for you.

AMEN.

St. Michael and All Angels

PSALM 103:19–22

LONDON (SEPTEMBER 29, 1957)

Today is St. Michael and All Angels Day. Who is St. Michael? He isn't anybody. He is an angel. Is he really a "he"? No, he is not, for angels are neither "he" nor "she." They aren't "it" either because they are persons and because Scripture so speaks of them. However, Scripture doesn't tell us a great deal about the angels, and we don't make much of what it does say. Nowadays we are a bit embarrassed by the angels, so we don't talk about them much. People may smile at us, for most people believe in a world into which angels don't fit. People have made their understanding of the world so small and so have made God small, and the angels have been quite pushed out of the picture.

As sinners we try to restrict God's scope as much as possible, so we try to bring the world into our grip, if not into our control, at least of our prediction. Then, on the basis of this construction, we declare what can and what cannot happen. What we can't see and measure we won't allow to exist. The very thought of God makes this ridiculous. We can't cage God up in our 2-by-4 conception of the world. God is free. God is almighty, and He doesn't wait to get our permission. "The LORD hath prepared His throne in the heavens; and His kingdom ruleth over all" (Psalm 103:19). God delights in creating. He can never have enough creatures to love, so He made lots and lots in a quite dazzling variety. No two of God's creatures are the same, for He would delight in the particular quality of each one. We should not be surprised if we someday get to know a whole lot of other creatures of His that we never even dream of now.

God has told us of one set of creatures rather different from ourselves. He hasn't given us a full account of angels. Perhaps he wants to whet our eager curiosity for making their closer acquaintance. But every now and then in Scripture, angels appear on the scene. Not usually with great fanfare and fuss but quite naturally. They are there all the time, but only now and then do they show themselves.

Three men dropped in on Abraham, and he and Sarah got busy to get something good on the table for them. Somehow Abraham knew who they were. We are told Abraham was God's friend. Abraham dealt with one of these men as with God. He is the one who in the Old Testament is called the Angel of the Lord. God made use of a human form, and when God thus deals with a man, we know it to be God the Son. But today we are not so much concerned with Him whom we know so much better from His having permanently taken on our human nature and become one of us by being born of Mary. Jesus isn't an angel; He is God and man.

In the psalm following our text, we are told God made the angels spirits. To say that they are spirits doesn't tell us much. It does say that they belong to a world we don't see, a world outside the limitations of place and time in which we have been placed. All our thinking is in terms of place and time, so we cannot comprehend angels.

Our text does divulge an important fact: The angels excel in strength. They have powers beyond our reach. They can do things we cannot even imagine. We are told what they do. They do God's bidding, which can mean an awful lot. Their name helps us. The word *angel* means "messenger," that is, one who is sent to bring a message or to do a job. A message was brought to Abraham. The heart of that message was the Gospel. The full, clear Gospel was proclaimed by an angel to Mary. That was the greatest message ever brought. It was entrusted to an archangel. There are angels and archangels, different ranks, different kinds, including cherubim and seraphim. We read of principalities and powers and dominions. We are told the names of only two, though they all surely have names, for God has names for all His creatures. In God's having names for all His creatures is the meaning that He cares for each individual one. The same is even said of us.

There is the great Gospel angel Gabriel and there is Michael, a prince among angels. Daniel tells of him as the angel who guards God's chosen people. He had a commission with regard to the body of Moses. He is mentioned three times in the New Testament. In today's Epistle, Michael plays the role of the commander in chief. He seems to be "Angel Number One," so the day the church has dedicated to the angels is called St. Michael and All Angels Day.

The Jews weren't content with knowing the names of only two angels. Two more names are added in the Old Testament Apocrypha: Raphael and Uriel. The number was later brought up to seven. This certainly wasn't a great wickedness so long as the Jews clearly distinguished between what they had been told and what their pious embellishments were. This is a distinction that we have to be careful to observe, particularly with regard to the angels, for most of our ideas about the angels derive more from artists' efforts to depict them than from the various statements in the Bible. Take the wings, for example. More often than not in Scripture there is no mention of wings. In the vision of Jacob while he slept at Bethel, he saw the angels ascending and descending on a ladder. Wings would obviously be redundant.

Some people get superior about this sort of thing. They say what a funny idea this is of a ladder from earth to heaven. Besides not reading the Bible carefully, they miss the whole point in God's revelation of Himself. If God and His world are to be made known to us, it has to be done through forms of our world, through things that strike our ear and eye. So when the angels show themselves, they do it by using perceptible forms of our world. They make use of the form of a man. Sometimes they appear with wings. Now the angels as spirits no more have feathers than the Holy Spirit has a beard. But they take to themselves these forms so we can get a glimpse of them and know something about them. The instruction of the wings is that they are not related to space as we are, that they are swift in performing their tasks and carry a meaning of protection. The angels are guardians especially, we are told, of little children.

In criticizing the artists who are admittedly doing their best with an impossible task, we should further mention two mistakes. The first follows from what has already been said about God's delighting in each one of His creatures whom He makes as a unique individual. It is wrong when an artist paints a crowd of angels and gives them all the same face. The angels all have different faces, each beautiful in a different way. But then, you see, they don't really have noses and teeth. These are all part of the human form angels use to make contact with us. The only way we can think of them is with faces, and that is the way they have chosen to show themselves to us. We can't get above ourselves, and while we recognize the inadequacy of these forms, to express them fully we are closest to the truth when we stay closest to those forms in which they have chosen to show themselves. That is why children often understand angels better than we, who try to be more clever than the mode of revelation chosen by God. These forms are not chosen by the angels' whimsy. The angels, above all else, are persons that do the will of God. The other thing against the artist, or rather those of the sentimental nineteenth-century school, is the sugary feminine angels they painted. We are told that the angels are without sex, but when they use a human form, it is always a masculine one, for that is more expressive of their strength. They excel in strength. From today's Epistle we see that there is nothing soft or womanish about Michael.

But to get back to our text: It begins with God and His complete dominion. That is important. The angels have no action independent of God. All that they do is His bidding, and the really big things God does Himself. He created us. God came as man to redeem us. To take hold of us through His Word, God sends His Holy Spirit. God is "Judge" and angels are His assistants. "The reapers are the angels" (Matthew 13:39), but God, in all things, has the glory. In the world of the New Testament there was danger from heathen sources of making too much of the angels. Angels were the cover for slipping in some heathen gods and making them mediators between God and people. St. Paul fights against this in Colossae, and Hebrews shows how Jesus far transcends every angelic being. There is no mediator between God and us, neither angel nor saint, only the one mediator, Jesus Christ.

Our danger is of making too little of the angels, for so much of our thinking is shaped by a closed-in, materialistic view of the world. Like Thomas, if we don't see, we won't believe. But if we learn to live with God more closely, though we don't see Him, we shall learn to live also with His angels, and we shall be the happier for it. The nearer to God, the nearer to His angels. We are most near to the angels when we join in with them in what they are doing, that is, when we do the bidding of God. Then we are working side-by-side with them. St. John was told by an angel that they were co-workers, fellow servants. An angel is really something to have as a workmate, particularly when the going is hard, for, unlike us, they excel in strength.

Working together, we share the joy of achievement, and the great joy of the angels is in the victory of the Gospel when a person is won for God. When you help in bringing someone to Christ, then the angels are shouting "Hurrah" with you. The highest joy of the angels is in their Divine Service, their worship. When we have the Divine

Service here today, we are joining with the angels. We sing their songs with them, "Glory to God . . ." When you sing that, you are putting yourself in the company of angels. The climax of this is in the Communion liturgy when, on the basis of God's great goodness, you chime in with the "angels and archangels and all the company of heaven to laud and magnify His glorious name, evermore praising Him and saying, 'Holy, holy, holy, Lord God of Sabaoth.' " This is the song of the angels in the presence of God. God is the Lord God of the angels. Sabaoth means host, the hosts of heaven, the angels. He is their God and ours too. That prompts some humility on our part. We are not the whole cheese. God isn't our private possession. He is the God of the angels and of us too. We must remember that we are the junior members of the family, but what a family, you and I in with the angels.

You know, in a way we are superior to the angels. We read, "For verily He took not on Him the nature of angels; but He took on Him the seed of Abraham" (Hebrews 2:16). The Son of God did not become an angel but one of us. We drew the greatest of all love from God, a mystery and magnitude of love that the Scriptures tells us surpassed the comprehension of the angels. If it is a love that angels could not understand, we surely cannot. Who can understand such a love that God as man should die for us rebellious and sinful people?

This is not a superiority of which we can boast, but this surpassing love is as sure as Jesus' redeeming death for us outside Jerusalem. It is the same incredible love that prompts His dealing with us in the Word and Sacrament today. He does for us what He has not done for angels. He gives us His body and blood. He does this to cleanse us of our sins and draw us on toward fitting us in closer with the angels. They have no envy. They are confirmed in the joy of those who do God's bidding. They have God's joy in seeing His family grow and marvel that God could do this for such unlikely specimens as you and me, and well may we marvel too. Yet confident of that staggering love of God guaranteed in the Sacraments, we call to the angels and archangels to join with us.

> Bless the Lord, ye His angels, that excel in strength, that do His commandments, hearkening unto the voice of His word. Bless ye the Lord, all ye His hosts; ye ministers of His, that do His pleasure. Bless the Lord, all His works in all places of His dominion: bless the Lord, O my soul. (Psalm 103:20–22)

> Amen.

St. Luke, Evangelist

Luke 1:1–4; 24:44–53

Concordia Seminary (October 18, 1983)

From today's Gospel comes our provision: They "returned to Jerusalem with great joy" (Luke 24:52). A good beginning calls for a good ending, which calls for a decisiveness and doneness. The Gospel for St. Luke's Day is the beginning and ending of the Gospel according to St. Luke. He tells us that he had done his research. That done, he begins to write his orderly account so Theophilus, when he is finished reading, may know the truth of it all. The ending of the Gospel draws it all together and sets the scene of the next beginning.

There is more to it than Luke's great literary skill—though that is something he has been schooled in and is using to tell what all of Scripture is there to tell. Jesus says, "While I was yet with you" (Luke 24:44)—so that is over. What comes next? A new beginning, and for that Jesus proceeds to equip the disciples. The vitality of an ending is in what it begins. "These are the words which I spake unto you" (Luke 24:44). They are to begin to grow into the confidence that is not propped up by their seeing Him but relies on His words, with which He is present bestowing what they say. They have the Scripture with everything written about God. Thus it is written that the Christ should suffer and on the third day rise from the dead. That has been done. It is finished. Now from that "finish" comes the beginning of carrying what He has finished to all the nations. The words that proclaim Jesus carry Him to all the nations.

The witnesses of these things Jesus sends to carry the words that carry Him. And they will be carried by those words. He promises that they will have His accompanying Spirit, for the Spirit and His enabling dynamic they are to wait. For the Spirit comes as a gift, the promise of the Father. The days of Jesus' being with them are over. His passion, death, and resurrection are finished. Now it is time for His disciples to carry on, to carry Him and what He has done, to carry His words out into the world. But Jesus does not say, "Go to it." He says, "Wait in Jerusalem."

Jesus has given them a load of exegetical work to do in Moses, the

Prophets, and the Psalms "with burning hearts," for He has opened to them the Scriptures. The time of working, waiting, and praying in the Upper Room bears fruit in Peter's first sermon, which began, "Men and brethren, this scripture must needs have been fulfilled, which the Holy Ghost by the mouth of David spake" (Acts 1:16). Jesus brings to an end His time when He is seen with them. He brings to an end His passion, death, and resurrection. And He will bring to an end also their time of working and preparation in Jerusalem. With each ending, Jesus makes a new beginning. And each beginning is more.

Their times are in Jesus' hands. The scars in His hands and feet made them sure of Him and of what He had finished. They are to proclaim forgiveness in His name. Sin is what ruins us, sin that takes us, cuts us off from the living. That death must be disclosed, that death that is ours by our sin. Repentance is called for, and the message that Christ's death has been died for us as the wounds of Christ declare. Repentance and faith are to be preached. Forgiveness of sins is to be preached in His name to all nations.

But not quite yet. "Stay in the city until you are clothed with fire from on high," Jesus says. From our Lord come our beginnings and our endings, which come to us on the level of His eating a piece of broiled fish, of our studying the Scriptures with burning hearts as He opens them to us by way of a broiled fish of a professor. Even so your times, your beginnings and endings, are in His hands. So also the beginning of each new day, and this day is particular because it is St. Luke's Day, the day when we rejoice in what our Lord gives us by way of His servant Luke. In Luke there is a continuity of the Upper Room. It is always the same Jesus. And the same Jesus giving more. Jesus gave them His blessing as He brought to an end their time of seeing Him. They returned to Jerusalem with great joy, not as those who had lost something by an ending but as those who had been given much more in a new beginning that was first a time of preparation.

In our days of preparation, we have now our Upper Room time. We are in the company of our Lord and His disciples, angels and archangels and all the company of heaven, as if the parousia had begun already. My Lord, what a morning! As He gives us His body to eat and His blood to drink, He makes a new beginning with us, as He makes an ending with repentance and the forgiveness of sins. Nothing then can hold us back, hold us captive, keep us from the great joy of a new beginning. "They returned to Jerusalem with great joy and were continually in the temple blessing God." That first. They also devoted themselves to the apostles' teaching and fellowship through the breaking of bread and the prayers.

Later the church at Antioch decided to call Paul and Barnabas. They laid their hands on them and sent them off. Then in Acts 16:10 at Troas, Luke slips into the scene. "We thought [*we* thought] to go into Macedonia, concluding that God had called us to preach the Gospel to them." No noisy "*Ta da*, here I am, watch out, just watch me when I get my own church!" Luke was given a new beginning in carrying the Word. That is what is going on—the Word. And he tells that story. The Word of God grew and multiplied. Luke is in on that also. And in our Lord's way, with our lives, of endings and beginnings, we also may, of His generous mercy and ascending blessing, have our joyful part. And toward that end, first now come and be given His body to eat and His blood to drink. Maranatha!

AMEN.

St. Simon and St. Jude, Apostles

JOHN 14:21–27

CONCORDIA SEMINARY (OCTOBER 28, 1997)

Simon and Jude. If only we had some good stories about them, though they might be a bit cooked-up, as stories of the saints sometimes tend to be. That could at least supply us with some moral example material. "Now you go and be like St. Simon and/or St. Jude." Sorry, it is pretty much a blank. So what are we to make of St. Simon and St. Jude?

We can't get it much more backward than by asking that question. Wrong question. The only good question is the one the Lord has, in fact, given us answers to. What did *He* make of Simon and Jude? Here we are on solid ground. The Lord made them apostles. Simon and Jude are named in the list. They were there when He instituted the holy ministry, Holy Baptism, Holy Communion, and Holy Absolution. Not only were they there, they were instituted themselves as apostles into the office of the holy ministry. No uncertainty—they are unmistakably identified: Simon the Zealous—not Simon Peter—and Jude, which is better than Judas. In Luke, he is Judas, son of James, and in Matthew and Mark, he is surnamed Thaddeus. In today's Gospel he is named Judas—not Iscariot.

Apostles may be interchangeable, but they may not be in any doubt that they are the ones whom the Lord has made to be apostles, so titled by Him. What the Lord chose them for, what He put them to do, is given with the Words of Institution, of holy ministry, Holy Baptism, Holy Absolution, and Holy Communion. He sent them on their way to make disciples by Baptism and teaching, to preach repentance and forgiveness of sins in His name to all nations, beginning at Jerusalem. To forgive the sins of penitent sinners and to retain the sins of the impenitent, to be the mouth of the Lord speaking His words, His hands to give out His body and His blood. That is all confessed with the word *holy*. If not, why bother?

A big point is made with the Twelve. Lined up at Pentecost, the Lord has His Twelve. The Twelve are mentioned again when they ordain seven men who were particularly designated to care for the poor. We hear no more of the Twelve. They disappear. They go, sent by the Lord. Others are also sent. Barnabas, Paul, Mark, Timothy, Titus, and thousands more on to our day, as we confess in Tractate 26 and with our chancel window. Of some we are told in the traveling on of the Word of the Lord, but not of St. Simon and St. Jude. Where did they go? We are not told. Therefore, wrong question.

That is a lesson that we may learn from Judas, not Iscariot, or better from the Lord in His response to Jude's question, "Lord, how is it that Thou wilt manifest Thyself unto us, and not unto the world?" (John 14:22). Jesus does not answer the question. Therefore, wrong question. But the Gospel says Jesus answered him, and these are the words He said, "If a man love Me, he will keep My words: and My Father will love him, and We will come unto him, and make Our abode with him. He that loveth Me not keepeth not My sayings: and the word which ye hear is not Mine, but the Father's which sent Me" (John 14:23–24). Whoa, hang on a minute. Jude gets a whale of a lot more than he ever asked for. Can't go into all of that in an itty-bitty sermon, yet there is always more there than we can ever learn or live our whole life long.

Risky business asking Jesus questions. The wrong question can only accommodate a wrong answer. In His patience, the Lord, in His boundless mercy toward us, does not suffer Himself to be confined within our questions. He does answer Jude's question, but with such an answer as bursts Jude's question that we can hardly find any trace of it left at all. Jesus was readying Jude and the others whom He sent. Today's Gospel ends with sending.

The Father's sending of the Son, who, when His saving work was done, said to them, "As My Father hath sent Me, even so send I you" (John 20:21). It is all one sending—the Lord's all the way. It goes forward as He sends and uses His instruments for His speaking His words, for His baptizing, for His forgiving and retaining sins, for His giving into our mouths His body and His blood. What is done according to the Lord's mandate and institution is surely done by Him. What He makes of Simon and Jude is for His use of His means of grace (Augsburg Confession V). So if you would like to try for some good questions, try working them out from Jesus' answers. That will help your praying, too, along with St. Simon and St. Jude, what He made of them and what He is working at making out of you.

AMEN.

Reformation Day

MATTHEW 18:20

WESTFIELD HOUSE (OCTOBER 31, 1963)

You have probably heard the remark or made it yourself about some church or other that it is "too catholic." What is meant by that? Too much liturgy? Too many candles or vestments? Is that what you mean by "catholic"? Every time we celebrate Holy Communion, we confess, "I believe in one holy catholic and apostolic church." Scarcely, but what has gone wrong? We had better start at the beginning.

Catholic is not a word used in Scripture. In ordinary Greek usage it means "universal." A stoic philosopher wrote a book about catholic things and dealt with matters found everywhere. The first Christian use of the word we find in Irenaeus, who died about the year A.D. 200. He says, "Wherever Jesus Christ is, there is the catholic church." Notice how this is rather like another way of saying our text, "For where two or three are gathered together in My name, there am I in the midst of them" (Matthew 18:20).

Whatever we say about the catholic church must have Jesus Christ as its center. Apart from Jesus Christ there is no catholic church, and there is only one catholic church, for there is only one Jesus Christ. Although we may muddle and contradict this fact, Jesus has His one church. The particular job the word *catholic* has is to affirm that no kind of distance divides us.

Those gathered together in the name of Jesus in two different places are not cut off by the miles, sea, or mountains between them for the compelling reason that Jesus is in the midst of them in both places. Both lots are with Him; therefore, they are together, united in Him. Not only both places are united but also any place where two or three are gathered together in the name of Jesus. *Catholic* also means not separated by any distance of time. The catholic church embraces Abraham, Athanasius, grandfather, Aunt Agatha who died three weeks ago, you, and me. All who were and are with Jesus Christ at any time or place are in His one catholic church. As a great Greek theologian observed about the house of the church, the important thing is not whether you are downstairs or upstairs but whether you are in or out.

In the fourth century the word *catholic* developed another meaning. The church was then particularly troubled by heresy. The leading heretic, Arius, denied that Christ is truly God. To say that you belonged to the catholic church meant that you confessed Jesus Christ as He was confessed at the Council of Nicaea and in the resulting creed. This meaning of the word *catholic* is not a foreign item but of a piece with our text and with what Irenaeus said, "Wherever Jesus Christ is, there is the catholic church." If you held with the Arians to a Jesus Christ who was not God from all eternity, then you were not with Jesus Christ and not in the catholic church, which is only where He is, true God and true man. This doctrinal and confessional significance of the word *catholic*, together with its affirmation that place and time do not divide Christ's one church, is beautifully expressed in Article VII of the Augsburg Confession and its Apology: "It is also taught among us that one holy Christian church will be and remain forever. This is the assembly of all believers among whom the Gospel is preached in its purity and the holy Sacraments are administered according to the Gospel."

Here the church is tied closely to Jesus Christ. As Irenaeus pointed out, only where He is, there is the catholic church. Where is Jesus Christ? You won't find Him up there or in here among flowers and birds, babbling brooks, or glorious sunsets. Christ is there, of course, but that is not the place appointed by Him, the place where He first does His real work with us. He addresses us, takes hold of us, and imparts Himself and His gifts to us through His Word and Sacraments. Where they are in action, there Jesus is present and in action, and wherever He is thus, there is the catholic church. Notice here how we have all solid factors, Jesus factors, His Word and Sacraments.

These factors, being divine and His, are sure foundation. Pushing in some other factors, human factors, will undo this certainty. This, sad to say, has happened. Other factors have been introduced that should guarantee the catholic church and also identify it. When these are human factors, the impudence is recognizably colossal. Certain forms of organization, institution, or government came to be insisted on as safeguards and guarantees of the catholic church. Thus rule by bishops was insisted on, and later rule by the pope, and still later some insisted that the church organization must be presbyterian while others said it must be congregational. Support was claimed for each one of these from the New Testament. You should look to see whether you can find anything of that sort in the New Testament. Nor will you find there anything special for a particular place or people. To say Roman Catholic, Greek Catholic, or Anglo-Catholic is to squash the meaning of *catholic*. If it is particularly Roman, it can't be particularly catholic.

There is one more use of the word *catholic* we should look at before we come to the tidying up that took place at the Reformation. This usage was started by the heretic Celsus who used the phrase "catholic church" to mean the "great church," the biggest one, as if you could be assured the catholic church was where there were the most Christian noses to count. This sort of thinking got worse when the church was approved by Caesar, and his way of thinking and ruling seeped into the church.

The tragedy of the Reformation was that when Luther raised questions of the Gospel, he was given no such answer. The government of the church felt itself bothered by some unheard of little Augustinian monk from the remote cow pasture of Wittenberg, and it told him to be quiet. Luther pleaded for discussion of the Gospel. He was met with the naked demand to recant and to submit to the pope. The Ninety-five Theses were no Declaration of Independence but a request for discussion and debate. When Luther recognized that the pope pulled one way and the Gospel the other, the Reformation began in earnest.

The Reformation may be described as cleaning out the human factors that had been intruded into the church and her message. On Reformation Sunday we most often consider what this meant in the basic relationship of God and us. This was expressed in the doctrine of justification by faith alone with its affirmation that we cannot stand before God on the basis of any human factors but only on the basis of Jesus Christ, His atoning death, and His victorious resurrection.

Something similar happens in the understanding of the catholic church that we are thinking about this Reformation Sunday. Irenaeus said, "Where Jesus Christ is, there is the catholic church." The Apostles' Creed puts it more closely: Wherever Christ's Word and Sacraments are in action, there is the catholic church. Everything else is subordinate to that—the pope too. In the early church some bishops who were guilty of false teaching were sacked. They were no guarantee, that alone is Scripture and its doctrine.

Now the Lutherans did not fall into the same error as the pope by saying that not the pope but some other form of church government was commanded by God. They held that no particular form of church government is laid down in the New Testament. They were even willing to have the pope continue running the affairs of the church by human right, so long as he did not hinder the Gospel. The pope, however, would not have that. He insisted on being Christ's vicar by divine right and cursed the Gospel held by the Lutherans. "Let it be anathema," said the Council of Trent concerning the doctrine of justification by faith alone.

The Lutherans, as their enemies called them, or Evangelicals, as they called themselves—we still carry both names, and *evangelical* tells you nothing about how many candles or vestments as *catholic* truly does neither—had no notion of starting a new church. Same old church there has always been; there is only one. They kept everything that did not contradict the Gospel. That is why the Calvinist Reformation regarded the Lutheran Reformation as only half a reformation and blamed the Lutherans for not throwing away the vestments, crucifixes, candles, altars, organs, stained-glass windows, and statues, as happened most notably north of the border in Scotland. Luther recognized that as the same old error in different clothes. The catholic church is not shown to be catholic by having or by not having candles, crucifixes, vestments, etc. It is catholic by having Jesus Christ, and He is there for us in His Word and Sacraments. Where they are, He is, and there is the catholic church.

Let us, then, rejoice in our catholic heritage centered in Jesus Christ and freed from the intrusion of human factors and reliance. Let us live our catholic heritage in relation to other Christians. Luther said, "Rome is surely worse than Sodom and Gomorrah but there they yet have the Sacraments and the Scripture and the name of Christ. There is the catholic church." No matter whether it be Rome, Geneva, Constantinople, Canterbury, or Timbuktu—no matter what the denominational label—if the Word and the Sacraments are there, if there two or three are gathered together in the name of Jesus, there is the catholic church. Even if the flow of the means of grace, the Word and the Sacraments, may be only a trickle, there is yet the catholic church. This does not mean that impeding the flow with human factors is not a fearfully dangerous thing. Luther was not exhorting people to affiliate with Sodom and Gomorrah. And if we love people, we will want to help them loosen their hold on the impeding human factors.

But we always have a considerable job of such loosening to do with ourselves. The Reformation certainly cleaned out the pipe, but that may not lead us Lutherans to suppose that we have a corner on the catholic church. We may put no confidence in the fact that there are a lot of Lutheran noses to be counted in the world or that we have an efficient organization. The only ground for confidence, and this is then a joyful and unshakable confidence, is Jesus Christ, who is there for us and imparts Himself through Word and Sacraments. Sharing them in Jesus' name, we know that He is in our midst and we are in the catholic church. All this comes to clear expression here in church, but it must be remembered that our being in the catholic church is not something that can be divided by place or time. We cannot be members of the catholic church in our homes and not members of the catholic church at our work. We cannot be members of the catholic church on Sunday and not on Monday nor hope to be much in the way of Christians on Monday if not on Sunday. That is flat contradiction of *catholic*.

When you stay away from church for no good reason, the bad reason is basically some diminishing of Jesus and intrusion of human factors. You are content with yourself and feel that you can manage another week without gathering in the name of Jesus and receiving forgiveness and strength from Him through Word and Sacrament. You can do without the catholic church. You know jolly well you can't, and if you allow these intrusions, this pushing off of Jesus, you are in danger, you need some reformation. Don't give up your reformation, your centering in Jesus Christ, your membership in the catholic church. That membership is powerfully expressed as you worship your way through the liturgy, which is a pattern of worship in which you join fellow members in the catholic church of many centuries and many places. This reaches a climax in Holy Communion when we acknowledge ourselves to be together with the angels and archangels and all the company of heaven.

Do you belong there? If you look at yourself closely, you may well doubt it, but look to Jesus. He says you do. He died and rose again for you. With Him there is forgiveness and the life that lasts, and from Him there is nothing that can separate you, neither time, distance, nor death itself. He holds you together with all who are His, together in His catholic church or, as we usually say, the Christian church—same thing, His church.

AMEN.

Reformation Day

VALPARAISO UNIVERSITY (OCTOBER 31, 1967)

"God is not far but near!" This cry of Martin Luther tells his trouble. He could not push God off. He could not get God caged. God was getting at Luther all along the line. He could not restrict God to the nice things. God's hand was in everything, and that hand was heavy. Luther spoke of God's grinding us between the upper and the nether millstone. For us, other things do the grinding—the screech of sirens and fanatics, famine, people splattered on the highway, violence, faces knocked in, and the needle and the advertising that can make people wag their tails at whatever they are lined up for. Luther cries, "There is no corner or hole in all of creation into which a man may creep, not even in hell, but he must let himself be exposed to the gaze of the whole creation, and to stand in the open with all his shame." "A rustling leaf becomes the wrath of God and the whole world, on which a moment before we strutted in our pride, becomes too narrow for us." "If you could probe a little grain, you would die of amazement."

We have grown out of the Romantic Age that palpitated at vast sunsets and breezes in the trees. The moon is a lump of dirt. We have learned the terror of specifics. Luther shuddered at a grain, we at the split atom. We try to disengage in a tranced calm in which we contemplate disaster as a rabbit looks into the eyes of a snake. World War I ushered in a period in which tension was overt, expressing itself freely in a brawling, extravagantly personal style in the arts, in bootleg liquor, assertive sex, traditional jazz with its ruthless drive, jive dancing that faithfully mimed the gestures of panic, the goon world of mad sports marathons, and all-in wrestling. After the A-bombs fell, this was replaced by the cool world of inward hysteria, where the most valued right is the right to dissociate from experience altogether, to opt out of life as the LSD addict does, and whose chief terms of praise are "trips," "gone," and "way out." We exchange one set of fig leaves for another. No bush can keep God at bay. There is no escape from the wrath of God.

Luther took refuge in a monastery. There he might be safe. The church can offer the best protection against God. Here we may find Him tied and taped. But Luther found the tapes did not hold. St. Augustine helped Luther take God straight, but in the Augustinian inheritance there was also a technique for keeping God at a distance. This had seeped in from Greek philosophy: the separation of the spiritual and the material, the heavenly from the earthly, God's world and our world. Our plight is then seen as being captive to earthly things here below. Our salvation is then in somehow getting up out of the earthly prison and rising to the spiritual and heavenly realm up above where God is only really at home. These two worlds are not on friendly terms. They do not really mix.

Luther recounts how he broke more than one limb trying the ladders designed to get you up out of the earthly to the heavenly realm. He remained flat on the ground before the high, holy, and heavenly God. All that could honestly be expected from Him was wrath, for Luther learned to see that his plight is not that he is an earthly creature but a sinner who would kill God and usurp His role. Then Luther learned to know God as the one cast on the arms of Mary and the cross. The Greek cages for God and humans were broken. Augustine's heavenly and earthly letter and spirit were replaced by the Law and the Gospel, God's two ways of dealing with His people. This liberated Luther from attempting to cage God. He was exposed to all of God: the inexplicable and the wrathful God, the God of the manger and the cross. When the blows of God fell on him, Luther crept to the cross and clung to God, his Savior and brother, clinging to God against God.

When Oecolampadius exhorted Luther at Marburg to elevate his thoughts up to the high and heavenly God, Luther would have no "other God than him who became man . . . for there is no other who can save. Hence he could not bear that the humanity be treated as so little worth and cast aside." Oecolampadius and Zwingli were following the tradition of assigning things either to the heavenly spiritual world or to the earthly material world. Obviously, then, the right hand of God belongs in the heavenly realm, and if that is where Christ has ascended to, you can hardly expect Him to be grateful for being dragged down to the earthly level again. This is what horrified Zwingli about Luther. As Luther puts it, Zwingli said to him: "Here you fool, open your eyes! Don't you see that heaven is high up there where Christ sits in his honour, while the earth where his supper goes on, is way down here? How can a body be seated so high and in honour and at the same time be down here allowing itself to be dishonoured and handled by hands, mouth and stomach, as if it were a fried sausage?"

Zwingli, you see, was defending Christ's heavenly honor, but he was doing it still captive to the two-story thinking of the world that would divide not only the world into up there and down here but also Christ Himself. Christ could be present in the Sacrament according to His divine nature but not according to His human nature. Even then His divine nature must not get too entangled with such earthly things as bread and wine. They may serve as signposts upward where Christ is alone fully at home.

Zwingli also took the commonsense view that a body is only a body as we know it if it is in one specific place. Therefore, the body of Christ is at one specific place, that is, at the right hand of God up there. Here what we know a body to be is imposed as a limitation on Christ and what He can do with His body. If He says He is doing something with His body that is not possible for bodies in our experience of them, then He simply can't do it and consequently can't be saying that He does. Whatever Christ does must remain within the limits of what we know a body to be. Luther was appalled at this laying down of limits for Christ, measuring out the confines within which Christ's action must be restricted. For Luther, quite simply, Christ does what He says

He does. How He manages it is His business, not ours. There may be no caging of Christ. Luther mocks Zwingli's right hand as a sort of celestial swallow's nest. Luther will not allow any of our ideas about the world to be imposed on Christ. We learn what Christ does from Christ.

This means that we cannot measure things out for Christ or tie Him to our notions as if He were some necessary part of them. There have been no end of cages constructed for Christ. One philosophy after another has sought to tie Him into it, so also succeeding views of the world and of us. Now there is some reason for this. When everybody is talking Platonic talk and you want to get the Gospel across, then it is at least good strategy to put as much of the Gospel as you can into Platonic talk, though there comes a point when this talk inevitably breaks down and the Gospel must go it alone with its own native words. Such alliances are risky, for alliances are usually something for something. If the Gospel has been staked on some philosophy or view of the world or humans and they give way, then the Gospel seems also to be giving way.

We need some working view of the world and of humans, but we should sit lightly by them. Luther had an old-fashioned view of the world. He thought the sun went round the earth, but that did no damage to his proclamation of the Gospel. That does not stand or fall with any philosophy or view of the world or of us. Luther's recognition of the right hand of God as the exercise of God's power, which he got from how the term is used in the Bible, liberated the right hand of God from its captive place in some scheme of how the universe and people are supposed to be put together. He was too ignorant of such things to be persuaded by Copernicus. Luther had little time for cosmology; his job was to teach the Bible. But he was liberated from the notion that Copernicus was doing something unfriendly to God with his scientific research. The introduction to Copernicus's great work was written by Osiander and seen through the press by the Wittenberg professor of mathematics. It was a later generation of Lutherans, who did not so fully realize what the Bible is about, who insisted that the sun had no alternative but to go round the earth because it had stood still over Ajalon.

Copernicus did not put God out of business. Kepler's freedom to pursue his scientific research did not mean any exclusion of God. It was men of the Renaissance and the Enlightenment who attempted that. In them we find the old error, again, of fitting God into a philosophy or particular view of the world and of humanity. When God is assigned a role within some such scheme of things, He is given progressively less and less to do by His masters. For a good while He retained the job of setting things up and giving the first push. Thereafter, God was allowed no more role than that of a spectator. Humans got so carried away with their growing competence to describe what was going on that they got the idea that they were more and more in charge. God lived only in the things they had not yet figured out, and, therefore, His realm shrank and shrank, and it was only a matter of time before His realm would disappear altogether. To such a God railways constituted a threat according to Feuerbach, and, more recently, Bultmann has pointed to the difficulties regarding God that arise when we are able to switch on an electric light. What has happened to God's right hand? An astronaut buzzing around our planet radioed back the observation, "Can't see any God anywhere up here," which makes him more old-fashioned than Zwingli.

Be not deceived, God is not threatened by railways, electricity, or the receding nebulae. As long as the world seemed limited, it provided schemes for fitting God in. Now that we know no limits to the universe it can no longer serve for caging him in. Nowadays, it is from an understanding of humans that limits are provided for God, and theology becomes anthropology. This development set in as God was forced to retreat from the world. Those who still had a care for Him thought a safe place could be found for Him in the heart of humans. Exiled from the world and from history, God might find refuge in my heart. An exiled king, of course, has to watch his step and mind the manners and values of the place that has taken him in—a sort of Duke of Windsor god, useful for social purposes but really rather pathetic and dispensable. Things can get along quite well without him.

Now, if we feel sorry that God is pushed around like that, we must be careful that we are not prompted by abstract notions of God that are set majestically above these foolish people with their pitiful little ideas. If we insist on God dealing majestically, He will deal with us that way. He has two ways to deal with us: majestic justice or brotherly forgiveness. The insistence on the humanity of God is nearer the truth than any grand, abstract notions. Feuerbach, who laid a number of eggs that we see hatching today, had read Luther, which is more than can be said for the Bishop of Woolwich. To what Luther says about God being a man, Feuerbach gave a fatal twist and concluded, "Then humanity is God." This thought had already been entertained by mother Eve, though for her weakness at abstract thought it was rather, "Then I would be as God." This indicated also that the God problem is not so much a problem of thinking as of takeover.

It is not enough to let God be God uncaged, for a God who is everywhere is no better than a God who is nowhere. It is harder to let Him become a man, and the man He became to be our crucified Savior and Lord who deals with us now by way of such common and unimpressive things as words, water, wine, and bread. Yet He can be no other than the God He is, that is the God as He has spoken and the God who was born of Mary and crucified under Pontius Pilate. "He came so near he could not be nearer."

Luther points out that we are creatures of five senses. If anything is going to get through to us, it comes by way of these. Christ deals with us as the creatures we are. We cannot swing up to a higher heavenly level to be within His range. Christ comes all the way to us. We may say "comes here" to exclude the notion that we cover part of the distance to Him, yet He does not come or go, up or down. We are liberated from the disjunction of heavenly world and earthly world. We are liberated from the vain endeavor of fluttering about, trying to go upward and get to God, for God has joined us here. He became a man and chose things of our earthly world to bestow Himself and His gifts: words, water, wine, and bread—media appropriate to us five-sensed creatures. We are liberated from fitting these into heavenly and earthly divisions. We are no longer sliced in two with an upper nature and a lower nature. Christ became the whole lump of man and joins the whole lump of you to Himself as He imparts Himself and His gifts with the words, the water, the wine, and the bread. He became a person to make a person of you. God has no finer thing for you than that you become a full person. Banished, then, is all scorn of us, all thought of making like a god, of talking god talk other than He Himself has spoken. Banished is all scorn of creation. We accept, probe, harness, and use it all to magnify Him. We accept that we are creatures located. Our life does not go on anywhere other than where God has joined us. Hence no desire to escape either out of ourselves by wafting off to heavenly regions or within ourselves by jagging our brains with drugs or dreams. There is only one world, God's world.

Zwingli's "up there" and today's "gone," "high," or "way out" are fictions. We are put. No escape means prison, but prison is only prison if we want to get out, which depends also on there being somewhere to escape to. Suicide perhaps, but you had better be quite sure God is dead before you join Him. He has, in fact, joined us here and taken us on in His work of deprisonizing the world for us. He calls with a call that fetches men out of their cells into the glorious liberty of the sons of God. He calls with a call that many reject, for He takes no prisoners in His company. God came to set the captives free. There can be pain as we hold back, clinging to the chains, but the chains are broken and He would have us free.

Luther's happiest proclamation comes at Christmas:

> Here God is not to be feared but loved, and that love brings the joy of which the angel speaks. Satan, on the other hand, brings home to me the Majesty and my sin, and terrifies me so that I despair. But the angel does not declare that he is in heaven. "You shall find the babe." He has come to us and put on our flesh and blood.
>
> Reason and longing would ascend and seek him above, but if you would have joy, bend yourself down to this place. I will stay with that boy as he sucks, is washed, and dies. There is no joy but in this boy. Take him away and you face the Majesty which terrifies. I know of no God but this one in the manger.
>
> O thou boy, lying in the manger, thou are truly God who hast created me, and thou wilt not be wrathful with me because thou comest to me in this loving way—more loving cannot be imagined.
>
> If you would truly love, let him be this way in your heart. If you regard the boy according to the flesh, he means nothing to you; but much, if this little Jesus is your God and Savior. (From the 1527 Christmas Day sermon found in the Weimar Edition of Luther's Works 23:732)

AMEN

All Saints' Day

MATTHEW 5:1–12

VALPARAISO UNIVERSITY (NOVEMBER 1, 1981)

This morning we name the names of our dead, those of our family and of this university who have died since last All Saints' Day. We name them here together before the Lord. For some of us there will be a name of a person we know a little or one whose life was intertwined with ours, intimately known, loved or not loved, or both. There will be a name of someone with whom we had happiness or pain or both. Before the Lord, we have courage to be honest. Nothing else will do before Him. Of those whom we mourn we remember things that we would rather not remember, things that make the funeral parlor talk ring hollow. "He was always such a good man." "She was always so sweet." Not true, yet we are prone to fall in with such pretenses. Pretenses do not change the facts, but in our grief, even the fact of death is something we are prone to make pretenses about. We are encouraged in this by those who encourage the pretenses out of social obligation, for profit, or even from friendship. But the fact remains a fact.

In Noel Coward's play *This Happy Breed*, a man's son is killed in the war and his friends try to help him with pretense talk and euphemisms for death. Out of the emptiness of his heart, he finally cries, "He didn't pass on, pass out, or pass over; he just bloody well died." Such honesty can crumble a man. His son was all that mattered to him. What is the point of going on living when the one most precious in all the world has died? Such grief is possible only when we know that life is to have a point, meaning, and worth, but you cannot read that looking into a grave. This we have to face, yet death is a fact that, for all its finality, is not the final fact.

You have not faced death fully unless you have faced the death on Calvary. Jesus was, in fact, a good man. Two bad men were dying along with Him. One of them acknowledged the truth, "We have it coming to us, but not this one." Jesus was different, yet He was on the center cross, dying along with them. He was not guilty. He cries, "My God, My God, why hast Thou forsaken Me?" (Matthew 27:46). That is ultimate death, the forsakenness of God. The death of no more brain waves, breath, or heartbeat has its final weight not in the nullification of any worth, meaning, or happiness that we may have known or hoped for, but in the fact that we are accountable for our lives. This fact is acknowledged also by those who deny God, for they would still justify themselves, claim some meaning, worth, or at least a little happiness, and make a case for themselves.

The greater the insistences, the greater the uncertainty, for we do not do the final judging. Who does? Today's Epistle answers, "God and the Lamb." Which of the two will be your judge? God? What God? The God of our God talk, of our construction or definition? If you insist, that kind of God will be your judge before whom you make your case. Yet they are not separate; there is one throne, the throne of God and the Lamb. "And they shall see His face; and His name shall be in their foreheads" (Revelation 22:4). On your forehead? Yes, for His name was put on you with the water of Baptism, as we confess with the cross put on your forehead and on your heart, the cross of the Lamb who was slain, the Lamb who bore the sins of the world, the Lamb who bore your sins for you in your place and was forsaken of God, where your sins put you but where He was for you in your place.

When Jesus cries, "My God, My God, why have You forsaken Me?" have God and the Lamb come apart, opposite each other? Yes, for the Lamb is where we are, opposite God, in our place as sinners. He bears our punishment of sin, the forsakenness of God. Anyone bearing his or her own sin is finally lost, but not Jesus. He is bearing not His own sin, but ours; He is not opposite God, but doing the saving will of the Father. He won't let go of us, and He won't let me let go of God. Out of the ultimate darkness of ultimate death comes the cry, "It is finished" (John 19:30). Jesus is through. He has done it. Then He goes through the little death also. The one who was crucified, the Lamb who was slain, is the risen one who sits on "the throne of God and of the Lamb" (Revelation 22:3). From that throne God is for us as the Lamb is for us, no other God for us but as He is for us in the Lamb.

To separate God and the Lamb, to insist that God is not like that for you, is to tear Calvary apart. It is to insist that the Lamb did not bear your sins for you but that you will answer for them yourself before God apart from the Lamb. That is the final folly of those who go into the final death, as it says: "Every one who loves and practices falsehood" (Revelation 22:15 RSV). This is the falsehood of separating God and the Lamb, the falsehood that denies your sin is answered for and forgiven. Forgiveness refused means that you answer for your sins yourself. This expunges His name put on you, and your name is not then in the Lamb's Book of Life.

We read the names this morning trusting in that forgiveness won on Calvary by the Lamb who was slain. It is He who is our judge, He who answered for our sins on Calvary. What Christ did is given us as ours, His death for us, His life for us, and so we are forgiven and righteous with His righteousness, holy, saints. That is all ours from the Lamb, and the Lamb who is our judge cannot deny Himself or what is ours from Him, no more than God can be undone by separation of God and the Lamb. We are justified by grace through faith for the Lamb's sake.

The Lamb is not one who coerces. He suffers Himself to be rejected. Such unbelief chooses to be judged differently, and we may have that option. The Lord knows whether any of the names we read this morning are those who rejected the Lamb and His forgiveness. We must respect that fact too. If some people insist that they are not Christian, we may not make pretenses that they are. There have been times when a person who committed suicide was not given a Christian burial, his or her last act an act of rebellion against God. That may be so. In confirmation class I used to suggest that the man who jumped over the cliff might repent on the way down. God knows, and how He is toward us is not according to this or that moment in our lives. If He is, who could ever be surely saved? The hands that hold us are the hands pierced on Calvary. They hold us while the wired-up body lies in intensive care and the machinery keeps some heartbeat going and we wonder whether the person is still there. Whether the body is inert or wrenching, we stand in reverence before what may be passing between that person and the Lord. He knows. With our prayers we draw closer. We hope that person is in the hands of the Lamb who was slain for him, for her, for you. No separation there either.

Knowing that, we are free, free to mourn with a mourning that is free of pretenses, free fully and truthfully to mourn, free to weep the tears that Jesus shares with us as we hear His words: "Blessed are they that mourn: for they shall be comforted" (Matthew 5:4). The sting of death is sin, and the power of sin is the Law. But thanks be to God, who gives us the victory through our Lord Jesus Christ. He, the Lamb who was slain, has been through it all and made the way through for us. He doesn't just talk comfort; He has done it at Calvary for us.

Calvary is for you, from Him, a gift. Blessed are those who are given to. They are "the poor in spirit" of the first Beatitude. If there is any hope of deliverance, it can only come from God. The poor in spirit wait on the Lord. As He gives, they are given to. His giving to them is not blocked or hindered by what they have crammed together and would use for bargaining. "God gives into empty hands," says Augustine, not into hands full of what we would boast of before God. There is no room for the gifts to be given into. Sometimes, with drastic mercy, our Father empties our hands so there may be room for His gifts. Blessed are those who are given to by God. Blessed are they who receive their death as a gift from His hands. Nothing is outside His hands. Despite the pain and perplexity of any way of dying, we are never outside His hands, and within His hands and from His hands our deaths are a gift by way of which He brings us to the fullness of His promises. "Blessed are the poor in spirit: for theirs is the kingdom of heaven" (Matthew 5:3).

In the Gospel this word *blessed* is always in relation to Jesus. It rings with gladness, as is pointed to by the translation that says, "Happy are those who know their need of God." But happiness is often something so fleeting or shallow, and here is something from our Lord, a lively, joyful gift for all our living and all our dying. Not spoonfuls, not bucketfuls, but the "river of water of life, clear as crystal, proceeding out of the throne of God and of the Lamb" (Revelation 22:1). "And of His fulness have all we received, and grace for grace" (John 1:16). You were "buried with Him in baptism, wherein also ye are risen with Him through the faith of the operation of God, who hath raised Him from the dead" (Colossians 2:12). You who were dead in sin God made alive together with Him, having forgiven us all our sins, having blotted out the charges of the Law against us. This He set aside, nailing it to the cross. "For ye are dead, and your life is hid with Christ in God. When Christ, who is our life, shall appear, then shall ye also appear with Him in glory" (Colossians 3:3–4).

Happy All Saints' Day. "Rejoice and be glad." "Blessed are those who mourn for they shall be comforted." "Blessed are the poor in spirit, for theirs is the kingdom of heaven." "The throne of God and the Lamb." "The Lamb's book of life."

Amen.

Harvest Festival

Deuteronomy 16:13–15

London (1954)

As long as God has been good to His people, they have given thanks to Him. In the days when the earth was young and harvest was done, Cain and Abel brought their offerings of thanks to God. God had been good to them and blessed their work in the field and with the flock. From God's hand they had thankfully received many good things; therefore, they chose the best, and with sacrificial use of fire gave it back to God. It was all from Him; it all belonged to Him. Abel's sacrifice was with glad and faithful gratitude and God was pleased.

So on down through the patriarchs, God's men made their sacrifices of thanksgiving. The response of God's people to His gifts is thankfulness. Each day for each person has its gifts, and from each person, therefore, thanks are owed to God each day. Now thankfulness to God is something we cannot do well by ourselves in isolation. Right thanking means right using, and right using means sharing.

In boarding school, when a lad receives a parcel of cakes and good things from his mother, he is surely a contemptible fellow if he hides the parcel in his locker and only sneaks to it secretly to eat all the good things by himself. We take it as natural that he will yell for roommates and they will devour the parcel with exclamations such as "What a lucky fellow you are!" and "What a colossal cook your mother must be." Happy times those parcels from home with the hearty sharing and the fun and thanks of one's starving friends. That is the sort of fun God wants us to have with all the parcels He sends us from home. Only He sends so many and sends them so regularly that we get so used to them that we do not recognize them as from Him, share them, and so do not have full joy in them and do not truly thank Him.

To remedy this dreary reception of His gifts, God, in the Old Testament, had Moses arrange great festivals of communal thanksgiving. The people were to come together in a sort of Christmas spirit, consider God's bountiful gifts, and rejoice together in thanks to God for His great goodness and in sharing His gifts. There were three great festivals of this kind. First came the Feast of the Firstfruits at the beginning of harvest. A sheaf of the first ripened grain was taken to the temple and waved before the altar of God. No new grain was used until, with this first sheaf, they had thanked God for the promised harvest and dedicated it to Him. Seven weeks later, when the grain harvest was gathered in, came the Feast of Weeks, also called Pentecost because it was fifty days after the Passover. Here the blessings of the completed grain harvest were thankfully offered to God. Two loaves of ordinary leavened bread, such as were daily used in every household, were presented before the altar of the Lord with festive prayers and song. That everyone might join in the celebration, special care was taken of the poor, the stranger, the widow, and the orphan. God's plenty was for all to share and rejoice in.

Yet the most joyous feast of the three was the Feast of Ingathering (Tabernacles), the culminating Harvest Festival when the barley, wheat, wine, and oil had all been gathered. At the temple the trumpets called to resplendent ceremonies. The people came in gay and colorful procession, bearing fruit in one hand and intertwined branches of the palm, the myrtle, and the willow in the other hand. Another procession went to the Pool of Siloam and brought water, without which people cannot live, and poured it out before the altar. In the evening there were illuminations, music, dancing, and singing. One commentator in his enthusiasm observes that whoever has not seen the joy of the Feast of Ingathering has never really seen what joyful festivity is. When Zechariah pictures the messianic promise fulfilled with people rejoicing together in the goodness of God, he calls it a great climactic Feast of Ingathering. If we today would take our place in the great company and line of God's people and have a right rejoicing Harvest Festival, we shall do well to consider God's directions for the celebration of the Feast of Ingathering, also called the Feast of Tabernacles.

Most obvious in the celebration are the fruits of the earth. The people brought these to the temple in glad thanksgiving. It was the recognition of God as the Giver. "For the earth is the Lord's, and the fulness thereof" (1 Corinthians 10:26). It is He that "covereth the heaven with clouds, who prepareth rain for the earth, who maketh grass to grow upon the mountains. He giveth to the beast his food, and to the young ravens which cry" (Psalm 147:8–9). "The pastures are clothed with flocks; the valleys also are covered over with corn; they shout for joy, they also sing" (Psalms 65:13). Such were the psalms they sang. As we learned last Sunday from the lily, this is God's world. He made it; He controls and uses it to serve His plans.

Some people get monstrously superior about the Old Testament, where hail and lightning and rain are under the personal direction of God. Nowadays we say that the rain comes from a low pressure area from the Atlantic Ocean. We know so much more now. Air currents, atmospheric pressures, positive and negative electric charges, cloud formations, and cold fronts—we understand all about them. When it rains, we know that it is a pressure area from the Atlantic that causes it. We are not so naive as those ignorant people of the Old Testament who supposed that God sent the rain. What is more, some people, with a great show of humility, declare that they hold God too far, too high, and too exalted to think that He would send rain to water their beans.

But this is not by any means as humble as it seems at first glance. For you see, it deprives God of His control and also pushes Him far away from the everyday things of our world. It puts God at a nice, vague, safe distance. It is only natural that people who make God quite remote feel themselves little indebted to Him. They feel they have been successful by their own actions (Deuteronomy 8:17). It is the old pride of trying to dispense with God, and it is a dismal business, for if things are not received as gifts from God, there is little joy in them. Then they are clutched as things that add up to make life worthwhile. No created thing or collection of them can stand the strain of being treated as God. They will crack under the strain, and as they do, the life that is built on them will crack to pieces also.

It is folly to attempt to remove God from control of His world. No matter how scientifically advanced we may be—and science rightly pursued can be the worship of God—no matter how full the description of what happens in the world, we may never conclude that God has been put out of business, given the sack. However much we may know about the world, and it is the bidding of God that we should know and use it to the uttermost, it still remains God's world, and He is in control of it—complete control.

There are, indeed, problems in this truth that baffle our understanding. Take, for example, the death of the Japanese fisherman who died a few days ago as a result of the radioactivity from the hydrogen bomb. We cannot blame God for that, yet it happened in His world. We may grope for answers in the problems of God's running His world and get lost. When we cannot understand the ways of God and they are shrouded in darkness, we do well not to get lost in these but to take hold of those words and deeds of God that are clear and unmistakable and be instructed by them and by Him. There are times when the only sure thing we have to hold on to is the Word of God. If, at such times, we have learned to hold on to that Word, we shall have a stronger understanding of how God deals with us and will not be at all eager to push Him away or exclude Him from "our" world.

We shall neither have any understanding of the ways of God nor rightly use what He gives if we do not know something of who He is and what He means to accomplish with us. Therefore, we must consider not only the words but also the deeds of God, what He has actually done. We build not on theories but on the acts of God.

Thus the Feast of Tabernacles commemorated God's great act of deliverance. It was so called because at this feast the people dwelt in booths, imitation tabernacles, or tents decked with branches and greenery. This, besides making a picnic of it all, was to remind them of the great deeds of God when their forefathers had dwelt in tents in the wilderness. They had been in slavery in Egypt and God had wonderfully delivered them from their bondage. This great saving act they were to recall and by it know that God was a God who was near to them, a God who heard their prayers, saw their need, and saved them.

When their forefathers had dwelt in the wilderness, God had miraculously given them their daily bread. He provided manna and quail for them, and He gave them water when there was none. He was a God also who had let them go hungry and suffer want, and by this He had blessed them. He had given them His promises, and He had shown Himself reliable. In considering the great deeds of God, they knew who God was and how He dealt with them and, above all, what He meant to do with them.

This salvation from Egypt's bondage was the pattern and promise of the great deliverance that would be effected by the promised son of Eve and seed of Abraham, the deliverance from sin, sin that had spoiled God's good world, separated us from God and person from person, and made us guilty before God and subject to death. At the Feast of Tabernacles there were not only the sacrifices of thanksgiving but also the sacrifices for sin, the propitiary sacrifices. The wages of sin is death. For our sin we must die. The only hope is that another die in our place. On each of the eight days of the Feast of Tabernacles a young goat was offered for the sins of the people. The death of the goat had no value in itself, but it told the people of the dread consequence of sin, gave promise of another dying in their place that they might escape the death that was coming to them for their sin, and that they might live to God as His people.

The fulfillment of those foreshadowings and promises is the act of God in that great deliverance that is at the heart of our Feast of Ingathering. The merciful and faithful God has kept His promises. He spared not His own Son but delivered Him up for us all. Christ died that we might be forgiven and have that happy life that God so abundantly plans for us. This is the God whom we thank and worship today. We can be sure of Him. After Calvary we can have no doubt of His love. He who sent His Son to die for us gives us the promise that whatever is necessary for our good He will give us. Our faith is confided in Him.

Therefore, our thanksgiving today is not with calculations such as Mr. Micawber's: income 20 pounds; expenditure 19 pounds, 19 shillings, and six pence; therefore, happy prosperity. God has not promised that our income will always exceed our expenditure. This year the farmers have had a hard time of it. Some of them will gather in little. Among us there are also those for whom business has been tightening up. We haven't made or saved as much as last year. Does a decrease in income mean a decrease in thankfulness at Harvest Festival? By no means. Ours is the God who at times may let us go hungry and suffer loss, and through these give us unthought-of blessings. There are times when our only certainty that God cares for us is in nothing of our circumstances but only in His Word. He has given His promise that His love will never fail us. He will not leave us nor forsake us. The God whom we know in Christ cannot lie.

But when we come to celebrate the Harvest Festival, it would be shameful to dwell on the things that we do not have. Our text points us to rejoice in what we do have and starts off a list. First, our families and homes, "thy son, and thy daughter" (Deuteronomy 16:11). What happiness has been yours this year in the mutual trust and dependence, sharing and affection of your home? The happy cares of helping your children grow sound in body and soul. And all the refuge, comfort, and strength given you by your home.

Next on the list, your work and business, "thy manservant, and thy maidservant" (Deuteronomy 16:11). You have had a job to do, a job in which to use and cultivate the strength and skill that God has given. Honest work that has enabled you to care for your own and to reach out for the helping of others.

Honored as we are by the presence of the mayor of our borough, we cannot but think of the blessings of good government. Order has been maintained and a law enforced that is just and humane. Many not able to care for themselves are given help. We enjoy the rights and responsibilities of freedom. These liberties that are ours under the British flag are precious indeed. They have been dearly bought. Many of the best and bravest of this country have given their lives that we may live in this freedom. Thousands of people expend their life's energies maintaining the fabric of our society. From the one who sweeps the street for us up through the police officer, the schoolteacher, the doctor, the magistrate, the mayor, the judges, the ministers of the Crown, to our Sovereign Lady Queen Elizabeth herself. All these combine to make possible our lives as they are protected and free. The occupation of many of you is involved in the defense of these great civil blessings. We are grateful that they have been preserved for us for another year.

Most precious is the liberty to worship our God according to His Word. That we may freely come together this morning to give thanks to God in our Harvest Festival is such a blessing that it would be peril to despise. Not many miles to the east from this place there are people who grew up celebrating Harvest Festival every year. It was the regular thing, taken for granted. Today they are either hindered in celebrating the festival or, if they bravely do it, they are under the shadow of tyranny and the danger of persecution. God has given us another year of liberty. It is of His mercy and not of our deserving.

How we are to use these and all the great gifts of God is suggested by the last four on the list of our text: the Levite, the stranger, the fatherless, and the widow (Deuteronomy 16:11). If we clutch the blessings of God to ourselves and think to enjoy them by ourselves, they will not only be no happy blessing to us but also become a curse. God may well grow impatient with us.

God gives to us that we may grow to be like Him. God has His delight in giving. The more we are like God, the more joy we have in giving and sharing our gifts with others. What He does for us, He wants us, in turn, to do for others. First, the Levite. He stands for the church and those who serve it. If we have really come to know God as our Father in Christ, we won't be able to keep it to ourselves, but we will want to share that which gives happy meaning and purpose to our lives. The church is given to us for giving on further the Gospel.

Next, the stranger, the one who feels that he or she doesn't belong. It is a hard thing to be a stranger. Loneliness can disintegrate a person. God has given you your home for another year so you may share it, there making the stranger welcome and to feel that he or she belongs.

Finally, the fatherless and the widow. These represent those who are defenseless and who can only get on with your help. You meet them quite often. But there are many that we don't meet and we want to help show them too. Church helps us do more together.

What you do for the needy is indivisible from the sort of thanks that you offer God today. If you are grudging toward them, you are grudging toward Him. But this is to put it negatively. Rather, God knows what makes us happy. God wants us happy. He bids us rejoice; therefore, He gives us gifts and bids us share them. "And thou shalt rejoice in thy feast, thou, and thy son, and thy daughter, and thy manservant, and thy maidservant, and the Levite, the stranger, and the fatherless, and the widow, that are within thy gates" (Deuteronomy 16:14). Thou shalt surely rejoice.

AMEN.

The Holy Innocents, Martyrs

MATTHEW 2:16–18

LONDON (DECEMBER 28, 1956)

In Friday morning's paper the tragic death of a little child was reported. The family was escaping over a lake from Hungary into Austria, and in the bitter cold the little child froze to death. The rest of the family, weak and injured, arrived in Austria, but the baby was dead. Friday was the day on which the church remembers the babies of Bethlehem who were put to death by the tyrant Herod. We did not observe the day together here in church, but in our family devotions the devotional booklet directed our attention to those little children so pitifully slain. The church calls them the Holy Innocents and gives them the name of "martyr," for they were the first to lose their lives for Mary's baby. For more than 1,500 years, the church has sung of them as the little flowers of the martyrs.

This beautiful name should not obscure from us the hateful wrong of their being put to death and of the heartbreak in those homes of Bethlehem that the soldiers of Herod entered to do their grim business. We have been so calloused by the statistics of death rained down from airplanes on crowded cities that when we learn there probably were not more than twenty babies killed in Bethlehem, we feel that it wasn't so bad after all. But love does not work by statistics. Love is personal and individual. Each mother in Bethlehem bore the whole weight of the loss of her child that she loved. The Hungarian mother whose baby froze to death is not comforted by the thought of other thousands also bereaved. She suffers the whole weight of wrong that humans have done. When we see such sorrow, our eyes are touched with tears as were Jesus' eyes when the two sisters wept for the brother they loved.

Tears, however, are not enough. Tears by themselves can be merely a selfish indulgence. Those tears are best that wash our eyes to see more clearly and are linked with the living, which shows their sincerity. There is little to the tears of a mother at the death of her child when she has allowed it to be shaped more by the television set than by loving, playing, and keeping company with her child. To weep for the loss of a child who wasn't given enough calcium or the right size shoes because the money went into cigarettes or the pools is to make empty noise. Tears shed at the funeral of a mother are made empty by following a pattern of life that has little place for what she held most dear.

No, tears are not enough, and our commemoration of the Holy Innocents has no point if it issues only in our feeling sorry for those little ones of Bethlehem and the bitter grief of their parents. We remember them best as we heed what their death proclaims so we see the basic facts more clearly, see what sin is like and what God is like, and live accordingly.

We see what sin is like most obviously in the damage when one sins against another. This is horribly clear with Herod. Herod loved Herod. Herod wanted himself to be big. He got power for himself no matter by what means and no matter at what cost to others. When he suspected his wife or sons of endangering his power, he simply had them executed. Herod shed so much blood to secure his power that the Jewish historian Josephus doesn't even mention the killing of a few children in Bethlehem—though there probably are other reasons for the omission, for Josephus was writing also to secure his own position.

When we are sinners, when we put ourselves first, then everybody else comes second. Herod had the power to subordinate people to himself. Most of us sinners do not have so much power; therefore, the damage we do others in putting them second is not so spectacular as Herod's efforts in Bethlehem. But the basic principle of sin remains the same, though its expression may be variously limited. When people get in our way, we do not have the use of Herod's sword, but we know how to get rid of them.

We do not grow in stature by merely looking at Herod and saying what a wicked man he was. For growth, first comes repentance, the recognition of our sins of putting ourselves first and the various ways we have of putting others second. However, we have not yet seen the true horror of sin so long as we have only looked at the damage that sin causes between us. The full and hideous enormity of sin is seen only when we recognize the damage that it does between us and God. If sin is only what hurts my neighbor, it is not such a problem. I, then, can do whatever I like, so long as I don't injure others. This is the level of morality of many with whom we associate. This is, however, rank rebellion against God, for it excludes God, denies that He is Lord, dethrones God, and has us take over the role of God. You can't push almighty God around like that and get away with it. When we try to overthrow God, it is not God who comes to grief.

The first fact about us is that we are creatures of God. This is what God made us to be, and if we insist on being something else, we are not what God wants. Therefore, we have coming to us the wrath and rejection of God. This direct insult and exclusion of God is not unrelated to our sins against others; rather, it is the cause. If I refuse to recognize myself as a creature of God, then, naturally, I also fail to recognize my neighbor as a creature of God. Then I do not value and deal with my neighbor according to his or her connection with God but only according to the connection with me. If my neighbor is not understood in connection with God, then he or she has value to me only as he or she is useful to me and I feel free to push him or her around to suit my convenience.

Facts, however, are not changed by denying them. No matter how much I may deny it and act contrary to it, I cannot ever change the fact that I am my father's son. It is the same with the fact that I am God's creature and that my neighbors are God's creatures also. If I damage someone in his or her health, welfare, or fulfillment, I am damaging a piece of God's workmanship, God's creature. God meant that person for something, and if I injure him or her, I am working against God.

When Herod killed those children, he was doing fearful damage to them, to their parents, to himself, and toward God. These were not separate actions, for what Herod did against the children he did against God. In each baby that Herod killed, he was guilty of killing Jesus, for three reasons: (1) that was what he intended to do; (2) each of those babies was a creature of God, and to do away with what God has made is the attempt to do away with Him; and (3) by God's being born a man in Bethlehem, He became each one of them and of us. After the incarnation it is unmistakably clear that to harm or damage any person is to harm or damage Jesus. Because He became each one of us, what we do to one another is done to Him. Jesus states this explicitly when he speaks of the judgment in Matthew 25. How truly we spoke in the confession when we called ourselves sinners and recognized our sin's enormity by acknowledging that each of them was against God.

All this sin is departure from God. This is not what He wants. This is not what He does. He cannot be blamed for it. Yet because we are eager not to face the responsibility for sin, we immediately look for someone else to blame. From the first sinner right down to you and me, when confronted with our sin we add to the sin of departing from God, of directly or indirectly blaming Him. With Adam it was "the woman that Thou gavest me"; with us it is usually that we have been put in a position in which we couldn't help but sin. Such pressure was put on us that we couldn't help it. Another form of blaming God is the question "Why doesn't God stop it?" If He is almighty and if He is a loving God, why did God let those babies perish by the sword of Herod or by the freezing cold on that lake on the border between Hungary and Austria?

What happened in a stable in Bethlehem gives the answer. God could have come with terrible power and slain Herod and all like him. But if He slew everyone prepared to put themselves first, there would be none of us left. He came the way of love, which knows that we are not made better by force. The only thing that can really change us is love. It changes us inside. Force deals only with the outside of a person. When God came to save us from sin, He used not force but love—love that brought Him to a stinking stable and a cruel cross.

Jesus did not put Himself first. He was there for us. His whole life was such action of love. It fulfilled the will of God. He lived the life that is expected of us, and He died the death that was coming to us for our sin. Thus was sin answered for and overthrown. Thus alone is there victory over sin. If that was Jesus' path to victory, we cannot expect that ours will be different if we could share that same victory with Christ.

Sin—whether in ourselves, that is, our flesh, or in the efforts of sinful people, that is, the world, or in the temptations of the devil—is always out to destroy us. In comparison with that destruction, having our throats cut is a trifling hardship. For that destruction is our separation from God, our utter ruin, our hell. It is because we know of a horror far worse than physical death that we were so glad at Christmas. We acknowledged ourselves as sinners, justly deserving that separation from God, and we saw in the babe of Bethlehem our God come to us to save us from the destruction of sin. He does not stop sin by an act of almighty power, for that would mean the killing of every sinner. He takes our sin on Himself and suffers it all, even to the agony of the cross, so sin may be forgiven and we may be changed and brought into the kingdom of God where He rules, not with a sword but with His love. Those who are God's no man or sword of man can destroy. The purpose of God's love for each of His children can never be overthrown. No bomb or sword of Herod can separate us from the love of God which is in Christ Jesus.

God carries through the plan of His love. When Herod would destroy Mary's baby, God saw to it that He escaped safely. Jesus still had His great redeeming work to perform. Joseph, at God's bidding, takes Jesus and Mary to safety in Egypt. The hard life of refugees in a foreign land is also part of His road of suffering for us. The other babies in Bethlehem who did not escape did not have so long a road before they came to their triumph. The parents who mourned for their children did not see how their deaths fit into God's plan: perhaps they heard something from the shepherds. Or perhaps later, when Jesus was crucified, those parents said to one another, "Our boy, if he had lived, would be as old now as that Jesus. Thank God he didn't live to come to that." They may have come to know and rejoice in the death of Jesus for them and their children. Or it may have been that they had nothing to rely on but God and had to wait until heaven before they saw how it all fit together.

We know the baby for whose sake their children were slain; we know His death for us on Calvary. We know that if God did that for us then no power of sin, world, or Satan can separate us from the love of God. No matter what onslaughts of sin we may have to endure, we know that we cannot be destroyed. We may have to suffer a lot. Jesus did too. We may be put to death. But through all this we know that the God who has joined Himself to us in Bethlehem and died for us on Calvary will not forsake us. By all this our being bound up with Him is tested and strengthened. We are challenged to show forth the victory with our lives and with our deaths. We will be His witnesses until God lifts us finally free of sin to the bright glory of His presence, where we shall find the Holy Innocents, the first witnesses that God has come on the scene to save us from sin for life with Him now and always.

AMEN.

Memorial Service

1 CORINTHIANS 15:56

MRS. RAE HUEGLI, WIFE OF VALPARAISO UNIVERSITY PRESIDENT A. L. HUEGLI (1980)

In Cleveland, over Thanksgiving, we saw that there was a Medical Care Center where there was once a hospital, a Learning Center where there was once a school, a Geriatric Center where there was once an Old Peoples' Home, and a Car Care Center where there had once been a service station. This summer we were glad to come on a playground that had not yet been changed to a recreational facility.

The day of 1984 is at hand. Even within our university, a university dedicated to the true thinking, writing, and speaking of true words, there is evidence of the leprosy of language, palsying jargon, and the putrifying sores of manipulative and counterfeit words. A university dies when its truthfulness atrophies and all the facts can no longer be faced and truly spoken. "Better a straightforward burglar than a sanctimonious manipulator" is Strietelmeier's word of wisdom in the last issue of the *Cresset*. If one were looking for a description of the way many deal with death and funerals, "sanctimonious manipulation" would accommodate much of the data. Manipulation of people is facilitated by the manipulation of language, which is the most precious gift from God, who speaks His words to us.

What does God say of Rae Huegli? Our Lord put His name on her with the water of Baptism: "You are one of Mine and precious." Into her our Lord gave His body and blood, given and shed for her for the forgiveness of sin, a sinner forgiven, justified by grace through faith for Christ's sake. By His forgiving words, by Baptism, by the body and blood, by His death and resurrection, our Lord redeemed Rae Huegli, sustained her, and finally brought her to the completion of His promises for her. True. As long as we are saying Jesus' things, we are saying what is surely true.

Within Jesus' truth, within His forgiveness, within His embrace of Rae, we, too, may truly cherish, embrace, forgive, and delight in all the good that was given into her and through her to us. How many beauties had she? Let us count the ways. A beguiling, womanly beauty she had and, more lasting than that, an engaging vivacity that deepened to a strength of determination to carry on even when her body was wracked with pain. Her devotions and her prayers strengthened her. When she stood receiving the long, long line of freshmen, you could not tell by looking what victories she was winning to continue standing there, warmly greeting each one, our university's gracious first lady.

Yet the surest thing we can say of her is that Christ died for her. To the death that He died for her sin and ours, He joined her by Baptism, and He joined her to His life that is stronger also than the little death of our mortality "that like as Christ was raised up from the dead by the glory of the Father, even so we also should walk in newness of life" (Romans 6:4). She, too, now walks in a newness of life brighter than we can imagine, all accusations of the Law left behind and with vivacity unimpaired. "The sting of death is sin; and the strength of sin is the law. But thanks be to God, which giveth us the victory through our Lord Jesus Christ" (1 Corinthians 15:56–57). This is most certainly true.

Amen.

Funeral Sermon
for a Suicide

John 6:68

Valparaiso University

"Lord, to whom shall we go? Thou hast the words of eternal life." Jesus had pointed toward His death, and "many of His disciples went back, and walked no more with Him" (John 6:66). Jesus went on to His death, leaving them with their ways of figuring things out to which they clung. Of Jesus' death we know. The Lamb of God bearing the sins of the world. The words that bring us that death bring us that forgiveness won for us on Calvary. They are the words of eternal life.

With our prayers today, we pull this woman's death together with the death of Jesus. We pray; we do not say what is only our Lord's to say. What He knows for sure, we do not. It seems likely that she committed suicide. That is a fearful thing. Her last act, an act of rebellion against God, yet we do not know if that was her last act. God knows; we do not. He spoke to her, but what He said we do not know. We may not arrogate to ourselves what is only His to say.

To turn away from God and carry on with our efforts to sort things out is to turn away from where alone the final answer is—with Him. "If I were her judge, this is how I would decide." To do that is to attempt to replace the Lord with myself. Or in His place we may put our talking of how we failed or did not fail. We did all we could—seeking to justify ourselves. We cannot make a compelling case for ourselves or for her. The only hope for any of us is that we might be forgiven.

We do not pray that she may be forgiven. She has died, and as Scripture says, now comes the judgment. But we would cherish her as one who did not die denying Christ, holding herself outside His forgiveness. She was wearing the cross. She had not thrown that away. We can pray stronger prayers on the basis of her Baptism, for then we are praying laying hold of the name of God that was put on her with the water at her Baptism.

God cannot but be true to His name. He remains faithful to His name. "For if our heart condemn us, God is greater than our heart"

(1 John 3:20). How He is toward us we know from the cross. He loves us so much. God loves us so much that He lets us go to hell if we insist. He does not coerce. He suffers Himself to be rejected.

Those of us who know something of this person affirm that she was no rejecter of Jesus. Only the Lord knows for sure. We cannot speak for Him or pose as more surely merciful than He, but we can say with certainty what He has said about Himself, all that is in His name, and at its heart the cross. As Martin Luther says, "We crawl to the cross" at such a time with all our doubts, anxieties, and uncertainties, and we lay them down there. There is forgiveness and healing, and from there the way and the words of eternal life. The strongest words I heard last Friday were "She was a Christian." Stronger still, "Jesus is the Lord," and strongest of all, "Jesus is her Lord." "Lord, to whom shall we go, you have the words of eternal life?"

AMEN.

Wedding Sermon

PHILIPPIANS 4:4–6

CAMBRIDGE (DECEMBER 11, 1966)

"Rejoice"—that is the note for today. Not simply rejoice, but "Rejoice in the Lord." That comes first. But perhaps you have been thinking of rejoicing in one another, and there is lots to rejoice in there. Of first importance, however, is the fact that these two rejoicings are not alternatives. When they are taken as alternatives, there is damage both ways. When embracing your spouse means turning your back to God, there is damage toward God and toward your spouse. The same is true when embrace of God means turning your back on your spouse. This is all tied up with rejoicing in the Lord coming first.

Let's take the first case, where embracing your spouse means turning your back to God. This is most dangerous. Yet when God says He comes first, that the greatest love in our lives is our love for Him, it does sound a bit as if He is wanting to cut back love of husband or of wife. In fact, the opposite is the case. It is only when we love God most that we love spouse best.

We are God's creatures. "It is He that hath made us, and not we ourselves" (Psalm 100:3). Our life and success come only from Him. God knows that only He can be God for us. The idolatry of putting people or things ahead of Him is ruinous both ways. If you make an idol of your spouse, your wife cannot possibly fulfill your idolatrous expectations. Your spouse will rebel or break under the strain, and if you have rested your life on this idol of spouse, then it, too, will go to pieces.

God is the number one fact of our lives. Every good thing is the gift of His hands, and His gifts have their full and happy value and blessing when received from His hands. Such a gift is marriage. Marriage is God's idea, and it is a characteristic sort of gift. You can tell a lot about people by the sort of gifts they give. Marriage is God's sort of gift. God has His happiness in giving gifts. In James He is acclaimed as the giver God, and in John He is characterized as love. God had more love than He could contain. He made man and set him up splendidly. But God wasn't selfish. Love can't be stopped. It must swing on. He made woman. More love. Male and female He created them. So children and so more to love.

Our happiness, like God's, is in loving and in being loved, and marriage is the perfect setup for this, a many-leveled being there for each other. Male and female He created them as two halves to fit together and make a completeness and fullness of person. As the Bible says, they two shall become one flesh, that is, one person. It is no longer my life and your life but these two put together into one life, our life. The oneness of that life is fulfilled as it receives its direction, resources, and achievements from God. This is disrupted when the life of one spouse is held back and is set to say and achieve something different from that of the other spouse. "I want my way" is set against "No, I want my way." It is vital, then, that both turn to God and inquire what is the way He would want for us.

Today, when you ask what sort of marriage you shall make, you find there are only two options: the marriage set up by God or that marriage degraded. You cannot make another sort. Actually, bride and groom don't make a marriage. The estate of marriage is there; bride and groom step into it and take their place. Their respective place and role God has arranged as He sets forth in His Word.

You come today to receive this gift of marriage from God. You are received into it, and within this estate ordained of God you receive one another. You don't need any help from me to help you recognize the manifold gifts you both receive. Today you make only a beginning. Love grows in substance not so much by our looking at each other as by traveling the hills and valleys of your life together. What happiness there can be in your two lives made one you cannot now even imagine. That takes more than a lifetime. Hence, rejoice in the Lord always. Each morning there is the gift to grow bigger through another day. You wake up and accept the gift of your spouse. Give your spouse a hug and receive each other from the Lord, thank Him for another day, and launch into it together, rejoicing in the Lord always.

Anxiety shall have no place, for anxiety comes only when God has been taken over from, when something has cut into God's place, or when something gets disconnected from Him. When anything gets disconnected from Him, there is trouble. Hence, keep everything tied up with God. "Be careful for nothing; but in every thing by prayer and supplication with thanksgiving let your requests be made know unto God" (Philippians 4:6).

There are many forces and pressures set to destroy marriage as ordained by God. What God's enemies hate most of all is to see His children blithe and gay. They can't stand it and will do all they can to destroy it. These enemies have stubborn and proud allies in your own hearts, and they will present your self-insistence as altogether reasonable. Then there will be hurt and disappointment. First, just a flicker. You would never expect that your wife would be capable of being so insensitive, ungenerous, or slow to understand. Just a flicker perhaps, but it is swift to grow if allowed to grow. And the bigger it grows, the uglier and the more destructive it becomes. Therefore, it must be taken hold of and laid out before God in prayer so there may be honesty in taking its size and in assessing the reaction it has prompted. It is vital that no such thing be allowed to grow, certainly not beyond the day. Therefore, at each day's end, put yourselves together under God's Word. You take it from Him. You offer your day to Him, asking that He may have use of it and that He may forgive and make good your shortcomings. You receive forgiveness from God, and that forgiveness swings back and forth between you, and the things that could push you apart are removed. Held within His forgiveness, nothing can destroy your marriage.

Oh, I almost forgot the case the other way around when we turn our back on spouse to hold to the Lord. This is a pretty tricky one.

When it is a straight conflict of loyalty, the Lord, of course, comes first. This is no denial of love. If spouse pulls to sin, you love spouse by saying no. To say yes would be the opposite of love. As the poet has it, "I could not love thee dear so much, loved I not honor more." We would say Christ rather than honor, but the point is quite clear.

We get into situations, however, that are not all that clear. She has been pestering you to get the storm windows on and you say, "I am sorry, dear, but I am afraid I really must get on with my sermon." Now that may be true, or it may be that you are just hiding behind the Lord where she can't get at you anymore. The Lord does not at all like being used as a defense against fulfilling your role as husband and father. We may not allow love of the Lord and love of spouse to be alternatives.

When you are married, you cannot be true in the one and not in the other. The bigger love encloses the lesser love. Today you are sure that your love for each other is a big one, but there will come days when you are not so sure. Then you will need the resources of the one absolutely reliable love, the love with which Christ has loved you. As you are drawn closer again to Him, you will be drawn ever closer to each other.

As God's children, you have been endowed with staggering gifts. We have mentioned the greatest—forgiveness for Christ's sake—with which comes our being taken on by God for the fulfillment of His happy purposes. He is pledged to see us through. We are guaranteed the lot. Hence, we are in a position to be what the Revised Standard Version translates as "forbearing," the King James translates as "moderate," the New English Bible translates as "magnanimous," Beck and Phillips calls "gentle," and if any one asked me, I would suggest "generous." In the Bible this is God's way of dealing or the way of a good king—one who has everything and is then generous. The opposite would be demanding, exacting, lording it, requiring dues and desserts, in a word, the way of the Law. This generosity is then the way of the Gospel with its delight in giving and forgiving. Thus God has dealt with us and heaped on us the resources for dealing similarly with one another.

When husband and wife live toward each other from the pile of these resources, they can be generous, forbearing, gentle, magnanimous. They do not have to prove anything, no chalking up of merit and good works on the basis of which demands can be made. Sinners who know themselves justified by grace for Christ's sake cannot make themselves bigger than that fact. That fact radiates through all the lower levels.

> Love is patient and kind; love is not jealous or boastful; it is not arrogant or rude. Love does not insist on its own way; it is not irritable or resentful; it does not rejoice at wrong, but rejoices in the right. Love bears all things, believes all things, hopes all things, endures all things. (1 Corinthians 13:4–7 RSV)

Love does not set itself limits, hence marriage, with its vows of love without limits or reservations. The only limits are the limits of love. Love will say no to what is not good in your spouse and love will strive to overcome it and love will not give up. The way of building each other up is the gentle, forbearing, generous way of the Gospel, not the demanding, exacting way of the Law. And it shows. "Let all men know your forbearance" (Philippians 4:5 RSV). It shows in the ease of your relationship and conduct. It is the ease born of the mutual confidence of love and the gifts God has endowed you with. It is the have-nots who are most bumptious and put on an act, who snatch and clutch and make a parade.

As Christians we may live with a royal confidence. We know who we are and we know our goal. The Lord has forgiven us and taken us on. We have His pledge that what He has begun He will see through to the consummation. "The Lord is at hand" (Philippians 4:5 RSV). Perhaps you wouldn't be so pleased if His Second Advent were scheduled for this evening, but even so, that could not mean deprivation, only enlargement of love and happiness. There may be some more years before He comes and winds things up, and each year the third Sunday in Advent will put you in mind of your wedding and its Introit that will ring again its happy notes for you: rejoicing, generosity, confidence clear of anxiety, prayer, thanksgiving.

There is His Advent now with you today. He comes into your hearts today in Word and Sacrament. He comes to join you together in His ordinance of marriage. He will come with you into your home and stay with you even to the end of the world. Your embrace of each other is held firm within the embrace of His love.

> Rejoice in the Lord always; again I will say, Rejoice. Let all men know your forbearance. The Lord is at hand. Have no anxiety about anything, but in everything by prayer and supplication with thanksgiving let your requests be made known to God. And

the peace of God, which passes all understanding will keep your hearts and your minds in Christ Jesus. (Philippians 4:4–7 RSV)

AMEN.

Wedding Sermon

MATTHEW 19:3

VALPARAISO UNIVERSITY

In Matthew 19 Jesus tells of discipleship—how life is lived by those who are His. The theme is wholeness—wholeness all the way through as one stage follows another: marriage, children, young man, possessions, and wholeness also in living each relationship. The young man wanted to be a partial disciple. He wanted to divide his loyalties. The whole area of his possessions he wanted to fence off from Jesus and retain the lordship for himself. With Jesus there is no negotiation of terms, no "ifs" or stipulations as safeguards against Him. He is Lord all the way. As His disciples we take it from Him; who we are is gift from Him. We are given to.

Little children are only given to. They simply receive, so they exemplify faith. "Of such is the kingdom of heaven" (Matthew 19:14), such as are given to and do not defend themselves against the gifts. They are so exposed, so bound up with their parents. We can make them so happy, or, if we deny them love, we can do them such pain and damage. Either way they remain our children indissolubly. Little children also exemplify wholeness. When little children laugh, there is none of them left outside their laughter. When they cry, they cry with the whole of themselves, without reservation. When Jesus hugged the little children, there were none of them left out of His loving embrace.

So back to Jesus' words about marriage, which we hear ringing with the theme of wholeness, of being given to, and undivided loyalty. You marry with the whole of you, without reservation, with nothing kept back or held outside. After you are married, a big part of the answer to the question "Who am I?" will be, "I am Kathy's husband. I am Mark's wife, the whole of me without reservation." To each other you give yourself and are given to, fully exposed and open to each other.

Nobody can give you such happiness as the other, nor such pain.

All of little child and parent is not so much as husband and wife. That is even bigger. "For this reason a man shall leave his father and mother and be joined to his wife, and the two shall become one" (Matthew 19:5)—wholly, together, for good. Twice in the chapter the disciples say, "This is too much. It is more than a man can manage." Twice Jesus agrees, "Yes, it is too much but not for God." His giving gives more than we can imagine or hope to achieve. Jesus who speaks to us here is the Jesus on the way up to Jerusalem to give Himself for us on Calvary and through Calvary to the resurrection and the life that sin and death cannot destroy. That is the way the apostle says husbands are to love their wives.

A new life begins with marriage. You begin to live husband-life and wife-life, two lives joined into one life. All that bountiful Creator God put into each of you as man and woman, all that you are as baptized Mark and baptized Kathleen, all is joined into one wholeness as you enter marriage, "the holy estate ordained by God." You enter, you are given to, you receive marriage, wide open for all wholeness, the shared creative living and loving, all the growing and happiness that His generosity built into marriage.

Receive each other as gift, and receive the gift of the new life as husband and wife. Gifts are more as shared. From you two together new life may be born of you, deputies of Creator God. Then, too, there will be all the possessions you get with their temptations to divided loyalties. They can separate and enslave you, but not if they, with all of you, are embraced within your undivided loyalty to Christ. He is your Lord. You are His. Held within His love you cannot fall apart. Only what is broken off and kept outside His love can destroy you. At the end of each day, you lay it all out before God, nothing kept back, nothing held outside His forgiveness and His love.

Confident in that forgiveness and love, you are bold to make the staggering full-size promises of marriage love without reservation. You think your love for each other may wear thin; Christ's love does not fail. Running with your love through its ups and downs is His love. Do not cut out even the tiniest piece and defend it against Him. That is to treat Him as enemy. That way lies disintegration and death. With Christ is life. Within His larger love, your love for each other need have no fear but can grow and deepen, including always more and more. There is more than you have even dreamt of, but now in the morning of the day, you make a good beginning as you are married, all of you, in His name.

AMEN.

Church Anniversary

EXODUS 20:3

GOOD SHEPHERD, COVENTRY (1966)

I don't know what it is like to live in Coventry. I imagine it can be pretty nice. There is so much here that is new and well planned. The bombing was certainly an ugly business, but it did get rid of a lot of the old town's old ugliness and gave to this generation the opportunity to build new and better. Much that has been built is really first class. In this attractive neighborhood there are streets of new houses with services and supplies laid on. Things are set up for the comfort and convenience of modern living. And this great industrial town is in the business of providing the equipment for modern living: cars, electrical equipment, household appliances, tools of all sorts—so many excellent things supplied for your use. If setting, tools, and equipment can provide it, then life in Coventry has the best chance of being good—indeed, among the best in the nation. Real poverty and want are seldom heard of. Essential needs are supplied, and for most there is much more than that.

All these things are laid out for our use, but then comes the vital question, "What about the users?" There is one man I know who bought a magnificent set of woodworking tools—all sorts of chisels. He had great plans, and for about a week he was excited about it all. Then he realized that using these tools called for a lot of skill and effort. It would cost him a good deal of time and patient concentration to master these tools before he could achieve much with them. It was not long before the fine set of tools lay rusting on a shelf in the garage. He never really mastered or possessed those tools, at least no more than a child does a toy.

Another friend bought some of those wonderful Black & Decker machines. You have seen them advertised on television, I am sure. This chap was simply captivated by the tool. He couldn't use it enough. He built all the cupboards and shelves his wife could use and some more besides. Then there were bookshelves and coffee tables and a box on legs for holding the shoe polishing stuff with a lid that fell back to reveal a mount for putting your shoe on for polishing. There was no end to it. His home became not so much a home as a place for installing things with his Black & Decker. You can imagine how his wife felt. She was, of course, delighted at first, but the multiplication of cupboards and shelves and so on really got in the way. When he suggested that the thing he would most like for Christmas was the bigger model because there would be so much more that he could do, she nearly popped.

Our tools, houses, appliances, and equipment are excellent in themselves, but in actual fact they are no better and no worse than the user makes them. They can soon become a bore, or they can take us captive. Sense and balance cannot be expected from them nor really, for that matter, from the people who use them. What looks like balance is often merely the result of limited money. The man who got bored with the woodworking tools would, if he had the money, go on buying one toy after another, while the other chap would go on getting bigger and better Black & Decker's and lathes and band saws and what not.

Did you see the trouble they are having with the center of gravity in the new Concorde? Past the sound barrier, the center of gravity shifts, so they are planning to move the weight of fuel from tanks in the front to tanks in the back. If the center of gravity is not right, they will have trouble. Without a sure center of gravity, we wobble. Without a solid point of reference, we can't tell which side is up. The astronauts have quite a time of it, but they get an angle on the earth or some star to know which side is up and where they are going. At sea the officer of the watch takes his sextant and gets a reading on the sun. His angle to the sun tells him where he is and which way he is heading and whether he is off course or on course.

That is why the First Commandment is of such crucial importance. It states the solid point of reference, our angle that tells us where we are and whether we are on or off course. We have no choice whether we shall travel or not. We are born to journey. We travel from birth to death. So much at least nobody would deny. The journey is more of minutes than of miles. How are you traveling? There is only one sure way of finding out, and that is by reference to the one quite solid point.

There are other points of reference, the other gods mentioned in the First Commandment. We know them quite well. To the question, "Are you traveling successfully?" one answers, "Yes, look at my bank account," another, "Look at my children" or "Look at my furniture" or "Look at my friends" or "Look at the car I drive" or "Look at the holidays I have." All excellent things in themselves, but can they bear the weight of your life?

In the Bible we find God's challenge: "Try the other gods and see what they are worth." There is nobody and nothing that can stand the strain of being treated as God except God Himself. Each of us will prove this truth one way or another. There was one man I knew when I worked in London who lived for his business. His shop burned down, and he went to pieces. Idols makes slaves to our ruin. They all break under the strain of being treated as God , then those who rely on them break with them.

The damage is bad enough when the idol is something or some pile of things. It is even worse when the idol is a person. The woman whose god is her children is preparing double damage. Her children cannot fulfill her idolatrous expectations of them, and these expectations can be a crushing weight on her children. They can't bear the weight, they rebel, and, in her resentful disillusionment, the mother will cry that she has lived for her children and given them everything she could. She has been their slave. She has clutched them for herself, thus harming both them and herself. We know what lazy and demanding little monsters children can become when their parents do everything for them.

The same is true of idolatrous marriage and idolatrous friendship. "Thou shalt have no other gods before Me" (Exodus 20:3). This may sound a bit like God thumping His own drum. I am the big cheese and you had jolly well better know it and kowtow. I suppose this really betrays how we would feel if we were God. Many people do estimate themselves according to how many people they have kowtowing to them. But God, who is the only one in a position to pull that sort of thing off, isn't like that at all.

When He says He is number one, it isn't for His own sake. He doesn't need us to make Himself big. It is for our sake. He knows that only He can be God for us. No created thing can take His place and pull it off. As created by Him, we can only derive our life and success from Him. There is really no other alternative. We are either in the fulfillment of His plan or we are that plan ruined. While there is no escaping these facts, God is not a tyrant who makes slaves as do the other gods. He allows the option of rejection. If we persistently set ourselves to do without God, God finally says, "You shall have it as you want it then," which means hell.

The negative possibility is bound up in the fact that God is no idol. He wants no slaves. He is not that sort of person. He wants sons and daughters, a family held together by the greatest of His gifts—love. That is the sort of God He is. Love in the solid sense of being there for someone, a love that can cause pain, but a love that holds firm. This is the staggering thing about God. He is there for us, there for our good. We may see this in the bounty of good things He has provided for us. Just walk around this neighborhood and look in the homes. A good deal of God's good gifts, however, have been badly mucked about. So much has gone wrong; He allows the option of rejection. The absolute certainty of Him being a God who is there for us is Calvary. He must have cared an awful lot to have gone through that for us.

God comes into the mess we have made of things. He is born as one of us, as we shall shortly celebrate. He makes a way through the mess for us. He takes our sin and answers for it. He takes our death and overcomes it. All this He did for you so you might know Him as the God who forgives you, the God who takes you on and would fulfill His happy purpose in you.

All this comes only from God. He is number one. We must take it from Him. What He gives and says goes. This can be rough. We are reluctant to let Him have the say so. We would rather like to keep that or, at least, some of it. We are prepared to fit Him in somewhere down along the line of other gods. We don't want to tell Him straight that He is redundant. Better to put Him on reduced time. We might need Him some day. This line of thinking betrays itself when things don't work out the way we want them to. There comes a day when we need God and He doesn't come up to specifications. He doesn't deliver the goods, so we sack Him. Well, not just like that. We use some polite dodge or another, but the effect is the same. What it boils down to is that God is not doing what number one tells Him to do.

Now this just won't wash. You can't expect God to play second fiddle, nor can you make Him your flunky. He is number one. Like it or lump it, that is how it is. I have known individuals for whom God has taken away their other gods, left them with nothing to prop themselves up with and nobody left to rely on but only God. That is the sort of love He may show you someday. Remember how Jesus dealt with the rich young ruler? Put everything else aside and start with God. It didn't work in that instance. But it has to work for each of us if we are going to make it. God is God. He can do what He likes and we are completely at His mercy.

Through the low doorway of this confession we must go on our knees with no specifications that we can impose on God. Those who have been brought through this find that when they have been cleansed of other gods, cleansed of trying to play God, cleansed of telling God how to behave, they find the solid fact of God, the solid point of reference, God in the stable and on the cross. There is a God you can rely on and love, a God from whose hands we live. Every good thing is then received and valued from Him. When everything is seen in relationship to God, it has this true and full value and meaning and blessing. Then things can't be ruined by being treated as idols.

When God says you must love Him more than wife or child, it sounds like He is wanting to cut back your love for them. The opposite is the case. You love wife and child best when you love God most. Then your love for them can be sound, healthy, full, and sure, and your love for them is held within His love for you. This is true also for your enjoyment of your car, refrigerator, and potatoes.

For one year now, this building has sat here and has been saying, "Here is a solid point of reference for all you people in this neighborhood. Here God's Word is spoken and brought home into lives, hearts, and homes. Here you may gather to take it from God. Here you can get things straight out from Him." When we gather for worship, we first get out our sextants and get our angle to God. We begin "In the name of God the Father and the Son and the Holy Ghost"—the solid point of reference. Before Him we can get things sorted out, see ourselves more clearly. We get rid of what has gotten in the way. We confess our sin and ask forgiveness. His forgiveness is given us in the name of Jesus. With sin forgiven, we then draw in close to acclaim God as the great God He is. We pray. We listen to Him speak to us through His Word. Then this Word is unfolded for us in the sermon and brought home to us. We say a big prayer that ties everything up with God. We receive His blessing. Then we go out, on into another week, forgiven, connected more strongly with Him. We can cheerfully tackle another week with strength and direction from God. We know where we are going.

Not that there aren't snags. You bump up against all sorts of contradictions of God. You want so much to share what means so much to you with your friends and neighbors, and they couldn't care less, they are quite all right, Jack. The hardest snags are closer to home. Someone in your own home is quite content with the short-term policy of running his life as if he has taken over from God. In your own heart there is stubborn resistance too. We like to keep some corner at least with a notice to God, "Keep out."

If God comes first, you are in for some struggle and pain. But as you come to know Him more fully for the astonishing God He is, you will come to be grateful for that too. One year is just a start. Already there are victories to show, lots we do not see, and many more lie ahead as Christ comes to have more and more His way with you. When you enlist with Christ, you get more than you bargain for. If you are quite satisfied with yourself and the way you are managing things, you would be well advised to stay away from Christ. You are really in for something when Christ takes over, when you call Him Lord. When you do that, you are onto something solid.

So today we give thanks to God for what He has done for us here this past year and we say, "We are yours, Lord, build us solid to You and use us."

Amen.

Pledge Sunday

Genesis 28:10–22

London (1957)

Jacob was fleeing for his life. His mother, Rebekah, had told Jacob to trick his father, Isaac, to get the big blessing. Jacob hadn't wanted to do it, but Rebekah pushed him into it and half-blind old Isaac had given him the blessing. Esau was furious and was out to pay his brother back. Rebekah got wind of it, and Jacob fled, a poor fugitive with only what he stood up in and with a staff in his hand. At night he slept on the rocks. But while he slept, he dreamed, and through his dream, God spoke to him. Jacob saw in his dream a ladder. The top reached to God and the foot of the ladder was beside him. On the ladder the angels went up and down between him and God. To the penniless outcast God spoke and gave the promise that the ground on which he lay would be his, that God would multiply him and make from him a blessing for all the people of the earth.

The experience of this dream shook Jacob. When he awoke, he was filled with fear. The mighty God was there about him and had lovingly spoken to him. But had God, or was it only a dream? How could Jacob be sure? If it were truly God, then His words would be fulfilled. Jacob took God at His word and declared, "If You keep Your word, I shall know that You are the true, the living God, and to You I pledge myself." Jacob set up the stone as a pillar and dedicated it with anointing oil for its sacred function as witness of God's promise. It was a sort of signature to God's promise and His pledge. If God brought Jacob to that place again and fulfilled His promise, then, beyond all doubt, Jacob would acknowledge the Lord to be His God and do Him service.

Jacob journeyed on to Haran. There, for many years, he was put through a hard school. As he had deceived, so also now was he deceived by Laban, both as to his bride and as to his wages. But through all this he carried the memory of God's promise and God did bless him. Jacob prospered despite Laban's double-dealing. After these years he stealthily removed from Laban to return again to the land of his father and the land that God had promised to him. Laban pursued him, and it was only by the doubtful stratagem of Rachel that Jacob escaped unscathed. At Peniel he wrestled with God and was not overthrown, for he held God to His promise. God is captive to His word. Jacob built on that. Then Jacob faced Esau, and by all human calculation of numbers and strength, Esau could keep him out of the promised land. But God had promised it, and Jacob entered. Upon his return, double sorrow overtook him. He buried his father and Rachel whom he had so dearly loved. Never could Jacob delude himself into thinking that he was the master of his life and the controller of his destiny. What good came to him he could not chalk up to his virtue.

All this that we are told about Jacob is not designed to glorify Jacob but to glorify the living God. When we are shocked by the shady and downright wicked things that the patriarchs did, it is perfectly clear that God didn't bother about them because they were such splendid fellows. That they certainly were not. So the reason for God's concern for them was not in them but only in God. The shabbier their record the more amazing is the grace of God that so patiently cared for them and brought them through. God had given them His promise, and He couldn't go back on His word.

Jacob, however, was never allowed to suppose that he had God in his pocket. Never in his life could he say, "Now I am it." There were often times in his life when everything contradicted that God was on his side. Many a time when he was with Laban he must have thought, "Hasn't God deceived me?" Jacob only had God's word. When he stood at the graves of his father and of Rachel, when his sons brought him the blood-stained coat of many colors, and when, as an old man, he bade good-bye to the promised land to go into the strange and distant land of Egypt, he must have questioned, "Is God a deceiver or is He true?" At many points in his life, it looked overwhelmingly to Jacob that God had deceived him. We have the advantage of seeing the outline of the whole course of his life and can see more clearly the fulfilling hand of God, but for Jacob this was mostly only a fact that he grasped by faith. But he did return to Bethel, and God did keep His promise that He had made to the fleeing fugitive with only a staff in his hand.

Jacob knew that God had broken into his life, that God was the Lord who, through all his ups and downs and despite his sin, had led him, blessed him, and kept His promise to him. God had proved Himself. His action proved it, for He is the active, the doing, the living God, who beyond all human calculation takes a hand in our lives and fits them into the fulfillment of His purposes. In doing this God involves Himself with us. God commits Himself to us by His promises and proves Himself by the specific action that fulfills the promises. Here is the living God who is not some notion or idea but is actively and personally present in our lives with His plans and actions. Jacob knew this, and the only way to respond to such a God is on the same basis of deed and action. If God involves Himself with us, then we are involved with Him. This is shown by His action and ours. Jacob vowed specific action to God.

> If God will be with me, and will keep me in this way that I go, and will give me bread to eat, and raiment to put on, So that I come again to my father's house in peace; then shall the LORD be my God . . . and of all that Thou shalt give me I will surely give the tenth unto Thee. (Genesis 28:20–22)

The only valid response to God's solid and specific promise is our solid and specific promise to Him. As the proof of His promise is in His action, so are we proven by our action. The evidence that God is involved with us is in His specific action. The evidence that we are involved with God is in our specific action.

That God has involved Himself with us we know more clearly than Jacob ever knew, for we know the action of God by which He became a man here among us, lived our life with us, and gave His life for us so He would be our God and we His people. He has done it. God kept His promises that He would. He is the true, the living God; His action proves it. He has committed Himself to us, so we are committed to Him.

We are dealing with the living, doing God, not with some idea or notion or vague abstraction. To the living God we cannot merely say, "I believe that there is a God" or even "That Thou art God." God is much more specific in word and action than that, and the only valid response is in the similar specific word and action. God said to Jacob, "I will bring you back to this place in prosperity." Jacob said, "If You do that, I pledge You a tenth of all that You will give me." That is solid. That means something. That takes God seriously. He means business and He expects us to mean business too. You can't deceive God with fine phrases. He knows the value of words without the corresponding action; so do we. If a fellow continually insists to a maiden how passionately much he loves her and never gives solid evidence of his love in generous action toward her, she doesn't take him seriously. She is sure he means business when he proposes and is willing to commit himself to her in marriage, to share his life and all with her. Similarly, we can't expect God to take our protestations of love too seriously unless they are accompanied by solid, generous action toward Him, and it is only in our willingness to commit ourselves to Him that is carried through in action that it is clear that we mean business.

At confirmation we committed our lives to Him. That promise is just so many lying words unless it is carried through in specific action. God has, quite incredibly, committed Himself to us in Christ. Whether this is so for us or whether we repudiate Him our action shows. It is meaningless to say, "Jesus is my Savior. I love Him dearly," unless there is specific undertaking and action in our lives to show that it is so.

Jacob pledged a tenth; Hannah pledged her son; Jephtha pledged her daughter. In the Psalms we often read of vows being made and paid to the Lord. In times of tribulation or sickness or grateful rejoicing, God's children made promises to God that showed that He counted in their lives, and that they took Him seriously. There are some among us today who are here because such a vow was made and kept.

Yet we must face the question of why there are few vows made by us. The usual explanation is that we don't want God too intimately involved in our lives, so we hold back from making the vows and keeping them, which would get us too closely mixed up with Him. We like rather to entertain the notion that we are in control of our lives and can fashion them to our own liking. God knocked that idea out of Jacob as He will also with us if we start acting as if we were God. Or we do not make vows to God because we are willing to get all we can from God and make no return. When we are sick, we ask God to make us better again quickly, but we make no promises of what we will do with the health and energy He will give us. We ask God to bless our work and our businesses but prefer to remain piously vague about how we will dispose of what He will give. Jacob knew He was dealing with the living God, and he took God seriously. God promised him prosperity. All right, if you are serious, I am serious. "Of all that Thou shalt give me I will surely give the tenth unto Thee" (Genesis 28:22). That is what Americans call "talking turkey." It means business.

We Lutherans are subject to a special temptation. We have been so much assured that our standing with God is based entirely on God's free and undeserved love and not on any action of ours that the devil is right there to suggest, "Well, if it is not based on any action of yours, your actions don't matter. You have a nice cushion to rest on there. You have complete forgiveness in Christ. So do as you please. You are always forgiven." There is no more hideous mockery of Christ and Calvary than that. Christ died in our place so we may not be condemned and punished for our sins. He takes all that for us so we may be forgiven and may know the living God as a God who graciously involves Himself with us and we with Him. Are we, then, to make of this the basis for a life that contradicts that we are involved with Him?

Our pledges today, whether written on our pledge cards or recorded in our hearts, are evidence that we are deeply and gladly involved with God, not that we think thereby to buy God's favor or put Him in our debt. We want to show Him how much it means to us that He rescued us from ruin and would make us members of His family and wants to have us always with Him.

Only as we come to solid undertaking and fulfilling action, only as we rise above the vague pious words on which hypocrisy breeds do we take God seriously. We are often at Bethel, whether in this house of God, when He speaks to us through His words from the pages of our Bibles or from some passage that we carry in our memory, in the Sacrament, or when we recognize the hand of God in our lives. It is the living God who deals with us, speaks with us, and gives us His promises. He is the living God as His fulfilling actions show. Faith takes hold of God as the living God who graciously involves Himself with us. It is taking God seriously. It is our lot thrown in with Him, the evidence of which is in our fulfilling action.

AMEN.

Mission Festival

ISAIAH 35

ST. PAUL'S, BOREHAMWOOD (1963)

"He will come and save you" (Isaiah 35:4). That is the message of Advent. The promise of our text was, in the first place, for Israel in exile in Babylon. They had lost their home and the land promised to their forefathers Abraham, Isaac, and Jacob. These patriarchs had lived as strangers in that land, but they lived there by the promise. Then Jacob went down to Egypt with his family and there became a large people, so large that Pharaoh got scared of them and tried to squash them. He laid on them hard bondage. Yet they had the promises given to their fathers. They had the body of Joseph, which they had promised to take with them when they came into their own land. They cried to the Lord in their need, and the Lord heard their cry and sent them a deliverer. When Moses led them out of Egypt, God showed that He had come among them to save them. The glory of the bright cloud was the guarantee that He was with them and leading them on to the land that He would give them. They were brought into the land promised to their forefathers, but just before entering it, they received the promise that a Deliverer, like Moses but greater, would be sent to them. They were to watch for Him. They were to know that when God fulfilled His promise of giving them the Promised Land, that was not the lot. There was more to His promise to Israel than His giving them the goodly land flowing with milk and honey. There was still much more that He had in store for them. God's promise was bigger than what they then received.

The same is true the second time God brought His people out of bondage. The promise of our text was for Israel, captive in Babylon, beside whose waters they sat down and wept when they remembered Zion. "Strengthen ye the weak hands, and confirm the feeble knees. Say to them that are of a fearful heart, Be strong, fear not: behold, your God will come with vengeance, even God with a recompense; He will come and save you" (Isaiah 35:3–4).

And God did. Israel was brought again into its own land. The ransomed of the Lord returned and came to Zion with singing. Great as their joy was in returning, it was not as big as the promise. Israel was God's servant for fulfilling His great purposes, and Isaiah also told of the Israelite, the Servant of the Lord who would suffer for our sins, bear our grief, and carry our sorrows. Stricken, smitten, and afflicted, He would be wounded for our transgressions, and by His stripes we would be healed. He, the virgin's son whose name is Wonderful Counselor, the mighty God, the everlasting Father, the Prince of Peace, whose name would be called Immanuel, God with us, God come to save us. So Israel, having her own land again, was not to let that become the be all and end all for her. The promise was bigger than that.

When Israel was again in bondage, this time in her own land under the hated rule of the foreign Romans, there were still those who lived by the promise. One of them was Simeon, who waited for the consolation of Israel as he knew promised by the mouth of the prophet Isaiah (chapter 40). Again God came and saved them, this time in person, Immanuel. They could know it was He from what Isaiah had said, "Then the eyes of the blind shall be opened, and the ears of the deaf shall be unstopped. Then shall the lame man leap as an hart, and the tongue of the dumb sing" (Isaiah 35:5–6). That part of the promise had not been fulfilled before; it was now. You may have noticed how the writers of the Gospels are at pains to record especially these particular miracles mentioned by Isaiah.

Here, then, comes the big deliverance wrought personally by God. He had shown Himself to Israel as a God who delivers His people out of bondage. He had taught them to expect this sort of thing from Him and something bigger. The former two major deliverances were from national bondage, but each time God told them that there was much more He had in mind. The tragedy of Israel is that when God came Himself for the big job of delivering them from the bondage of their sin and freeing them for the vibrant liberty of the sons of God, all they wanted was the little deliverance of their nation from the Romans. The big thing still outstanding in God's promise to Israel they did not want. That was too much for them.

Their rejection became God's occasion for swinging wide into the whole world with the Gospel of Christ's forgiveness and victory. Christ achieved the great deliverance, then He bade His men "Carry on!" They should share in the victory of Christ by carrying its conquest throughout the world. Christ made His men His messengers and representatives. "He that heareth you heareth Me" (Luke 10:16). "Go ye therefore, and teach all nations, baptizing them . . . and, lo, I am with you always even unto the end of the world" (Matthew 28:19–20). "Where you go, I go with you." So out from Israel went Christ's men—Christophers all, carriers of Christ, east and west, north and south from Palestine. Across into Europe came Paul. He moved across the upper Mediterranean world, bringing Christ to Macedonia, Philippi, Athens, Corinth, and to the then center of the world, Rome, and, perhaps, later to Spain. Christianity began fanning out, for wherever Christ's men traveled, Christ traveled with them.

Phoenician traders may have brought the Gospel early to Britain, to Cornwall. At the Council of Arles in A.D. 314 there were representatives from London, York, and Lincoln. British bishops were at the Council of Nicaea in A.D. 325. In A.D. 410 the Romans withdrew from Britain leaving the A1 and Huntingdon Road behind them and the country in chaos. Then came the barbarians from northern Europe. That is where you and I come in. This is our crowd, our forefathers, and a pretty wild lot they were. They plundered and ravaged the land. Some settled here and pushed the people that had been here before to the fringes, into Cornwall, Wales, and Ireland. These were the Dark Ages. Into this darkness came Christ's men from the west, from Ireland came Columba to Iona and beyond. From the north, from Northumbria came Aidan and the men of Lindisfarne. They brought the

Gospel to our then barbarian forefathers. From the south there came also Augustine and his men working out of Canterbury. They had been sent by Rome and made a bold takeover bid for the British church, which succeeded at Whitby in A.D. 664. With these men Christ came again to our forefathers in Britain. What that has meant for this land is beyond calculation. For you it has meant that there was somebody to carry Christ to you, your parents, perhaps to a friend, or perhaps oddly enough, to your pastor from Australia, though he, too, comes from the same set of barbarians.

There are different barbarians today who no longer come in long boats, plundering the land and destroying its Christian heritage. They may come wrapped up in your newspaper. They face you charmingly from your television screen. They are your workmates who mock Christ or even members of your own family whose cool indifference would make you ashamed of Christ. With Columba and Aidan we do not retreat but go after these barbarians as Christ's men to make them His also. Thus God may come and save them, bringing Christianity once again through this land. That is to say Christ comes to Boreham Wood nowadays with you and through you.

But no place is the end stop of the route that Christ takes. He takes His way to the ends of the world, and He would go there by way of you. Most of us are not so fortunate as to be carriers of Christ to the ends of the world. We carry Christ around Boreham Wood and perhaps some little spot in London. That is a full-time job. Each day of our lives confesses Christ directly or by implication, or each day denies Him. But still there is more. There is always more to God's promises. His bidding about "into all the world" is for us too. If we are too old or too young for that job or not equipped for it, then somebody must go in our place, someone equipped and eager to go but who cannot go unless we buy a ticket and support the work that is our work too: going into all the world, teaching, and baptizing. Thus God comes and saves. But not "into all the world" as if "into all the world" meant everywhere in general and nowhere in particular. Christ's work is always particular work—Nigeria, New Guinea, India, Swaziland.

The person who goes is quite particular, too, and goes to a quite specific place and task. Our Evangelical Lutheran Church of England has Nora Mitchell teaching in India at Kodaikanal. Our church would be much richer and alive if there were more such particular people. The measure of a church or organization is not what it does for itself but what it does outside itself and beyond itself, for Christ becomes more for us as we give Him away to others as their Savior and Lord also.

It was thrilling while we were in St. Louis this last year to meet a goodly number of missionaries: the young Larsons heading back to New Guinea where the whole community is reshaped with the coming of the Gospel; the Jim Mayers returning to India (he is Dr. H. A. Mayer's son). He has a responsible task in administration and overall planning, but he is itching to get back to the those particular villages he has already served for years. The Kreylings were eager to return to Japan where he trains men for the ministry. They all tell of God keeping His promise to come and save, also that there is more to the promise not yet fulfilled. There are neighboring towns and regions where no one has yet carried Christ. In our mission field in New Guinea, there are no schools for girls. Particular men and women are needed for these places, as is the support to send and sustain them there. You? Only you can tell.

You are a particular person. Are you particularly involved in all this? Indeed you are. Every time you read or hear God's Word, by every sermon, Christ is carried to you, coming and saving. Perhaps all you want is your lumbago cured, or it is nice for the children. You may put up your defenses against Him, or He moves closer in helping you to drop the thing you have been holding between you and Him, moving in closer so He has more His way with you. And Christ has more His way with you as He has more His way through you.

So Christ's promise will be fulfilled for you: His coming and saving. But there is always more to His promise—more than you have yet known or experienced. As He comes and saves more and more with you, you will know more of the happy fulfillment of His promise. Spectators can know none of this, only those involved do, and they do indeed.

Yet however rich and happy your experience of God's fulfillment of His promise, there is still more in store, more than we can take in while yet hampered by sin that still limits and crumples us. That is the meaning of the rather odd things in our text. "Waters shall break forth in the wilderness, and streams in the desert; the burning sand shall become a pool, and the thirsty ground springs of water; the haunt of jackals shall become a swamp, the grass shall become reeds and rushes" (Isaiah 35:6–7). We have never seen anything like that nor are we likely to. This is not a description of a fantastically successful irrigation scheme, but our world is pictured here as bursting out and beyond itself, doing things unimaginable as we know it. There is a glory it cannot depict or contain. That is part of the promise as yet unfulfilled: the everlasting joy on their heads and sorrow and sighing fled away.

That is also part of God's promise to you, the ultimate fulfillment. We come to that by way of the earlier fulfillments, the part of the promise fulfilled today and this week. Each fulfillment stretches and points us to a larger fulfillment until our pictures and language burst trying to express them. You don't know half of what God has in mind for you. It is probably more than you want right now. So many play safe and try to protect themselves from God, and we know where that leads to. But God has kept some of His promises to you, and each fulfillment stretches you for more. When you can't take any more, you will burst and get the lot.

AMEN.

Synod

HEBREWS 11:31; JAMES 2:25–26

(1967)

Rahab is something of an embarrassment all around—though the prostitute who turns out right in the end is a stock sympathetic character in numerous novels and films. But how does Rahab come to be the cover girl for our Synod in the 450th year of the Reformation? It looks as if there must have been someone from the advertising game among those who drew up the plans for this Synod. It should sell with Rahab as the cover girl. As if that is not enough to raise our eyebrows, we have Hebrews lauding her faith and James praising her works. Was Rahab a Lutheran or not? Yet the theme prescribed for this sermon is "Faith Alone Justifies the Sinner."

Well, what are we to make of it all? The one thing we may not do is suppress any of the evidence. The story is certainly one that Hollywood could play up. Two spies equipped with the latest scientific know-how of that great power Egypt. They stroll into Jericho with all the brass of James Bond. The counteragents spot them, and they, playing it cool, find lodging at a place strategically placed for observation where not too many questions will be asked. Enter Rahab, a striking woman, but not what she used to be, so she is grateful for any business. She has had to take on a sideline in flax, and she also does bed and breakfast. That is not what the police thought, but Rahab had their number. She was a shrewd woman; she had been knocked about a good deal in her time. Rahab knew how to put people off who asked too many questions. She soon got rid of the police. The way she did it was no more honorable than her profession. She told them a clever and thumping big lie. So that is Rahab, resourceful and clever, but on the other side of the ledger, there are all the dark entries. Her life was a mess and she was damaged.

Then comes the staggering thing. Rahab makes a mighty confession of faith in the God of Israel, the God who delivers and leads His people, not some little, local god she had been taught to believe in, but the Lord who is God in heaven above and on earth beneath. Rahab cannot stand against Him. She throws in her lot with His people. She risks her life on this God whom she had just recently come to know from the great things He had done for His people. She believes in Him, and she does not perish. She becomes one of the grandmothers of Jesus. She has a place in the list of the great heroes of faith in Hebrews 11.

But as we have already seen, Rahab does not simply know about the people of Israel and the God they thank for His deliverance of them as we might merely know something that we read in the newspaper. It didn't just stay in her head. Rahab faced up to it, saw that she and her people were being challenged and called in question. She did not try to hide from the God of Israel. Rahab acknowledged Him to be the Lord. She would belong to Him. All her life had been so far was questioned. It couldn't stand before the Lord. It fell away, and she was swung into His service.

Now if Rahab had just said, "Yes, I suppose it is so. The God of Israel is the Lord, but you chaps had better get out fast. I don't want any trouble. I have had enough of that. I don't want to get involved in your operation." If she had said that, she would have had faith in the way that James uses the word *faith*, faith that is only in your head or your words but that doesn't go beyond that. This is the faith that knows the right words to say but refuses to risk our lives on God, rest them on Him, and be taken over into His service. This is the faith that James is talking about and says won't do. The real thing is involved with God and His program. Works flow naturally from such a saving faith, the real thing. James isn't talking about the real thing, saving faith, but the faith that only knows the right words to say.

Rahab said the right words and made a mighty confession, but hers was a genuine faith, for it took over her life. Martin Luther didn't get this clear in James, thus he said some foolish things about James. In this 450th year of the Reformation, it is good to recognize that Luther was not infallible—and he would be the first to agree. Luther did not get what James was driving at, or rather he did not get it from James. Luther puts the matter clearly in one of his sermons: "Those who like to hear and who understand this doctrine of true faith but do not begin to serve their neighbor, just as if they wanted to be saved by a faith devoid of works, do not perceive that their faith is no faith."

Our largest gratitude to Luther this 450th anniversary year is for his clear and bold declaration of what saving faith really is. This is first the recognition of what saving faith is not. Saving faith is not just knowing the right words to claim credit for. It is a gift of God; more exactly, it is our receiving and living the gift. The gift is, first, the forgiveness of our sins and life as the children of God for Jesus' sake. This is the big gift, and it brings us to accepting it. Faith is nothing apart from the gift it receives, but receiving the gift, it is, in Luther's words, "a living, energetic, active, mighty thing this faith. It does not ask whether good works have to be done, but before the question is put it has already done them and is forever doing them. Faith is a living, daring confidence in the grace of God."

All of faith is God's gift. A floppy piece of rubber becomes a balloon when it is filled with air. When God bestows His gifts, we become His children, unless we reject them, which is unbelief. With respect to God, there is grace. He is the giver. With respect to us, there is our being brought to receive, that is, our faith. The gift is such that when it has worked its reception it cannot merely be looked at or have nice words said about it. It does things, it energizes and activates, it does things with us.

Thus Rahab, when she had God straight, didn't just sit and say the right words. She really got cracking. She knew herself involved, linked up with Him. That meant sorting some things out. Rahab had quite a lot to throw away as rubbish, though her first thoughts were not of herself. Her actions flowed swiftly from the faith she had confessed. She had her father and mother to think about and her brothers, aunts, and cousins. I think her family must have been a pretty shiftless lot, mother a trollop and father couldn't stay off the bottle. Anyway, Rahab had to go out to work, and the wages they paid at Woolworth's were not enough. She may have been driven into prostitution or cheated into it or led by her own lust. We don't know. Rahab doesn't attempt any defense of herself: "I couldn't see my poor old Mum starve." "Nobody else would help, so I had to do what I could." "It hasn't been easy, and after what I have been through, I have a right to expect something back for it." No. Her confession is not based on herself—she has rather forgotten that. It is all God, but when she has gotten that straight, then things get underway with astonishing efficiency. The arrangements and plan are quite clear, and everyone knows the part they have to play.

With this opening service, we make our confession of God. In the Creed we have acclaimed Him the great God He is. Scripture and hymn tell of the great things He has done for His people. In our Redeemer and Deliverer God is the certainty of our salvation. This is faith's certainty. We know to whom we belong. Such saving faith does not just say the right words. It is involved with God, it pitches into His program, the work and challenge He has set before us. With faith's eagerness to follow through the push of God's gifts to us, we would also bring Rahab's swift efficiency that sees what has to be done and sets to it.

"Faith alone justifies the sinner." Sinner Rahab was, there is no denying that, even those with a limited notion of sin would agree with that. Justified she was, there is no denying that, even those with a limited notion of sin would agree with that. Justified she was, there is no denying that, for she knew the Redeemer and Deliverer God as her Lord. In Him rested all her confidence, so she was justified by faith alone. All gift of God, and that gift of God had its way with her as she saw what needed to be done and swiftly got on with it.

AMEN.

Confessional Address

JOHN 20:11A, 14–17A

LONDON (1955)

Our reading today is one of the most moving moments in the life of our Lord. In two words—*Mary* and *Rabboni*—we have an exchange of love that no other words could express. But when Mary would embrace the feet of Jesus, He speaks those strange words, "Touch Me not" (John 20:17). As we prepare to embrace our Lord in the Holy Sacrament, we should ponder the deep significance of these words.

The word *Mary*—so heavy with love—was spoken by the same voice that had driven the seven demons from the sordid soul of the woman of Magdala. With joyous recognition, she would lay hold of the Master whom she had lost and was now hers again, just as He had always been. That was Mary's mistake. Jesus was not as He had always been. No longer did He bear the burden of everyone's sin. No longer was He under the Law that condemned and required a death for sin. All that was finished. Now Jesus was the risen and victorious Lord who was about to ascend.

The Son of God had drawn near to us, nearer He could not come, and this He did to draw us to God. He came down to earth so we might go to heaven. Mary was wanting to hold Jesus to earth and clasp Him with earthly hands. Jesus responded, "Touch Me not." Mary must grow beyond a merely earthly sight and communion to embrace Him with the hands of faith. She must rise from an earthly love to a heavenly love, not with hands but with the heart. Jesus touched Mary with awakening love, then took a step back so she could move that step of love toward Him and learn to follow Him as He goes from earth to heaven, even if He is no longer seen in earthly eye and fellowship.

Jesus still draws close to us in His Word, most especially in the Holy Sacrament, where He is giving us His body and blood. Some, with Mary's error, say that they see and touch the body and blood of Christ. But Christ is not earthly wise received, for He calls to a closer, deeper communion. He calls us from our Baptism by our name, awakening us to a lovely recognition expressed in our "Rabboni!" We join Christ's fellowship at His Table. Then He takes a step back from us so we may move that step of faith toward Him. Our earthly eye and hand see only bread and wine, but to our mouths our Lord gives His body and blood. We receive into ourselves His real body and blood and are cleansed, forgiven, and invigorated. In Christ's steps we move toward heaven, toward that final and perfect communion with Him, the blood of whose dying love cleanses and creates us as the children of God.

Our Savior comes near to us to draw us after Him to heaven. He is no less near to us because we cannot touch Him. We are nearer to

Him when we grasp Him not with the hand of our earthly body but with the hand of our spirit. We don't pull ourselves up to heaven by the shoestrings of earthly things. They drag in the other direction. We are drawn to heaven by the magnetism of Christ. Within the magnetism of His love, blessed are we if, not seeing, we yet believe, for we are closer to that glad and blessed heavenly communion of which we today receive a foretaste and toward which we today are strengthened.

Let us this glad Easter Day open and stretch out the stained and empty hands of ourselves and embrace our Master. We seek not a dead Jesus but a living, victorious, and risen Lord who ascends to draw us from the tears of our earthly eyes and feelings to a closer, more joyous heavenly communion with Him. God grant that we may rise from the death and tears of our sins, from our cramped earthly mindedness, and embrace within our inmost selves His body and blood given into death for our sins so cleansed, forgiven, and filled with new power for our heavenward way, our every thought and act and word may cry our ardent "Rabboni!"

AMEN.

Confirmation Service
"Hold That Fast Which Thou Hast"

REVELATION 3:11

LONDON (1951)

Just a few moments ago, you showed that you have a basic knowledge about God, yourselves, and this world. Your confirmation text bids you to hold fast to that which you have. To promise to hold fast is to confess that left to yourselves you would collapse, that you cannot stand in your own strength, and that the strength and meaning of your lives are outside of yourselves. We find no solid foundation on which to plan and build our lives in ourselves. We must have that solid something outside ourselves onto which we can hold with certainty.

An honest consideration of ourselves will show that we are not what we are meant to be. Deep down in each of us there is the knowledge that we are designed for something more, something higher than this world allows. There is something more to us than a few years working, eating, sleeping, chatting about the weather, football, then dying. If that were the whole meaning of a person, why go on? Why endure the uncertainties, the chances and changes, the pettiness and meanness if that is all there is to being a man or a woman? We revolt against such an answer from the inmost depths of our being. We know that we are created for a purpose and for strength. We would not feel our weakness if we did not know that we are meant to be strong.

The fearful tragedy is that so many seek for this purpose and strength in themselves. Being in need of strength, they seek strength just where it is lacking—in themselves. They are rather like the famous Baron Munchhausen, who told the story that once, while riding in winter, he was tossed by his horse into a deep snowdrift. He found himself sinking fast into the powdery snow. Already his ears were smothered by snow, but being a man of resource, as he would say, he was not at a loss. He took a firm grip of his boot laces and pulled strongly till he was clear of the snow. My dear friends, no matter how desperately we may try, no matter how we may hate to admit it, we cannot find a firm basis in ourselves on which to build our lives. We cannot save ourselves by tugging at our boot strings.

The answer to our need must be from the outside, a rock certainty not from ourselves but from another. Just as there is no meaning, strength, or life in lungs without air, in a heart without blood, in a car without an engine, so there is no meaning, strength, or life in us without God. We were made to work from God, to be powered by Him. What is the sense of a light bulb without electricity? What is the sense of you without God?

My dear young friends, during the past year and more we have been learning the theory of Christianity, the rules of the game. Sometimes I am sure you wondered why we were learning certain things that seemed to have little relation to life. That is the way the person training to be a pilot feels about the mathematics and physics that he or she has to study for months before touching an airplane. But when this person gets up against the real job of flying, he or she proves the value and necessity of the mathematics and physics learned theoretically. So also the theoretical study we have made of Christianity will prove its value and necessity when you come up against the real job of living. Then what you learned theoretically will become tested and strong truth for you. So many of the things you have learned you hold as only theoretically true. These lessons will come to full reality of truth for you when put to the test in your lives. The truths of Christianity are not known by argument or logical deduction but by participation. If you want to know whether Christ is your God and Savior and His Word the truth, don't try to figure it out or argue about it, give it a go. Try it out. The proof of the pudding is in the eating.

However, the fact of God does not depend on your recognizing it. Whether you believe in God or not doesn't put God out of existence or into it. What you may think or feel doesn't alter any of the facts. But all that we said before about God being to us as air to lungs, engine to car, electricity to light bulb will only become a valid fact giving life, strength, and meaning for you when you take God at His Word, take Him into your life or, rather, when you give your life to Him. You will find it works. God is the center of all things not you, not your bank account, not the clothes you wear or the house you live in. God is the one certain and utterly reliable fact. Everything else has its meaning and value only when it is connected to that one unshakable fact of God.

My dear catechumens, today you step forward before God and this body of Christians as young men and women who are responsible for their lives. You will make your oath of allegiance. You will confess the creed, which is to declare that you will live your lives by God and His truth. You promise that He shall be the controlling center of your lives today and even to death. God shall be your rock tower of strength, at the center, unmovable, a sure stronghold. Each part of your life shall have its true value and meaning in being connected to God. You shall know that Christ and His Words are true, for you mean to live them. We have often said how when the greatest love in our lives is the love of God, then all the other loves in our lives will be larger, healthier, and happier. We love our parent, spouse, child, or friend best when we love God most. With God at the center, all other things and relationships will fall into their proper place, each with its true value and meaning. Today you give your word that God will be in control in your life. You confess Him as your Lord. You belong to Him, and your life you plan to build according to His plan and on the rock foundation of His Word.

What was it that got hold of you and brought you to this? It is not because it pays. You have to give up an awful lot if you mean to be God's child. It isn't compulsion that brings you here. It is something you cannot understand, something quite wonderful. It is the love of Jesus. Yet God, merely as God the Almighty and all-holy, is a terrifying thought. If we think only of the just and holy God who is so utterly different apart from us and above us, in the light of whose holiness all our best efforts are as filthy rags, before whom we are guilty—to see God only as righteous judge is to come to hate Him. As Luther says, we would like to kill this God in whose light we see ourselves for what we are. In this withering light of God's holiness, we are reduced to nothingness, crushed to our knees in self-rejecting repentance. Seeing ourselves as sinners whom in justice God might well have done away with, we cry, "God, be merciful to me, a sinner." In ourselves we have no hope of being answered. God doesn't need us. Yet this is the miracle of love: God sent His Son to take your sin and guilt on Himself as your substitute He answered for your sin. He died where you should have died that you might escape the death of being cut off from God. It is this love of Jesus that has got hold of you, that brings you this blessed night to this place to say to Jesus, "Thou gav'st Thy life for me. I give my life for Thee." Having dedicated your life to God, having relived your Baptism, you will go forth from this place tonight with clear purpose, high courage, and firm faith. Should you this night be seized by evil and given the choice of renouncing Christ or die, I do not doubt that you would bravely take your place with the heroic martyrs.

But you will probably not be granted that privilege. You will be put to the harder test of making the love of Jesus a live reality in the flat ordinariness of everyday life. The heroic strength of Jesus is shown most gloriously in a martyr's death, but that same cheerful strength and Christlike quality can also be a part of such things as drying the dishes or doing your math homework. Everything you do should be something different because you are God's child. This difference isn't always obvious, but those near you should observe something different about you because you are God's child. They will find a cheerful helpfulness and a patient kindness. In short, they should see the love of Jesus at work in you. This is far from easy. The cultivation of the art of Christlike living takes a lifetime, and nobody masters it. But we keep at it. So long as we have our hold on Jesus, we cannot but strive to get nearer to what He wants us to be.

This hold on Jesus is faith, the acceptance of all that He did as our substitute and the trusting surrender of our lives to Him. It is this hold of faith that must remain fast and firm, for it is this faith that takes hold of Jesus and makes ours all the blessings that are won for us by Him. All love and kindness, all true courage and right purpose for our lives come through this living connection with Jesus.

Hold fast that which you have, that is, let faith be firm. How is faith made firm and strong? Faith was created in you by the power of the Holy Spirit in the Word with the water in Baptism. It is that same Word that preserves and strengthens faith. For in that Word there is Jesus and the truth of God for you. To know Jesus truly is to love Him greatly. The more we know Him, the firmer our faith, the stronger our love. We are drawn nearer to Jesus in deeper knowledge, which is ours as we take in the Word of God, read, spoken, preached, or sung. If you are to hold fast, you must stay close by the Word of God. The Word of God is the means the Holy Spirit uses to create and confirm faith. Therefore, let your hearts be stored with its precious truths that, strong in faith, you may make a worthwhile job of your lives; that your lives have their significance, strength, and achievements according to the plan of God; that when your time is up and your life has been lived, God will not sadly shake His head and sigh, "What a waste of time that was."

Live by the strength and purpose that are ours in Christ so you may hear at the end, "Well done, thou good and faithful servant" (Matthew 25:21). It will be well done, well lived, if it has been lived by faith in Christ and by the power of His love. May the Spirit of God ever confirm your faith through the life-giving Word of God that your hold on Jesus may never slacken so your life shines forth Jesus and is a life beautiful and worthwhile, a life ever watched over by the care and love of your heavenly Father. May He bring you safely to your first Communion that there you may receive the pledge and proof of the redeeming love that died that you might have life as the child of God. May you there be confirmed in faith and hold fast to your Savior and your Lord throughout the life that you this night do solemnly dedicate to God.

AMEN.

Dedication of Westfield House

Luke 8:4–15

Sexagesimal
Cambridge (February 25, 1962)

"In the beginning God created the heaven and the earth . . . And God said, Let there be light: and there was light" (Genesis 1:1–3). In God's words is His power to effect what they say. The centurion of Capernaum understood this: "But say in a word, and my servant shall be healed" (Luke 7:7). God's words are His tools and instruments to do His will. The psalmist speaks of God's words as a person, His agent:

> He sendeth forth His commandment upon earth: His word runneth very swiftly. He giveth snow like wool: He scattereth the hoarfrost like ashes. He casteth forth His ice like morsels: who can stand before His cold? He sendeth out His word, and melteth them: He causeth His wind to blow, and the waters flow. (Psalm 147:15–18)
>
> Fire, and hail; snow, and vapours; stormy wind fulfilling His word. (Psalm 148:8)

Yet in such words of God we may only recognize His almighty power, a power that may well strike us with doubt and dread. Looking only at what goes on in His creation may bring us to despair and resignation. God evades our attempts to grasp Him.

"Mummy, where is God?"
"My dear, God is everywhere."
"Is He in my ink bottle?"
"Well, yes, I suppose He must be."
"Whammo! Got Him!"

We cannot capture God in this or in any other way. We cannot find Him by seeking Him in the atoms or beyond the stars. There was that silly Russian astronaut who remarked while whizzing around our little planet, "I don't see any God about." Nor can we find God by peering into ourselves with an eye cocked for some flutter of emotion or flight of fancy. God is, indeed, everywhere, but the critical question is whether God is there for you.

Remember Elijah. After the big spectacle on Mount Carmel, he had to flee for his life. Was Elijah the only crazy one left who trusted the Lord? Where had that brought him? Cowering in a cave on Mount Horeb, the word of the Lord came to Elijah.

> And He said, Go forth, and stand upon the mount before the Lord. And, behold, the Lord passed by, and a great and strong wind rent the mountains, and brake in pieces the rocks before the Lord; but the Lord was not in the wind: and after the wind an earthquake; but the Lord was not in the earthquake: And after the earthquake a fire; but the Lord was not in the fire: and after the fire a still small voice. (1 Kings 19:11–12)

Elijah heard the voice of the Lord. He had heard the wind, the earthquake, and the fire. In the Lord's way of doing things, you might say He was in the wind, the earthquake, and the fire, for they are His to do with as He pleases. But it was with the words of the still small voice that the Lord spoke to Elijah. The Lord also speaks to you. It is the same voice, the same God speaking to you as to Elijah. You have His words; there you have Him. With God's words He makes appointment with you, speaks to you, deals with you. After that, you are never quite the same. His words work plus or minus, life or death.

The way God uses His words Jesus illustrates in the Parable of the Sower. The seed is the Word of God. We are the dirt. Life does not derive from us. Our sins serve to form a hard crust that has to be cracked and broken open. God does this with the ploughshare of His holy Law, which ploughs us over and lays bare what lurks there. Then comes the seedtime, when the little seeds of the Gospel are sown into our scarified soil. In those seeds is life. The winter is past, the rain has come, flowers appear in the earth, the time for singing has come (Song of Songs 2:11–12). In the parable Jesus is the sower sowing the seed into those gathered on the shore, as the Messiah was expected to do. Before His ascension, He provided for sowers to carry on.

Not one of us here today in Cambridge is a farmer. We can all do a bit of seed sowing, but we would have a lot to learn about farming before we could do a good job at seedtime. That takes years of training and experience. Just ask a farmer. Those who will be farmers with the sowing of the seeds of the words of the Lord need even more instruction. That is why they are to be given the best possible training. Just think what they are handling. If when they trundle you into the operating theater, the surgeon picks up the wrong card and takes out your gall bladder instead of your appendix, the consequences may be physically serious but nothing in comparison to what may happen if your pastor botches his job with your spiritual body.

It is vital that the pastor knows the seeds and the diagnosis of the soils. He needs to know when the Law must be preached to humble the proud and self-satisfied and when the still, small voice of the Gospel is to be spoken to the troubled and the despairing. Senior apostle Paul said to junior apostle Timothy: "Study to shew thyself approved unto God, a workman that needeth not to be ashamed, rightly dividing the word of truth" (2 Timothy 2:15). It is also vital that the pastor knows the words of the Lord and is able to recognize their pollution, but he also needs to revere those words so he speaks them not as his own but as God's (Apology of the Augsburg Confession VII, 28; XXVIII, 19). The vestments help us to forget the man who is in them and focus on the words the Lord is speaking to us by His use of the mouth that He has put there.

The Lord puts seeds into your soil. With His words He is sowing into you what those words say and convey with their potential fruit. Thus to be receiving into us, from outside ourselves, His words with what they say and bestow, that is one of the glories of our liturgy and Lutheran heritage. It isn't so important whether your pastor is some dashing Gregory Peck type or a bit of an old dodderer. The seeds are the same, and that is what matters most. The words are the Lord's; He grows them. As Paul confesses, "I have planted, Apollos watered; but God gave the increase. So then neither is he that planteth any thing, neither he that watereth; but God that giveth the increase" (1 Corinthians 3:6–7). The Lord is doing His sowing by use of Paul, Apollos, Timothy, and all the sowers He sends to sow. "You are God's field." The seeds He sows and waters, He controls the growing of. They are as sure as God is. They do not derive anything from us. His words come to us from outside ourselves. They are what God gives us to hold on to Him by. There are times when there is nothing else to hold on to, that He has hold of us by.

Without God's words we are barren soil. At times we reach for the words of the Lord we desperately need and cannot find them. We need help. Thanks be to God that the words of the Lord are not only there, loaded with His deeds and doing, but that He has instituted the office of the holy ministry for their delivery (Augsburg Confession VII, 14, 28). Those whom He puts into this office are His servants and sowers of His words, not derived from them, but His, delivered as He has ordained, thus not doubtful by reference to anyone else. By His words we are faced up to the Lord. Thus in Holy Absolution, thus His name that baptizes us with the water, thus His words He speaks to us in Holy Communion. Christ says He gives His body and blood for us Christians to eat and to drink for the forgiveness of our sins. Where we find forgiveness of sins, we find life and salvation.

Faithful treasuring of this clear Lutheran confession was the beginning of our Evangelical Lutheran Church of England, which lives on now in what is dedicated to our Lord's words and their sowing in this house today. Such a house may be called a seminary, a plot for the Lord's seeds. His words here engage us, received in liturgy, studied in the ways our Lord has taken our words into His use, lived in community, and readied for sowing skillfully, wherever the Lord may put us for His use.

The little handful we are recalls the other sowing parable of the mustard seed, the tiniest of seeds. Our work in Cambridge is like a mustard seed. What can we claim of ourselves? If we look to ourselves, we may soon be discouraged. It is now six years since the sainted Dr. Arndt was in Cambridge exploring possibilities and seeing his dictionary of New Testament Greek through the Cambridge University Press. His death seemed a setback, yet here we are today, celebrating the dedication of Westfield House. We look to the Lord and thank Him for the faithful prayers, gifts, and love that were His way of bestowing on us such a gift.

Our theological studies are underway, strong in Scripture's Hebrew and Greek—loaded words being loaded for delivery. The Cambridge University Lutheran Society engages Lutheran students and their friends who come from all over the world. Divine Service has been held, enjoying the hospitality of St. Michael's and All Angels, as also at bases of the United States Air Force in East Anglia for the Lutherans stationed there.

St. Augustine observed that the Lord gives only into empty hands, confessing what comes only as a gift. Thus today we extol the Lord's generosity that has brought us to this day in this house, and we reach out our empty hands toward Him. He is able to do far more abundantly than all we ask or think, where and when He pleases. "Except the LORD build the house, they labour in vain that build it" (Psalm 127:1). "I wait for the LORD, my soul doth wait, and in His word do I hope" (Psalm 130:5). "And bring forth fruit with patience" (Luke 8:15).

AMEN.

www.ingramcontent.com/pod-product-compliance
Lightning Source LLC
Chambersburg PA
CBHW020218170426
43201CB00007B/252